The World Is Our Home

Society and Culture
in Contemporary Southern Writing

Edited by
Jeffrey J. Folks
and Nancy Summers Folks

THE UNIVERSITY PRESS OF KENTUCKY

Publication of this volume was made possible in part by a grant from the National Endowment for the Humanities.

Scholarly publisher for the Commonwealth,
serving Bellarmine College, Berea College, Centre
College of Kentucky, Eastern Kentucky University,
The Filson Club Historical Society, Georgetown College,
Kentucky Historical Society, Kentucky State University,
Morehead State University, Murray State University,
Northern Kentucky University, Transylvania University,
University of Kentucky, University of Louisville,
and Western Kentucky University.

Editorial and Sales Offices: The University Press of Kentucky
663 South Limestone Street, Lexington, Kentucky 40508-4008

04 03 02 01 00   5 4 3 2 1

For permission to reprint, we wish to acknowledge *masculinities* 3.2 (1995): 43–66, in which a version of Suzanne W. Jones's essay "New Narratives of Southern Manhood: Race, Masculinity, and Closure in Ernest Gaines's Fiction" appeared under the title "Reconstructing Manhood: Race, Masculinity, and Narrative Closure in Ernest Gaines's *A Gathering of Old Men* and *A Lesson Before Dying*." We also acknowledge *Critical Survey* 9.2 (1997): 15–42, in which "New Narratives of Southern Manhood: Race, Masculinity, and Closure in Ernest Gaines's Fiction" appeared. In addition, we wish to acknowledge the publication of an earlier version of "'Trouble' in Muskhogean County: The Social History of a Southern Community in the Fiction of Raymond Andrews" by Jeffrey J. Folks in *Southern Literary Journal* 30.2 (1998): 66–75.

Library of Congress Cataloging-in-Publication Data

The world is our home : Society and culture in contemporary southern writing / edited by Jeffrey J. Folks and Nancy Summers Folks.
    p. cm.
  Includes bibliographical references and index.
  ISBN 0-8131-2166-3 (cloth : alk. paper)
    1. American literature—Southern States—History and criticism. 2. Literature and society—Southern States—History—20th century. 3. Southern States—In literature. 4. Social problems in literature. I. Folks, Jeffrey J. (Jeffrey Jay), 1948- II. Folks, Nancy Summers, 1946-

PS261 .S618 2000
810.9'975—dc21
                                  99-089784

Contents

The World Is Our Home

An Introduction

Jeffrey J. Folks and Nancy Summers Folks

As James Agee wrote at the beginning of his now classic study of southern sharecropping, *Let Us Now Praise Famous Men*: "The world is our home. It is also the home of many, many other children, some of whom live in far-away lands. They are our world brothers and sisters" (xviii, quoted from *Around the World With the Children* by F.B. Carpenter). In his writing, Agee was greatly concerned with the experiences of southerners from social groups distinct from his own. His artistic practice also insisted on reading literature within the discernible world of historical realities that shaped, and often constrained, the lives of those social groups. Similarly the essays in *The World Is Our Home: Society and Culture in Contemporary Southern Writing* increase our understanding of recent southern writing in relation to particular social and cultural issues and to various classes of southern people—the many "worlds" about which Agee wrote. Focusing on southern narrative from the early 1970s to the present, these essays address such issues as racial justice, gender roles, class equality, and cultural alienation. *The World Is Our Home* thus provides insight into the momentous changes that have taken place, and that are still under way, in contemporary southern society. As we have come to understand the ways in which southern writers have registered and interpreted this process of change, we may better grasp the South's relationship to larger social developments in the national and international culture.

From the 1970s on, critical approaches that insist on the contingent and historical nature of literary production have come to occupy a major position in literary studies. The nature of the relationship of literary texts to their social and cultural contexts is suggested, for example, by Stephen Greenblatt's phrase in his essay "Shakespeare and the Exorcists": "the permeability of [the text's] boundaries" (165). As Greenblatt notes in the same essay, "I believe that the most important effect of contemporary theory upon the practice of literary criticism, and certainly upon *my* practice, is to subvert the tendency to think of aesthetic representation as ultimately autonomous, separable from its cultural context and hence divorced from the social, ideological, and material matrix in which all art is produced and consumed" (164). In "Criticism and History," Fredric Jameson provided an eloquent rationale for the necessity of exploring the "historical dimension" of literature. Jameson wrote that the exploration of the social and historical context "involves what is properly a transformational process, conversion techniques, a shift in mental perspective that suddenly and powerfully enlarges our field of vision, releasing us from the limits of the various, purely literary methods, and permitting us to experience the profound historicity of their application, as indeed of all mental operations in general" (577). *The World Is Our Home,* in its focus on the social and cultural aspects of contemporary southern writing, contributes to the critical endeavor of historicizing and contextualizing literary narrative. It is our hope that the essays in this collection will expand the "field of vision" of southern literary studies by illuminating the historical dimensions of contemporary southern narrative.

The degree of interest of recent American criticism in social and cultural approaches can be explained, in part, as a reaction against an earlier formalist bias. The "sociological" approach, as it was sometimes termed, was largely dismissed by a generation of New Critics during the 1940s, 1950s, and early 1960s. In Mark Schorer's well-known essay "Technique as Discovery" (1948), the author disparaged the need to study "the materials of art" and warned against "the urgent sense of the importance of the materials— whether these are autobiographical, or social ideas or personal passions" (391). The climate of New Criticism—much of it, we need not be reminded, an invention of southern critics—deeply influenced the shape of the southern canon as it was first studied, and it determined to a great extent the available critical approaches to that canon. To an important degree, the New Criticism did not favor the study of what was termed "social ideas."

In the past twenty-five years, critics of southern literature have redressed the situation in their efforts to focus on social and cultural issues. Indeed, many would agree with the postmodern critic Charles Newman, who writes that he "tend[s] to see cultural and aesthetic conflicts as explicitly social and economic" (12). The South, of course, has always been a region of cultural admixture and often of social and political conflict, but in geographical, social, and ideological terms, recent southern writing has become markedly more heterogeneous, a development that compels us to assess more explicitly the relationship of imaginative works to the historical reality that they represent and embody. One of the aims of the present collection is to document and analyze the diversity of narrative interests of recent southern writers in terms of their heterogeneous identities and subjects.

Why should an interest in social and cultural issues be so fundamental to southern fiction and drama and yet, as it has been at times, so muted in southern criticism? The history of the South since the Civil War has shaped a literary culture in which a prevailing sense of loss and defeat is a crucial factor. The continuing economic and cultural imbalances—and the South's need to refute charges of cultural and economic underdevelopment—helped to produce a literature that was keenly aware of social differences within the South and between the South and other regions, and yet one that, particularly in its critical writing, developed an elaborate cultural means to explain these differences. In such a climate the "attacks" of critics such as H.L. Mencken were either dismissed or championed, depending on the southern writer's orientation to his or her homeland, but the underlying historical causes for the region's lack of development were rarely credited.

If an earlier generation of defenders and "monumentalists" refused to admit the extent of the South's social problems, critics from outside the region did not always regard the South's failings in a disinterested manner. As Walker Percy argued in "A Southern View" (1957), the social problems of the South, especially its slow progress in civil rights, was used as a pretext by those critics motivated by "an ideological hatred of the South and Southern tradition" (90). As Percy noted, critics who were eager to point up the South's failings did not always demonstrate an understanding of—or wish to understand—the complex historical reasons for these failings, nor were they always willing to credit the South's valuable heritage and cultural accomplishments. A criticism that is focused only on social ills may well be termed, in Percy's phrase, "gratuitously offensive" (90), for it may be grounded in a cultural bias against the South as a region and against the values of its cultural tradition.

One would hope that more recently, a more evenhanded and informed view has prevailed. There is increasing understanding of the South's position within a system of "internal colonialism" that relegated the South after the Civil War to a lower status in the national economy and culture. C. Hugh Holman was exceptional among earlier critics of southern literature in his understanding of the South's colonized status in relation to the national culture and in his interest in the sociological aspects of southern writing. Working at a time when Agrarians and New Critics dominated the study of southern culture, Holman argued for a pluralist view that spoke of the many "Souths." At a Davidson College symposium on southern writing (edited as *Southern Fiction Today* by George Core), Holman argued for the relevance of the "other" southern canon—that body of social realism that focused on everyday lives of southerners throughout the region. Against the reigning New Critical persuasion—evidenced among those at the conference who defined southern writing in terms of its traditional cultural value, "religious" qualities, or formal aesthetic properties—Holman urged the consideration of a tradition of social realism that reflected the dependence of art on common human experience, and he stressed the value not only of a "representational" realism but of a socially committed activism capable of critiquing the weaknesses of society. Rather than supporting writing that merely celebrated the southern past and monumentalized its culture, Holman recognized the need for a literature devoted to cultural critique and social change.

In discussing the social content of southern writing, Holman wrote that "the Southern writer tends to be a social critic, a portrayer of a region, a pointer to its social ills, a suggester of means for their correction" (qtd. in Core ix). In an important essay, "The View from the Regency-Hyatt," Holman identified different "Souths" in "a heterogeneous land" (18), noting that a "socioliterary method . . . essentially that of social realism" (20) represented a separate tradition from that of the southern aesthetic writers. The southern social realists were more influenced by Sinclair Lewis and H.L. Mencken than by Gustave Flaubert and James Joyce. In Holman's view, "one of the generating forces for the [southern] renascence was the energy of this social anger and regional criticism" (21).

Holman's interest in the southern tradition of social narrative was shared by other important critics. In his long and productive career, Louis D. Rubin Jr. often addressed the problem of defining the distinctive qualities of "southern" literature. At various times he would offer different explanations, pointing to its essentially "religious" nature, its aesthetic of "concreteness," and (more often) its artistic rendering of its subject. By 1989, in a talk presented at a National Endowment for the Humanities Summer Institute at the University of North Carolina at Chapel Hill (published in 1990 in *Virginia Quarterly Review* as "From Combray to Ithaca: Or, the 'Southernness' of Southern Literature"), Rubin's view had come to accord more with that of Holman. At the beginning of his paper, Rubin stressed that while elements such as "a sense of place, language, a sense of evil, an historical consciousness, an attitude toward nature or God or tradition" are not unique to southern writing, what *is* distinctive is "the particular and special ways in which such elements are arranged, the characteristic shapes that they assume in respect to one another, the manner in which they cause people to behave and writers to choose metaphors" (62). So far, Rubin was holding rather closely to the New Critical practice of stressing the formal elements of the work—the arrangement and "characteristic shapes" and "metaphors"—yet his next sentence revealed a significant shift in thinking, as he noted that these formal relationships and aesthetic choices "come out of the Southern community experience, a community that . . . so shapes the imaginative response of its literary people that when they write their stories and poems they do so, to a markedly recognizable degree, as *Southern* authors" (35). Elsewhere, in an essay on Mencken's anti-Semitism ("The Mencken Mystery"), Rubin's criticism seemed even more a model of social investigation. In these and other examples, Rubin's later critical writing forms a significant bridge between the New Critical emphasis on formalist reading—a criticism that was heavily indebted to such southern theorists as John Crowe Ransom, Allen Tate, and Cleanth Brooks—and a newer, post–New Critical criticism that is marked by an investigation of the literary work's cultural, historical, sociological, biographical, and autobiographical elements.

As co-editor (with Robert D. Jacobs) of *Southern Renascence,* Rubin had much to do with the creation of an early "canon" of southern letters. As elaborated by Rubin, Jacobs, and the other contributors to *Southern Renascence,* this early canon was hardly illiberal or culturally monolithic, but it did reflect the temper of criticism in the late 1940s and early 1950s. By the 1960s there was need for a revisionist study of southern writing that would expand the limited canon and reassess the accomplishment of many individual figures. One such study was John Bradbury's *Renaissance in the South: A Critical History of the Literature, 1920–1960* (1963). As Bradbury wrote, in opposition to the canon of the "new traditionalists" of the 1950s:

> The more one reads in the modern literature of the South, the more compelling becomes the desire to redress the critical balance. A strong and wide-spread liberal wing, covering both urban and rural subjects, has been largely ignored. Problem novels have proliferated; those dealing with industry and the farm are matched by a similarly diverse group centering on the family and group relations. A highly significant area of this development has been the serious Negro point of view story, chiefly written by white Southerners, a sub-genre which has exhibited remarkable growth and maturity. The South boasts its "tough school," its realistic, as well as romantic, historical novelists, its humorists, even its existentialists. (5)

As a bibliographical survey of Southern Renascence writing, Bradbury's work began to redress the balance.

The sixteen essays in *The World Is Our Home* are an effort to continue redressing the balance in critical practice by dealing with social and cultural issues that were largely excluded from earlier criticism. Clearly, no other group had been so neglected in the southern literary canon as the work of African Americans and other ethnic minorities, despite the efforts of such early critics as Alvin Aubert, Sterling Brown, Blyden Jackson, Saunders Redding, and Margaret Walker. The importance of admitting ethnic writers to the southern canon was widely recognized only after the 1960s with the work of William L. Andrews, Thadious M. Davis, Henry Louis Gates Jr., Lee Greene, Minrose Gwin, and Charles Rowell. Hazel V. Carby's *Reconstructing Womanhood: The Emergence of the Afro-American Woman Novelist* (1987) documented a tradition of African American women's writing, including the work of southern writers such as Zora Neale Hurston, and it positioned this writing in historical terms. Anthologies such as *Black-Eyed Susans* (1975) and *Midnight Birds* (1980), edited by Mary Helen Washington, and *Southern Black Voices: An Anthology of Fiction, Poetry, Drama, Nonfiction, and Critical Essays* (1992), edited by Jerry W. Ward and John Oliver Killens, demonstrated the contributions of African American writers to the southern canon.

Several essays in this collection study the treatment of racial issues in the works of contemporary southern writers. Susan Goodman's "Competing Histories: William Styron's *The Confessions of Nat Turner* and Sherley Ann Williams's *Dessa Rose*" considers the issues of construction and "ownership" of history in two works of historical fiction dealing with nineteenth-century slave revolts. Goodman considers charges against Styron's 1967 novel based on his "fictionalizing history." Like some earlier critics, Sherley Anne Williams was outraged by her sense that Styron distorted the Nat Turner figure into a dehumanized image of his own racial and cultural assumptions. In *Dessa Rose* (1986) Williams writes a parodic rebuttal that positions her narrative of slave revolt in an "other history" in which the victim of slavery retains heroic and loving qualities. Both novels, however, constitute a "meditation on history" as they assert that the making of history is shaped by the parochialism of the historical and ideological perspectives of the author.

In "'Trouble' in Muskhogean County: The Social History of a Southern Community in the Fiction of Raymond Andrews," Jeffrey J. Folks examines the fiction of an African American writer whose work constitutes a fictionalized social history of one county in east central Georgia. In novels such as *Appalachee Red*, Andrews carefully documents the intricate racial observances of the small-town South before and during the civil rights era. Most important in Andrews's social history is the evolution of race relations in the South, extending from a period when Jim Crow laws were still firmly in place to the period of the civil rights protests. In an essay on Ernest Gaines's *A Lesson Before Dying*, John Lowe analyzes issues of social control and imprisonment, and he connects the novel's "lessons" with contemporary problems of racial justice. Drawing on the theory of Michel Foucault, Lowe examines the ways in which society's "gaze" exerts control over the social underclass of America.

Increasingly, literary critics have begun to recognize the interrelatedness of race, gender, class and other "spheres" of social and cultural inquiry. Indeed, a special issue of *American Literature* edited by Cathy N. Davidson ("No More Separate Spheres!" volume 70, number 3 [September 1998]) suggested a revised critical practice that would bridge the "separate spheres" of race, gender, and class and that would study the ways in which these spheres are interrelated. Inevitably, issues of racial justice intersect with problems of gender and class equality; ethical questions are inextricably connected with the spheres of race and gender; religious convictions exist in relation to, and are assumed to address, the historical conditions of everyday human existence. In many of the essays in *The World Is Our Home,* the authors have explored the relationship between the "separate spheres," attempting to discover connections between a variety of social and cultural issues.

Like several other critics in this collection, Keith Byerman finds that the spheres of race and gender overlap and intersect. In "Gender and Justice: Alice Walker and the Sexual Politics of Civil Rights," Byerman considers the portrayal of the civil rights movement in three of Walker's works: *The Third Life of Grange Copeland, Meridian,* and "Advancing Luna—and Ida B. Wells." In these works, Byerman demonstrates that the political struggle for civil rights is interpreted in gendered as well as racial terms. Similarly, Suzanne W. Jones's essay, "New Narratives of Southern Manhood: Race, Masculinity, and Closure in Ernest Gaines's Fiction," crosses interpretive boundaries of gender and race as it analyzes the construction of "manhood" in two important works of African American narrative. Jones views Gaines's mature fiction as moving beyond a traditional image of southern masculinity and toward a more communicative, nonviolent, and cooperative definition. Jones considers the interrelationship of the South's race and gender ideologies as she shows how southern codes of masculinity were formed within the historical crucible of racial conflict.

If the early southern canon failed to include works by African American writers, it was also remiss in excluding works by women writers and by the limiting critical vocabulary it employed to discuss those women writers who were included. In "Making Peace with the (M)other," Barbara Bennett documents the emergence of an important genre of southern women's writing that focuses on the relationship of mothers and daughters. While mother figures were generally ignored or disparaged in southern fiction before the 1970s, more recent fiction offers a positive image of the mother-daughter relationship—a change, Bennett suggests, that is based on the evolution of southern society as a whole away from rigid patriarchal norms of behavior. Studying the examples of Jill McCorkle's *Ferris Beach,* Tina McElroy Ansa's *Ugly Ways,* and Josephine Humphreys's *Rich in Love,* Bennett shows the development of a positive model for a mother-daughter relationship and acceptance of the mother figure. Linda J. Byrd's "Toward Healing the Split: Lee Smith's *Fancy Strut* and *Black Mountain Breakdown*" also focuses on the depiction of maternal roles in recent southern fiction. In Smith's novels one may trace the splintering of women's sexual and maternal qualities as a result of a patriarchal conception of gender and the "masculinization" of divinity.

The masculinization of divinity is likewise a crucial issue in the works of Sheila Bosworth, a Catholic novelist from Covington, Louisiana, who, as Gary M. Ciuba stresses, defines her formative experience as that of being "a female child in the Catholic church in the 1950s." In his study of "sacred violence" in *Slow Poison,* Ciuba relates Bosworth's experience to a tradition of religious devotionalism within which the believer forms an identity based on the idea of "giving oneself up" to the authority of a cruel or indifferent God. Such behavior has important psychological and social consequences, especially for women who structure their lives along the lines of the scapegoat identity learned in childhood. Linda Watts's "Stories Told by Their Survivors (and Other Sins of Memory): Survivor Guilt in Kaye Gibbons's *Ellen Foster*" positions Gibbons's heroine in an equally repressive social milieu. Approaching Gibbons's fiction from the psychological theory of "survivor guilt," Watts's essay traces Ellen Foster's self-doubt to its sources in the economically disadvantaged and dysfunctional family structures that shape her childhood. In her struggle against these restrictive conditions, Ellen turns to a nurturing tradition of women's storytelling. Similarly, Moira P. Baker's "'The Politics of They': Dorothy Allison's *Bastard Out of Carolina* as Critique of Class, Gender, and Sexual Ideologies" studies gender and class issues in the fiction of a significant southern woman writer. Allison's fiction, including her story collection *Trash* (1989) and first novel, *Bastard Out of Carolina* (1997), depicts southern women living in conditions of poverty and gender subjugation. Baker analyzes the ways in which society's prejudices and myths concerning gender and sexuality overlap with "white trash" images of illegitimacy, incest, and other transgressive forms of behavior.

Just as a study of the South's social and cultural practices includes attention to its construction of race and gender ideologies, it must also consider the existence within southern culture of a vigorous religious and spiritual tradition that has exerted much influence over southern mores and social attitudes. Several essays in this collection center on the continuing impact and legacies of this religious culture, particularly in terms of the phenomenon of cultural dislocation as the subject of contemporary southern writing. As monolithic standards of ethical value and religious belief have been replaced, in the South and the nation as a whole, by more tentative sources of faith, many writers engage in an anxious search for meaningful existence.

Like James Lee Burke, Jayne Anne Phillips, and other contemporary southern writers, Walker Percy was deeply concerned with the apparent sense of spiritual malaise and moral confusion in American society—a phenomenon that he represented in *The Moviegoer, The Last Gentleman,* and, perhaps most acutely, in *Lancelot.* In "Walker Percy's Lancelot Lamar: Defending the Hollow Core," Julius Raper studies Lancelot Lamar's explanations of his own violence as a reaction to "evil" and relates these explanations to "the southern tradition of evasive idealism and high-minded violence." Contrary to what Lamar himself says, the "truer motives" for his violence lie in a defense of his own fragile "borderline" state resulting from parental abandonment and intrusion. Drawing on the work of James Gilligan and Heinz Kohut, Raper locates the causes of Lamar's narcissistic rage in the context of a lifelong effort to repress the knowledge of his own oedipal conflicts. Raper's analysis contributes much to our understanding of Percy's important novel—a novel that has larger implications for comprehending a contemporary culture in which violence is often glamorized.

Frederick Barthelme's *Painted Desert* and the earlier companion novel, *The Brothers,* deal with themes familiar in the work of Walker Percy: the alienation of middle-class existence and the consequent loss of a sense of individuality and selfhood. For Barthelme's characters, as Robert H. Brinkmeyer Jr. shows, the American West (as opposed to the South that they inhabit) holds powerful symbolism as an empty space of "endless possibility"—an opportunity to escape the endless routine of bourgeois existence. In Del and Jen, characters with an unusual "capacity to wonder," Barthelme suggests the possibility of transforming this existence, not through geographical escape but through imagination and love. Frank W. Shelton demonstrates a similar sense of alienation and loss of selfhood in James Lee Burke's Dave Robicheaux novels, in which Burke's hero describes his small-town, working-class origins with a nostalgic and elegiac tone, as the simpler and more meaningful life in which he grew up is seen to be disappearing. The house in which Dave grew up and to which he and his wife return "evokes his roots and the permanence of the past . . . the essence of what Dave seeks to defend," writes Shelton. Burke's novels, however, are not a nostalgic paean to the "lost South" but only to those modest values of small-town America that were so vividly a part of southern life in Burke's generation. As his fiction details the historical origins of racial prejudice and the pervasiveness of violence in southern society, "the novels embody a complicated vision—both nostalgia for and criticism of the southern past" (Shelton). As James Grove demonstrates, the same quality of ethical questioning and cultural estrangement permeates Jayne Anne Phillips's fiction. In her second novel, *Shelter,* set at a West Virginia girls' camp in the summer of 1963, Phillips depicts scenes of horrific abuse to children and suggests a cycle of future violence and distrust. In his analysis of the novel,

Grove stresses the difficulty of comprehending and responding to the pervasiveness of evil in contemporary American society.

A "hunger for the spiritual" is equally evident in the plays of Horton Foote. As Gerald C. Wood demonstrates, Foote encourages an acceptance of "any belief system" that will ameliorate the emotional anguish and social disorder that he sees in contemporary society. Especially in the nine-play cycle *The Orphans' Home,* Foote depicts the need for humane and responsible behavior and for a belief system based on "a merciful, androgynous God" rather than on a punishing Calvinist deity. In Foote's view, social change is dependent on individual acts of empathy, imagination, and love. As Wood writes, "When freely chosen, sanctified by the human will, loving attachment can become a powerful force for peace and justice."

Lacking a transcendent order of ideas, Richard Ford's fiction nonetheless evinces, as Joanna Price notes of characters like Frank Bascombe, "a yearning for something to put in the place of the sacred," but Frank's attempts in this regard amount merely to "simulation" of closure. The "acceptance of cultural and historical contingency" in Ford's writing is radical, and it affects every aspect of his art. Price's essay on Richard Ford studies the ways in which, in the case of a postmodern writer from the South, "the cultural and economic formations of postmodernity take the place of former regional culture as the subject of art." As Price stresses, Ford conceives his settings as mutable spaces in which cultural permanence is hardly essential or even imaginable.

While the perspectives and assumptions of authors discussed in this volume vary greatly, all share a common historical experience as artists who have arrived "late" at the end of a period of regional self-examination and change. They are gazing at the South, as it were, from beyond a historic period of social transformation: a civil rights movement that has often been compared to the Civil War in its transformative impact; an examination of gender that involves every person and institution in the South; an alienating metamorphosis, in less than fifty years, from a largely provincial culture of smaller cities and towns into a region of suburban sprawl. Given their historical experience, it is hardly surprising that southerners write out of the "urgent sense of the importance of the materials," to appropriate Schorer's phrase, if also out of a commitment to fiction as art and from within a useful tradition of southern social narrative.

Works Cited

Agee, James and Walker Evans. *Let Us Now Praise Famous Men*. 1941. New York: Ballantine, 1966.

Bradbury, John M. *Renaissance in the South: A Critical History of the Literature, 1920–1960*. Chapel Hill: U of North Carolina P, 1963.

Core, George, ed. *Southern Fiction Today: Renascence and Beyond*. Athens: U of Georgia P, 1969.

Greenblatt, Stephen. "Shakespeare and the Exorcists." *Shakespeare and the Question of Theory*. Ed. Patricia Parker and Geoffrey Hartman. London: Methuen, 1985. 163–87.

Holman, C. Hugh. "The View from the Regency-Hyatt." *Southern Fiction Today*. Ed. George Core.

Jameson, Fredric. "Criticism in History." *Criticism: Major Statements*. 3rd ed. Ed. Charles Kaplan and William Anderson. New York: St. Martin's, 1991. 574–94.

Newman, Charles. *The Post Modern Aura: The Act of Fiction in an Age of Inflation*. Evanston: Northwestern UP, 1990.

Percy, Walker. "A Southern View." *Signposts in a Strange Land*. Ed. Patrick Samway. New York: Farrar, Straus and Giroux, 1991. 89–93.

Rubin, Louis D. Jr. "From Combray to Ithaca: Or, the 'Southernness' of Southern Literature." *Virginia Quarterly Review* 66 (1990): 47–63.

Schorer, Mark. "Technique as Discovery." *20th Century Literary Criticism: A Reader*. Ed. David Lodge. London and New York: Longman, 1972. 387–400.

Competing Histories

William Styron's THE CONFESSIONS OF NAT TURNER and Sherley Ann Williams's DESSA ROSE

Susan Goodman

> History should not be so much an account of facts as an account of illusions, because men act according to their illusions, and myths, much more than on the guidance of facts.
>
> Bernard Berenson, *Conversations with Berenson*

A month after the publication of *The Confessions of Nat Turner* (1967), William Styron received an honorary degree from Wilberforce University, an Ohio institution named for the British abolitionist. Addressing the mostly black audience, he hoped that an increased awareness of history, particularly of slavery, "would allow people of both races to come to terms with the often inexplicable turmoil of the present." His speech prompted a round of enthusiastic applause before his listeners, perhaps thinking of relatives in Vietnam, rose to sing "The Battle Hymn of the Republic." "I felt gratitude at their acceptance of me," he recalled, "and, somehow more importantly, at my acceptance of them, as if my literary labors and my plunge into history had helped dissolve many of my preconceptions about race, which had been my birthright as a Southerner and allowed me to better understand the forces that had shaped our common destiny" (*Confessions* 434–35).

Styron had—as his comment suggests—his own ghosts to appease. Weaned on antebellum stories of his slaveholding grandmother, he could scarcely remember a time when the idea of slavery had not haunted him. The division between blacks and whites had always bemused and angered less than it intrigued him. "I fell under the spell of *négritude*," he explained. "Most white people were, and are, racist to some degree but at least my racism was not conventional; I wanted to confront and understand blackness" (436). Styron assumed a monolithic entity called "blackness," a state or condition as misleading for him as it has been for his opponents. Any generalizations about

"blackness" seem inadequate, though Styron's in the late 1960s—a time of black empowerment—seemed especially presumptuous. To many African Americans, he sounded like a man seeking expiation;[1] to anyone unsure of a "common" past or "destiny," merely naive.

Although the faculty of Wilberforce and the Pulitzer Prize committee sanctioned Styron's motives, most black readers have not.[2] They expressed, and continue to express, concern about Styron's characterization of Turner, his fictionalizing of history, and his adoption, if not theft, of Turner's voice.[3] According to his critics, Styron perpetuated the very "preconceptions" he hoped to have shed. Where, they wanted to know, had Styron discovered any evidence that Turner lusted after a white woman or that his one sexual experience occurred with another man? Above all, they thought that the narrative voice, Turner's supposed language, psychology, and religious perspective, belonged to a white man—never to the Turner they esteemed as a virile leader. Styron seemed to offer a revisionary history that diminished the real Turner's significance and the painful legacy of slavery.

Unfortunately, Styron's running commentary on the novel has become virtually inseparable from the novel itself. Styron castigated his antagonists for forgetting that he had written a *novel*. Certain historical facts, he insisted, are either unimportant or unnecessary and yielding to them compromises the novelist's aesthetic honesty. Yet despite his vehement defense of artistic freedom, Styron shifted the focus of the debate away from the novel to the integrity of history—a topic that Ralph Ellison shrewdly warned would be better left alone (130–32). At the thirty-fourth annual meeting of the Southern Historical Association, Styron repeated the argument that he had been making to college audiences across the country. Some facts happened to be more important than others, and the novelist had to exercise reason. He had not given Turner a wife, for example, because he had not uncovered "substantial evidence" of one (West 135). Nothing, however, prevented Styron from imagining Turner's adolescent sexual encounter with another man or his fantasies about white women. Neither had he read any accounts that would alter his opinion about the character and extent of slave resistance. Critics who derided Styron's historical sources thought he had consciously manipulated evidence to fit his prejudices. His book revealed the workings of the white power structure, not the history or the character of Nat Turner.

Knowing that writers should probably refrain from granting interviews, Styron still did, and his stubborn defense of his novel's most contested "facts" kept the controversy (and his book) alive. The quarrel always had more to do with the present than the past; but its location in history, its focus on something not "real" (a novel), permitted a freer dialogue about race relations—perhaps the single most difficult topic for Americans to address.

The cultural controversy surrounding *The Confessions of Nat Turner* indicates how we have defined ourselves and our society in history. Twenty years after the publication of *The Confessions*, Sherley Ann Williams, still "outraged by a certain, critically acclaimed novel . . . that travestied the as-told-to memoir of slave revolt leader Nat Turner" (*Dessa* ix), ventured something rare in literature, a novelistic rebuttal of another novel. *Dessa Rose* (1986) or this "other history" (*Dessa* x), as Williams calls it, relates what she saw traditional histories and Styron's historical novel ignoring: the life of a black slave woman and rebel leader told from her point of view. Intentionally parodying the form of *The Confessions*, Williams presents Styron as Adam Nehemiah, a crazed writer of manuals on slave management. She speaks in the voice of Nehemiah as he becomes increasingly violent, lustful, and infantile. Apart from a few quibbles about her portrayal of Styron, no sustained argument surrounds *Dessa Rose*, a novel that looks at the past (much like *The Confessions*) from the superimposed perspective of the present and draws on a limited number of historical sources. Critics have generally accepted Williams's "facts" as credible and praised her "faithful" imagining of history (Stone 375).

Williams might object with some justification to the old adage that imitation is the highest form of flattery. But though her novel directly rebuts Styron's, *The Confessions of Nat Turner* and *Dessa Rose* remain strikingly similar books.[4] Each, for example, claims its authority from historical accounts: Styron extrapolates from Turner's *Confessions* as recorded by T.R. Gray, and Williams uses two "historical incidents" taken from Angela Davis and Herbert Aptheker, the author of *American Negro Slave Revolts* (1948). The first concerns the 1829 decision to delay the hanging of a Kentucky woman, convicted of leading a slave revolt, until the birth of her child. The second grows from a report the following year that a white woman gave sanctuary to runaway slaves on her farm in rural North Carolina.

Both Williams and Styron begin their novels with an author's note. Styron makes an argument for including *The Confessions of Nat Turner* in a tradition that begins—at least for those readers of the Marxist Hungarian philosopher Georg Lukács—with the Waverly novels of Sir Walter Scott. Lukács wrote that the "greatest" historical novels focus on the "poetic awakening" of ordinary people affected by past events, not on the events themselves (42). Styron, thinking that "historical novels" had acquired a pejorative connotation, aims to separate his book from romantic chronicles or costume dramas that depict the past through an accumulation of detail. *The Confessions of Nat Turner*, he explains, "is less an 'historical novel' in conventional terms [that is, bound by '*known* facts'] than a meditation on history" (*Confessions* "Author's Note"), a form that can expand to the parameters of its author's imagination.[5]

Styron's choice of the word "meditation" has continued to prove problematical.[6] For readers familiar with Scripture, it recalls Psalm xix: "Let the words of my mouth, and the meditation of my heart, be acceptable in thy sight" (Ps. 19:14). The word draws author and subject together by suggesting a connection between literary creation and religious ardor. Styron explained that he called his book a "meditation" because he wanted to emphasize the intimate process of his own thinking. His critics interpreted his explanation of the autobiographical impulse behind much writing as an admission.[7] What readers had now, they argued, was nothing more than "The Confessions of William Styron." The conflict surrounding Styron's *Confessions* suggests that a "real" or acceptable history may never be written. After three decades in which Styron has figured at the center of an often ferocious debate about the nature of history,[8] his use of the word "meditation" ironically acknowledges the recursive and elusive nature of understanding.

In her author's note, Williams echoes exactly the responses of Styron's contemporary critics. Irritated by everything from Styron's pronouncements to his methods, she writes: "Afro-Americans, having survived by word of mouth—and made of that process a high art—remain at the mercy of literature and writing; often, these have betrayed us. I loved history as a child, until some clear-eyed young Negro pointed out, quite rightly that there was no place in the American past I could go and be free. I now know that slavery eliminated neither heroism nor love; it provided occasions for their expression" (*Dessa* ix-x). This passage indicates how much the conception of Williams's novel parallels that of Styron. It also shows her coming perilously close to implying that slavery had its beneficial aspects, that it was the cause, rather than a condition or circumstance, for human valor. Her difficulty with tone results from the "meditative" nature of looking back, from the wish, in Williams's case, to pay homage to those who endured.

Williams's effort to distinguish her novel from Styron's has served to underscore their similarities. Both authors assume, for example, that personal experience, whether Styron's birthright as a southerner or Williams's as an African American, sanctions their parochial versions of history. Asserting the same poetic freedom, they feel a kind of self-congratulatory catharsis. Styron takes pride—as he said of his visit to Wilberforce—in his acceptance of "them" (*Confessions* 435), whereas, Williams declares that what she has written "is as true as if I myself had lived it" (*Dessa* x). Why, might Styron ask, can Williams "own"—as she claims in her author's note—"a summer in the 19th century" (*Dessa* x) and he, nothing of a few months in 1831? What conceit, Williams might wonder, had prompted Styron to presume that he could actually *be* Nat Turner? What blindness, Styron might reply, could allow Williams so much borrowing with so much animosity? In the end, their conflict comes down to two issues: Who writes the history of the South? And how should it be told?

If Styron was genuinely shocked at the outrage his novel generated, he must partly blame himself for repeatedly confusing history and fiction. The genres of history and fiction have always intersected.[9] Novelists before and after Styron have given themselves permission to do what the historian does in reconstructing the past. And historians, such as Francis Parkman, have tried to transmit the essence of culture through the imagined lives of actual people and their biographical import for the writer. History no less than fiction and fiction no less than history demand an act of social imagination. In the spirit of Henry Adams, Styron desires for widely diverse individuals to achieve a new consensus through the study of history, which he views as an organic process of conflicting and resolving forces capable of determining the present (Stocking 38).

Styron hoped that his act of imagination would create "a spiritual harmony between the human soul and its environment" (Morris 81), that art would resolve the differences preventing blacks and whites from participating equally in a national past. In retrospect, his assumption proved narcissistic. The forces that have biographical import for the writer may or may not relate to what Styron called "our common destiny" (*Confessions* 435). The "aesthetic dimension" of art—to use Herbert Marcuse's phrase—provides an entry into an ahistorical realm of letters (ix), a land where one can simultaneously explore and escape the past. Writing "fixes" the past by allowing its revision and containing what at times might seem engulfing.

For Styron, the past and the present have the power to exist contemporaneously because places retain significance through time. Visiting the Whitehead house, the scene of the historical Turner's murder of the adolescent Margaret, he hears "a mad rustle of taffeta, and rushing feet, and a shrill girlish piping terror; then that day and this day seemed to meet and melt together, becoming almost one, and for a long moment indistinguishable" (*Quiet Dust* 30). Styron's wish for "a past once intimately shared by blacks and whites" (Stone 47) reflects a personal need to know and thereby atone.

It seems ironical that *The Confessions of Nat Turner*, a novel that has stirred so much passion about history, would itself be viewed ahistorically, that is, apart from a long tradition of authors, both black and white, who have considered race central to American literature.[10] Yet that is largely what has happened. Controversy has obscured the connection of Styron's novel to literary history. From Mark Twain's Jim to Julia Peterkin's Scarlet Sister Mary to Ellen Glasgow's Parry Clay, white writers have written in black dialect. While readers have tended to respond according to the dictates of their era, they have not automatically responded on the basis of race.[11] In the 1920s, for example, Carl Van Vechten's dubiously titled novel *Nigger Heaven* (1926) seemed to capture the spirit of Harlem in the voices of its inhabitants, and readers such as Langston Hughes discussed its depiction of a segment of black life in aesthetic terms.[12] The danger of Styron's choice lay in its seeming parody of slave narratives and its evocation of the blackfaced minstrel.[13] Not surprisingly, his critics considered Turner a literate cousin of Amos and Andy. Maybe nothing would have worked for Styron given his time and place and pure bull-headedness. But he did have a choice of narrative strategies that for one reason or another he chose to disregard, including those of Willa Cather's *Sapphira and the Slave Girl* (1941) and William Faulkner's *Light in August* (1932)—works not far removed from his own. Though as different as their authors, these novels ponder, without seeming to appropriate, black experience.

Unlike Styron, Cather decided to tell the story of a historical woman's bondage and escape almost exclusively from the outside. In the last chapter, however—dated twenty-five years later and narrated by an "I" who seems to be Cather herself—she shifts from limited third-person omniscient to first-person narration. Cather forestalled criticism by reserving her meditation on history until the end and openly acknowledging her autobiographical stance. Styron may have rejected a similar model because its form maintains a conscious distance between author and subject. Styron admired Cather, whom he credited—along with Ernest Hemingway, F. Scott Fitzgerald, and Sherwood Anderson—for inspiring a literary resurgence in the 1920s. Known primarily as a western writer, she did not, however, seem an immediate predecessor or rival. The same is not true of William Faulkner, whose vision of the South and its history has become *the* vision for many readers. And few, maybe no, novels have better captured southern ambivalence about race than his peculiarly American version of Dr. Jekyll and Mr. Hyde, *Light in August*. In Faulkner's scheme, Joe Christmas feels driven in one direction by his "white" blood, in another by his "black," though he may be white or black, neither and both. If Faulkner seems, like Styron, to perpetuate certain racial stereotypes, they become with Christmas's alternating identity successively muddled, inverted, and cleverly broken down.

Styron realized, like Faulkner, the amorphous nature of race, decided according to shifting formulas of blood. He wanted to lessen the gulf between the races, which even a writer as "supremely knowledgeable as William Faulkner" could not bridge. Although Faulkner's characters seemed to Styron "marvelously portrayed," they also seemed more "*observed*" than "*lived*" (*Quiet Dust* 13). Refusing to accept Faulkner's belief that a white person could never fully understand a black person, Styron decided to assume Turner's voice. At the time, while it struck some people as a radical choice, Styron himself might have thought that it logically and more candidly extended Faulkner's strategy in *Light in August*.

Styron's struggle to embody his protagonist is reflected in the difficulty he has even beginning his novel. Trying to solve the inherent problems of speaking in Turner's voice, he uses a series of narrative frames that subvert their own integrity. In a sense bookends, the frames contain what he described as "an imagined vision within a vision" (*Quiet Dust* 8). They lead the reader into Turner's consciousness and also outward: to other ways of knowing, in which personal testimony is dispersed into history and myth. The ending frame makes a further demand by returning readers back to the beginning, where they must reevaluate both the author's note and the frames themselves. Styron does, in this way, "meditate" on history, and—contrary to his (mis)statements—his meditation critiques the historian's as well as the novelist's assumption that "we" can understand "blackness."

Styron purposely undercuts his narrators to focus attention on the larger issues his novel generated. How is history recorded? What is its value? Whose voice takes precedence? From the outset, he alerts his readers that they will need to read differently, that they are entering spaces that resemble a series of Chinese boxes. After the dedication and before his author's note, Styron inserted a symbol of the alpha and the omega, the beginning and the end. It may mean that nothing or everything changes, for its significance depends entirely on one's interpretation of the novel. Styron uses the symbol to provide a kind of ground plan for reading. Its presence challenges the hierarchy that places the word above sign. In contrast, Sherley Ann Williams elevates both the oral and the written word.

If Williams presents the voices of Dessa and Nehemiah reversing like sand in an hourglass, Styron creates a tower of Babel through different accounts of the same events. He places his own gloss—the author's note—first, then follows it with a notice to the public from T.R. Gray and an epigraph from the Old Testament. None of his narrators can be trusted, especially Styron himself. In this regard, *The Confessions of Nat Turner* most differs in tone and intent from *Dessa Rose*. Styron realizes that both fiction and history grow from competing exchanges that confirm the boundaries, the values, the kind of knowledge and prestige of a particular culture at a particular point in time. His frames provide the "competing exchanges." Whether or not we accept his vision, Styron seeks a moral engagement with history—a legacy he thinks the responsibility of every southerner.

Styron uses the section titled "To the Public" to stress the same idea that Williams criticizes him for in *Dessa Rose*. His characterization of Gray almost begs the reader to make unflattering comparisons between his process of transcribing and the act of authorship—exactly the idea that most infuriated Williams. Williams and other critics refused to see some of the ironies of *The Confessions*, including Styron's parody of himself, partly because of Styron's public pronouncements. But, in fact, Styron presents his own writing process as analogous to Gray's. Lending an aura of historical accuracy, Gray's polemic emphasizes the problem of first-person accounts. As Styron demonstrates, Gray's testimony is tainted by his personal failings, social circumstances, and his role as Turner's interlocutor—a role that prevents Turner from ever being heard. "I have been amazed by the phenomenon of Nat Turner *alias* William Styron," a reader wrote the editor of *The Nation*. "Or is it: the alien phenomenon of Nat Turner *via* William Styron. . . . This man [Nat Turner], this object of attention, attack, and vast activity, cannot make himself be heard, let alone be understood. *He has never been listened to*" (Stone 120). This is precisely Styron's message. Introducing the victims as "remorseless murderers," Gray inverts the historical reality and perpetuates racist stereotypes to alleviate white misgivings. *"It will thus appear,"* he explains, *"that whilst every thing upon the surface of society wore a calm and peaceful aspect . . . a gloomy fanatic was revolving in the recesses of his . . . mind schemes of indiscriminate massacre to the whites"* (xvi). Styron's characterization of Gray begs readers to question the received history of the novel and also that of the original manuscript on which it is based: Turner's 1831 confession recorded by a historical figure named Gray.[14]

In *The Confessions of Nat Turner*, Styron makes three points about writing that might also apply to history: it is collaborative, political, and often unintended—an aspect that Styron forgot when trying to refute his detractors. Gray does not perceive, for example, that Turner's confession gives him a social and political being otherwise denied. He confesses, as he explains to Gray, so *"that all the nations may know"* (15). The distinction places guilt on Turner's listeners; however, the "truth" of what they know remains cryptic. Not only does Turner withhold and edit information, but then Gray translates his confession. The so-called historical document in this fictional work is—in Gray's words—"more or less a reconstitution and *recomposition*" (30) of their various discourses, authored finally by neither Turner nor Gray. How can we separate the characters of Turner and Gray, who, in the notice to the public, acquire one voice? "His words (mine? ours?)," Turner thinks (37), as he is propelled (foreshadowing Styron's address at Wilberforce) into the maelstrom of history—or is it fiction?

For all his talk about history, Styron does not elevate it above other epistemologies. Instead he suspends Turner's own story for one more moment by following Gray's frame with an epigraph from the twenty-first chapter of the Revelation of Saint John the Divine. The epigraph introduces another reality or way of ordering experience ahistorically. As the symbol of the alpha and omega offers an alternative to the word, the epigraph offers an alternative to history:

*And God shall wipe away all tears from
their eyes; and there shall be no more*

> *death, neither sorrow, nor crying,*
> *neither shall there be any more pain:*
> *for the former things are passed away.*

The epigraph, which imputes Gray's chronological structuring of Turner's narrative, also comments ironically on any "confession" and its aftermath.

Only after a series of frames—the symbol of the alpha and omega, the author's note, the notice to the public, and the epigraph—does Styron tell Turner's story. His "confession" subverts accepted notions about the constitution and exercise of power. Exposing both the inherently racist structure of society and the tenuous nature of identity itself, Styron suggests an unholy collusion between blacks and whites that no acts of contrition can absolve. Turner and Gray alternately manipulate and minister to each other. Turner knows Gray inside and out, smells his rotting oversweetness before he sees him, and adjusts his language and manner accordingly. The gulf between the man Gray thinks he is initially interviewing and the man who sits opposite him contemplating the metaphysics of existence seems almost unbridgeable. Gray appears so limitedly stereotypical of whites that Turner wonders whether he has made him up. Turner plays with him as though he were a cat, a word that Judge Cobb, the one man who recognizes him as a human being and sentences him to death, asks him how to spell. Like the grandfather in Ralph Ellison's *Invisible Man* (1952), Turner has lived with the lion's head in his mouth; he has overcome them with "yeses," agreed them to death and destruction.

Styron makes it clear that Gray, assured in his own ignorance and vulgarity, presents no comparable threat to Turner's sense of identity. Yet, perhaps for just this reason, Gray becomes the means of Turner's self-explorations. As the lawyer shows an increased understanding of people and events beyond his immediate ken, Turner gradually allows him deeper into his consciousness. Gray's counting for so little frees Turner to speak so much, and that speech forces Gray to recognize Turner's humanity, to "pass" psychologically into his skin. Before Turner's execution, Gray brings him a Bible forbidden by the court. Turner thinks that he has never seen this man. He also knows as Gray reaches through the bars to grasp his hand that his "last white man" (35) has never before shaken a black hand. Turner feels "a wrench of pity" (425) for Gray, whom he now realizes wore his own version of the mask that grins and lies and bears what cannot be borne. Gray becomes Turner's convert, the purveyor of a legend the power of which Styron himself barely intimated. And Styron does, with Turner's "resurrection," recreate "a past once intimately shared by blacks and whites" (Stone 47).

The design of Styron's text—as opposed to his statements about it—

suggests that history's "truth" is a Lear-like warning (so different from the healing vision of *Dessa Rose*) that nothing can come of nothing. Where is his novel's moral center? Gray submits Turner's confession to the public *"without comment"* but not before making an argument for more repressive measures to restrain *"this class of our population, and to induce all those entrusted with their execution, as well as our citizens generally, to see that they are strictly and rigidly enforced"* (xvii). Styron draws a parallel between Gray's edited version of Turner's account and their invented speeches in the ensuing narration. His use of Gray's frame implicitly begs readers to rethink concepts such as "revenge," "anger," and "fanaticism." It undermines the findings of the members of the Jerusalem court and by extension the "law" of the nation.

As the multiple frames illustrate, Styron successively topples the very structures he has erected. The text ends after Turner's confession—idiosyncratic, self-serving, and no less problematic or racist than Gray's—with another quotation from the Revelation of Saint John the Divine:

> *And he said unto me, It is done.*
> *I am Alpha and Omega, the beginning and*
> *the end. I will give unto him that is*
> *athirst of the fountain of the water*
> *of life freely. He that overcometh shall inherit*
> *all things; and I will be his God and*
> *he shall be my son.*

Styron seems to be commenting on the artist's role as much as the preceding narrative or any prophesied future. He has and does not have the final word, which belongs singly and collectively to John, Turner, and the disembodied "I."

Styron concludes his novel with the same doubts with which he began. What is an author's moral responsibility to his subject? Styron frames this question both verbally and physically by placing an excerpt from an actual "history" after the verses on the last page. He took the excerpt from *The Southampton Insurrection* (1900), written at the turn of the century by William S. Drewry, "an unreconstructed Virginian of decidedly pro-slavery leanings" (Styron, *Quiet Dust* 16). It concerns the disposal of Turner's body, which doctors skinned before converting the flesh into grease—a detail that, in Styron's mind, links the practice of slavery to the atrocities of the Third Reich. According to Drewry, at least one person owns a money purse made of Turner's "hide," though his skeleton has disappeared. In choosing this passage, Styron emphasizes the resistance and commodification of Turner first into purse, then text. Drewry gives a racist version of the Eucharist and the process of immanence: the absorption of Turner, the historical figure, into legend. The parallel passages, in content and placement on the page, work, complexly interact, rivaling, transforming, even canceling one another. The overarching structure of Styron's novel (maybe better called a "decomposition") seems at odds with what many readers think its central message of redemption. It is not, however, at odds with a vision that borders on nihilism.

In *The Confessions of Nat Turner*, Styron subverts and promotes a faith in history, whose "fragile testimony" (387) misleads no less than it inspires. What is the history of Nat Turner? he asks. Is it what others have observed and recorded any more than what Turner himself has sworn? The novel's multiple endings give readers a chance to write their own history. For some, Nat's story ends with his final sentimental vision of Margaret Whitehead, the girl he desired, hated, and killed, calling him to love and God. For others, it ends with Drewry's summary of Nat's physical remains, or with the words: "It is done . . . and he shall be my son." The shifts in time and reality underscore the historian's difficulty in trying to communicate the ephemeral nature of human experience—never separable from the forces that shape it. Nat's vision of heaven, so like Harriet Beecher's Stowe's in *Uncle Tom's Cabin* (1852), suggests that the novel's last words might belong, after all, to Gray, who tells Turner that "God is a God durned lie!" (114).

As a writer, Styron himself seems pulled by two conflicting forces: the imperatives of modern history and the allure of deeper mysteries. "One of the enduring marvels of art," he wrote when accepting the Howells Medal, "is its ability to soar through any barrier, to explore any territory of experience, and I say that only by venturing into strange territory shall artists, of whatever commitment, risk discovering and illuminating the human spirit that we all share" (Stone 101). *The Confessions of Nat Turner* acknowledges the impossibility of what Styron's spirit craves, a moment in which an individual can forget oneself in a body of souls. That yearning helps to explain what feelings fuel the continued debate about his novel and why he himself has refused to be silenced.

Sherley Ann Williams first published the short story that would become her novel, *Dessa Rose*, in a 1980 volume titled *Midnight Birds*. The volume's editor, Mary Helen Washington, selected pieces that made women their own historical subjects (xiii). In the statement that precedes her story, "Meditations on History," Williams writes: *"I am the women I speak of in my stories, my poems"* (198). She is also, as she writes, a man in her previous book, *Give Birth to Brightness*, and a sexual voice in an essay on the blues in Afro-American poetry. Like Styron, she wants to soar through barriers, but in the process she also wants to retain an essential self. While Williams's stance may be mitigated by her awareness of her position as author, it seems dangerously close to duplicating Styron's in *The Confessions of Nat Turner.*

Williams, attempting to reconstruct the private and public history of black people, prefaced her "Meditations" with an excerpt from Angela Davis, to whom she respectfully and affectionately dedicated her story. Davis calls for a resurrection of the black woman in her true historical contours: "*We, the black women of today, must accept the full weight of a legacy wrought in blood by our mothers in chains . . . as heirs to a tradition of supreme perseverance and heroic resistance, we must hasten to take our place wherever our people are forging on towards freedom*" (qtd. in Sherley Williams, "Meditations" 200). With this statement, Williams boldly locates herself as subject, an act that she thought Styron avoided, yet the personal and political intent of her work raises the same specters that haunted his *Confessions.* What is its relationship to history? How do we determine its tone apart from the exegesis of its author?

The two versions of Dessa's story further complicate Williams's point of view. The short story, which begins in limited third-person omniscient from Dessa's perspective, focuses on her loving relationship with her husband, Kaine. What follows is a section composed of dated journal entries titled "Meditations on History," recorded by an unnamed white male narrator, who in the novel becomes Adam Nehemiah ("Nemi"), the author of *The Complete Guide for Competent Masters in Dealing with Slaves and Other Dependents.* Although the meditations are in his hand, their authorship becomes collaborative to the extent that he transcribes Dessa's words without understanding their import: "Onlest mind I be knowin," she tells him, "is mines" ("Meditations" 237). The story ends with her escape and the narrator's keen sense of loss: "Gone . . . just—just gone" ("Meditations" 248). The narrator fails to realize that Dessa has never been present to someone incapable of compassionate interpretation.

In the novel, Williams retains Nehemiah's journal entries while increasingly telling the story from Dessa's point of view. An italicized prologue follows the author's note, and the body of the novel consists of three sections that suggest the personal and cultural evolution of the protagonist: "The Darky," "The Wench," and "The Negress," each introduced by epigraphs successively from Frederick Douglass ("You have seen how a man was made a slave. . . ."), Sojourner Truth (". . . I have plowed and planted and no man could head me. . . ."), and Taj Mahal ("*Ma négresse, voulez-vous danser, voulez-vous danser avec moi, ici?*"). The epigraphs place the novel in relationship to African American history and popular culture. Accenting different avatars of Dessa's social identity, they fetishize her in a manner analogous (though perhaps unavoidable) to Styron's Turner. An italicized epilogue set years later further recalls the circular structure, the alpha and the omega, of *The Confessions.*

In *Dessa Rose*, Williams sometimes seems, no less than Styron, to be working at cross purposes. The novel honors certain kinds of history, such as slave narratives and oral histories, which are absorbed—some might argue subsumed—by Williams's own written narrative. Dessa begins as text, a body literally inscribed by the lash, and ends as author. The shift highlights how the dueling narratives give way to a comforting, more collective voice that allows the stories of every character, black and white, to coexist. This ending especially appealed to reviewers, who saw the relationship between Dessa and Ruth, the white woman she learns to trust, as promising a new era of interracial sisterhood.

The plot follows Dessa: her participation in a slave uprising, her imprisonment awaiting the birth of her child, her escape, her respite on Ruth's farm, and her new life in the West. Over the course of the novel, Dessa's ideas about herself and her past go through several transformations. Williams's vision of history, more political than organic, presents Dessa as both subject and author. As Nehemiah records her talking to herself, she comes to understand the past as process: "White men existed because they did. Master had smashed the banjo because that was the way he was, able to do what he felt like doing. And a nigger could, too. This was what Kaine's act said to her. He had done [attacked the master]; he was. She had done also, had as good as killed Master, for wasn't her own punishment worse than death? She had lost Kaine, become a self she scarcely knew, lost to family, to friends. So she talked" (56).

Dessa's version of the past, as well as her ways of exploring it, stand in opposition to Nehemiah's so-called truth-seeking. He asks questions and expects answers that will allow him to categorize human experience and human beings and that support existing political and social structures of domination. She burrows into the past. Trying to make her present congruent with her past, she hunts what is almost a Hegelian explanation that will permit her to have a continuous self or identity. For her, history rests in "the persistence of memory . . . in lost hidden places." According to Eudora Welty, those places "wait to be found and to be known for what they are. Such history is barely accessible, the shell of it is only a fraily thing held together . . . the continuity is *here*" (7). Dessa's memory of the past, indeed of Dessa herself, will live through the telling and retelling of her story, written down and "said back" (260) by her grandchild. Dessa's two accounts of the past, which unite written and oral traditions (and recall in this way Cather's *Sapphira and the Slave Girl*), reinforce the novel's promise of integration. The novel ends with Dessa's vision of the past being something tangible, a text she can pass on to her descendants.

Williams contrasts Dessa's knowledge, through communal stories and lived experience, with Nehemiah's, rooted in his Calvinist, working-class childhood and deformed by his social ambitions to marry into the planter class. Possessing Dessa, Nehemiah hopes to fix who he is. In this mad and futile pursuit, he resembles the narrator of Henry James's *The Aspern Papers* (1888) as much as William Styron. James's narrator will do anything—marry a woman he does not love, even murder—to own the remains of his alter ego, Jeffrey Aspern. The self, as all three of these authors show, remains finally ineffable.

The change in Dessa from subject to author, to someone who both feels and constructs knowledge, results largely from her relationship with Ruth. Ruth or "Miz Rufel," whom Dessa renames "Miz Ruint," is indeed ruined. Her gambling husband has left her with a run-down, half-built farm and a child. Her protector and surrogate mother, a black woman she calls "Mammy," has died. When Dessa and her fellow escapees, Nathan, Harker, and Cully, arrive, she needs them as much as they need her.

Williams would seem to endorse, rather than condemn, the act of sympathetic imagination that motivated Styron. Her heroines grow because they learn to see from the other's point of view. Their disparate perspectives, shaped by historical realities, intersect through their shared experiences as women. Dessa is offended when she wakes to find Ruth breast-feeding her newborn baby. The act upsets what has been beaten into her about the order of the world. Ruth outrages Dessa, because she, like Nehemiah, seems to think that everything rightfully belongs to her, from Dessa's son to her friend Nathan, who becomes Ruth's lover. Dessa begins softening to Ruth when she realizes, as they work their way west as mistress and maid, that white women are also vulnerable to rape. Their masquerade—Ruth's selling of "slaves" who then escape—recalls the cons Mark Twain devised for Jim and Huck or the Duke and Dauphin in *Adventures of Huckleberry Finn* (1885). The masquerade allows all participants to explore their own roles from a distance, to adopt and discard masks that are just that: masks, not some inherent self. Destabilizing their identities, the masquerade provides a space where Dessa and Ruth can be friends.

In *Dessa Rose*, Williams offers the American public what W.D. Howells thought it craved: "a tragedy with a happy ending" (qtd. in Wharton 65). For all her ignorance, innocence, and liberality, Ruth persists in seeing Dessa as "the wench." Indeed, no matter how much she loved Mammy, she never knew—as Dessa, thinking of her own mammy, taunts her—that Mammy's given name was Dorcas. The pain of that knowledge impels Ruth to "know," not to "own," Dessa. When Ruth surprises Dessa naked and sees her scars, she realizes Dessa's right to hide her pain and, more important, her own right to the private self denied slaves. "Odessa," she tells her: "Your mammy birthed you, and mines, mines just helped to raise me. But she loved me . . . she loved me, just like yours loved you." Ruth's recognition of Dessa's feelings makes it possible for Dessa to answer without anger or regret, "I know that" (167). Dessa has wanted to misname Ruth (and Ruth, Dessa), to hold her at a distance out of fear: "Where white peoples look at black and see something ugly, something hateful, she saw color" (184). In these ways, Williams makes a distinction between "owning" ("possessing") and "owning" ("acknowledging"). Naming means something entirely different in these separate contexts: the first robs a person of his or her identity, whereas the second expresses a wish to share a small part of that person's life.

At the novel's end, Williams gives "owning" one more, and perhaps disturbing, twist, making it resemble a confession that recalls the complicity between Styron's Turner and Gray. "I will never forget Nemi trying to read me," Dessa writes, "knowing I had put myself in his hands" (260). How had Dessa put herself in the hands of this "last white man" (241)—a phrase that echoes Styron's characterization of Gray in *The Confessions*? By not trusting Ruth, by talking to herself? Williams's meaning remains ambiguous, yet it suggests Dessa's collusion through the shame she feels. "Nemi knowed me without looking at scars," she thinks. "I couldn't hide them no way and they told plain as day who I was" (246). Dessa learns, however, that to Ruth they signify her courage and will to survive. Aunt Chloe, whom the sheriff asks to verify or deny their existence, pays tribute to them with a touch, then wills them out of being with a few words: "I ain't seed nothing on this gal's butt. She ain't got a scar on her back" (254). This promise of healing and renewal prompted readers to suppose that relationships such as Dessa and Ruth's most likely did exist in the antebellum South. Ironically, Williams's novel, as did Styron's, served political ends that they did not consent to endorse.

Williams's version of southern history makes *Dessa Rose* seem a far more sentimental book than the one it parodies, if not imitates, and critiques. Her view of the past matches Turner's view of heaven. Although Dessa and Ruth go in separate directions (Dessa west and Ruth east to Philadelphia, a major terminal on the underground railroad), their stories exist alongside. Dessa wonders whether Ruth calls her name to her daughter as she calls Ruth's. The process highlights the transmutation of family stories into myth and national allegory. Ironically, Styron's vision will not allow this kind of amalgamation. He maintains that the past holds no place where people, any people, can go and feel secure.

As *Dessa Rose* and *The Confessions of Nat Turner* illustrate, there is no recipe for calling history into being. It should not surprise us that Styron inspired Williams's anger or that so many people have misread Styron, including Styron himself. Authors, responding to the changing needs of their immediate worlds, have always reformulated the past. Williams and Styron demonstrate that there are as many histories as there are Souths, that history finally becomes—as Ralph Waldo Emerson wrote—subjective: "In other words there is properly no history, only biography" (40). Like many writers, Williams and Styron had to learn this lesson for themselves, so as to live, in Emerson's words, what they would know.

Notes

1. Bennett argues that Styron tries "to escape the judgment of history embodied in Nat Turner and his spiritual sons of the twentieth century" (4).

2. See Stone 101–76, Mellard, and Tragle.

3. See, for example, Bennett 4; Killens 36; and Harding 32.

4. See Henderson.

5. In the afterword to the 1993 edition, Styron interprets Lukács's argument in the following way: "The creator of historical fiction . . . should have a thorough—perhaps even a magisterial—command of the period with which he is dealing, but he should not permit his work to be governed by particular historical facts" (441).

6. See Bryer.

7. Thewell states that the real history of Nat Turner has yet to be written (91).

8. See Mellard.

9. John A. Williams argues that a novelist writing a historical work becomes in effect a historian (46).

10. Kaiser discusses the problem of creating black characters and gives a survey of novels dealing with slave uprisings (50–51).

11. See Hairston 68–69.

12. There were objections to the book itself. James Weldon Johnson notes that whites could not believe that there were intelligent, well-to-do blacks in Harlem, and middle-class blacks thought Van Vechten's depiction of dissolute characters "a libel on the race" (381).

13. For a discussion of minstrel, see Baker. Also see Bennett 5.

14. See Fabricant 342.

Works Cited

Baker, Houston A. Jr. *Modernism and the Harlem Renaissance*. Chicago: U of Chicago P, 1987. 17–24.

Bennett, Lerone Jr. "Nat's Last White Man." *William Styron's Nat Turner: Ten Black Writers Respond*. Ed. John Henrik Clarke. Boston: Beacon, 1968. 3–16.

Bryer, Jackson R. "William Styron: A Bibliography." *The Achievement of William Styron*. Ed. Robert K. Morris with Irving Malin. Athens: U of Georgia P, 1975. 242–77.

Ellison, Ralph, William Styron, Robert Penn Warren, and C. Vann Woodward. "The Uses of History in Fiction." *Conversations with William Styron*. Ed. James L.W. West III. Jackson: UP of Mississippi, 1985. 114–44.

Emerson, Ralph Waldo. "History." *Essays: First Series*. New York: John B. Alden, 1886.

Fabricant, Daniel S. "Thomas R. Gray and William Styron: Finally, a Critical Look at the 1831 *Confessions of Nat Turner.*" *American Journal of Legal History* 37.3 (1993): 332–61.

Hairston, Loyle. "William Styron's Nat Turner-Rogue-Nigger." *William Styron's Nat Turner: Ten Black Writers Respond.* Ed. John Henrik Clarke. Boston: Beacon, 1968. 66–72.

Harding, Vincent. "You've Taken My Nat and Gone." *William Styron's Nat Turner: Ten Black Writers Respond.* Ed. John Henrik Clarke. Boston: Beacon, 1968. 23–33.

Henderson, Mae G. "(W)riting *The Work* and Working the Rites." *Black American Literature Forum* 23.4 (1989): 631–60.

Johnson, James Weldon. *Along This Way.* 1937. New York: Viking, 1967.

· Kaiser, Ernest. "The Failure of William Styron." *William Styron's Nat Turner: Ten Black Writers Respond.* Ed. John Henrik Clarke. Boston: Beacon, 1968. 50–65.

Killens, John Oliver. "The Confessions of Willie Styron." *William Styron's Nat Turner: Ten Black Writers Respond.* Ed. John Henrik Clarke. Boston: Beacon, 1968. 34–44.

Lukács, Georg. *The Historical Novel.* Boston: Beacon, 1963.

Marcuse, Herbert. *The Aesthetic Dimension: Toward a Critique of Marxist Aesthetics.* Trans. and rev. Erica Sherover. Boston: Beacon, 1978.

Mellard, James M. "The *Unquiet Dust:* The Problem of History in Styron's *The Confessions of Nat Turner.*" *The Critical Response to William Styron.* Ed. Daniel W. Ross. Westport, Conn.: Greenwood, 1995. 157–72.

Morris, Wesley. *Toward a New Historicism.* Princeton: Princeton UP, 1972.

Stocking, George W. Jr. *Victorian Anthropology.* New York: Free Press, 1987.

Stone, Albert E. *The Return of Nat Turner: History, Literature, and Cultural Politics in Sixties America.* Athens: U of Georgia P, 1992.

Styron, William. *The Confessions of Nat Turner.* New York: Vintage, 1993.

———.*This Quiet Dust and Other Writings.* New York: Vintage, 1993.

Thewell, Mike. "Back with the Wind: Mr. Styron and the Reverend Turner." *William Styron's Nat Turner: Ten Black Writers Respond.* Ed. John Henrik Clarke. Boston: Beacon, 1968. 79–91.

Tragle, Henry Irving. "Styron and His Sources." *Massachusetts Review* 11.1 (1970): 135–53.

Washington, Mary Helen, ed. *Midnight Birds.* Garden City, N.Y.: Anchor, 1980.

———. "In pursuit of our own history." *Midnight Birds.* xiii-xxv.

Welty, Eudora. "The House of Willa Cather." *The Art of Willa Cather.* Ed. Bernice Slote and Virginia Faulkner. Lincoln: U of Nebraska P, 1973.

West, James L.W. III, ed. *Conversations with William Styron.* Jackson: UP of Mississippi, 1985.

Wharton, Edith. *French Ways and Their Meaning.* New York: D. Appleton, 1919.

Williams, John A. "The Manipulation of History and of Fact: An Ex-Southerner's Apologist Tract for Slavery and the Life of Nat Turner; or, William Styron's Faked Confessions." *William Styron's Nat Turner: Ten Black Writers Respond.* Ed. John Henrik Clarke. Boston: Beacon, 1968. 45–49.

Williams, Sherley Ann. *Dessa Rose.* New York: Berkley Books, 1986.

———. "Meditations on History." *Midnight Birds.* Ed. Mary Helen Washington. 195–248.

New Narratives of Southern Manhood

Race, Masculinity, and Closure in Ernest Gaines's Fiction

Suzanne W. Jones

In memory of Herbert Lee Blount

In *A Rage for Order: Black/White Relations in the American South Since Emancipation*, Joel Williamson explores the conjuncture of race, manhood, and violence peculiar to the American South. He argues that for southern white men the traditional Victorian masculine role of provider and protector was directly linked with violence because of plantation society's "necessity of controlling a potentially explosive black population." As early as the seventeenth century, a patrol system, made up of masters and overseers, enforced the laws of slavery. By the nineteenth century, the duty of patrolling was extended to all white men, who had authority over all blacks (even free blacks) and over whites who conspired with blacks. Thus a system for controlling slaves became a practice "of all whites controlling all blacks . . . a matter of race" (11). The martial role white men created for themselves became entrenched particularly in the last decades before the Civil War as slavery came under attack by northerners from without and by rebellious slaves from within. Whites created a complementary stereotype of black people as "simple, docile, and manageable," who if properly handled were like children, but if improperly cared for became animals. Williamson argues that this "Sambo" figure was a figment of white wishful thinking, which functioned "to build white egos" while masking their fears of black rebellion. Many black people played the Sambo role in order to survive slavery and its aftermath: "Downcast eyes, shuffling feet, soft uncertain words, and a totally pliant manner were white-invented signals to be used by a black person to say that this individual was no threat." Williamson believes that the Sambo role saved not only blacks from white hostility but whites themselves "from the wild and murderous behavior that did damage to their flattering image of themselves as protecting parents to these childlike people" (15–16). The convergence of conventional Victorian gender ideology with southern racial ideology operated to make black males boys and white males men. Slavery and segregation fostered stereotypes and kept white people ignorant of black people. In Ernest Gaines's *A Gathering of Old Men* (1983), the white characters are surprised when the black men do not act "like frightened little bedbugs" (15). In Gaines's *A Lesson Before Dying* (1993), white lawyers argue that the falsely accused black defendant is not a man but an "animal" (6–7).

In his fiction Ernest Gaines is interested not only in deconstructing stereotypes but also in presenting new models of southern manhood, for both black and white men. While Gaines has employed traditional definitions of manhood in his fiction, the vision he presents in *A Lesson Before Dying* is similar to that of Cooper Thompson and other contemporary theorists of masculinity, who believe that young men must learn that "traditional masculinity is life threatening" and that being men in a modern world means accepting their vulnerability, expressing a range of emotions, asking for help and support, learning nonviolent means of resolving conflicts, and accepting behaviors that have traditionally been labeled feminine (such as being nurturing, communicative, and cooperative) as necessary for full human development (586–91).[1]

Gaines's *A Gathering of Old Men*, set in the late 1970s in rural Louisiana, seems to have two definitions of manhood, one for young southern white men and one for old southern black men—a difference based on the social construction of race and masculinity and the history of race relations in the South. Gaines structures his novel with parallel maturation scenes that involve white and black men coming to terms with southern society's race and gender ideology. A young white man comes to maturity when he rejects his society's equation of masculinity with violence, while the old black men become men when they enact this definition. The young white man Gil attempts to break the cycle of racial violence that his father is known for by refusing to join his family in avenging his brother's death, allegedly at the hands of a black man. The old black men break a cycle of paralyzing fear that has led to passivity by responding, first verbally but then violently, to the attempt of white men to wield power over them. In doing so, while they do not provoke the racial conflict, they do not end it as soon as they could have. Ernest Gaines allows the old men briefly to wield power over whites, perhaps as revenge for having been at the mercy of whites in the past, perhaps as the only message racist white men, like Luke Will, who instigates the shoot-out, can understand. These two definitions of what it means to be a man lead to an ideologically contradictory, though emotionally satisfying, double ending. This ending—first a shoot-out and then a trial banning guns—seems to be determined as much or more by literary conventions than by ideological considerations. As a result, *A Gathering of Old Men*, while reconstructing race relations and reversing historically southern social constructions of black and white manhood, does not go as far in questioning traditional definitions of masculinity and writing new masculine endings as does Gaines's *A Lesson Before Dying*. The model of manhood that Gaines confers on his young black male characters in *A Lesson Before Dying* converges with Gil's. With these two portraits Gaines suggests that in order to reconstruct the South, both black and white men must reject the traditional Western model of manhood that links masculinity and violence. Both novels enact Gaines's belief that the South needs new narratives of manhood.

In *A Gathering of Old Men*, Gaines focuses on a group of old black men in their seventies and eighties, who have been "boys" all their lives, not only in the eyes of the white men they have worked for but also in their own eyes. Born after Reconstruction failed in the South, they have grown up only to be beaten down by racial prejudice and boxed in by Jim Crow laws that have kept them in an inferior position socially and economically. The civil rights movement and its resulting laws have had little effect on their lives, which continue to be shaped by segregation and economic dependency on whites. These old black men, who once worked in various capacities on the white-owned plantations, continue to live gratis in the old slave quarters. Many of the old men who were once sharecroppers or skilled artisans find the prospects for their children's lives even less promising than their own because their children are now working as laborers for Cajun farmers who are renting the land that they used to sharecrop. Social customs of deference to whites—looking down, going to the back door—remain unchanged. These social and economic facts, conditions Gaines has termed "de facto slavery,"[2] give *A Gathering of Old Men* the feel of a historical novel rather than one set in contemporary times.

The subordinate position of these old black men has not only lowered their self-esteem but caused doubts about their manhood, which they, like the white men they work for, define in traditional terms as providing for and protecting their families. This blurring of gender identity with maturity reflects the power of gender ideology to shape conceptions of the self. Hazel Carby argues in *Reconstructing Womanhood* that manhood as traditionally defined by Western society could not be achieved or maintained by black men "because of the inability of the slave to protect the black woman" (35). In this regard, Gaines's old black men have lived lives not very different from those of slaves. Each tells a story of a sister or brother, son or daughter, who was at the very least treated unfairly by whites, at the worst raped or killed. Each knows that he did nothing to stop white injustice, not only because he felt powerless to do so but also because he feared for his life if he stood up for equal and just treatment. The old men's feelings of fear and powerlessness, which keep them socially impotent, have created problems for black women as well. The men have taken out their frustrations with white society and with themselves by verbally and physically abusing their wives. Citing similar scenes in James Joyce's *Dubliners* and William Faulkner's "Dry September," Gaines sees such behavior as universal: "All men have hopes, and all men brutalize other things near them at home, when they cannot fulfill such hopes" (Gaudet and Wooton 44). The sociologist Clyde Franklin, who has researched the effect of institutionalized racism on black men in the United States, argues that "structural barriers to Black male sex-role adoption, then have produced a Black male who is primed for a conflictual relationship with Black women" (347). The question has become what part the social construction of race, class, and masculinity plays in causing male frustration to be enacted as violence.

When Mohandas Gandhi worked with the nonviolent struggle in South Africa, he argued that passive violence (such as that practiced by racist whites in the American South) must be eliminated to rid society of physical violence: "Passive violence in the form of discrimination, oppression, exploitation, hate, anger and all the subtle ways in which it manifests itself gives rise to physical violence in society."[3] In *A Gathering of Old Men*, the mostly passive violence of white landowners and the mostly physical violence of the white working class produce black violence. For Charlie to explain why he killed Beau Boutan in self-defense, he must begin forty-five years earlier, when he first ran from someone who abused him. Beau's abuse pushed Charlie over the edge: "It took fifty years. Half a hundred—and I said I been 'bused enough. He used to 'buse me. No matter if I did twice the work any other man could do, he 'bused me anyhow. . . . And long as I was Big Charlie, nigger boy, I took it. . . . But they comes a day! They comes a day when a man must be a man" (189). A similar day finally comes for the old men as well, a day when they will take no more abuse, when they are ready to take a stand. To explain their behavior to Sheriff Mapes, they, too, return to the past and tell stories of white injustice.

According to Mathu a man is not afraid to do "what he think is right. . . . That's what part him from a boy" (85). The other old men have never done what they thought was right. They have never stood up to whites to protect themselves and their families and friends from rape and murder and discrimination—until the day on which this novel takes place. Responding to white plantation owner Candy Marshall's request to protect the man who has been influential in her growing up, they rally around Mathu with their twelve-gauge shotguns. It is not surprising that the one black man, Clatoo, whom Candy does not have power over emerges as the leader of the old men, insisting on their right to congregate alone and to make decisions without Candy. Because Clatoo owns his own land and gardening business, he does not depend on Candy for his home or livelihood, a fact she threatens the other men with: "'Y'all can go on and listen to Clatoo if y'all want,' she said. 'But remember this—Clatoo got a little piece of land to go back to. Y'all don't have nothing but this. You listen to him now, and you won't even have this'" (174). Sheriff Mapes's assessment, "you want to keep them slaves the rest of their lives" (175), suggests that Candy's desire to help the black people is combined with a desire to control them and take responsibility for them that is reminiscent of nineteenth-century planters' paternal roles.[4]

Standing up first to white injustice and then to Candy's paternalism is not enough to make the old black men feel like men; rather, it takes an act of physical force to certify their manhood. They have no doubt that Beau's father, Fix Boutan, who has allegedly fixed the fate of several black men and women in the past, will seek revenge for his son's death and give them the opportunity to stop him with force. Although some of them are afraid, they know that they have only their fear to lose and very much to gain. Facing death, the old men are determined to act like "men" before they die, thereby winning self-respect and respect from Mathu, the only man in their community thought to be "a real man" (84). Previously only Mathu has stood up to whites who demean him. Thus, before Charlie Biggs confesses, everyone assumes that Mathu has killed Beau Boutan. Sheriff Mapes's certainty of Mathu's guilt and Mapes's easy equation of violence and masculinity is testimony to the casual, often unconscious, way language is used to reinforce gender ideology: "He killed him, all right. The only one with nuts enough to do it" (72).

The novel turns on an interesting paradox in defining manhood as it relates to "race." In order for Fix's youngest son Gil to be a man, he must refuse to kill the black man who has killed his brother Beau; in order for each old black man to be a man, he must be ready to kill a white man, following what Bob Connell has identified as the "hegemonic masculinity" in Western society, a model associated with aggressiveness and the capacity for violence (197). The white man becomes a man when he rejects this model. The behavior that Gaines deems manly for each racial group is based on the history of race relations in the rural South. The old black men long understandably to get even for all the injustice their families have experienced at the hands of white people. The young white man Gil wants to put a stop to the misunderstanding, hatred, and violence that have characterized southern race relations and come to epitomize his family's reputation in the community.

As a football player at Louisiana State University, Gil has grown to respect, like, and depend on Cal, a black player on his team. Together they are Salt and Pepper, destined to become All-Americans and win the conference title for their university. Together they have become a symbol of improved race relations in a new South. The "publicity people" (111) at the university have invented the nickname, encouraged the symbolism, and profited from the alliance: "It would be the first time this had ever happened, black and white in the same backfield—and in the Deep South, besides. LSU was fully aware of this, the black and white communities in Baton Rouge were aware of this, and so was the rest of the country. Wherever you went, people spoke of Salt and Pepper of LSU" (112). For Gil and Cal the relationship is more than symbolic. Gaines uses their relationship to suggest that when diverse people live and work together for common goals, stereotypes fall on rocky soil and racial hatreds wither and die.[5]

Gil's decision not to join his father in vengeful and violent behavior is seen by his father and the older men in his family as unmanly, and they impugn his manhood by identifying Gil's restraint as feminine: "He [Gil] says sit, weep with the women" (145). Furthermore, Fix doubts Gil's racial pride because he views his behavior as choosing black over white: "Your brother's honor for the sake to play football side by side with the niggers" (143). Gaines emphasizes the difficulty Gil has in opposing conventional masculine behavior by having Gil repeatedly ask the old white men gathered, "Haven't I been a good boy? . . . Aren't I a good boy?" (147). The power of gender ideology makes Gil blur gender identity with obedience and family loyalty.

While in some respects Gaines portrays this conflict between Gil and his father as generational and in doing so projects a more hopeful future, at the same time, he creates several young white "rednecks," who subscribe to the old conventions. The leader of the group, Luke Will, publicly tries to shame Gil and his brother Jean into avenging Beau's death by attacking their manhood and appealing to racial solidarity, but his attempt to shame Gil and Jean Boutan for refusing to fight does not work because Gil and Jean have become members of a larger, racially mixed community and have left behind the violent practices of what southern historian Bertram Wyatt-Brown identifies as "primal honor."[6] That Gil is college-educated is certainly significant. While Gil's father thinks that an education at LSU should reinforce the old southern code, Gaines suggests otherwise. An education opens Gil's mind to the racial discrimination and oppression in the rural community in which he grew up. In Wyatt-Brown's terms, because Gil puts individual conscience before reputation in the community, personal guilt before public shame (22), he is able to make an unpopular stand in his family, which seeks to defend its honor, and in his parish, which seeks to keep black people in their customary place.

For Gaines, Gil becomes a man when he refuses to use or sanction violence, a reversal of the primal code of honor practiced by Gil's Cajun family and working-class whites in the community. In refusing to participate in the accustomed masculine behavior, Gil takes the fictional step for his social class that Faulkner's Bayard Sartoris took for upper-class whites in *The Unvanquished* when he withstands both family and community pressure to kill his father's murderer. Because of Gil's compassion for the old black men, his father flippantly calls him "a regular Christ" and sarcastically quips, "Feels sorry for the entire world" (145). Gaines expects the reader to take this comparison more seriously, as a new vision of southern white working-class manhood. This new vision includes the ability to express emotion other than anger (Gil cries in this scene), to articulate one's feelings, to empathize with black people, and to resolve conflict in nonaggressive ways.[7] Gil's and Jean's experiences indicate that solidarity is predicated not on race, or class for that matter, but on community, whether on the football field at LSU or in the town of Bayonne, where Jean is a butcher.

With the scene between the professor of African American literature from the University of Southwestern Louisiana and Jack Marshall, who owns the plantation where Beau has been shot, Gaines suggests a reconstruction of masculine identity for upper-class southern white men as well, a definition that includes trying to find solutions to continuing racial tensions in one's community, regardless of whether one is personally involved in them. Whereas Jack Marshall escapes the conflict by leaving the plantation and drinking himself into oblivion at Tee Jack's bar, the professor suggests that in ignoring the situation, Marshall passively contributes to the violence. The professor asserts that "in the end, it's people like us, you and I, who pay for this," and "the debt is never finished as long as we stand for this" (165).

Whatever his accomplishments are in the classroom, this articulate, open-minded professor is unable to convince Luke Will and his cohorts to change their behavior by reasoning with them for a few minutes in a bar. The professor's call for restraint is met with Luke Will's physical intimidation to leave the bar. When Tee Jack, the bar owner, protests that the professor is a white man, Luke Will responds, "If he's a white man, let him act like one" (165). Ernest Gaines suggests that Luke Will cannot follow the professor's advice because he has not been socially conditioned to perceive such beliefs and behavior as worthy of "real white men." Luke Will has defined his manhood in terms of his ability to make life hard for "niggers" (159) and to keep the parish segregated. This aggressive behavior allows him to assert his power not only over the black people whom he antagonizes but also over the educated white men of a higher social class than himself (like the professor) who have created new laws to end segregation, and thus life in the South as Luke Will knows it. As a result, he can define masculine bravery only as fighting, not as refusing to fight. It is telling that during the shoot-out Luke's buddy Sharp defines the old black men as "brave" (204) at the point when they physically defend themselves, behavior the white men do not expect from black men.

To help rationalize his decision to take the law into his own hands, Luke Will asserts that the "next thing you know, they'll [black men] be raping the women" (149). The Deputy Sheriff's comment, "If they can't get you one way, they'll bring in the women every time" (149), is evidence that white men have played the sex card in the past, especially during the 1880s and 1890s, when they lost political power to northern Reconstructionists and to black men and when they lost economic power to an agricultural depression and to black male competition for jobs. Joel Williamson argues that because southern white men could not play the role of "protector-as-breadwinner" for their women as well as they expected during this time, they focused on another part of the traditional masculine role—"protector-as-defender of the purity of their women, in this instance against the imagined threat from the black beast rapist" (182).[8] During this period they revised their "Sambo" image of black men so as to justify their own violent behavior. The power of rhetoric to shape perceptions is particularly evident during this time in the case of Thomas Dixon Jr.'s novels and plays, especially *The Clansman* (1905), which D.W. Griffith made into a film, *The Birth of a Nation* (1915), thereby purveying to millions of people the image of black men as brutes and rapists. Joel Williamson points out that it was Dixon's novel *The Leopard's Spots* (1902), not "scholarly" articles or political tracts, that popularized radical, white southerners' racist views (98–99).[9]

With *A Gathering of Old Men*, Gaines rewrites Dixon's narratives of white masculinity. Although working-class Luke Will certainly thinks of himself as a man because of his willingness to defend the white community against blacks who have forgotten "their place," Ernest Gaines represents Will and his cohorts as boys and portrays their bravery as braggadocio. Big-talking Leroy, who can't wait to wield his gun against the old black men, turns into a "sniveling" (202) little boy when he is grazed by a bullet in the shoot-out. His ineffectual pleas for mercy from the Sheriff, "I'm a white boy, Mapes," and "I ain't nothing but a child, Mapes," (203), are among the funniest lines in the novel. The irony, of course, is heavy and twofold. First, being white no longer automatically gives one protection in the eyes of the law. Second, from the protected distance of Tee Jack's bar, this "child" had been "ready to kick me some ass" (166), but he crumples when he finds himself in the crossfire of live ammunition. Also, unlike Charlie Biggs, who as proof of his maturity takes responsibility for his actions and admits to killing Beau, Leroy will not admit that his cohorts have shot Sheriff Mapes; he falsely accuses the old black men.

In "Rereading American Literature" James Riener argues that manhood for the old black men in *A Gathering of Old Men* is "to be found, not in wielding power over others, but in a man's response to the attempts to wield power over him" (292). This is certainly true—the old men withstand Sheriff Mapes's slaps and Luke Will's bullets. Plus, they are willing as Riener suggests "to accept the consequences for the murder and for their defiance of the sheriff" (292). The willingness to accept responsibility for one's actions is especially true in the case of Charlie, who shoots Beau in self-defense but initially allows his parrain Mathu to take the rap for the murder because he is afraid that given past workings of the white-dominated legal system, he will never get a fair trial.[10]

The scene in which Charlie returns and confesses in front of his relatives, the sheriff, and the old black men parallels the scene in which Gil changes the pattern of behavior expected of him and emerges as a man, willing to accept responsibility for his actions. The main differences, of course, are that Gil is a young white man and Charlie is a fifty-year-old black man. Charlie declares before all gathered that at fifty years old, he is finally a man: "I want the world to know it. I ain't Big Charlie, nigger boy, no more, I'm a man. Y'all hear me? A man come back. Not no nigger boy. A nigger boy run and run and run. But a man come back. I'm a man" (187). Referred to by whites as "Beau's nigger" and Beau's "boy" because he works for Beau, he demands to be called "Mr. Biggs" by Sheriff Mapes, the reporter Lou Dimes, and the other assembled whites. With Charlie's demand, Gaines once again underlines the power of language to construct identity. The use of the appellation "Mr.," which signifies respect and has heretofore in southern society been reserved for adult white men, redefines Charlie as a man, not a boy.

While James Riener is correct to point out that it is not important that the old black men's defiance of the white establishment culminate in a fight because they have proven their manhood to themselves (292), most of them don't think so. Ironically, the manly behavior that the old black men are eager to exhibit comes in part from their capacity for violence and from a desire for revenge, which has the potential to threaten the emerging new relationship between the races as symbolized in the cooperation of Gil and Cal on the football field. Indeed, Gaines originally titled the novel "The Revenge of Old Men" but says he changed it "because these guys don't get any revenge; they're just gathering" (Gaudet and Wooton 118). After Charlie's confession, both Clatoo and Mathu suggest that the old men go home, pointing out that they have proven their manhood, just by standing up to Sheriff Mapes. They have gained self-respect and the respect of everyone there, black and white. But Rooster's reaction is typical of the majority:

> I was thinking now about all the hurt I had suffered, the insults
> my wife had suffered right in front of my face. I was thinking

about what all the old people musta gone through even before me. I was thinking about all that—and this was the day we was go'n get even. But now here Clatoo was saying we ought to go back home. Go back home and do what? I hadn't even fired a shot. Just one, in that pecan tree, so I could have a empty shell. No, that wasn't enough. Not after what I had put up with all these years. I wanted me a fight, even if I had to get killed. (181)

At this point the old black men are ready to take their memories of injustice out on any white man, similar to the way white men have treated them in the past. Earlier in the afternoon Gable says he is ready to kill Fix because "he was just like them who threw my boy in that 'lectric chair and pulled that switch. No, he wasn't born yet, but the same blood run in all their vein" (102). The old men are very disappointed when Fix does not show up to avenge Beau's death because they have projected onto him the responsibility for all past injustice.

Sheriff Mapes expresses the paradoxical nature of contemporary race relations when he blames the old men for Fix's failure to arrive: "Y'all the one—you cut your own throats. You told God you wanted Salt and Pepper to get together, and God did it for you. At the same time, you wanted God to keep Fix the way Fix was thirty years ago so one day you would get a chance to shoot him. Well, God couldn't do both. Not that He likes Fix, but He thought the other idea was better—Salt and Pepper. Well? Which do you want?" (171). But God can do "both," as Ernest Gaines illustrates. Although Fix does not show up, Luke Will does—giving the old men a chance not simply to stand up to attempts to wield power over them but to respond violently. To many readers, it seems only poetic justice, although hardly indicative of a new southern masculine order, that the old men get to fire their shotguns. Although they have proven their courage and Mathu's innocence before Luke's arrival, fighting seems necessary to prove their manhood, at least to them, if not to Gaines.

But it is Gaines, of course, who creates the fight and allows the men to do more than "gather." And Coot says he hasn't felt so good since World War I. Using slapstick humor, Gaines makes the fight more comic than tragic, even though two men are killed: the black "boy" who becomes a man when he admits to shooting Beau Boutan and the white man who remains a "boy" because he refuses to leave justice to the courts. When Luke Will wants to stop the fight and turn himself and his boys in, it is Charlie Biggs who encourages the old men to continue the fight, perhaps another reason Charlie must die in the end—because he encourages the black men to take justice into their own hands as the white men have done in the past. For Charlie, "standing up to Luke Will" (208) is equally as important as standing up for his rights. When Lou Dimes tells him that Luke Will wants to turn himself in and warns Charlie that if he continues to fight he will be charged with murder, not self-defense as with Beau, Charlie refuses to stop fighting, and he even enlists the old men to help him. One could argue that the old men lose some moral ground by following Charlie's lead rather than Mathu's and Clatoo's.

Gaines's novel has two resolutions to the black-white conflict: first a shoot-out and then a trial. These dual resolutions allow readers to have it "both ways" because they get an emotional catharsis resolved by traditional masculine behavior in the shoot-out but re-resolved in the trial that follows, by talk rather than aggression. The judge sentences all the men involved, both black and white, to a life without guns for the next five years. Gaines seems to have thought the shoot-out necessary to fulfill readers' expectations because in an interview he said, "They brought guns, and I still believe in the old Chekhovian idea that if the gun is over the mantel at the beginning of the play, the gun must go off by the time the curtain comes down. And I thought that the only way the gun could go off in my book was Charlie and Luke Will out on the street shooting at each other" (Gaudet and Wooton 97). Gaines's reply when asked to compare the novel's ending with that of the television movie is significant. The movie ends with Luke Will backing down once he sees that the old men have guns. There is no shoot-out, but there is not a trial banning guns either. When asked whether the ending of the television movie made a different point than that of the novel, Gaines replied, "I don't know if there's any difference at all. I think what I was trying to do in that entire book was show a group of old men standing" (Gaudet and Wooton 97). It is interesting that when Gaines thinks of the novel's impact, he focuses on the old men gathering to support Mathu, finally taking a stand against white injustice and discrimination—not on the shoot-out that follows. Indeed, in the novel Gaines states that most of the old men are not very good shots, and he gives them comic roles in the fight as if to distance them from the deaths caused by this tragic encounter. While Gaines refers only to Charlie and Luke Will when he talks about the shoot-out, the old men are certainly emotionally as well as actively, if ineptly, involved in this event.

Unlike Gaines, I think the double ending he chooses for the novel does make a difference. The two endings support contradictory themes about violence and masculinity. The first ending suggests that fighting is the only emotionally satisfying and manly way to resolve an argument; the second reaffirms what Gaines has already proven in the novel—that talking can produce results. While Fix suggests that talking is the equivalent of doing "nothing" (144), Gaines proves otherwise in the gradual change that Sheriff Mapes undergoes as he listens to Charlie's and the old men's personal accounts of injustice and discrimination. Granted Gaines does not suggest that talk always works. The conversation the English professor has with Jack Marshall is disappointing, and his exchange with Luke Will is ineffective. Similarly Gil, too, struggles to make his father understand his new views about race relations. Begging his friend Sully to help him, Gil is still unable to move his father beyond football to civil rights, beyond Gil's chance at being an All-American to his heroic attempt to stop the cycle of violence. Gil's father views him as a coward rather than the brave young man Gaines presents him as. In contrast, the storytelling of the old black men is incredibly effective, particularly that of Tucker, Johnny Paul, and Charlie. They recreate scenes and situations so that the people listening, Sheriff Mapes and Gaines's readers, can see and feel the injustice they are talking about.

Gaines does have a point about readers' expectations and the convention of the gun. Many viewers of the television movie who had also read the book found the television ending disappointing: they preferred the shoot-out to the gathering (Gaudet and Wooton 98). Perhaps their disappointment is the natural reaction to viewing a movie ending that departs so radically from the novel. But perhaps these readers, like Gaines, expect guns to go off if they appear. Or perhaps they are used to violence as a tool to settle men's disputes and to conclude men's plots. In *Before Reading*, Peter Rabinowitz explains that "in a given literary context, when certain elements appear, rules of configuration activate certain expectations." Rabinowitz goes on to explain, however, that the writer can make use of readers' expectations in a variety of ways: "not only to create a sense of resolution (that is, by completing the patterns that the rules lead readers to expect, either with or without detours) but also to create surprise (by reversing them, for instance, or by deflecting them, or by fulfilling them in some unanticipated way)" (111). Gaines could have had Luke Will back down when faced with so many guns, which is what the television scriptwriter did, or he could have had Charlie heed Lou Dimes's advice and end the fight. Either ending would have been more in keeping with Gaines's stated focus on "a gathering of old men" rather than "the revenge of old men." Gaines speculates that television movie producers found his original resolution too sensitive for a large viewing audience given the current racial climate: "Maybe they just didn't want a black and white shootout, killing each other off" (Gaudet and Wooton 97). To me, the ending of the novel sends an ambivalent message about violence. Gaines clearly is more interested in talk than in violence, in the power of storytelling rather than the power of guns. If he had banned the guns before the courtroom, thereby using the guns in a surprising way rather than the expected way, his novel would not have required two endings to get his point across.

While five years may be enough time in Gaines's fictional parish for blacks and whites to start dismantling racial stereotypes, reconstructing manhood, and learning to solve disagreements without violence, it took ten years for Gaines to find a way of writing beyond the conventional endings of stories about race and masculinity.[11] In *A Lesson Before Dying* he reconstructs black manhood in a way very different from his definition in *A Gathering of Old Men*. Though set in 1948, *A Lesson Before Dying* speaks to several contemporary issues: the racially imbalanced use of the death penalty, the responsibility of middle-class blacks for the larger black community, questions of gender-role egalitarianism, and new definitions of manhood. In "A New Vision of Masculinity," Cooper Thompson delineates attitudes and behavior that he says boys do not often learn but that he thinks boys should be taught. He includes "being supportive and nurturant, accepting one's vulnerability and being able to ask for help, valuing women and 'women's work,' understanding and expressing emotions (except for anger), the ability to empathize with and empower other people, and learning to resolve conflict in non-aggressive, non-competitive ways" (586). These are the behaviors that Gil exhibits in *A Gathering of Old Men* and that Gaines's black male characters in *A Lesson Before Dying* must learn in order to become men. But before they can implement these lessons, they must learn one key fact: that the white power structure has defined, and thereby confined, black people. Grant Wiggins, an elementary school teacher, has learned this lesson in college; he must teach it to Jefferson, who is in jail, in order for him to become something other than the "animal" white society has said he is. Although this lesson cannot free Jefferson from an unfair execution for a crime he did not commit (Jefferson is sentenced to death in the electric chair), it frees him to create himself mentally and emotionally within white society's prison.

To emphasize the white construction of black social reality, Gaines opens his novel with three versions of what happened the night Jefferson, in the wrong place at the wrong time, entered a store with two black friends. Their attempt to rob the store results in the white store owner and Jefferson's friends fatally shooting each other. Jefferson, who is a bit slow-witted, is unable to process what has happened before his eyes. He takes a drink to calm his nerves and then steals from the open cash register because he has no money and there are no witnesses. But to explain his actions, both the prosecuting attorney and the defense attorney tell stories that reveal assumptions of biological racial differences, the kinds of assumptions that white southerners used first to defend slavery and then to justify segregation. The prosecuting attorney argues that Jefferson is an "animal" who "celebrated the event by drinking over their still-bleeding bodies" (6–7). The defense attorney, trying to prove that Jefferson is not capable of planning a robbery, also argues that he is not a "man":

Gentleman of the jury, look at him—look at him—look at this. Do you see a man sitting here? Do you see a man sitting here? I ask you, I implore, look carefully—do you see a man sitting here? Look at the shape of this skull, this face as flat as the palm of my hand—look deeply into those eyes. Do you see a modicum of intelligence? Do you see anyone here who could plan a murder, a robbery, can plan—can plan—can plan anything? A cornered animal to strike quickly out of fear, a trait inherited from his ancestors in the deepest jungle of blackest Africa—yes, yes, that he can do—but to plan? To plan, gentlemen of the jury? No, gentlemen, this skull here holds no plans. What you see here is a thing that acts on command. A thing to hold the handle of a plow, a thing to load your bales of cotton, a thing to dig your ditches, to chop your wood, to pull your corn. . . . Why, I would just as soon put a hog in the electric chair as this. (7–8)

After the trial, Gaines underlines the power of the white man's words by having Jefferson become the "hog" that his lawyer has named him—dirty, unkempt, and rude. When Grant first visits Jefferson at the request of Jefferson's godmother who wants Grant to make him a man before he dies, Jefferson shows no concern for his godmother and eats the food that she has sent without using his hands. He acts this way both in reaction to and as a result of being called "a hog" at the trial—a cause-and-effect sequence of scenes that is emblematic of the social construction of black manhood in southern society.

Grant's first sessions with Jefferson have no effect. Grant's pedagogical techniques include modeling polite behavior for Jefferson, trying to make Jefferson feel guilty for hurting his godmother's feelings, and exploiting the bad relations with whites by telling Jefferson that they are betting against Grant's project with him. At first Grant fails with Jefferson for the same reason he is failing with his elementary school students: he does not want to teach, he is cynical about the prospect of making a difference, and thus he is angry about being forced into such a position.

Grant does not reach Jefferson until he changes his tactics. Only when Grant shifts the focus of their meetings from himself to Jefferson—which is where the focus should be, given that Grant has agreed to help Jefferson—does Grant begin to have a positive effect. First, he establishes a rapport with an open-minded and congenial young white deputy, who gives him important information about Jefferson's daily life and his state of mind. Then he has a conversation with Jefferson about the purpose of their meetings, which unlike his previous lectures allows Jefferson to talk about what is most important to him—dying—rather than what is most important to Grant—making Jefferson's godmother feel better. Also, Grant becomes more patient and empathetic, focusing on the reasons for Jefferson's rude behavior rather than on the behavior itself. For example, when Jefferson insults Vivian, Grant's lover, Grant wants to hit him but thinks before he strikes him, "I recognized his grin for what it was—the expression of the most heartrending pain I had ever seen on anyone's face" (130). Finally, Grant asks Jefferson philosophical questions that make him think about how to live.

When the date is scheduled for Jefferson's execution, Grant instinctively adds another strategy to his plan, asking Jefferson if there is anything he wants. He brings him a radio, comic books, and a pad and pencil. Grant's students send pecans and peanuts, and Grant promises Jefferson that he will have what he wants to eat on his last day. Finally, Grant tells Jefferson he would like to be his friend. The care and respect that Grant shows Jefferson have an effect. Jefferson begins to care for and to respect Grant and to show concern for those who have shown kindness to him. When Jefferson thinks of others as well as himself and tells Grant to thank the children for the pecans they sent, Grant feels he has made a breakthrough.

The third stage of Grant's lessons with Jefferson involves defining four crucial words for him: friend, "a friend would do anything to please a friend"; hero, "a hero does for others"; scapegoat, "someone else to blame"; and myth, "a myth is an old lie that people believe in. White people believe that they're better than anyone else on earth—and that's a myth" (190–92). With the first two words Grant challenges Jefferson to fulfill his potential, to become both friend and hero. Grant's definition of "hero" matches Gaines's: "It occurred to me one day that the only black people I knew as a child *were* heroes. . . . My hero is a person who will get up and go to work every damn day, and see himself not accomplishing much that day or maybe the next day, but will get up anyway and try it again, against the odds, to make life a little bit better" (Gaines, "Southern" D2). With the final two words, "scapegoat" and "myth," Grant enables Jefferson to see how white people have shaped his identity: "To them, you're nothing but another nigger—no dignity, no heart, no love for your people" (191). It is this knowledge of the social construction of black masculinity that frees Jefferson to be a man in his own mind and a hero in his community. Gaines suggests that because Jefferson has internalized white racism, he has limited what he expects of himself, and he has accepted mistreatment and disrespect as his due. Jefferson tells Grant, "Yes, I'm youman, Mr. Wiggins. But nobody didn't know that 'fore now. Cuss for nothing. Beat for nothing. Work for nothing. Grinned to get by. Everybody thought that's how it was s'pose to be. You too, Mr. Wiggins. You never thought I was nothing else. I didn't neither" (224).

Gaines shows that while language can be used to construct reality, it can also be used to deconstruct and redefine it. It is significant that at Jefferson's trial he does not speak for himself; white lawyers speak for and about him. When the judge asks if Jefferson has anything to say before the sentencing, he keeps his head down and says nothing. Grant gives Jefferson the encouragement to voice his thoughts and emotions and the words to understand and articulate what has happened to him. Gaines uses language, the diary that Jefferson has kept, as moving proof of Jefferson's dignity, integrity, and humanity. Despite the grammar, spelling, and punctuation mistakes, the diary is proof of Jefferson's ability to "stand, and think, and show that common humanity that is in us all" (192). Until Grant's interest in him, Jefferson writes that "nobody aint never been that good to me an make me think im sombody" (232). Abandoned by his parents, he says no one has ever shown him affection, or complimented him, or asked him what he wanted. One of the most poignant passages in Jefferson's diary regards the effects of this emotional deprivation: "mr wigin i just feel like tellin you i like you but i don't kno how to say this cause i aint never say it to nobody before an nobody aint never say it to me" (228). Although white people have made Jefferson an "animal," Grant dismantles white notions of black masculinity and reconstructs Jefferson's manhood. Before his death Jefferson exhibits the "grace under pressure" that Gaines so much admires in Ernest Hemingway's heroes.[12]

But it is in his depiction of Grant's coming to manhood that Gaines moves beyond Hemingway's model of manhood, for Gaines is ultimately more interested in how to live than in how to die, in the creation of new worlds than in the death of old ones. That Jefferson learns the lessons that Grant teaches, that he makes something of himself even within the confines of a jail cell and in the space of a few weeks, becomes a lesson for Grant, who by succeeding with Jefferson, learns that he can make a difference by teaching in the rural South. In becoming a teacher, Grant has thought that whites have controlled his fate as much as they have controlled Jefferson's because teaching is one of the few careers that educated blacks are allowed to have in the 1940s South. Gaines shows that although this may be true, Grant can control how and what he teaches. Plus Gaines suggests that Grant's teaching is necessary to deconstruct white definitions of black manhood. But when the novel opens, Grant is pessimistic about the chances of making a difference in his students' lives: "I teach what the white folks around here tell me to teach—reading, writing, and 'rithmetic. They never told me how to keep a black boy out of a liquor store" (13). Gaines juxtaposes Grant's thoughts of Jefferson's fate with the illegible papers that he is grading, with the memories of boys he went to school with who have been killed or sent to prison for killing someone else, and with the sight of his young male students who act exactly like the illiterate black men who bring wood to the school. Grant's thoughts depress him: "Am I reaching them at all? They are acting exactly as the old men did earlier. They are fifty years younger, maybe more, but doing the same thing those old men did who never attended school a day in their lives. Is it just a vicious circle? Am I doing anything?" (62). But when he is teaching Jefferson about the social construction of identity, Grant realizes how he has shortchanged his own students for six years: "I have always done what they [the white school board] wanted me to do, teach reading, writing, and arithmetic. Nothing else—nothing about dignity, nothing about identity, nothing about loving and caring" (192). Given the effect Grant has on Jefferson by teaching him just such lessons, Gaines suggests that these other subjects are equally as important as the three Rs.

In *A Lesson Before Dying*, Gaines revises the ending of his first novel, *Catherine Carmier* (1964), in which a young college-educated black man, Jackson, decides he cannot remain in the South and face the daily indignities of oppression and institutionalized racism. Unlike Jackson, Grant remains in the South, but he continues to question his decision to stay and teach.[13] When the novel opens, Grant cynically asks how he is supposed to teach a man how to die when he himself is "still trying to find out how a man should live" (31). His most influential childhood teacher, Matthew Antoine, has taught him a lesson that he cannot forget: "He told us then that most of us would die violently, and those who did not would be brought down to the level of beasts. Told us that there was no other choice but to run and run. . . . He could teach any of us only one thing, and that one thing was flight. Because there was no freedom here. He said it, and he didn't say it. But we felt it" (62–63). When Grant decides to return to rural Louisiana after college, Matthew Antoine discourages him: "You'll see that it'll take more than five and a half months to wipe away—peel—scrape away the blanket of ignorance that has been plastered and replastered over those brains in the past three hundred years" (64).

Grant learns Antoine's lessons well. Although he stays in the South, he is bitter about white racism and cynical about whether he is having any effect on his students. These factors combine to keep him alienated and on the verge of leaving. That his aunt should ask him to help Jefferson die with dignity presents a special problem for Grant. He himself has gained dignity and self-respect by leaving the plantation, and he worries that the humiliating encounters he must have with the white power structure in order to help Jefferson—going through the plantation owner's back door, being made to wait by whites, and having his body searched at the jail—will slowly strip him of his hard-earned self-respect: "Professor Antoine told me that if I stayed here, they were going to break me down to the nigger I was born to be" (79).[14]

But in the course of this novel, Gaines gives Grant some new teachers, most remarkably his own pupil Jefferson. Perhaps equally influential in guiding Grant to manhood is his lady friend Vivian. Their relationship is very different from any other male-female relationships in Gaines's fiction. Unlike Phillip and Alma in Gaines's *In My Father's House* (1978), who do not have an equal or emotionally intimate relationship, Grant and Vivian are very much equals, and they talk with each other about their lives. Thus Vivian provides Grant not simply with emotional support but with crucial advice when he most feels like giving up on Jefferson. In *A Lesson Before Dying* Vivian, who is also a teacher, is more than a love interest: she provides the role model for Grant that Mathu provides for the old men in *A Gathering of Old Men*. But unlike Mathu, Vivian teaches Grant the lessons that Cooper Thompson says are attitudes and behaviors boys traditionally have not learned. When Vivian visits Grant at the house he shares with his aunt, she gets him to help her do the dishes rather than leaving them for his aunt to do, thus teaching him that domestic work is not by definition woman's work. Because Vivian must be prudent in her relationship with Grant so that she will not lose her children before her divorce is final, Vivian teaches Grant that in family relationships the individual cannot always fulfill his or her desires first. Also, since Vivian is a committed elementary school teacher, she shows Grant that individual fulfillment involves commitment to others.

While Grant's most important lesson for Jefferson is about the social construction of race and masculinity, Vivian's most important lesson for Grant is about violence and manhood. She teaches him this lesson after dragging him out of a barroom brawl. Grant has started a fight with two mulatto brick-layers whom he overhears maligning Jefferson as a discredit to men of color. At first, Grant effectively deflects his own anger into thoughts about why the men were making such insensitive remarks: "They were probably out of work, and it was just plain frustration that made them go on like that" (198). But Gaines uses the Old Forester that Grant has been drinking to instigate a fight, much like the fights that occur elsewhere in Gaines's fiction. This fight, however, is a brief three pages, very different in length and function from, for example, the fight in *Of Love and Dust* (1967), which begins as a squabble over cards and sprawls over two chapters. While such violence in *Of Love and Dust* seems gratuitous and the violence in *A Gathering of Old Men* results in a battle between ideology and literary convention, the fight in *A Lesson Before Dying* functions as a key scene representing the necessity to redefine masculinity. Gaines devotes much more narrative time to a discussion between Vivian and Grant about the violence he has provoked than to the fight itself. With Vivian's lesson ("That's how you all get yourselves killed" [206]), Gaines underlines consequences for men who fight rather than talk or walk away from potential violence. The placement of this scene is crucial. It comes right after the pivotal scene in which Grant has succeeded in making Jefferson understand that he is as much a man as any other man, white or black. During Grant's discussion with Vivian about his fight, he tries to change the subject from his behavior in the bar to what he has accomplished with Jefferson, which he expects will make Vivian "proud" of him (207). But for Vivian, Grant's readiness to fight overshadows his success with Jefferson. Thus Vivian feels "disgusted" (209) not only by Grant's failure to control his behavior but also by his failure to think about the consequences of his fighting, both for himself and for her and her children. At this precarious time when she is awaiting a divorce from her first husband and trying to keep custody of her children, she must be the model of propriety. Just as Grant asks Jefferson difficult questions about friendship, love, and family, Vivian asks Grant hard questions about meaningful relationships between men and women, about sex and love, and about marriage. Grant's first emotion is anger, and his first inclination is to run out on her, but he thinks better of both. This chapter ends with the sentence, "I knelt down and buried my face in her lap" (210)— a striking contrast to the previous chapter that ends with Grant "standing up" after the fight (203). Gaines makes Grant's kneeling courageous, more an act of manhood than his ability to win the fight with the bricklayers. Kneeling before the woman he loves suggests an ability to learn from her and to commit himself fully to their relationship.

Throughout his fiction Gaines uses the physical act of standing as a symbolic representation of coming to manhood. In this novel, though, Gaines adds kneeling and broadens the definition of manhood to include behaviors traditionally associated with women. In the very next scene after Grant's crisis with Vivian, Reverend Ambrose visits a rude, unkempt, and cynical Grant in his bedroom, much as Grant has visited Jefferson in the same state in his cell. This parallel indicates that Reverend Ambrose is to be Grant's third teacher. Reverend Ambrose argues that despite Grant's college education, he does not know himself or his own community very well. Reverend Ambrose questions Grant's manhood, in part because of the rivalry between them over whose services Jefferson needs most and because Grant refuses to cooperate with Reverend Ambrose, but also in part because Grant does not understand the role that the black church and the black community have played in creating traditions that have sustained black people in a racist society. In a scene with echoes from the one in *A Gathering of Old Men* in which Charlie asks to be called "Mr. Biggs," Reverend Ambrose tells Grant, "When you act educated, I'll call you Grant. I'll even call you Mr. Grant, when you act like a man" (216). Because Reverend Ambrose knows of Grant's success with Jefferson, he wants Grant to ask Jefferson to kneel and pray for forgiveness in front of his godmother. But Grant does not believe in heaven or in the black church's placation of oppressed people, which he believes has had the effect of bolstering the white power structure.[15] Although Reverend Ambrose's remark, "You think a man can't kneel and stand" (216), makes Grant dig in his heels in their argument about institutionalized religion, it reverberates powerfully for the reader as regards issues of masculinity because it echoes the previous scene in which Grant kneels with his head in Vivian's lap.

A Lesson Before Dying ends with Gaines's vision that coming to manhood involves more than "standing." On the day that Jefferson is to be executed, Grant spends the early afternoon outside his school awaiting word of the execution. After an introspective walk through the quarters, Grant admits to himself that Reverend Ambrose is "brave" because he is with Jefferson, and Grant fervently hopes that he has not done anything to weaken Jefferson's belief in God (249). When Paul, the young white deputy, brings Grant the news the Jefferson has died with dignity, he also congratulates Grant for transforming Jefferson, "You're one great teacher, Grant Wiggins" (254). Gaines ends A Lesson Before Dying with Grant asking Paul to return and tell his students about Jefferson's dignity and courage. This upcoming lesson and pedagogical method will be very different from the reading, writing, and 'rithmetic and the rote memorization Grant has employed in the past. This change is reminiscent of the introduction to The Autobiography of Miss Jane Pittman, in which the history teacher explains that he needs to record Miss Jane's life story because it has been left out of the history books: "I'm sure her life's story can help me explain things to my students" (v).

Up to this point in the novel, Grant has internalized most of his emotions except for his anger. He has held back tears for Jefferson, both tears of joy at his progress and tears of sadness at his fate. While Grant waits to hear word of the execution, he thinks, "I felt like crying, but I refused to cry. No, I would not cry. There were too many more who would end up as he did. I could not cry for all of them, could I?" (249). Grant's last action in A Lesson Before Dying, which is to stand before his class and to cry while telling his students of Jefferson's execution, is a powerful redefinition of masculinity that makes crying a strength. With this act, Gaines signals that Grant has finally become a man, both because he knows who he is and what he can do for his community and because he is not afraid to express his emotions. That Gaines's final portrait of Grant is similar to his portrait of Gil in A Gathering of Old Men, despite racial difference, suggests that Gaines thinks both black and white men must reject traditional models of manhood that link masculinity with the capacity for violence and embrace a new model that includes empathizing with others, resolving conflict in nonaggressive ways, and expressing a wide range of emotions. With these final words, "I was crying" (256), Gaines has expanded the possibilities of masculine endings—in more ways than just the fictional.

Notes

I wish to thank Susan Donaldson and Michael Kimmel, whose comments and questions have been helpful in my work on this article, which appeared in *Critical Survey* 9.2 (1997): 15–42 and in a slightly different form in *masculinities* 3.2 (1995): 43–66.

1. See other essays in *Men's Lives* by Matt Groening, Joseph Pleck, Harry Brod, Bob Connell, Norm Radican, and Pip Martin, which explore new definitions of masculinity.

2. In an interview with *Washington Post* reporter Ken Ringle, Gaines describes the contradictory nature of growing up black in rural Louisiana in the 1930s and 1940s:

> There's such beauty in this place. Such peace, and such beauty. As a kid here there were times I was the freest kid in the world, and times I was in de facto slavery.
>
> There were places I couldn't go, things I couldn't say, questions I couldn't ask. You had to work for nothing and take what they gave you. Yet at the same time, you had all the fields to run in, the river to fish in, the swamp to hunt in. . . . I was freer than any white kid, and at the same time, not free at all. What a paradox. (Gaines, "Southern" D1)

3. In an editorial in the *Washington Post*, Arun Gandhi quotes these lines from his grandfather's letter.

4. While I agree with Mary Helen Washington that the society Gaines depicts is a sexist one, I do not agree with her assessment of this scene. In her review in *The Nation*, she suggests that the old black men exclude Candy from their discussion because she is female, "just another threat to manhood" (24), but I think that Candy's exclusion has more to do with the power and privilege of her race than with her sex. Notice that Candy's fiancé, Lou Dimes, who is sympathetic to the old men, is excluded as well. For once, the old men want to direct their own actions, not have them dictated by the white power structure. With the final tableau in which Candy seeks Lou Dimes's hand after Mathu has refused her offer of a ride, Gaines indicates that Candy must redefine her identity as other than a caretaker of black people.

5. Some readers have suggested that Gil is still prejudiced. They cite as evidence his cutting behavior to Cal when Gil hears that a black man has killed his brother. Although he does react to Cal briefly at this point "because of his color" (115), I think Gaines has him behave this way to depict the complexity and difficulty of overcoming the racism one has been raised with. This scene shows how stereotypes can lie latent but potent in one's consciousness. In the discussion that follows among Gil and his family, Gaines makes it clear that he is no longer the bigoted young man his father raised him to be.

6. See chapters 2 and 3 in *Southern Honor: Ethics and Behavior in the Old South*, where Wyatt-Brown argues that the harsh southern code of primal honor can be

traced to the Indo-European tribes that created Homeric Greece and destroyed Rome, and he links the persistence of these archaic values in the South to "the Southern conviction of life's transience" (31). He identifies the following elements as "crucial in the formulation of Southern evaluations of conduct: (1) honor as immortalizing valor, particularly in the character of revenge against familial and community enemies; (2) opinion of others as an indispensable part of personal identity and gauge of self-worth; (3) physical appearance and ferocity of will as signs of inner merit; (4) defense of male integrity and mingled fear and love of woman; and finally, (5) reliance upon oath-taking as a bond in lieu of family obligations and allegiances" (34).

7. Gaines's vision here is similar to Cooper Thompson's.

8. See chapters 4 and 5 in Williamson's *A Rage for Order*. The turn-of-the-century decades were an incredibly violent time in southern history; a dramatic rise in the number of lynchings of black men and in riots against black people occurred in cities such as Wilmington, New Orleans, and Atlanta. Williamson states that whereas before the 1890s lynching had been a "Western and all-white phenomenon, often having to do with bands of cattle rustlers," in the 1890s lynching became a southern practice with black victims: "In the decade of the 1890s, 82 percent of the nation's lynching took place in fourteen Southern states. In the three decades from 1889 to 1918, that proportion increased to 88 percent. . . . In 1892 the number peaked at 156" (84).

9. See Gossett's *Race: The History of an Idea in America* for a discussion of the "scholarly" articles that articulated the racist ideas that Dixon popularized.

10. In *A Lesson Before Dying*, which takes place a generation earlier than *A Gathering of Old Men* (during the time period that the old men speak of in their oral histories), Gaines actualizes the legitimate fears of black people, such as Jefferson, who could not get fair trials in the white criminal justice system and who were swiftly sent to the electric chair. In an interview with Ken Ringle, Gaines revealed that *A Lesson Before Dying* "is the product of a lifetime of nightmares about execution." Ringle writes, "It is not, he says, that he is a particular zealot against capital punishment, just that he has long been obsessed with wondering what it must be like to know in advance the exact moment one is going to die" (Gaines, "Southern" D2). Gaines's obsession is surely fed by the number of executions that took place in the South when he was growing up, the time period in which he sets this novel.

11. Here I use DuPlessis's phrase and her theories about the endings of women's narratives in *Writing beyond the Ending* to help me think about the endings of men's narratives.

12. In conversations with Gaudet and Wooton, Gaines spoke about Hemingway's relevance for black readers and for himself as a writer: "I've always said to students, especially black students, that somehow I feel that Hemingway was writing more about blacks than he was, really, about whites when he was using the grace-under-pressure theme. I see that Hemingway usually puts his people in a moment where they must have grace under pressure, and I've often looked at black life not only as a moment, but more as something constant, everyday. This is what my characters must come through" (Gaudet and Wooton 22).

13. Gaines wonders whether, if he had not left the South and gone to school in California, where his writing talents were nurtured, he would have become an embittered teacher who hates the world for not offering him the opportunity to write (Gaudet and Wooton 48). In his fiction Gaines vacillates in his depictions of teachers: from the flattering portrait of Jackson's former teacher, Madame Bayonne, in *Catherine Carmier*, who is the only person at Jackson's homeplace that understands his frustrations and desires, to the unflattering portraits of Grant's teacher, Matthew Antoine, and the apolitical teachers in *In My Father's House* (1978), who have lost interest in the civil rights movement. Gaines's portrait of Grant at the end of the novel, however, seems to combine the heroism of other black male characters who are social activists, such as those in *The Autobiography of Miss Jane Pittman* (1971) and his other fiction, with the duties of teaching, thus broadening the definition of both teacher and activist.

14. Grant's fears about remaining in the South resemble Richard Wright's as expressed in *Black Boy* (1945). Both protagonists resist white definitions of black inferiority, both recognize the power of these constructions of black identity, and both feel it is chance that has kept them from becoming the "nigger" they were supposed to be. But Wright ends his autobiographical narrative with leaving the South so that he can "understand" the South (228), while Gaines has Grant stay to try to change it. Thus, in some respects, Gaines rewrites Wright's ending and revises Wright's vision of black manhood, which is premised on solitude and repudiation of community and region. But then, Gaines is writing fifty years later—after political and social change has occurred in the South and after Gaines himself has returned to Louisiana to teach creative writing there for one semester each year.

15. The exchange between Reverend Ambrose and Grant mirrors Gaines's own ambivalence to organized religion, which surfaces in his portrayals of less than admirable ministers in his other novels, such as Reverend Jameson in *A Gathering of Old Men*, who is the only old man reluctant to stand up for Mathu.

Works Cited

Carby, Hazel V. *Reconstructing Womanhood: The Emergence of the Afro-American Woman Novelist*. New York: Oxford UP, 1987.

Connell, Bob. "Masculinity, Violence and War." *Men's Lives*. Ed. Michael S. Kimmel and Michael A. Messner. New York: Macmillan, 1989. 194–200.

DuPlessis, Rachel Blau. *Writing beyond the Ending: Narrative Strategies of Twentieth-Century Women Writers*. Bloomington: Indiana UP, 1985.

Franklin, Clyde W. II. "Black Male-Black Female Conflict: Individually Caused and Culturally Nurtured." *Men's Lives*. Ed. Michael S. Kimmel and Michael A. Messner. New York: Macmillan, 1989. 341–49.

Gaines, Ernest J. *The Autobiography of Miss Jane Pittman*. 1971. New York: Bantam, 1972.

———. *Catherine Carmier*. 1964. New York: Vintage, 1993.

———. *A Gathering of Old Men*. New York: Random House, 1983.

———. *In My Father's House*. 1978. New York: Vintage, 1992.

————. *A Lesson Before Dying*. New York: Knopf, 1993.

————. *Of Love and Dust*. New York: Norton, 1967.

————. "A Southern Road to Freedom." Interview by Ken Ringle. *Washington Post* 20 July 1993: D1–D2.

Gandhi, Arun. "The Problem with Peace Movements." *Washington Post* 17 Feb. 1991: C7.

Gaudet, Marcia, and Carl Wooton. *Porch Talk with Ernest Gaines: Conversations on the Writer's Craft*. Baton Rouge: Louisiana State UP, 1990.

Gossett, Thomas F. *Race: The History of an Idea in America*. Dallas, Tex.: Southern Methodist UP, 1963.

Rabinowitz, Peter J. *Before Reading: Narrative Conventions and the Politics of Interpretation*. Ithaca: Cornell UP, 1987.

Riener, James D. "Rereading American Literature from a Men's Studies Perspective: Some Implications." *The Making of Masculinities*. Ed. Harry Brod. Boston: Allen and Unwin, 1987. 289–99.

Thompson, Cooper. "A New Vision of Masculinity." *Men's Lives*. Ed. Michael S. Kimmel and Michael A. Messner. New York: Macmillan, 1989. 586–91.

Washington, Mary Helen. "The House That Slavery Built." *The Nation* 14 Jan. 1984: 22–24.

Williamson, Joel. *A Rage for Order: Black/White Relations in the American South Since Emancipation*. New York: Oxford UP, 1986.

Wright, Richard. *Black Boy: A Record of Childhood and Youth*. New York: Harper and Brothers, 1945.

Wyatt-Brown, Bertram. *Southern Honor: Ethics and Behavior in the Old South*. New York: Oxford UP, 1982.

The Snake and the Rosary

*Violence and the Culture of Piety
in Sheila Bosworth's SLOW POISON*

Gary M. Ciuba

When Sheila Bosworth discussed religion with Walker Percy, her fellow novelist from Covington, Louisiana, they frequently argued about being Roman Catholic.[1] Bosworth admired Percy for letting his faith vitalize his fiction without becoming didactic, but she disagreed with him about their experiences in the church. "His church and my church were two different churches," Bosworth observes. ". . . He didn't understand what it was like to be a female child in the Catholic church in the 1950s" ("Interview" 163, 150–51). She would sometimes summarize the difference between her own and Percy's church by joking that hers had mean nuns (Tolson 457). Although Bosworth's jest might sound like a Catholic-bashing cliché, her memory epitomizes how violence is often associated with the culture of popular piety in her novels. Bosworth's fiction explores the violence in the devotional religion of Catholic families and the religious implications of the violent desires in her family members' hearts.

As a minority church in the South, Catholicism survived as "a miniature culture," according to Walker Percy, ". . . a small besieged enclave in which Father said such-and-such, Sister said so-and-so," a world "redolent . . . with incense and candlewax and all the vivid parochial particulars" (320). Bosworth grew up in this devotional culture, which Percy the adult convert never knew during his formative years. Born in 1916, Percy became a Roman Catholic in 1947 after discovering that the southern stoicism in which he had been raised and the scientific humanism in which he had been educated throughout college and medical school did not adequately respond to his increasing sense of mystery in life. Although the church that Percy entered as an adult was essentially the same as the one into which Bosworth was born in 1950, being a "cradle Catholic" meant that she was much more deeply formed by its religious practices and traditions.[2] Raised in New Orleans, "a very, very Catholic city," as she describes it, Bosworth acknowledges, ". . . I can't imagine anything that's been as far-reaching in my life as the church has been. It's like breathing or eating; it has been simply a fact of my life, as long as I can remember" ("Interview" 147, 148). Although Percy notes that in New Orleans, "Catholics tend often to be more Catholic than the Pope" (19), Bosworth does not recall her parents as being overly zealous in their devotion. Rather, they quietly passed on to her the heritage of their family faith and reinforced their example by their daughter's formal education. When Bosworth was five, she began attending a school taught by the Sisters of Mercy; after the fourth grade she went to the Academy of the Sacred Heart, where she remained throughout high school. "Oh, as Catholic girls, we had benediction and incense and the white veils, and let's cleanse our souls, and oh, it's very interesting, yes," she remembers ("Interview" 169). In school, Bosworth attended retreats where she prayed, kept silence—even during meals—listened to priests lecture about hell and eternal life, and read pamphlets about the lives of the saints or the dangers of attending a non-Catholic college.[3]

Although Bosworth admits that she might have been more sensitive as a child than her peers, she faults the culture of faith during her youth because it inculcated fear, mindless compliance, and a sense of personal worthlessness. "The message of Christ, supposedly, is love; the 'new law' is love," Bosworth objects, "and yet I felt precious little of that in the Catholic church when I was growing up" ("Interview" 159). Instead, she recalls an unfeeling priest who terrified her in confession—an experience recounted in *Almost Innocent*—and mean nuns who frightened her as a six-year-old—the basis of a set piece in *Slow Poison*. Percy, the moviegoer, used to tell Bosworth that he imagined all nuns to be like Loretta Young, the Catholic actress who played a sister in the 1948 film *Come to the Stable*. Irritated by lapsed Catholics who wrote plays and novels ridiculing priests and nuns, Percy advised his friend not to be overly critical of the church (Percy 321; Bosworth, "Interview" 151).[4]

When Bosworth paid tribute to Percy by having him appear anonymously in the opening pages of her first novel, she glanced at the kind of piety that made her disagree with him about the Catholic church. While dining at Galatoire's, Clay-Lee Calvert, the narrator of *Almost Innocent*, notices that amid all the odd patrons of the restaurant there is "a noncrazy, a famous writer who lived in Covington" (15).[5] Clay-Lee recalls that as twelve-year-olds, she and the writer's daughter planned to seek special permission from the Pope to enter the Carmelites, "a religious order famous for its romantic iron grilles and nervous breakdowns among the novices" (15). Unlike the sane stand-in for Percy, the young Clay-Lee risks seeming like one of the eccentric crowd because of her infatuation with the mystique of the convent. The would-be nun is attracted by what also makes the childish Miranda Rhea fantasize about the cloister in Katherine Anne Porter's "Old Mortality": both schoolgirls take dark pleasure in the prospect of self-sacrifice because they essentially want to sacralize themselves through violence. Knowing at first hand the danger of such obsession with suffering, Bosworth recalls how as a youngster she wanted "to die a martyr's death, to be spotless and holy" ("Interview" 169).

If such violence may bear away the kingdom of God, it follows that the sacred itself may be violent. Bosworth criticizes Catholicism for making "a great show of thanking God for things, but of never blaming God for anything." Bosworth was raised to believe in a protecting God, but she is troubled by a Lord who seems less than benevolent. "He might help you, then again He might harm you," she reasons ("Interview" 149, 150). At the end of *Almost Innocent*, a doctor comments, "Not even God Himself should have to take the blame for this one" (262) after Clay-Lee's pregnant mother dies, partly as a result of her young daughter's negligence. Bosworth's fiction expresses her anger at a God that she would like to hold responsible for such catastrophes; however, it moves beyond rage at such divine improvidence by its complex analysis of human responsibility. Each of her novels reveals the surprising and terrible complicity of her characters in the violations of the heart. "I think I got a lot of the anger out in the second novel, *Slow Poison*," Bosworth admits ("Interview" 150). Fiercer and funnier than *Almost Innocent*, *Slow Poison* confronts the violence in church and family devotion so that its characters may discover the final blessing of going in peace.

The faithful in *Slow Poison* belong to the mid-century church that so profoundly shaped Bosworth's early religious life. Indeed, the Cade family and their fellow Catholics in the novel might have stepped out of *Dynamics of a City Church*, Joseph H. Fichter's pioneering 1951 study in the sociology of a New Orleans parish, published a year after Bosworth was born. Fichter's analysis of Mater Dolorosa Church in the Carrollton area of the city revealed a spiritual life centered more on cultic observances than on a community of believers. This form of piety began in the America of the 1840s and reached its acme in the decades after World War I (Dolan 211–40). Whereas the eighteenth-century plain style of American Catholicism tended to emphasize the internal life and imitation of Jesus, the new devotionalism, brought from Europe by such groups as the ancestors of the very Irish Cades, stressed external observance. Strongly sensing their sinfulness, the faithful turned to the laws of a highly authoritarian church and the spiritual exercises that the church regulated as the means to overcoming their evil inclinations. Although Percy's novels have occasionally portrayed representatives of this devout life (for example, Lonnie Smith in *The Moviegoer* and Marva More in *Love in the Ruins*), Bosworth's fiction has made this pious tradition more completely its own. The Catholics of *Slow Poison* make novenas and recite the Morning Offering. They give up liquor during Lent and abstain from meat on Friday.

They wear communion veils, religious habits, and clerical garb. They honor the crucifix and the blood-stained gloves of a local stigmatist. They fast for hours before receiving the Eucharist, go to Communion on the First Fridays and First Saturdays of the month, and offer Masses in remembrance of the souls in purgatory. Above all, they pray the rosary.

Midway through *Slow Poison*, Rory Cade dreams of the violence that underlies what Flannery O'Connor criticized as "the novena-rosary tradition" of Catholicism (139). She watches her older sister Jane Ann stand on the gallery outside her bedroom, wearing her First Communion dress and holding a sparkling crystal and silver rosary. But as Jane Ann listens to a serenade of "The Old Rugged Cross," she becomes frightened and begins to blow on a silver police whistle. Rory notices that "Jane Ann's rosary was really a snake, and the silver snake's cross-shaped head was biting into Jane Ann's thin wrists, again and again, while Jane Ann screamed and blew on the police whistle and 'The Old Rugged Cross' played on" (175). Rory's dream of the rood uses the premier devotion of pre-Vatican II pop spirituality to reveal a terrifying violence that may lurk in such approaches to the sacred. Fusing images of snakes and rosaries that appear separately and together throughout the novel,[6] her vision gains its peculiar horror by inverting the way that the Gospel of John imagines the Crucifixion. Jesus looks to the glory of his death and resurrection when he identifies himself with the brazen serpent that Moses raised in the wilderness to heal the sinful Israelites of their snakebites (John 3:14–15). Rory dreams not of the love that reaches to the cross of Christ, however, but of the violence that poisons her family from the crucifix of popular belief and practice.

Rory's daytime nightmare vividly comments on the catechesis she had just received from her father before falling asleep. Eamon and Rory had been talking about Jane Ann, who had recently opened two letters that violated Rory's sense of the theodicy. Rory liked to imagine God as bound by old-time southern honor. In 1967 she "still held a belief in certain gentleman's rules for the Creator, a certain cosmic code of ethics. She still believed that tragedy confers transitory immunity from further tragedy, that trouble intrinsically, if temporarily, precludes more trouble" (171). Yet if God were so considerate in appointing destiny, Jane Ann would not have received an untimely letter from her husband, who had recently been killed in Vietnam, and another from her husband's overbearing mother, who wants to claim the child in Jane Ann's womb for her fundamentalist faith. Rory's father counsels her to "leave this to the guy in the sky" (173). Almost a decade earlier he had explained to her that the "Guy in the Sky" oversees an essentially equitable order that allots to everyone chances to go to ball games and movies as well as occasions to visit hospitals and funeral homes (128). But after Jane Ann has been devastated by the two letters, Rory cannot trust in such a divine wheel of fortune or the facile accommodation of her father's uncritical Catholicism. "You know what would be a lot easier on you, kid?" he counsels. "Just buy the whole program, no questions asked. You've got to believe in something, right? Why not the grand old Church of Rome?" (174).

Rory's subsequent dream about the snake and the rosary imagines how the religion that has been her patrimony conceals a cult of sacred violence. Like the cross that becomes a biting snake, its God may be a holy terror. Rory cannot be resigned to the deity implied by the faith of her father but believes that any intelligent person is either angry at or afraid of God. She sees such fear in a friend of her aunt's, who gave birth to a malformed baby. Rory observes, "She goes around saying, Isn't God good! every other sentence, in case He's listening and is in a bad mood again. It gives me the creeps" (174). Unlike Mrs. Buck, Rory is angry at this seemingly unpredictable and malevolent deity. Immediately after she wakes from her dream, Rory appears to have good reason for shaking her fist at heaven. She learns that her beloved Johnny Killelea has received his own disturbing letter, a notice to report in twenty-four hours for his army physical. The snake of God seems to strike again.

Rory's Lord is a version of the God with Thunder that John Crowe Ransom once sought decades earlier as an antidote to the too comprehensible and benevolent deity created by modern science and humanism. Ransom's Jupiter Tonans rules by whimsy rather than by order and design, desires the sheer wastefulness of sacrifice, and brings evil as well as good according to no predictable plan (27–52). Such a divinity seems to preside over the whole history of Rory's family, for the Cades do not know any respite from mishaps but only tragedy compounded by tragedy. Before her dream Rory has lived through her mother's fatal stroke and her young stepmother's multiple misfortunes: a brutal assault, the death of her unborn child, and a fatal car wreck on the Causeway. When Rory rides across this same road with one of her family's African American employees years after the accident, she thinks of how Aimée Desirée and her black maid crashed during a similar stormy night. "What if God happened to take note of the similarities and decided to stage a tragic reenactment?" Rory wonders. "God had a history of staging tragic reenactments" (152). After her dream Rory lives through the marriage of her own Johnny Killelea to her sister Jane Ann, a long separation from Johnny while he covers the war in Vietnam as a journalist, the stillbirth of Jane Ann's child, the deterioration of her alcoholic father, and his slow death from a stomach malignancy. The Cade family history seems to confirm Eamon's sly retort when a pious nun blathers about how God never sends people greater burdens than they can bear, "And Our Lord sure enough ain't going to hit you over the head with more happiness than you know what to do with, either" (17). Rory is angry at a God who is not as just as she would like to imagine, at the deity whom Bosworth herself has decried as "the Great Instigator of Tragedy" ("Interview" 149).

Although the God of devotional Catholicism frequently seemed a grim master, the religion of the Cades has an even older origin than the immigrant spirituality of the preceding century. René Girard's work suggests that its foundation can be traced to the way primitive cultures set aside violence as the sacred in order to establish peace amid a community in crisis. In *Violence and the Sacred*, Girard contends that the mutual antagonists of such a society ended the escalating competition and conflict among themselves by polarizing their fury onto a single individual. They turned the violence that divided them into the violence that united them, the violence against all into a violence against one. Since the killing of this surrogate restored peace to society, the slain outcast was viewed as both accursed and holy. The victim became the source of the malevolent violence that nearly led to the destruction of the community and of the beneficent violence that led to its instauration. Girard traces the very origins of culture to this scapegoating. Such institutions as law, kingship, medicine, theater, and religion not only developed in the peaceful aftermath of surrogate victimage but put into practice the principle of using some violent exclusion to establish harmony. Yet even as culture was founded on a series of metaphoric displacements of scapegoating, it still continued to worship violence as the sacred.

Girard views Judaism as breaking with this culture of violence by demythologizing its furious divinity. The founding stories of Judaism, like that of Cain and Abel or Joseph and his brothers, exposed the perils of violent reciprocity, its laws sought to eliminate violence and counterviolence, and its prophets denounced the mistaken priority given to sacrificial ritual. Jesus culminated this long tradition of revelation. Girard's reading of the Gospels interprets Jesus as the innocent victim who died because he preached the good news of nonviolence. His death exposed the violence that hides as the sacred even as it revealed the love that was truly sacred. Girard maintains, however, that historical Christianity never completely renounced a cult of rage, for it viewed Jesus' death in sacrificial terms, looked to a vengeful God of apocalyptic judgment, and scapegoated the Jews (*Things* 224–31). One trace of this more primitive religion can be seen in the way the statue of the martyred Saint Sebastian was honored during the late Middle Ages. Violence made the image so salutary. Thought to protect from the plague because he had been pierced by arrows, the statue of the scapegoat-saint was "brandished like the serpent of brass in front of the Hebrews" (Girard, *Scapegoat* 61).

Rory's dream about the rosary makes terrifyingly clear how the holy fury of the serpent lingers in the popular piety of the Cades. The cross in Rory's nightmare actually reimagines the sacrificial cult that has haunted her since girlhood. As a child she dreams that a typewritten schedule for executions is posted on the bulletin board of the bedroom she shares with Jane Ann. It announces that Children's Crucifixions are scheduled for three o'clock, the traditional hour when Christ died. "In the dream, this came as no surprise to Rory; children's sacrifices, as everyone knew, pleased Christ the most" (22). Rory feels this bloodthirsty Moloch continually darkening her childhood. Rory believes that she murdered her grandmother by failing to offer the necessary sacrifice—a novena to Saint Jude, patron of the most desperate causes, that could have undoubtedly saved Grandolly's life.[7] Rory is fearful of a club for such young sacrifice, the St. Dolores' Daughters. Members of this dolorous sodality wear such severe expressions as they grandly process to First Friday Communion in Marian blue veils that they look like "life-soured, middle-aged matrons" despite being no older than thirteen (67).

Rory finds that the sacrifice of children is conducted most often by the nuns of her girlhood. None is the saintly Loretta Young that Walker Percy idolized in the movies. Rory remembers how at her mother's funeral Sister Devotia once again used her "sweet voice to say things that make children cry" (15). Sister Devotia personifies the cruelty that Rory sees underlying much of devotional Catholicism. Although everyone else assumes that the nun is praying her rosary, the young Rory realizes that she is mumbling about Honor Cade's supposedly hereditary insanity. The sister then lies about her lack of charity when she discovers that the eight-year-old has actually overheard her callous comment. The Sisters of Mercy institutionalize the mercilessness of Rory's faith at Holy Shroud School.[8] Built in the "bomb-shelter motif" of the 1950s (71), the school is meant to provide a bastion from the threats of the Cold War. But the academy of the church militant offers not so much a haven from violence as a fortress of rage in the name of religion. The Sisters of Mercy are driven "to a frenzy that appeared to be almost beyond their control" by students who deface school desks and church pews (50). Infuriated by tardy children, Sister Marcella is "pushed over the edge of tolerance by a class of seven-year-olds who had apparently refused to seize their parents' car keys and drive themselves to school at dawn" (71). Sister Francesca conducts her version of Rory's Children's Crucifixions at the climax of the school day. After Father Byrd reprimands the nun because two unruly students were wandering the halls, she returns to the classroom and seeks a victim for her anger. "With a single sweep of the hand that wore Christ's wedding ring," Sister Francesca conjoins violence and the sacred to knock off Paul Sclamba's desk the sign from his father that dares to proclaim "Mr. Sclamba." When Paul tries to salvage the wreckage of his desk, the nun restrains his arm, "her voice husky with satisfied rage" (77). The violence of Sister Francesca is not sacred at all; it is the rage for a scapegoat that Girard identifies as all too human.

Although Rory feels that a God of violence presides over her family history, *Slow Poison* traces that violence back to the hearts of its antagonists. It is their drug of choice. Bosworth recalls the "down side" of her own childhood quest for holiness as "the religious version of cocaine withdrawal. You are very high, and then dangerously depressed. Because you're never quite good enough" ("Interview" 169). The Cades practice the converse—the pharmacological version of religion—in the way they find the divergent poles of the sacred in the ambiguous powers of drugs. Like the *pharmakos,* or scapegoat, which is both blessed and baleful, the *pharmakon* encapsulates the ambiguity of divine violence. Girard observes that the Greek word means that which causes and that which cures sickness, "a drug that possesses a simultaneous potential for good and for bad, one that serves as a physical transposition of sacred duality" (*Violence and the Sacred* 288). The *pharmakon* turns the power of the *pharmakos* into a substance that can be injected, absorbed, or ingested to contradictory ends. Rory recognizes how a drug may bring the benefits and risks of violence when she rages at remembering her grandmother's advice not to care whether her father is drunk or sober: "Goddamn Grandolly's prescription from the grave. Who wanted a remedy like that one, the purgative kind that nearly kills you?" (220). Like the serpent in Exodus that heals and kills, like the cross in Rory's dream that may bless or bite, the *pharmakon* is both salvific and poisonous.

"Beware of the love of women," Bosworth's epigraph from Turgenev's *First Love* warns, "that ecstasy, that slow poison" (119). Her title seems to do its own violence to the prefatory quotation by simplifying its contradictory description of "the love of women." Its reduction of the *pharmakon* might almost be carrying out the program that Jacques Derrida sees as typical of Western thought in "Plato's Pharmacy." Like the translators of Plato who have rendered *pharmakon* as either "remedy" or "poison," Bosworth's title tends to suppress the ambiguity of the logos by excluding one of the opposites in her epigraph. *Slow Poison,* however, works against its own name by restoring the paradox of the *pharmakon* and the sacred. The Cades encounter the duality of Girard's divinity in the drugs they love and the loves that drug them.

The characters in *Slow Poison* turn to many remedies/poisons in their cult of sacred violence. They smoke dope, cigars, Camels, Picayunes, and Lucky Strikes. They drink punch, sherry, champagne, Chivas, Ripple, Royal Beer, Old Crow, Jim Bean, Johnny Walker, Jack Daniels, and Dewar's White Label. They take mescaline, Seconals, Paragoric, and Percodan; they sniff nail polish and find a twenty-one-inch TV "almost as good as morphine" (284).

Each item in this litany promises a taste of the sacred, the "ecstasy" of stand-ing outside oneself, but each only intensifies its user's misery. The remedies finally lead to poisonous ends—Eamon's alcoholic collapse, Jane Ann's near-suicides, Arabella's detachment, Rory's and Johnny's anesthetized hearts. Yet *Slow Poison* is hardly a study in substance abuse. As in Percy's *The Thanatos Syndrome*, drugs merely make available for consumption the paradox of the sacred as benevolent and malevolent. There is really only one ingredient in the Cade family pharmacopoeia: violence. Rory testifies to this drug of drugs when she says of Johnny, "He knows the Cades; he knows anything could have happened" to provoke the mysterious summons from a family servant that brings the two of them back to Covington at the beginning of the novel. "Murder, mayhem, involuntary manslaughter, suicide, accidental poisoning. Paragoric" (8). The characters in *Slow Poison* find their *pharmakon* not so much in what they consume as in what consumes them, what the epigraph ambiguously calls "the love of women." The subjective and objective genitive points to how women's love and love for women bring the ecstasy and poison of the violence that gets consecrated in sacrificial religions.

"Decades" (Book One) chronicles how Rory's father and stepmother discover in each other the pharmacological equivalent of sacred violence. The love of Eamon and Aimée Desirée is, like the *pharmakon*, alternately "a magic drug or volatile elixir" that brings rapture as well as ruin (Girard, *Vio-lence and the Sacred* 95). Years after the death of Aimée Desirée, Rory recog-nizes her stepmother's potency: "Aimée Desirée Vairin Kemp Stafford Cade, she would hear herself say, what a powerful potion you were!" (123). Like Zinaida in *First Love*, Aimée Desirée has all the allure of a femme fatale. To tell of her is "a job for the coroner, a police reporter, some hard-boiled spe-cialist in catastrophe" (40). Before her marriage to Eamon, the twenty-three-year-old heartbreaker has already left too many lovesick men in her wake—most recently, an anonymous jazz musician whose child she aborted. Yet if Aimée Desirée seems a southern version of a film noir dame, she is also immensely therapeutic for the Cade family health. Her vast wealth, attention to details of food and furnishings, and demanding but considerate treatment of the staff bring a domestic economy to the household that it never knew under Rory's feckless mother. Whereas Honor Cade had become so desperate with desire for the indifferent Eamon that she neglected her baby and pined to be as pretty as Rory, Aimée Desirée is so self-possessed that she regards her stepdaughters as neither obstacles nor rivals. Rather, gentle and generous with her love, she inspires Rory and Arabella to climb "all over her like cats, as if they couldn't get close enough to her" (103). Eamon is right to view the enchanting Aimée Desirée with appropriate ambiguity—"with a blend of wonder, delight, and fear in his eyes" (102) as if he were a small boy at a magic show—for his ominous and invigorating new wife embodies all the contradictory violence in the *pharmakon*.

Aimée Desirée finds her own drug in the brutal but appealing godhead of Eamon Cade. Like every other devotee, Aimée Desirée was attracted to Eamon because he seemed an absolute lord. "What was it that made waiters, gardeners, priests, oil kings, state troopers, judges, and everybody else truckle to Eamon Cade?" Rory wonders. She finds the answer in "a paradox: Eamon Cade drew worshippers because he was indifferent to the opinion of almost everybody" (84). Since Eamon did not care about idolatry, he became a god, especially in his own family, where he was invoked as the "Amen" of daily life. "Our father, Eamon," Rory entreats and explains. "His daughters said his name, like it or not, at the end of all their prayers" (58). Rory herself demonstrates a filial piety worthy of an ancient Roman. When Eamon advises his daughter to believe in the Church of Rome, Rory affirms her belief in her paterfamilias instead.

Although the imperious Aimée Desirée might have been drawn to her perfect counterpart in the arrogant Eamon Cade, she conceals a girlish dependency behind her divine self-sufficiency. Merrill Shackleford believes that Aimée Desirée marries Eamon, who is almost twice her age, because the only daughter of the deceased Dreuil Vairin is looking for a lost father. "As are we all, God help us. As are we all," he adds (43). But if Aimée Desirée saw in Eamon a protecting parent, she found in him the other face of the sacred as well. Aimée Desirée might have sought in a surrogate father someone who would not just cherish her as daddy's girl but chastise her as a daughter of the church. Her former lover's wedding present dramatizes how Aimée Desirée's piety makes her need such punishment. He delivers a cross with a note explaining how wellborn women from French families would hang such a gift on the wall by their marriage beds. The present from "an Irish Catholic music man" does more than just turn a traditional benediction into a jeering valediction. The black iron crucifix, "the length and weight of a baby's coffin," connects Eamon with the venomous cross in Rory's dream (84). Aimée Desirée's jilted lover explains to her future husband, "She's got this Catholic Church crap in her head, telling her she's going to hell for getting rid of my kid! And now she's got this goddamn martyr fixation, so she set herself up to get pregnant by the first guy who comes along. You!" (89). Since a drunken Aimée Desirée grieves when her former lover departs before the ceremony, his analysis of Eamon's noxious role may have gotten to the heart of her violent religion. In marrying Eamon, Aimée Desirée lives out the cult of Rory's childhood by sacrificing herself.

The side effects of the marriage are severe: Eamon and Aimée Desirée slowly poison each other and themselves. After Aimée Desirée is assaulted and robbed while leaving her lover's apartment, Eamon discovers that his wife has resumed her romance with the jazz musician. He responds to the violation of their marriage with a calmness that "is akin to serenity in the double-crossed professional criminal; it is the prelude to final retribution" (122). Eamon exiles his wife from the house, leaves not one memento of her standing, and never says her name again. Her exclusion is complete when her car crashes off the Causeway. Although Aimée Desirée was not driving on that stormy night, her accident gratifies "the unmistakable, underlying passion for wreckage and ruin" that Eamon heard in her singing when she first enchanted him (129).

Aimée Desirée's legacy is ultimately as harmful and healthful as the *pharmakon.* "When my father swore you off," Rory invokes the overpowering presence of her stepmother that she sometimes feels years later in her sleep, "he and my sisters and I suffered severe shock and a lasting decline. After you went from our house, the structure itself took on a doomed air, as if it were a dwelling marked for demolition" (123). Eamon lives forever without her ecstasy. "It was obvious that a part of Daddy was always in hell now," Rory observes, "no matter where the rest of him happened to be" (128). Just as Eamon once turned to alcohol as "salvation" from Honor's too-needy love (48), he drinks again to recover a lost rapture. The social drug becomes his bane for the next decade. Rory speaks to the spirit of Aimée Desirée with "a shifting blend of anger and awe, perplexity and pain" because the woman who helped to bring such disaster to the house of Cade was also its surprising savior. In naming Eamon as the sole beneficiary of her enormous estate, Aimée Desirée guaranteed that the Cades would forever live in unexpected comfort and style. "And Eamon must have blessed you, in spite of himself, for that love letter," Rory concludes (123, 124). Blessed and accursed, beneficent and maleficent, the love of and for Aimée Desirée makes heartfelt the paradox of sacred violence in all of its ecstasy and slow poison.

Ten years later, in Book Two of "Decades," Rory and Johnny Killelea find that their love shares the same ambiguity of the *pharmakon.* Its anthem is the song that Rory hears in Johnny's '67 Corvette convertible at the very beginning of Book Two. Like Aimée Desirée's siren song of lament that captivated Eamon when they first met, "I Put a Spell on You" testifies to their mutual passion for destruction. When the record was made, a drug-crazed Screamin' Jay Hawkins, "out of his mind with ecstasy and rage," and his reefer-smoking band turned what was supposed to be a rather restrained love song into a "celebration of obsessive humping and the sacred violence of love" (133). Violence makes Johnny, like Aimée Desirée, as much a heady tonic as a toxic substance for the heart. "Violence in the name of honor: the Irishman's and the Southerner's constant passion," Rory thinks when Johnny goes to help a comrade who has been defending young women against riverfront assailants (138). Johnny would like to challenge every rival, whether to smash the head of his feverishly hateful stepfather with a brick or to shoot his best friend for eventually winning Rory's devotion. However, Johnny carries the gentleman's code so far that he comes to find honor in the name of violence. His gallantry conceals a furious machismo. And so Johnny hunts and brawls, smokes "lethal" Picayunes (3), drives his Harley while drunk, and crashes his Corvette on Magazine Street. He knows the warning that his friend Dr. Fox Renick offers about such recklessness, "I'm poisoning myself with demon rum and tobacco" (310), but what really poisons and possesses Johnny is not so much alcohol and cigarettes as the violence in him that they nurture.

Johnny himself is so much of a drug that he intoxicates Rory. She loves to repeat his name, for it is "a kind of sugar cube, saturated with a recreational hallucinogen that transported her to scenes from their love affair" (165). He offers her an "erotic olfactory cocktail" blended of smoke, beer, and the muskiness of his own strut and swagger (136). Typical of the inebriating violence of their romance is that the two have dates in which Johnny teaches Rory to shoot while both are drunk. Rory is so enchanted by this homme fatal that she does not protest even at the end of the novel when Johnny barges into her wedding party to give her away as the bride. As she explains, "That old black magic, the self-destructive urge, was upon me" (313).

If the violence of Johnny's ecstasy offers Rory an antidote to the slow poison of family life, she comes to see how his remedy actually repeats the sacrificial religion of her youth. Although Johnny scorns marriage as bourgeois, he agrees to a meaningless wedding with Jane Ann to avoid the draft. When Johnny tells Rory of his plan, she imagines her victimization in terms of classic biblical images for the triumph of sacred violence. "Something had gone wrong," Rory thinks. "Imagine King Solomon letting the woman who wanted the child hacked in half have her way. Imagine Abraham cutting his son's throat and then taking the ram back down the mountain with him" (188). Girard views both stories as testimony to how the Bible moves away from believing in a bloodthirsty deity. When Abraham receives the ram to be slaughtered in place of Isaac, the surrogate victim marks a turn from child sacrifice, especially of the firstborn, to the substitution of animal sacrifice. When Solomon gives his famous decision, he raises the specter of child sacrifice only to reject it in favor of the life of the infant and the love of the true mother (*Things* 237–43). Rory's imagination places ending her devotion to Johnny in the same tradition as the heinous acts of piety that Scripture renounces: "Imagine Rory Cade, unwilling, unable to cease loving Johnny Killelea, even under the present circumstances" (188). When Johnny decides to marry Jane Ann, Rory feels as if she is once again facing the child sacrifice about which she dreamed.

Victimization in love makes Rory want to be the victimizer. She longs for the blood of Jane Ann and Johnny. Girard has traced the communal conflict that gets resolved in scapegoating back to the clash between individuals who seek too much to be like each other. Such mimetic desire causes the model to see the disciple as a threat and the disciple to see the model as an obstacle (*Things* 290–91). Since Jane Ann has become Johnny's wife, Rory feels resentment toward the sister who is at once her ideal and her rival. On the night of Jane Ann's marriage, Rory's murderous rage blends with a sorrowful affection to create a heady emotional brew. "Hatred and pity for Jane Ann broke over Rory's heart in a bitter, poisonous foam she could taste on her tongue, a mysterious potion that made her want to break Jane Ann's neck, mend it tenderly, then break it again." The antithetical desires can be traced to a single element in the *pharmakon*: "Blood must be the key ingredient in this particular potion, Rory thought; you had to have this girl's blood running in your own veins in order to want to kill her and comfort her at the same time" (187). Blood is the main component of this drug, for blood makes vivid the duality of sacred violence. Girard recognizes its paradoxical effect when he writes that "the same substance can stain or cleanse, contaminate or purify, drive men to fury and murder or appease their anger and restore them to life" (*Violence and the Sacred* 37). Rory is overpowered by the contradiction that the blood that joins the Cade sisters in kinship is also the blood that may be spilled in killing her sibling and rival.

Filled with such violence, Rory eventually uses religion to poison the possibility that the marriage of convenience between Johnny and Jane Ann may deepen into romance. After deciding that she would no longer compete for Johnny's heart, Rory allows Jane Ann to think that she still loves her one-time boyfriend. Rory even lets her rival go to Reno for a divorce, although she suspects that Jane Ann is actually falling in love with her pro forma husband. "She had just buried her baby," Rory later admits to Johnny, "and I let her believe that God would allow something else terrible to happen to her, if she didn't give you up" (320). Appealing to the same unforgiving God that might have frightened Aimée Desirée into abandoning her lover, she uses the threat of divine displeasure to punish her enemy sister. Rory puts sacred violence at the service of the human violence that is its source.

Rory brings this same violence to her wayward romance with Johnny. Passion for her lover and rage at her sister's husband make her want the same single element in the *pharmakon* that aroused in her such contradictory emotions toward Jane Ann. Rory desires nothing less than blood on the night she consummates Jane Ann's marriage by making love with Johnny for the first time. She "was frantic to possess him, to own him in some tangible way, to leave her mark upon his body, to recklessly avenge this terrible theft that, unfortunately, had been committed with the full cooperation of the stolen goods." The next morning as the couple hears the bells of St. Louis Cathedral "ringing out an ancient love song, the Angelus," Rory tells Johnny that he is bleeding from the scratch marks all over his back (192). In commemorating the Annunciation to Mary, the Angelus celebrates in prayer how the God of the Gospels became human without any of the fury and antagonism typically associated with the divine conception of heroes in myths (Girard, *Things* 220–23). Rory and Johnny know not the sacred love that the popular Marian devotion remembers but the sacred violence that it rejects.

This blood lust gradually corrupts the love between Johnny and Rory. Much as Rory recalls how a family servant accidentally destroyed a century-old oak tree by pouring weedkiller too near it, Rory charges that Johnny has slowly poisoned her. He has killed their relationship by a recklessness less flamboyant but more insidious than the violence that first attracted Rory to him. Once when Rory asked Johnny why he tried so hard to wreck their relationship, he explained the presumption that eventually poisons it: he knows that he can do nothing that will make Rory stop loving him. Filled with reciprocal violence, Rory wanted to kill her lover right then because she realized the truth of his arrogance. When Rory finally accuses Johnny of this neglect, he not only accepts responsibility for his role as poisoner but even relishes it. Rory notices that Johnny gets the same frightening look that he wore before crashing his car into a lamp pole or smashing his fist into somebody's face, "Out of control, and enjoying it" (310).

The violence is mutual. As Johnny grasps Rory's head as if on the verge of some climactic mayhem, he charges that she used a rope to kill their love. She gave him the slack of too much freedom by not complaining about his proud indifference until Johnny at last became a hanged man. Rory foundered on the paradox of the *pharmakon,* for she tolerated and perpetuated violence to achieve peace. She resorted to the remedy that poisons, the love that kills. Rory never warned Johnny about his negligence or threatened to leave him because she feared the pain of his ultimate rejection. So, just as Rory once sought "a magnificent but fragile numbness" toward her alcoholic father "as if she were one toke over the line, sweet Jesus, one toke over the line" (223), she turned to another analgesic. But the cure for heartache caused its own adverse reaction. Rory anesthetized herself to Johnny's constant inattentiveness, matched his insensitivity with the slow cultivation of her own, until she finally became anesthetized even to his love. "I was too much of a coward," Rory admits to herself, "to undergo the operation of faking you out without an anesthetic, and now the operation's for real and the anesthetic won't wear off; the feelings won't come back. The operation was a success, but the patient died" (311). Rory could only survive Johnny's heedlessness by a drug beyond all the drugs that get consumed in *Slow Poison*, a self-medication whose overdose deadened the very love it was meant to keep alive. Unable to stop loving Johnny, she became like those biblical scenes of victimization that she imagined. Rory sacrificed the responsiveness of her own heart.

Both Rory Cade and Sheila Bosworth seek to get beyond the consecration of violence in *Slow Poison* through a religious use of narrative.[9] At the beginning of the novel, Rory has been away from Covington for two weeks on a publicity tour as a writer. When Johnny invites Rory to start her tale by telling about how a family servant used to fret over the possibility of insanity among the Cades, she recalls the words Sister Devotia recited at her mother's funeral, "Insanity in the family, in the genes, in the blood." Rory hears this triple intonation as echoing the rhythm of the Sign of the Cross, made in the name of the Father, the Son, and the Holy Ghost. "The signal for the beginning of affirmations, repetitions, mysteries, supplications," she remembers (11). Begun with such a benediction, the narrative is thus a ritualized retelling of the Cade family history over which Rory presides as hierophant. Although she initially imagines her account of family history as a way of "exorcising the demons of the Cade sisters, who even unto this night torment the soul of John Benedict Killelea," Rory completes it as a way of expelling the evil spirits that torment her own soul (303). "Fight, you devils, fight," Rory's grandmother once challenged the warring Cades at the dinner table, "I hate peace" (55). Her invocation is appropriate because devils, as Girard observes, are the very spirits of disorder and violence in the Gospels (*Scapegoat* 166). Whereas Johnny tells Rory to leave his demons alone because "I've grown attached to them, down through the hellish decades" (303), Rory wants freedom from such discord and division. She wisely honors Johnny's requests to tell about these infernal years in the third person, for the shift from a first-person viewpoint helps the bedeviled narrator to gain a necessary detachment from the emotional chaos of the past. Rory seeks dispossession through story.

Rory tries to gain peace by making her story into her own version of one of the central acts of piety in her family's faith. As if reversing her dream in which the First Communion prayer beads once bit into Jane Ann's wrist, Rory hopes to free herself from the violence of the snake through the rosary of her narrative. She was christened Rosary Maria Cade after the prayer to Mary that Catholics were enjoined to say for world peace. The rosary was so popular when Rory was born that Fichter's study of Mater Dolorosa Church notes how it was recited at wakes, missions, holy hours, Lenten services, and

Marian devotions. Schoolchildren prayed it at Mass, and families listened to it on the radio. The characters in *Slow Poison* repeatedly join the ranks of these faithful. Jane Ann prays the rosary daily to overcome the nightmares that follow her husband's death, disturbances that Fox Renick characterizes as "Violent ejection images" (242). When Eamon views a television replay of Robert Kennedy's assassination, he wonders about who might have given the slain senator a rosary. He tells Rory that Jane Ann should not be discouraged if an occasional bad dream still torments her despite her nightly rosary: "Because these evil spirits that have started hanging around now, they must be a stronger breed. Like the goddamn Louisiana cockroach. Mutating. Resisting the repellents" (259). When Eamon himself lies dying, his sister-in-law Tipping helps him to confront his own demons by placing in his hand a rosary.

Rory makes the arch-practice of devotional Catholicism the subliminal prayer of *Slow Poison*. The fifteen mysteries, or important events in the lives of Jesus and Mary, that are remembered during the rosary become the background for Rory's recollections of the "mysteries" of her past (11). Divided into the joyful, sorrowful, and glorious mysteries, the rosary encompasses the ecstasy and poison of Cade family life. The Angelus bell that rings after Rory and Johnny make love for the first time proclaims the Annunciation, the first joyful mystery. The "Visitation" (123) of Aimée Desirée's ghost to Rory echoes the name of the second joyful mystery, Mary's visit to her kinswoman Elizabeth, and the Christmas celebrations of the novel honor the third joyful mystery. Rory describes her stepmother's death as "the last *sorrowful* mystery of Aimée Desirée's life" (124) and recalls the same sad mystery again when she sees Eamon's death in terms of the Crucifixion. After Jane Ann's husband dies in a burning parachute over Vietnam, the fatality makes his wife and sister-in-law think of Jesus' Ascension into heaven, the second glorious mystery. Rory reaches to the end of the rosary when she views Aimée Desirée's generous legacy to the Cades as the "final, glorious mystery" of her life (124).

"I was brought up in the novena-rosary tradition too," Flannery O'Connor wrote a friend, "but you have to save yourself from it someway or dry up" (139). Bosworth saves herself from the ill effects of her girlhood religion and from her own reciprocal anger at its violence by Rory's imaginative appropriation of the rosary. Bosworth does not try to create any neat pious parallels between the bittersweet Cade family history and the events of faith remembered in the rosary. Nor does she give the prayer any talismanic magic. Although the suicidal Jane Ann recites the rosary nightly, she has been hospitalized before the novel begins because a possibly accidental combination of alcohol and Seconals has caused her to suffer cardiac arrest. Rather, as Rory recalls the events of "Decades," the name for the two central parts of her narrative that focus on the late 1950s and 1960s, Bosworth lets the decades of the rosary, the groups of ten "Hail Marys" that are prayed with each mystery, look to the peace that Rory and all the Cades need.

Bosworth's fictional practice of her faith is the ultimate demonstration of Walker Percy's quip, "In the end, ten boring Hail Marys are worth more to the novelist than ten hours of Joseph Campbell on TV" (370). Percy saw art as grounded not in the eternal recurrence of myth but in the world of particular times, places, and things that Judaeo-Christianity so deeply respects. He claimed that Catholic artists who rejected their religious heritage were seeking a romantic escape from such specificity (321). *Slow Poison* illustrates how a writer can criticize the culture of the church without losing the virtue of the parochial. Immersing her novel in the richly detailed milieu of devotional Catholicism, Bosworth writes a discerning commentary on the "novena-rosary tradition" and then does something more: she makes her peace with the world of the "Hail Mary" by writing the rosary into *Slow Poison*.

Rory has based her life on the intention for which Catholics frequently prayed the rosary. Because she was easily upset, Rory developed the reputation for being the peacemaker in her family. She carried this irenic spirit so far that she was afraid to challenge Johnny lest he dismiss her: "You're going? Well, so long. Go in peace, Cade, and Dominus vobiscum" (311). Rory kept the peace with Johnny, tolerated his violence, and responded with her own counterviolence, for fear of departing in peace without him. In "Ite in Pace," the epilogue of *Slow Poison*, Rory comes closer to realizing the concluding benediction of the Mass that she once dreaded as Johnny's farewell, the wish to go in peace. The blessing answers the title of the novel's prologue "Introibo," the opening word of the Mass in Latin that announces how the priest will go unto the altar of God. Like Bosworth's use of the rosary, her framing device is a peace offering of its own. It draws from the contested tradition of Catholic piety to turn the whole novel into a passageway, by way of the stormy plane ride and into the equally turbulent past, toward such peace.

Rory finds the beginning of such peace through her marriage to Fox Renick. Although he initially seems Johnny's double in drinking, hunting, and defending young women from unwanted advances, this old-time southern gentleman is a much gentler man than Johnny Killelea. After learning of Rory's plan to marry Fox, Johnny is amazed that his friend and rival suitor did not give his liquor a dose of some sulfuric acid from the medical school lab. But as a doctor, a master of the *pharmakon,* Fox does not use the powers of medicine for such violent ends. Rather than poisoning Rory of the weak stomach and diminished appetite, he romances her through restaurants, as if continued indulgence in the cuisine of New Orleans might be the antidote to her heartsickness. The non-Catholic Fox shows such tenderness and attentiveness to Rory that he is privy to a supreme moment of devotional faith in the novel: Rory explains how to say the rosary to him. "Didn't they lynch Catholics for this sort of thing in Fox's home state of Mississippi?" she wonders while giving such instruction (244). Fox is no violent nativist but a southerner so catholic that he is genuinely interested in the central prayer of the novel to bring peace.

Although even at the end Johnny's violent charisma makes Rory almost wish that she did not love Fox anymore, she knows that peace lies with her husband and baby daughter who wait for her at home. Whereas Rory once vengefully tried to frustrate any possible love between Johnny and Jane Ann, she now makes possible their reunion. Johnny had not visited his ex-wife in the hospital when she attempted suicide once before. But after Rory entices him to fly to New Orleans with her by pretending not to know which of her sisters they have been summoned home to help, she invites Johnny to join her in seeing Jane Ann. He agrees. "That one took ten years off my life," one of the flight attendants exclaims after the harrowing plane ride to New Orleans (317), but Rory's narrative of the two ten-year periods in "Decades" may have helped to renew not just her life but Johnny's and Jane Ann's as well.

Before visiting Jane Ann in the hospital, Rory celebrates her newfound serenity as she and Johnny enjoy the last drinks of the novel. Their toasts at Radosta's Airline Hi-Time at once comprehend and transcend the family history that has just been recounted: "To Jane Ann's healing heart and to Arabella's continued contentment. To Johnny Killelea and to Rory Cade. To Eamon and Honor and Aimée Desirée and all the poor souls in purgatory and Ireland, kid, in the coming times" (322). The drinks ritualize how Rory has gotten beyond rage and resentment to a capacious acceptance of the entanglements of her past. Whereas she once felt that she "couldn't afford to have a jolt of pity knock her back into full sensibility right now" (223), she at last includes pity as part of the libation, the "pity beyond all telling / [that] Is hid in the heart of love" according to the epigraph for "Decades" from Yeats's "The Pity of Love." "Drinking the transcendent blend of passion and trouble and sweet pity," *Slow Poison* ends. "The bourbon, the bitters, the sugar" (322). At the beginning of the novel, Rory complained that outside Louisiana, Mississippi, and Alabama, she could not get a proper Old Fashioned. On the plane she longed for precisely that drink's ingredients to make palatable the long revelation of family mysteries. Rory turns the annals of the Cades into such an elixir. Like the "genius" of a barman who prepares her Old Fashioned at the end, Rory has blended the contradictions of her family history into a narrative that is sweet and bitter, ecstatic and poisonous. After the violence of her past, Rosary Maria Cade lives up to the devotion of her name and finds her peace in that transcendent story.

Notes

1. Bosworth was part of the Sons and Daughters of the Apocalypse, the irreverent gathering of artists and writers that met with Percy for Thursday lunches at a restaurant in Mandeville (Samway 337–38). For Bosworth's memories of Percy and an admiring appraisal of the female characters in *The Moviegoer* and *Lancelot,* see her "Women in the Fiction of Walker Percy."

2. When Percy wanted to know if his wife should wear a black mantilla to meet the Pope in 1988, it was Bosworth whom he asked (Samway 397).

3. Bosworth eventually attended Sophie Newcomb College of Tulane University because it seemed like the best local alternative when her father would not let her go away to any school except to a Catholic college (Bosworth, "Fate" 90).

4. Percy was not blind to the failings of institutional Catholicism. See Gandolfo 40–43 for a discussion of Percy's criticisms of the church.

5. *Almost Innocent* impressed Percy so much that he wrote a blurb for the novel praising its Jamesian use of a child's viewpoint to portray evil.

6. For other snake images in *Slow Poison,* see pages 11, 125, 153, 276, 299, and 318.

7. In the religion of the Cades, piety often seems a magical means for averting violence by propitiating a demanding God. After Grandolly's death, Eamon pays for a hundred Masses to be offered for the soul of the woman who supposedly gave him a lucky tip on the races just before she died. "'I want you to spring her from purgatory as fast as possible, Father,' he says, handing over the ransom money for the Masses" (143).

8. Holy Shroud School was inspired by memories of Bosworth's own student days ("Interview" 163).

9. Clay-Lee Calvert also seeks peace and order through storytelling in *Almost Innocent.* Susan Donaldson, however, argues that like the New Orleans meals that provide so many occasions for such tales, Clay-Lee's narrative cannot contain the chaos of her family's insatiable desires. Rory is more successful than Clay-Lee because her narrative accepts the complexities of Cade family life rather than trying to exclude them in the name of absolute unity and total control.

Works Cited

Bosworth, Sheila. *Almost Innocent.* New York: Simon and Schuster, 1984.

———. "Fate, Fortune and the First Novel: An Interview with Sheila Bosworth." By William A. Francis. *Southern Quarterly* 29.1 (1990): 85–102.

———. "Interview." Susan Ketchin. *The Christ-Haunted Landscape: Faith and Doubt in Southern Fiction.* Jackson: UP of Mississippi, 1994. 146–71.

———. *Slow Poison.* New York: Knopf, 1992.

———. "Women in the Fiction of Walker Percy." *Louisiana Literature* 10.2 (1993): 76–85.

Derrida, Jacques. "Plato's Pharmacy." *Dissemination.* Trans. Barbara Johnson. Chicago: U of Chicago P, 1981. 61–171.

Dolan, Jay P. *The American Catholic Experience: A History from Colonial Times to the Present*. Notre Dame: U of Notre Dame P, 1992.

Donaldson, Susan V. "Consumption and Complicity in Sheila Bosworth's *Almost Innocent*." *Southern Quarterly* 30.2–3 (1992): 113–22.

Fichter, Joseph H. *Dynamics of a City Church*. 1951. New York: Arno, 1978.

Gandolfo, Anita. *Testing the Faith: The New Catholic Fiction in America*. Westport, Conn.: Greenwood, 1992.

Girard, René. *The Scapegoat*. Trans. Yvonne Freccero. Baltimore: Johns Hopkins UP, 1986.

———. *Things Hidden Since the Foundation of the World*. Trans. Stephen Bann and Michael Metteer. Stanford: Stanford UP, 1987.

———. *Violence and the Sacred*. Trans. Patrick Gregory. Baltimore: Johns Hopkins UP, 1977.

O'Connor, Flannery. *The Habit of Being: Letters of Flannery O'Connor*. Ed. Sally Fitzgerald. New York: Farrar, Straus and Giroux, 1979.

Percy, Walker. *Signposts in a Strange Land*. Ed. Patrick H. Samway. New York: Farrar, Straus and Giroux, 1991.

Ransom, John Crowe. *God without Thunder: An Unorthodox Defence of Orthodoxy*. London: Gerald Howe, 1931.

Samway, Patrick H. *Walker Percy: A Life*. New York: Farrar, Straus and Giroux, 1997.

Tolson, Jay. *Pilgrim in the Ruins: A Life of Walker Percy*. New York: Simon and Schuster, 1992.

Turgenev, Ivan. *First Love*. In *First Love and A Fire at Sea*. Trans. Isaiah Berlin. New York: Viking, 1983. 11–124.

"Because God's Eye Never Closes"

The Problem of Evil in Jayne Anne Phillips's SHELTER

James Grove

Life is made up of many dark fissures.

Stendhal, *The Red and the Black*

Contemporary American writers who *think* about evil in their art make an ethical decision that often places them in an uneasy relationship with their audience. Although evil has been ubiquitous in the murderous twentieth century, Americans have had difficulty recognizing, defining, and facing evil, except in superficial and ephemeral ways. In *The Death of Satan*, Andrew Delbanco writes that with the breakdown of traditional notions of religious certainty and transcendence, Americans have persistently discarded the potent words, images, symbols, and myths once used—for better and worse—to objectify evil. In turn, Americans have generally not found resonant replacements for them. The consequence of this is that there has not been enough "serious moral thinking" about evil (228). Too often, then, it is a subject that escapes "the reach of our imagination" (234).

Thus America suffers from a moral atmosphere of evasion that often dissociates evil from the self, from beliefs in human responsibility, and from the tragic side of human existence—although we remain fascinated by the probability that evil exists near us on Main Street. As a result, there is "an enormous appetite" in the popular culture for the bizarre, titillating, morbidly sentimental stories of serial killers, slashers, domestic abusers, sex criminals, and sinister aliens.[1] This dissociation, inextricably linked to the culture's Peeping Tom sensibility, has led, Delbanco argues, to "an unprecedented condition of inarticulate dread" (*Death* 9). People yearn to think deeply about evil and respond persuasively to it (*Death* 16–18). But they often do not follow through, for they get too lost in the noisy rush and confusions of modern/postmodern life; in the urge to blame and project evil onto an "other" (*Death* 229–30); in the temptation to embrace an optimism that refuses to look closely at the darknesses in human nature; or in the ironic willingness to deconstruct arguments about evil in order to empty them of their moral significance (*Death* 208–9).

Despite this deep cultural confusion, many of America's most prominent contemporary writers have centered their fiction on the problem of evil.[2] They use the language of narrative to fight the idea that evil—with its many shades, secrets, taboos, and dangers—is beyond the reach of a complex human response. In the process, they examine the basic, risky, prevailing questions that have haunted literature, philosophy, the social sciences, and religion: What is evil? How do we find words and symbols to name evil? If God exists, why is there so much undeserved suffering? Does evil preclude the belief in a benevolent God or the existence of any overriding presence? How do we explain the continuous human capacity for evil? How can we avoid seeing evil only as an abstraction? What is the relation of evil to sin, pride, guilt, and death? How can human beings most responsibly react to evil? To face such questions is emotionally, intellectually, and theologically risky because it leads writers, and then their readers, to entertain the probability that we live in a world where human beings are often the playthings of accidental, destructive forces beyond our control; that evil might not be an aberration in human beings but a constant inner quality as powerful as our will toward goodness; and, finally, that the individual's struggle with this darkness can be so profound and consuming that eventually very little is left undamaged.

Jayne Anne Phillips has faced and thought about evil throughout her writing career, for the world of her fiction is driven by the threat and reality of moral corruption at all levels of human experience. Phillips's much praised short story collections, *Black Tickets* (1979) and *Fast Lanes* (1987), intensely portray the 1970s and early 1980s as a post-Vietnam, postmodern nightmare in which, as Irving Malin writes, "life is a dangerous series of movements, unknown exits, and entrances. Her protagonists, for the most part, don't really know where they are going. They live moment by moment, day by day" (319). Her first novel, *Machine Dreams* (1984), while covering many of the same nightmares, is more ambitious, as it ranges from the 1930s through the trauma of the Vietnam War. In it, Phillips historicizes her soundings of the twentieth century's immeasurable evil.[3] Finally, the tragic mix of the short stories and *Machine Dreams* is preparation for her major work, *Shelter* (1994), the most southern of her works with its strong sense of place, its dense anti-minimalist texture, its climate of violence, its portrayal of fundamentalist religion, and its absorption with the burden of memory, time, guilt, and family history. *Shelter* is also one of the most intensely realized depictions of evil in contemporary American fiction.

In Phillips's short stories, characters are always wary that some sort of new "black ticket" might destroy them in hollow, violent, incoherent, and morally ill America. They are placeless and existentially anxious. Often despairing, drugged, and alienated, they search for the "fast lane," for a way to float away from responsibility, from whatever is trapping them. They dive into a random sexuality often empty of much meaning. Accident and change rule their lives. Their morbid attraction to the horrific, tied to visions of apocalypse, fearfully and obsessively broods on the probability that death brings no transcendence. Physical and mental illness are everywhere. Human aspiration is stunted by exterior/interior forces that defy understanding or control. This is the world that Maya Koreneva justifiably sees epitomized in Phillips's story "Home": "Here is a world of endless evil and vice, dominated by dark desires and vile passions, a world beyond redemption. . . . Here, virtually everyone is doomed" (272).

In short, there is a queasy atmosphere of pervasive Bad Faith. For Phillips's characters, the world frequently appears like "One Goddamn big lie" ("El Paso" 85), where people are "like a squirrel on a wheel," underneath a sky that "opens like a hole" ("El Paso" 95); where towns uneasily sleep remembering wars ("Snow" 208); and where people, no matter how intelligent, have their lives ruined in the most matter-of-fact ways ("Blue Moon" 103). It is true that some of her characters desperately dream of angels, love, and redemption—dream of making the "one right move" that might illuminate the darkness ("Fast Lanes" 65). They dream of a "universe controlled by a benevolent, all-mighty authority" ("Blue Moon" 110). Yet too often these desperate hopes are riddled with secrets that might save but can just as easily corrode and destroy. That is what makes the possibility of some hidden meaning so alluring yet so frightening. As the serial killer in "Gemcrack" notes, the people reading clippings about his murders "are looking for secrets. I'm pushing them. I could tell them light comes in one quick flash to the seeker" (260).

Reading Phillips's unsettling short stories is like reading an "inside" version of these clippings; it often feels as if we have gone down into the dark fissures of life. In fact, Phillips has explained what the "assaultive nature of some of the stories had to do with—I felt very much like an outcast. I felt very outside of everything" ("1986 Conversation" 57). Without much to hold onto, we experience these "quick flashes" with a strange mix of exhilaration and apprehension because they often reveal the "primal terror" at the heart of human existence ("Home" 11). At these moments, the issue of evil is often up front, and Phillips invites us not to turn away, invites us to fill in and connect the silences, tensions, and gaps in her narratives—even though the corruption in these "flashes" defies any sure explanation or amelioration, even though she questions fundamental hopes of justice, even though many of her characters appear irrevocably lost. Much of the time it seems like a damned world without salvation.[4]

Machine Dreams—fraught with alienation, fragmented families, devalued traditions, violence, ravaged landscapes, and miscommunication—certainly has an affinity to Phillips's stories. The novel is dependent on her memories of growing up in the South (although the representation of West Virginia is deliberately and elusively fragmented since the characters are losing their sense of place), and its portrait of evil centers on its take of the "Machine in the Garden" theme that has energized so much American literature.[5] Lost and betrayed by their faith in technology, the male characters face evil firsthand because of their machine dreams, thus becoming lost to themselves and to their loved ones. Their dreams are always haunted: from Mitch Hampson's persistent memories of bulldozing decaying dead bodies during World War II to his son Billy's death when his chopper is shot down in Vietnam; from the rapacious destruction by mining of their beautiful West Virginia landscapes to the closing of Mitch's concrete business that leads to the rusting away of his machines and his identity. At the same time, the novel's females wonder where all the sadness, placelessness, and evil come from; and this uncertainty makes Jean Hampson, as she tries to endure the losses of her husband and son, yearn for the simpler times of World War II, when it seemed easier "to tell good from evil" (8).

Again Phillips exposes how the times have become ill. Again the characters reflect her feeling that "everyone suffers" ("Interview" [Stanton] 42). And again they lack the prevailing faith or moral energy to escape a paralysis that subverts their finding any legitimate way to fight evil. As Phillips's impressionistic, gap-filled narrative moves back and forth between the five Hampsons, their need for answers, order, and justice leads to "flashes" that usually confirm that "bad things can happen anywhere" (267), that "you never know what can happen" (273), and that no one is ever safe. For the reader, this novel—with all of its familial, social, and individual destruction—is like the "dream" Danner Hampson experiences while listening to Jimi Hendrix's version of "The Star Spangled Banner": "She shut her eyes and heard the loud song: a translation into a language deciphered in darkness. How could anyone play an instrument like that? Even the silences between notes were full" (239).

As with Phillips's stories, the reader must actively enter into the performance of this novel. We enter into its suffering and secrets, trying to fill in its ellipses, its silences, while recognizing that Phillips deciphers her story in a darkness that does not lead to definitive answers but to an accumulation of questions in the novel's brilliant final chapter. As Danner Hampson faces her family's tragedies and failures, she also faces the legacy of the Vietnam War, her own placelessness, the fact that too often nothing can forestall evil, and the dangers of living in the moral chaos of an ahistorical, self-consuming present tense. *Machine Dreams* is therefore demanding—for writer and reader—because it demonstrates Phillips's belief that the "real risk is to be strong enough to understand and accept what you're going to find out so that you are not destroyed by what you find" (Phillips, "PW Interviews" 66).

Reading *Machine Dreams* is finally a more ample experience than reading the stories because it develops, with much more complexity, the idea of "connection" that Phillips talks about so often in interviews, an idea that undercuts the occasional critical presumption that her writing reveals a predominantly postmodern sensibility.[6] Rather it more deeply embodies both sides of the modernist tension that Baudelaire describes: there "is the transient, the fleeting, the contingent; it is the one half of art, the other half being the eternal and the immutable" (qtd. Harvey 10). Through its emphasis on memory, *Machine Dreams* demonstrates Phillips's contention that fiction must rescue and hold things long enough so that we can see them. It is an act "very similar to prayer, and even more similar to meditation" as it "witnesses," connects, and redeems through connecting ("Interview" [Douglass] 187). Jean and Danner persistently try to connect the scattered parts of their domestic world in attempting to realize Jean's desperate faith that when "suffering seems reasonless, people come together and want to understand" (*Machine Dreams* 100). Connecting. Witnessing. Warning. Redeeming. Throughout *Machine Dreams*, characters wonder what can be saved when there is so much discontinuity, so much damage, and when any kind of illumination is, at best, flickering.

At its heart, Phillips's world fits John Kekes's description of the human condition in *Facing Evil* (1990): human life is tragic because our persistent aspirations are made vulnerable by the inevitable "contingency of human existence, the indifference of nature to human merit, and the presence of destructive forces as part of human motivation" (5). Evil is so common because it finds so many openings in a world so much in flux. As a result, saving anything is always a difficult yet necessary task. This need to rescue and to preserve is why the female characters in *Machine Dreams* cherish their memories, why Phillips repeatedly stresses that *connection* is possible at all levels of human experience, and why *Machine Dreams* leads us into *Shelter*, which has been described as a new riff on the Southern Gothic tradition and has been compared to the work of Flannery O'Connor, James Dickey, Carson McCullers, Cormac McCarthy, and especially William Faulkner (the novel's title directly alludes to *Sanctuary*).[7] Moreover, what Cleanth Brooks says about Faulkner's "theology" also applies to this novel: "His characters come out of a Christian environment, and represent whatever their shortcomings and whatever their theological heresies, Christian concerns; and that they are finally to be understood only by reference to Christian premises [original sin, the conflict between flesh and spirit, the necessity of discipline, trial by fire, and redemption through sacrifice]" (22–23).

Shelter is set in 1963, just before the chaotic times Phillips relentlessly depicts in her short stories. Specifically, its claustrophobic narrative occurs at a West Virginia girls' camp, the summer before the trauma of the Kennedy assassination. From its prologue (a saturated, oppressive description of the camp, which reads like the humid calm before a great storm) to its muted, elegiac ending, there is a sense of foreboding.

This tenuous atmosphere is perfect for Phillips's intention to "think about evil, the idea of whether evil really exists" ("Interview" [Douglass] 188). Still believing in the pieties of the 1950s, while already feeling the cultural upheaval of the 1960s, the divided world of *Shelter* allows Phillips to dive into the quandaries of evil that have consistently intrigued moralists. Central to the novel is the question: What kind of world, what kind of God, what kind of ethical system, what kind of human being perpetrates, tolerates, or justifies harm to children? Moreover, Phillips is interested in exploring the problem of human accountability for evil, especially if evildoers have been "damaged" by uncontrollable forces severely limiting their ability to choose. She thus tests what Kekes calls the *soft* and *hard* reactions to evil: the *soft* emphasizing that such damage must influence and mitigate our view of evildoers who act according to unchosen vices; the *hard* warning that this damage should not deter us from condemning and acting against the evildoer, regardless of whether evil is chosen (6–7).

Phillips's intentions are objectified through four overlapping, impressionistic, third-person limited consciousnesses that accumulate images of everyday evil while gradually moving toward their raw confrontation with extreme malignity in the person of Carmody, an ex-convict. Two of the consciousnesses belong to Lenny and Alma, sisters attending the camp. With the scare of the Cuban Missile Crisis just behind them, these girls will soon know where they were when President Kennedy was shot and will mature in the late 1960s and early 1970s—perhaps becoming like the lonely, drifting, sensation-seeking characters in Phillips's short stories.

Right from the start, Phillips portrays how something reliable, safe, and good has already been eroded from their childhood. Indeed, they come to the wilderness as scarred refugees from the treacheries, secrets, and tragedies of unraveling home lives. They are not innocents who *fall* as they face the forest's darkness. Instead they reveal that Phillips's vision of childhood is similar to Graham Greene's (as Garry Wills describes it): "Greene often argued, innocence is like all other illusions, pleasant but dangerous. Children are not innocent. No one is innocent. Thinking that one is defies reality" (70–71).

Lenny's and Alma's memories of their daily life in Gaither, West Virginia, takes us back to the broken worlds of Phillips's earlier work. The economic situation is grim. Many people are searching for protection. Many are trying to float and empty themselves so that they cannot be further damaged. They are wandering without any kind of viable moral map in a landscape being emptied of spiritual meaning. They sense that evil is shadowing and depriving them, yet they lack the resources to define or combat its oppression. So there is fear, silence, and paralysis. Specifically, Lenny and Alma's father is a vaguely sinister alcoholic lost in his increasing self-absorption. Sometimes his daughters longingly remember how he once played with them in the fields; other times, he comes to them in dreams as a possible child molester (and we remain uncertain if these nightmares have some basis in reality). Their mother, Audrey, is "a canceled zero" (*Shelter* 8), emotionally lost to them after Nickel Campbell, with whom she is having an affair, commits suicide. This man is the father of Alma's best friend, Delia, whose sleepless nights at the camp betray how haunted she is by his death, which no one has helped her face. Delia's nightmares, in turn, make Alma feel more lost, guilty, and protective toward the girl because, more than anyone else, Alma knows the truth that Campbell was crushed by the irresolvable tension and shame of his adultery.

The sisters, therefore, live in a household turned morally upside down by these dark secrets that become even more potent in "awful" Gaither, where "everybody knows everything, except they get it all twisted" (169). In examining the ethics of secrecy, Sissela Bok writes that a secret can be "something sacred, intimate, private, unspoken, silent, prohibited, shameful, stealthy, or deceitful" (7). Keeping a secret can poison and estrange, infecting daily relationships. Yet revealing a secret can make us too exposed, too vulnerable. Keeping a secret may leave evil undisturbed, thus avoiding more suffering. Yet revealing a secret may purge the evil by bringing it out into the open (9). Finally, receiving secret knowledge may give us more insight, more power. Yet it also may carry the "fear of what learning will entail—of being drawn into a guilty secret, perhaps, entangled in its protection, or polluted through mere contact with it" (33). Bok's dissection of the ambivalent, tangled experience of secrecy is expertly caught in Lenny's and Alma's relationships with their mother, whose secrets are "next to her skin, as though she were wrapped in yards and yards of stories, like bandages . . . standing in the kitchen in Gaither, wrapped like a mummy in her complaints. Only her eyes peering out" (*Shelter* 229). As these secrets obsessively come unwound, with their murmurings of a lost marriage and a lost affair, the mother's indiscreet, grief-ridden confessions stunt the girls at home and in their community, which is always turning partial knowledge into the ripe secrets of luxurious, dark half-truths.

Lenny more successfully fends off Audrey's insinuating stories about her secret life, probably because she is older than Alma and already very alienated from her mother. Yet she is scarred, too. Her most clear-cut knowledge of the affair occurs when she catches a glimpse of Campbell kissing her mother. It is a "mundane and mildly horrifying" evil that festers inside her—especially the memory of Campbell's "sucking on her neck, like a vampire" (130). This memory is something dangerous that she cannot tell her father—hidden in a code she dares not understand. At the same time, because it makes her permanently distrust Audrey, the girl's everyday world becomes a tissue of lies beneath a "fallen and burning" sky (43). Wanting no more secret knowledge because its insights erode meaning, power, and love, Lenny retreats into imaginary games that create worlds where "things that really happened seem as though they never had," where "things that were magical, dangerous, waiting, fade into shadows" (130). With Lenny, then, Phillips raises the dramatic question of whether the fifteen-year-old's psychological damage will always keep her in these shadows. Will she always be too wary of life—not willing to break through to new worlds because she fears that these worlds will also be one "secret opening against another" (131)?

Alma, however, is much less insulated from Audrey. Desperately, the mother has made Alma her confidante: taking her along as a "cover" for her clandestine meetings with Campbell, telling her all the secrets of the affair, haunting Alma with speculation about Campbell's suicide, and filling the girl with her dark view of life. As a result, Alma's childhood is ruined. Audrey's lack of discretion and inability to respect her daughter's selfhood become malign, putting Alma in the impossible, guilt-ridden, polluting predicament of knowing too many secrets. She hears and sees too much, while wishing to share her knowledge with someone, while wishing that she were more like her friend Delia, who is never told anything about the suicide.

At the same time, Alma makes the moral decision to hold everything in, never passing the evil on, thus consciously deciding to reject her mother's example. Alma makes this choice because she knows that her privileged knowledge, while giving her some power, has also left her with no sure feeling of what is true or what is right or wrong. Alma will not burden someone else with it, for she knows that the world is filled with dangerous secrets that should be exorcised. But how to exorcise when the secrets accumulate so much fear, deceit, and shame so quickly? Yearning for some kind of purification, Alma apocalyptically wonders,

> What did it mean, the wrong life? . . . Alma knew the facts, but it seemed to her that Audrey [more than Campbell] was guilty. Well, Audrey had always been guilty . . . but the guilt was secret. Now

the secret was bigger, deeper. And a secret had to be paid for. . . .
Alma wanted to feel the anger rain down on her, wanted a series
of screams that opened out until the earth shook, howls that would
shatter glass and stone, cries that were empty like the wind is
empty, a voiceless keening that would let Alma go, let her betray
her mother. (138)

It is no surprise, then, that Alma responds so favorably to her camp director's
statement that everyone wishes for an organized and productive environment, "for a world attentive to our needs, a world perhaps wiser than we are"
(238). Both Alma and Lenny hope that the wilderness camp in its "emptiness, full" (8) will temporarily provide them with such a world. In this circumscribed, yet strangely wild sanctuary, the sisters want to refashion their
identities, to connect with the other girls, to try to find the right life, and to
experiment with ways to deal with evil.

On one hand, they want to be emptied of the past so they can lose their
fear and guilt and find a state of present-tense innocence. Thus they walk in
the woods or swim in the Turtle Hole, full with individual physical effort,
sometimes floating in a sense of emptiness, sometimes safe in the routinized
bonding with the other girls: "The common movements of the group, were
oddly pleasant: nothing to be thought of, nothing to be decided, only this
chore or that chore" (7).[8] At other times, they daydream about remaining
secure by becoming invisible—like ghosts; or by becoming orphans who never
leave the camp unless someone much wiser than their parents finds them; or
by rescuing time so that when the camp ended "they might all return to the
old life and find it unchanged. Audrey would never have begun Saturday
trips to Winfield to see Nickel Campbell" (83).

The girls, however, cannot escape the memories of the fallen world
they have left behind, no matter how deeply they lose themselves in the moment. Of course, when Alma sees a fish jump, she reads it as possible sign of
renewal. But it does not make her forget the evils of her past. Rather, it eventually brings her back to Audrey and to more hard questions about sinfulness, secrecy, and salvation: "A soul could be like that too, Alma thinks, that
silver color, or a kind of smoke. . . . But Audrey's words only waited in Alma's
head. It was Alma who seemed to push them, remember them, try to hold
them up. She wanted to move them. A soul could fly: hadn't Wes let his go,
drifted upwards and blown about like hair?" (258–59).

Lenny and Alma slowly come to realize that the woods are part of the
fallen world, too. The wilderness is full of natural and human wonder, natural and human danger—this mixture making the novel's sense of place so
inexplicable, so open to good and evil, and ultimately so resistant to any

immediate promises or answers. This is also true for the novel's other two narrative consciousnesses, who are trying to find safety and salvation in the woods, too. They are Buddy, the fear-ridden, seven-year-old son of the camp's cook, and Parson, a deeply conflicted, conscience-driven young man evangelically readying himself for a stark struggle with evil. Both are obsessed with the demonic Carmody; and through their "Carmody watching" (always on alert because of the omnipresence of his danger), Phillips works to give dramatic substance to this man's evil without reducing either its horrific mystery or accountability.

But such a characterization, built primarily through Buddy's and Parson's perspectives for most of the novel, is a difficult task, and some readers have been troubled by it. Miranda Schwartz writes that the "simplicity of his baseness stands in stark comparison to the richness of other characters" (11). Delbanco echoes this judgment by saying that Carmody is "something of a Gothic cliché—evil incarnate." Then he argues that the character becomes even more bothersome because Phillips wants to deepen Carmody by grounding his behavior in the "damage theory of evil—a favorite platitude in our culture" ("Child's Garden" 40)—a theory that Delbanco suggests is morally questionable because it can too easily explain away, excuse, qualify, or evade. This is the *soft* approach toward evil that, according to Kekes, has increasingly hamstrung our culture's capacity for facing and combating the malign (66–83).

These arguments, which cut to the heart of Phillips's aesthetic in *Shelter*, cannot be ignored, for they point to the limitations and risks of her fragmented presentation of Carmody. Of course, this piecemeal strategy is essential to Phillips's plan for revealing impressionistically Buddy's and Parson's very incomplete yet complementary knowledge about Carmody. Through them, Phillips gives us peeks into Carmody's past to show how his malevolence is rooted in his having "been down some hard roads" (177). These glimpses are important, for Phillips does not want to make him so completely alien that his evil has no connection with the human condition. Carmody must remain, however tenuously, one of us; thus Phillips sometimes foreshortens our distance from him by these patches of early biography.

We learn quite a bit about Carmody. After nearly murdering his mother, whom he describes as "a sot, a whore, and then a sot" (160), he was incarcerated and continually abused on a work farm before escaping when he was sixteen by entering the service, only to experience unspeakable punishment as a prisoner of war in Korea, then coming home burned out yet trying to lead a respectable life with Buddy's "Mam" while working in the mines, until finally committing a terrible crime and going to prison, where he met Parson. Prison drained away what was left of his humanity. Truly, he fits Kekes's description of the malevolent person, whose "disposition is to act contrary to what is good. Its emotional source is ill will, a desire for things not to go well" (79). Like this person, Carmody's evil is active, usually unprovoked, and leads to no gain. As Parson remembers, Carmody's rages in prison were sometimes about the past: "I gotta be a good boy, good boy, gotta be a good boy, *kill them, fuck them . . .*" (12). Other times, the past flowed into the future: "*cleaning up piss, all my life been cleaning up piss. . . . I get out of here, I'm gonna piss on the world*" (160).

From Buddy and Parson, we finally learn enough about Carmody to entertain the questions that Phillips asked herself while writing *Shelter*: "Is evil just a function of damage? The fact that when people are damaged they damage others?" ("Interview" [Douglass] 188). Certainly, Phillips wants us to fill in parts of this story and to believe that Carmody has been severely damaged by events he could not control. She wants us to take seriously Parson's early comment about him: "*Poor devil*, the country people would say of a man in the grip of poverty, disease, dissolution. . . . Wasn't the Devil a fallen child, too hungry to eat, starving, ravenous, alone so long he didn't remember who'd first cast him out, a body child, abandoned, lost?" (12). Suffering has had a large hand in creating this man, who was on the road to evil long before he could consciously choose another life, whose vices soon became habitual, and who now can only self-pityingly strike out against a world that has never been attentive or wise to him.

Clearly, there is enough evidence to understand Delbanco's concern about how Phillips is using the damage theory of evil. The incompleteness of Carmody's characterization, in fact, makes this issue difficult for the reader who must strain to find a coherent, workable connection between the unrelieved moral monster haunting the novel's present and the vulnerable child/young man severely abused in the past. Yet, despite these problems, Carmody is ultimately the catalyst that persistently helps Phillips to think most deeply about evil. That is, he is a malignant touchstone setting off narrative sparks everywhere— and not primarily because of what has been done to him but because his evil threatens, challenges, mystifies, galvanizes, and defines the moral sensibilities of the other major characters. In short, Phillips uses him to intensify the novel's self-interrogation—especially in Buddy's and Parson's sections; and in the process she interrogates and tests her own ideas about evil, too.

By filtering so much of our knowledge of Carmody through Buddy's victimized perspective, Phillips makes sure that we can never forget, ignore, or mitigate the consequences of Carmody's acts of undeserved cruelty against the boy. Buddy is most comfortable wandering in the woods, away from his "stepfather's" verbal, physical, and sexual abuse. In fact, Phillips hangs much of the boy's character upon his need to find some kind of respite or protection from this evil. Some critics, however, have dismissed Buddy as just another example of today's trendy child victim (in this novel of child victims) or as another version of the fundamentally innocent nature child.[9] But, like Lenny and Alma, Buddy defies such reduction because his deeply introspective narration is so concrete, individualized, introspective, and perceptive. Buddy is an extremely prescient evaluator of his environment: it is the only way he can hope to survive Carmody. As he works to separate his identity from Carmody's, Buddy yearns for invisibility and play-fights imaginary, evil Russians who "have faces like Dad's" (109). He also follows the camp girls, hoping he will be able to share adventures with them, planning strategies to save them from his stepfather's violence, and never losing his vague faith that within this shelter of a green world (with its holy dust, sounds, and smells) a blessed secret, a grace, a savior waits to release him from evil. Almost everything Buddy does is tied to his hope for such a connection.

The boy can never forget, however, that he is not safe in the woods because the nature-estranged Carmody sometimes intrudes even there. Nor is Buddy's safety guaranteed with his gentle Mam, whom he loves and depends on, whose large physical presence and deep religious faith give Buddy some relief and stability. For the boy's dreams of churches burning, with his mother's prayers fragmenting, suggest Buddy's awareness that Mam cannot stop Carmody either. Despite her assurance that she stands between Buddy and trouble, he knows that this man also brutalizes her. Furthermore, her faith and protection have not been tested by the worst: Buddy's secret that Carmody sexually molests him. The boy rightly senses that telling her would probably endanger them both. But he does hint about this "dark crack Dad filled if she left the house too early in the morning, too late at night, so it wasn't safe for Buddy to sleep late, not safe to say he wouldn't go to church of an evening. Not safe to sleep at all because all of night was cracked . . ." (244).

Phillips's use of Buddy as a narrator calls to mind Phillip Hallie's point in *Tales of Good and Evil, Help and Harm:*

> Good and evil have much to do with perspectives, points of view. If you want to know whether cruelty is happening and just how painful it is, do not ask the torturer. . . . The victimizer does not feel the blows, the victim feels them. . . . Victimizers can be blinded by simple insensitivity, by a great cause, by a great hatred, or by a hundred self-serving "reasons." Victims too can be desensitized, but usually they are the best witnesses to their pain. They feel it in their flesh and in their deepest humiliations and horrors. (71)

Phillips is, in fact, always "asking" the victim, even as she reveals all the damage to Carmody. Buddy's perspective is so important to Phillips's tough moral vision because the boy has suffered from Carmody's cruelty more intimately and persistently than anyone else. Therefore, when Mam attempts to convince him that Carmody has been greatly wronged by life and that even his evil can be forgiven (by God? by her? by Buddy? by his earlier victims? by the human race?), Buddy instinctively recoils from her "soft" reaction. He does not reject what she is saying as totally unfounded. This abused boy certainly understands how someone can be damaged early and often. But he cannot accept any hope for Carmody because he rightly senses that his stepfather's evil has become habitual. There can be no forgiveness; so he must be destroyed.

This distancing causes the reader to stop short of pitying Carmody too much. For Buddy's perspective shows how Carmody, the malignant human being, embodies the Augustinian premise that evil is essentially a shadowy, prideful, and self-hating "privation of good." Carmody's corruption threatens anything he comes into contact with. As Hans Schwarz states, for evildoers like Carmody, "the horizon of an ultimate meaning is lost that unites and transcends all human beings. . . . [They] wish to have their own limited horizons recognized as universally valid, thereby denying others the same rights and viewing them as virtually nonexistent." This can lead to an "introverted isolation" and to "life-threatening excesses" (200). Estranged from everything within and without themselves, they crave physical power so they can prey on others and make them empty, too.[10]

For Buddy, then, Carmody is an emptiness with only negative potential, with no desire to respect or love anyone. He is a poison that sleeps "like a bomb." He is a moral black hole that sometimes sexually uses the boy. His words steam "like an animal's insides steam when it's gutted and the entrails lay out sudden in the air smoking" (247). He is "like a sack of stones and the sack smelled sour . . . the stones were full of rot and pulp, breaking inside the bags of Dad's clothes" (206); and his tiny black, shattered irises always threaten "to pull at Buddy, suck him in" (209). Carmody lacks the moral imagination to see beyond his own needs, and his evil turns people into objects for his irrational, despairing, self-pitying, life-indulgent will.

If Phillips is asking the *victim* through Buddy, she is asking Carmody's *double* through Parson, the most elusive character in *Shelter*. As Parson admits, "Carmody was surely his brother" (74), and this affinity, which begins immediately after they meet in prison, gives Parson a special intuition into his cellmate's dark self. Like Carmody, Parson has been orphaned young, sexually abused, committed to the work farm after acting violently, and finally sent to prison for murder. Like Carmody, "he knew he was born dark" (10), for as a youngster he had experienced damning visions: "Creatures had appeared to him, creatures that feared light. He knew the creatures were bad and thought that he was one of them" (221). He has consequently felt the emptiness, the soul-destroying hungers that Carmody feels (we see this, for example, in Parson's ambivalent sexual hunger toward Lenny; we are never completely sure whether he wants to save or rape her). Yet whereas Carmody's sufferings and appetites reveal a self-consuming spirit that curses God, Parson sees his misfortunes as a sign of the divine struggle between good and evil within himself, which in turn indicates his anguished but real connection with God. As a result, Parson sees himself Calvinistically as a sinner who not only deserves God's retribution but who also might be blessed by God's unfathomable, miraculous grace.

Parson, who began his religious journey long before he meets Carmody, believes in an extreme version of "that old time religion," southern fundamentalist style. Rejecting the idea of human perfectibility, skeptical about beliefs celebrating human possibility, believing in hellfire and the devil, Parson sees evil everywhere—so much so that the reader occasionally questions the young man's sanity. Certainly Phillips never lets us rest too easily within his fanaticism, even though we can understand why Buddy believes Parson is an avenging angel come to save the children.[11]

Parson's sense of sinfulness has been reinforced by his early victimization, his recurrent visions, his criminal behavior, his being nurtured in the religious beliefs of his surrogate father (a corrupt populist preacher), and his continuing contact with all kinds of hypocrisy and depravity. Thus, for Parson, evil is a concrete, personal, everyday presence. It is in himself. It is in the deep waters of the Turtle Hole, in the dangerously ambivalent sexuality of women, in the hordes of grasshoppers, and in the cackling chickens. It is in "the sounds in the woods, the crackle and slide of evil slunk from its host. How evil moved like sun through trees, in patches, dappled and patterned" (185). It is in the emptiness of the camp directress, who tries to escape her own knowledge of darkness (especially her husband's suicide) through endless, Cold War demonizing of the Russians. She has made evil so exterior to herself that she is helpless to protect the camp girls. She is no "mate for the Demon, no match. But she was empty and evil; she scared Parson because the evil would work through her to get to someone else . . . the Demon was near her like a shadow, never left her. She knew about evil, she was afraid" (71). Because she evades the evil within herself, she cannot recognize or stop Carmody. Her righteous gaze, so filled with communist-sightings and abstract cries of retribution, has become lost in ideology.

Parson, in contrast to the directress, obsessively *watches* Carmody. He follows him to the woods because he knows that Carmody is "an evil unafraid of good, an evil thriving as shadow of every gesture and desire, every future. Time moved that way, and disease, and fire ate that way, catching the edge and burning toward the center" (46). Parson tracks him because he knows how much Carmody has been victimized and damaged, and he knows that one must never "pity those who are sick with evil" (15). Parson's righteousness—his hard vision of justice—is not only built on his inside-out doppelganger understanding of Carmody's terrifying emptiness (as with Buddy, Parson often describes Carmody's evil as a kind of irredeemable privation). It is also built on his passionate need to expiate his sins, especially his guilt over once recklessly killing a young woman in a car accident—a need tied to his belief in individual salvation and in the potential for everyone to have direct access to God.

The voices of Parson's desperate faith have thus led him to this "right place" (11). As with Lenny, Alma, and Buddy, the promise of some overriding meaning or some salvation is hovering for Parson in the atmosphere, just out of reach and out of understanding, yet always waiting to sooth his spiritual anguish. The promise of grace is in the moonsmoke, in the banks of clouds, in the rustling of the leaves at night, in the water's ghostly surface, just as evil is there. Everything is tropological for Parson, whereas nothing has meaning for Carmody.

And that is why snakes so enthrall Parson. Wound around him, the snake helps Parson demonstrate his faith in God's protection, while also symbolizing his fundamentalist vision of human beings' place before God. Wound around him, it is the "probe of God," primarily because snakes "are the living memory of evil, respect and fear them. As Lucifer himself was an angel fallen from grace, so these shades of the Devil are fallen from the mantle of evil . . . humbled, crawling on their bellies toward the scent of redemption" (126–27). As the memory and shade of evil, the snake is the way Parson reminds himself of his own capacity to sin, especially when he links the snake to his voyeuristic attraction to Lenny. It also reminds him that he must redeem his own abject soul by stopping Carmody, who has taken up the mantle of evil in the wilderness. He especially feels this duty, in a strange way, when he studies and identifies with the snake's gaze, which reminds him of the Angel of Death who "swallows [children] whole before the evil can touch them" (125). Finally, the snake's intimate, sensuous, abject journey through the rich, whispering, secretive, expectant, and evil world reminds Parson of his own sin-ridden pilgrimage.

As the sin-riddled Parson waits for his "dark brother" to act, Phillips is showing us, again, that her novel is not a trendy exploitation of the damage theory of evil. This is why Delbanco, despite his reservations, finally praises *Shelter* for resisting the formulaic explanations it sometimes courts:

> How is one to explain why one suffering child grows up demented, reviling the world, while another lives to love and save the inno-

cent? How is one to explain why some people see evil only outside themselves, while others sense it welling up as the "frantic . . . focus" of their own sexuality—as a kind of carnal solipsism? . . . Phillips's novel listens to its own contradictions, and declines to solve its own riddles . . . as fiction it has the tact to refrain from answers while persuading its readers of the mystery of the question. ("Child's Garden" 39)

In *The Paradox of Cruelty*, Phillip Hallie writes that the meaning of cruelty is best understood in relation to the force of resistance it provokes among those whom it victimizes. Through the degree of their outrage and pent-up power, the sufferers of evil "show just how destructive the cruelty they have experienced has been . . . the opposite of cruelty is not kindness. . . . *The opposite of cruelty is freedom*" (139, 159).

The climax of *Shelter*—as Carmody rapes Lenny at the Turtle Hole before being totemistically beaten to death by the girls, Buddy, and Parson—demonstrates Hallie's point that the terror of evil is best understood by the nature of the resistance against it. After Parson is knocked nearly unconscious trying to save Lenny, the children take turns trying to stop Carmody by attacking him with stones. Phillips describes them as a fierce tribe protecting its own, killing the threat by destroying Carmody physically, so that his inner emptiness no longer has a body—an instrument—for its life-denying work.

First, they fight back. Then they take responsibility for the harrowing necessity of their action, especially ensuring that the effects of Carmody's evil are not passed on. As a result, they ritualistically pledge to keep this murder a secret—to protect themselves from having to explain endlessly why they murdered him. As Lenny says, "If we tell someone, it'll never be over. We'll have to tell it and tell it. We'll never be able to stop telling it. Nothing else will matter anymore, ever" (278). By following Lenny's instructions, they will avoid having Carmody's evil survive vicariously. They will stop all of it from getting perversely twisted in Gaither, from taking on a tabloid life in the general imagination. They will instead take on the moral burden of each "hearing everything they're going to think and not tell, even to each other, years of phrases turned round and round, left here in the dark" (297). Their carrying the rape and retribution in their memories, dreams, imaginations, and consciences is an act that Buddy envisions in religious terms. As the children laboriously drag the body toward its tomb in a water-filled hole in Buddy's cave, the boy sees them as angels holding a divine net, flying while crawling toward the water, "and the water leaping up; there were dragons in the water but the angels weren't afraid. That was the kingdom of heaven and the dragnet in their hands, and the good and the evil all taken up" (297).

CIGAR ADVISOR

Q. How is a cigar held together after it is rolled?

A. In most factories specializing in hand-rolled cigars, you will see a little pot of glue-like substance, which is in fact a vegetable-based adhesive. Rollers use the adhesive to seal the head of the cigar with a cap.

places culturally appropriated
Brinkmeyer: "Cultural taxidermy" (182)

Kitschy theme parks, but also like
Williamsburg + these reserved
places frozen at 1850 or 1836

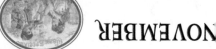

The moral complexity of these climactic actions ties together Phillips's abiding interest in the human capacity for action, secrecy, connection, and responsibility in a frightening world that somehow seems to damage and diminish everyone. The novel's final pages, then, resist one critic's evaluation of them as "a horror movie/fairy tale ending—it's almost as if the girls have stumbled into the wrong story, out of something open-ended and into something pat" (Deb Schwartz 588).[12]

Of course, the evil Carmody is dead, and, yes, Buddy is now free to run through his kingdom of the woods without fear, to live with Mam without fear, to dance away his memories of the "black world" (319) without fear, and to end the novel by tenderly bringing home a one-eyed rabbit for Mam to protect. Yes, the evil has been destroyed, and Parson has now fulfilled his holy duty to stop Carmody. And, yes, the girls have come together to stop the assault, so Lenny can apotheosize how the everyday sounds, sights, and activities of the camp, as well as the girls' reactions to the natural world and to each other, were the natural prayers that bound them together during the attack, so that no one ran away. They were their unspoken and natural spiritual glue.

But these affirmations, although powerful, do not hide the fact that there are many dark fissures remaining after Carmody's death. "The world would not be as it was," Lenny thinks. "She saw that there was no world but this one now . . . they were born into it, mourning" (279). For Lenny will never forget that she has been assaulted. All the children will never forget that they have murdered. All of them will have to live with the lingering psychological costs of confronting this evil, especially when they wonder whether they did "a terrible thing" (302). Parson's spiritual anguish/isolation will continue on the road, although it has been eased momentarily in the woods. As Phillips suggests the long-range damage to these decent people, we recognize with respect, discomfort, and perhaps anger what it costs to fight evil. We are also left wondering why this rigmarole of evil exists, especially if the world is divinely run?

Phillips has no pat answers for this moral conundrum. But she does show Buddy, in early November 1963, waking up from nightmares about Carmody and thinking that he, too, is a devil for helping kill his "father." Then the boy tries to find comfort from "the God's eye" hanging over his bed as protection. But although it is supposed to remind him that "God's eye never closes," it only causes him to ask Mam questions about what the eye thinks, sees, knows, and *does* (318). These questions remain unanswered for Buddy. So Phillips leaves us on the eve of the Kennedy assassination, Mam already worrying about the Vietnam War, with no certainty that there is any real shelter from evil except in the fragile beauty of tenuous human connections.

Moreover, we finish with Lenny wondering about where the evil that was in Carmody has gone. With all the evil in the world, it must have gone somewhere. Perhaps it is already "ripping along the two-lane to Gaither," toward her mother "alone in the house, opening the door" (303).

Notes

1. See Edmundson for a wide-ranging analysis of why contemporary American culture is so obsessed with these popular Gothic visions of evil.

2. Dorothy Allison, Russell Banks, Thomas Berger, Clyde Edgerton, Peter Matthiessen, Cormac McCarthy, Toni Morrison, and Jane Smiley are the best-known contemporary writers who have devoted novels to the problem of evil.

3. Phillips has said, "I think *Machine Dreams* in a way was a look further back, to see what engendered that time [the 1970s]; so it was a larger world view, and probably a more compassionate one, a more forgiving one" ("Interview" [Stanton] 42).

4. Creating such a world rests behind Phillips's statement "that art involves incredible psychic risks. . . . I don't think writers are intrinsically crazy, or that that is why a lot of them commit suicide. I think it's because they are under a kind of stress that would kill anyone else inside of two years" (Hill 349).

5. See Gainey for a helpful discussion of this theme, which is also implicit in *Shelter*.

6. Phillips has said, "It seems to me that the point of existence is certainly not happiness; happiness is entirely a transitory state, like excitement or depression. The point really is to understand the connection between one thing and another" ("Interview" [Douglass] 189). Also see Phillips ("1986 Conversation" 69) and Lassner (195–97) about this matter. For postmodern readings of *Machine Dreams*, see Koreneva, Price, and Willis.

7. See Sheppard, Radin, and Deb Schwartz. Carmody is certainly somewhat mindful of two other evil southern father figures, Pap Finn and Faulkner's Popeye in *Sanctuary*, and there are shades of Darl Bundren's tortured introspection in Buddy.

8. The theme of connection was the initial stimulus for *Shelter*: "When I started the book I thought I wanted to investigate bonding, particularly between adolescent girls, but I didn't want it to be simply about that" ("Interview" [Douglass] 188).

9. See Sheppard and Hulbert.

10. Delbanco makes the intriguing point that Augustine's "idea of sin as privation has proven to be almost inaccessible to the modern mind, in part because we think that without materiality there can be no existence. We tend to confuse a privative conception of evil, which should imply no reduction of its hideousness and virulence, with our own attenuated versions of evil as a concept that disappeared into relativism" (*Death* 50–51). Phillips faces this problem not by ignoring the explanations that Carmody has been damaged and unfortunate but by never reducing or relenting on the essential hideousness of his character, which always remains uncompromisingly dark as it shadows everything. In some ways, her portrayal of Carmody adheres to Erich Fromm's description of the "necrophilic" character, who aggres-

sively values death over life because of early life experiences. But Phillips, like Ernest Becker, distances herself from Fromm's trust in the notion that the nurturing of human reason will limit this kind of behavior. Instead Phillips sees evil as a permanent, irreducible feature of human existence. Concerning Augustine's view of evil, see Peterson (11–12, 191–96); and Hans Schwarz (101–6, 112–26, 138–42).

11. See the analyses of southern religion in Young and in chapter 12 of Grantham.

12. Sheppard denigrates the ending, too, by seeing it as violently fanciful and trendy; because the children, after much abuse, "carry out feral justice, it should satisfy current assumptions about victimization and empowerment" (82).

Works Cited

Becker, Ernest. *Escape from Evil*. New York: Free Press, 1975.

Bok, Sissela. *Secrets: On the Ethics of Concealment and Revelation*. New York: Vintage, 1983.

Brooks, Cleanth. *The Hidden God: Studies in Hemingway, Faulkner, Yeats, Eliot, and Warren*. New Haven: Yale UP, 1963.

Delbanco, Andrew. "A Child's Garden of Evil." Rev. of *Shelter*, by Jayne Anne Phillips. *New Republic* 26 Dec. 1994: 39–40.

———. *The Death of Satan: How Americans Have Lost the Sense of Evil*. New York: Farrar, Straus and Giroux, 1995.

Edmundson, Mark. *Nightmare on Main Street*. Cambridge, Mass.: Harvard UP, 1997.

Fromm, Erich. *The Heart of Man: Its Genius for Good and Evil*. New York: Harper & Row, 1964.

Gainey, Karen Wilkes. "Jayne Anne Phillips's *Machine Dreams*: Leo Marx, Technology, and Landscape." *Journal of the American Studies Association of Texas* 21 (Oct. 1990): 75–84.

Grantham, Dewey W. *The South in Modern America: A Region at Odds*. New York: Harper Collins, 1994.

Hallie, Phillip. *The Paradox of Cruelty*. Middletown, Conn.: Wesleyan UP, 1969.

———. *Tales of Good and Evil, Help and Harm*. New York: Harper Collins, 1997.

Harvey, David. *The Condition of Postmodernity*. Cambridge, Mass.: Blackwell, 1990.

Hill, Dorothy Combs. "Jayne Anne Phillips." *Contemporary Fiction Writers of the South: A Bio-Bibliographical Sourcebook*. Westport, Conn.: Greenwood, 1993. 348–59.

Hulbert, Anne. "A Heart Like a Coiled Serpent." Rev. of *Shelter*, by Jayne Anne Phillips. *New York Times Book Review* 18 Sept. 1994: 7.

Kekes, John. *Facing Evil*. Princeton: Princeton UP, 1990.

Koreneva, Maya. "Hopes and Nightmares of the Young." *Dialogues: Literary and Cultural Exchanges Between Soviet and American Women*. Trans. Maya Koreneva. Ed. Susan Hardy Aiken. Durham: Duke UP, 1994. 266–78.

Lassner, Phyllis. "Women's Narrative and the Recreation of History." *American Women Writing Fiction: Memory, Identity, Family, Space*. Ed. Mickey Pearlman. Lexington: UP of Kentucky, 1989. 193–210.

Malin, Irving. Rev. of *Fast Lanes*, by Jayne Anne Phillips. *Studies in Short Fiction* 24 (1987): 319.

Peterson, Michael L., ed. *The Problem of Evil: Selected Readings*. South Bend: Notre Dame UP, 1992.

Phillips, Jayne Anne. *Black Tickets*. New York: Delta, 1979.

———. "Blue Moon." *Fast Lanes*. 89–121.

———. "El Paso." *Black Tickets*. 75–95.

———. *Fast Lanes*. New York: Washington Square, 1987.

———. "Fast Lanes." *Fast Lanes*. 35–65.

———. "Gemcrack." *Black Tickets*. 251–65.

———. "Home." *Black Tickets*. 5–25.

———. "Interview: Jayne Anne Phillips." By Thomas E. Douglass. *Appalachian Journal* 21.1 (1994): 182–89.

———. "An Interview with Jayne Anne Phillips." By David M. Stanton. *Croton Review* 9 (1986): 41–44.

———. *Machine Dreams*. New York: Dutton/Lawrence, 1984.

———. "A 1986 Conversation with Jayne Anne Phillips." By Dorothy Combs Hill. *The South Carolina Review* 24.1 (1991): 53–73.

———. "PW Interviews Jayne Anne Phillips." By Celia Gilbert. *Publishers Weekly* 8 June 1984: 65–66.

———. *Shelter*. New York: Delta, 1994.

———. "Snow." *Black Tickets*. 205–24.

Price, Joanna. "Remembering Vietnam: Subjectivity and Mourning in the American New Realist Writing." *Journal of American Studies* 27 (1993): 173–86.

Radin, Victoria. "No Hiding Place." Rev. of *Shelter*, by Jayne Anne Phillips. *New Statesman & Society* 10 Feb. 1995: 45–56.

Schwartz, Deb. "Look Homeward, Angels." Rev. of *Shelter*, by Jayne Anne Phillips. *The Nation* 14 Nov. 1994: 585–88.

Schwartz, Miranda. "To Bury the Violence." Rev. of *Shelter*, by Jayne Anne Phillips. *Belles Lettres* 10.2 (1995): 11.

Schwarz, Hans. *Evil: A Historical and Theological Perspective*. Trans. Mark W. Worthing. Minneapolis: Fortress, 1995.

Sheppard, R.Z. "Southern Gothic, '90's Style." Rev. of *Shelter*, by Jayne Anne Phillips. *Time* 19 Sept. 1994: 82.

Willis, Sue Meredith. "Witness in the Nightmare Country." *Appalachian Journal* 24.1 (1996): 44–51.

Wills, Garry. "Two Sides of Innocence." *Time* 14 July 1997: 70–71.

Young, Thomas Daniel. "Religion, 'the Bible Belt,' and the Modern South." *The American South: Portrait of a Culture*. Ed. Louis D. Rubin Jr. Washington, D.C.: Voice of America Forum Series, 1979. 118–26.

Gender and Justice

Alice Walker and the Sexual Politics of Civil Rights

Keith Byerman

In her novel *Meridian* (1976), Alice Walker depicts a northern white civil rights worker very concerned with her impulse to see southern blacks as aesthetic objects: "To Lynne, the black people of the South were Art. . . . 'I will pay for this,' she often warned herself. 'It is probably a sin to think of a people as Art.' And yet, she would stand perfectly still and the sight of a fat black woman singing to herself in a tattered yellow dress, her voice rich and full of yearning, was always—God forgive her, black folks forgive her—the same weepy miracle that Art always was for her" (128).

This essay argues that for Walker herself, just as for her character, southern black folk are Art, in the sense that they serve as a fixed standard by which to measure the moral significance and achievements of the central actors in her narratives about civil rights. It is necessary to understand that region and class are as important as race in establishing this standard. Those who retain their status of being close to the land, with a southern mind-set that rejects abstraction, are the model.[1] This does not mean that Walker has a nostalgic view, though she may have a romantic one. The folk she presents are capable of change and of political action; it is simply that change must be connected to concrete experience.

Corollary to this narrative concern is the related issue of sexuality; desire in Walker's stories tends to produce distortions of itself in that characters generate abstractions of the sexual Other that they then manipulate out of motives of class or race ideology. In this case, the folk become the standard by consistently demonstrating innocent desire in the concreteness and authenticity of their relationships. Consistently in the texts under consideration here—the last part of *The Third Life of Grange Copeland* (1970), *Meridian*, and "Advancing Luna—and Ida B. Wells" (1981)—a complicated modern (even modernist) way of being and doing is set over against a folk model of (relatively) simple virtue in matters of gender and racial justice, and the modern approach is found wanting. Part of the problem is, in fact, that the modern characters confuse and conflate matters of desire and of justice.

The earliest version of this pattern occurs late in Walker's first novel, *The Third Life of Grange Copeland*. The book as a whole is almost naturalistic in its depiction of the repetition of racial hatred and attacks on women. It sets up a social pattern in which the powerlessness of black men in the face of white hostility leads them to victimize black women, especially their wives. Grange, having undergone an earlier transformation, has established his farm as a fortress to protect himself and his granddaughter Ruth from the effects of white racism and black self-destructiveness. While most of the novel is devoted to narratives of domestic violence, interracial antagonism, and self-hatred, it turns, in the penultimate chapter, to a story of civil rights.

Each of the episodes in the chapter links a sensual experience to the effort to attain justice, with the implication, at this stage in Walker's writing, that civil rights is an object of desire in the personal as well as political sense. Into Grange's sanctuary, through the device of television, come images of the civil rights movement. The initial viewing is contextualized by being presented as an item on the news, specifically the *Huntley-Brinkley Report*. Before the message, Ruth notes the messengers: "She became almost fond of Chet Huntley and David Brinkley, especially David Brinkley, who was younger than Chet and whose mouth curved up in a pleasingly sardonic way" (231). This representation of white male authority as "pleasing" marks a break from the images of whiteness that dominate the book. Brinkley's presence in Grange's fortress, through the media, is also a breakdown of the black man's separatist principles, principles developed over a lifetime of abuse, self-hatred, and racial intimidation. The visual image is at once intrusive and distant, allowing Ruth and Grange to come to terms with it without directly engaging it.

They receive their knowledge of the movement through these white images. When the narrator comments that "integration appealed to Ruth in a shivery, fearful kind of way" (231), the term "integration" can be understood as applying to the cross-racial experience of media producer and consumer as well as to the movement that is depicted. Moreover, the language of the appeal—"shivery, fearful"—can be linked as easily to sensual experience as to political activity. Thus it can be argued that Ruth is in part seduced into belief. At the same time, the medium keeps the events at a distance from her reality, allowing her to encounter them safely. Change can come to her in an attractive package, not in the dangerous action that shaped her grandfather's attitudes and behaviors.

The extent of this generational difference is apparent in the story of Fred Hill, an old friend of Grange's. He is killed, and Grange concludes that it is because his grandson "is making news" by trying to integrate the schools. The shooting is officially labeled a suicide, though no gun is found. For Grange, this is evidence that the world will not and cannot change. For his grand-daughter, the interest is elsewhere:

> "Tried to get into one of the cracker schools?"
> "And did he make it?"
> Grange leaned back his head and looked at the ceiling, his chair tilted back on two legs. "Naw," he said, "he didn't make it. How you going to study in a cracker school with half your granddaddy's head missing?"
> "Well," said Ruth, attempting to see a bright side, "you don't need your granddaddy's head to study. You just need your own." (234)

The assumption that there is a "bright side" to the story reflects a sanitized, dehistoricized relation to reality that is reinforced by the media. Ironically, it can be contended that it is also one means by which hope can be sustained, especially in the primarily secularized world in which Walker's characters operate. Without the church as a source of faith, the only alternatives seem to be ahistorical optimism and experiential despair.

Desire, politics, and history come together in the culminating scene of the chapter. The movement from television physically enters their realm when two couples, one black and one white, appear at the farm to encourage Grange to register to vote. The young black man is someone Ruth has seen in town with the demonstrators. The sensual nature of her response is evident even to her grandfather: "Grange looked over at Ruth. She was standing at the edge of the porch with one arm around a roof support. Her eyes were shining! He could almost feel the hot current that flowed through her, making her soft young body taut and electric with waiting" (237). Her desire continues throughout the scene, even when she learns that the young man is married to the pregnant woman with him. She reacts with a twinge of jealousy and then regret. It remains for her a "charged" moment, in which desire reinforces admiration for political activism.

What is important here is the innocence of Ruth's response to the young man, a response not followed in either *Meridian* or "Advancing Luna." This difference reflects Walker's representation of the folk as pure. The black activists in this novel are themselves part of the folk. They are locals whose families Grange knows well. They are engaged in the movement, not out of some abstract notion of virtue or justice but because it serves the needs of their community. Helen's father was killed trying to vote, and her mother was evicted from her lifelong home for aiding the activists. What is evident is their simple belief in the cause and their attendant refusal to be discouraged or dissuaded by hostility or resistance. Grange's life experience does not permit a sharing of their faith, but it does inspire a protective impulse: "He felt a deep tenderness for the young couple. He felt about them as he felt about Dr. King: that if they'd just stay with him on his farm he'd shoot the first cracker that tried to bother them. He wanted to protect them, from themselves and from their dreams as much as from the crackers. He would not let anybody hurt them, but at the same time he didn't believe in what they were doing. Not because it wasn't worthy and noble and inspiring and good, but because it was impossible" (241).

Through the black couple the young whites are granted standing. Because they are with the blacks and because they have also been threatened for their efforts, their commitment cannot be doubted. Ruth immediately accepts them, but Grange cannot overcome his suspicion, especially of the white woman. She represents for him the opposite side of desire, a racialized, gendered object used to justify oppression and violence against blacks. In his view, the white woman cannot be separated from this objectification. Ironically, his position is the correlative of that of white racists, who call one of the women participating in the march "you nigger-fucking whore" (235). In both instances, she is an eroticized image distorted for purposes of power. She cannot be an individual self. In this text, the figure of the white woman is the measure of the moral enlightenment of the characters. Grange recognizes the limitations of his own feelings but cannot quite get over them. They are too deeply embedded in his personal experiences and cultural conditioning.

The relatively straightforward interaction of gender, race, and civil rights in *Grange Copeland* is deeply complicated in *Meridian* and "Advancing Luna," in part because of Walker's decision to distinguish between the folk and the activists. By making this distinction, she can introduce questions of motive that challenge some of the conventional wisdom about the movement. She can retain a fixed moral standard while examining modern, secular characters and perspectives. The key figures in both of the later narratives have no direct links to the folk but must establish such links primarily through the movement itself. The quality of the connection is one measure of the moral development of the central characters.

But aspects of life in the modern world—education, cosmopolitanism, individualism, urbanization, middle-class culture—work against such connections by focusing on private rather than communal concerns. Whatever their political commitment and ideals, modern characters bring into the movement their personal conflicts and desires and find ways to play them out.

The three central figures in *Meridian*—Meridian Hill, Truman Held, and Lynne Rabinowitz—are educated young people who participate in civil rights activities out of a complex of motives that include idealism, guilt, self-assertion, and rebellion. Each is in some way self-absorbed. Meridian cannot come to terms with her own mother; Truman believes in his own importance; Lynne seeks to escape her northern bourgeois life by identifying the black folk as "Art." In contrast, the folk, whether local young men, poor families, or the religious elderly, are characterized by simple dignity, honor, and love; they can be confused or troubled by circumstances, but their underlying moral strength is never in doubt.

On matters of both desire and politics, the position of the folk community is very clear. In terms of sexuality, they are not tempted to dehumanize others. For example, after raping Lynne, Tommy Odds urges a group of young men active in the movement to sexually assault "it." "'It? *It?*' [Altuna] said. 'What *it* you talking about? That ain't no *it*, that's Lynne'" (162). Similarly, the refusal of some to register to vote is never the result of cowardice or indifference; they simply make it clear that they have higher priorities: God, family, or personal honor. Lynne attempts to argue with a mother of the church; she succeeds only in offending her by insisting that God has not gotten her anything of value. When Truman and Meridian try to register a husband whose wife is dying, he questions the purpose of registering, given his need to care for her and their son on his meager earnings. This time, instead of arguing, the activists bring back groceries for the family. Some time later, apparently after the wife has died, the husband comes bearing gifts and signs the registration list. In these cases and many others throughout the novel, the spiritual and moral strength of the folk is asserted and demonstrated.

In one sense, it could be argued that for them civil rights as an ideology and a movement is largely irrelevant. As Truman and Meridian admit in their recruiting visits, voting will have little immediate or direct impact on individual lives. The people who sign up do so largely out of gratitude for the kindness and attention of the civil rights workers rather than because they have any belief in the efficacy of the political system. At the same time, the folk do not question the moral power of the movement or the courage of the activists. But that power and courage already exist within the people, so the movement cannot transform their basic character; it can only confirm it.

In contrast, because the central characters and others are not part of the folk, they are subject to a variety of inconsistencies, self-induced problems, moral quandaries, and complications of race, gender, sexuality, and class. They cannot simply *be*, as the folk can; they must do and think and become and desire. If desire is the response to a lack or absence, as contemporary theory suggests, then it may be said to be the primary motivation for the key characters of the novel.

For Truman Held, desire is connected to status. He prefers, in his conversations with Meridian, to speak French because "he believed profoundly that anything said in French sounded better, and he also believed that people who spoke French were better than people (*les pauvres, les misérables!*) who did not" (95). She responds positively to him in part because he is clearly more sophisticated than other black men she has known: "He was a man who fought against obstacles, a man who could become anything, a man whose very words were unintelligible without considerable thought" (96). This last phrase suggests the irony with which he is viewed by the narrator, since it refers to the fact that Meridian knows very little French, not to the profundity of Truman's ideas. This commitment to white culture extends to his preference for northern white women. He tells Meridian, in an especially cruel moment, that he is attracted to them "because they read *The New York Times*" (141). The cruelty is based on his awareness that she has led a provincial life, with little access to the privilege inherent in the lives of the exchange students. Sex becomes the means by which he vicariously joins the world of white privilege; it is vicarious because his relationships do not literally enable him to enter the realm of white status and wealth. When Lynne's parents, for example, learn of their marriage, they disown her and her offspring. Moreover, Truman loses interest in her once she becomes his wife rather than a precious, almost unattainable object of desire.

He consistently links his sexual impulses to ideology. He justifies his interest in white students with his interpretation of W.E.B. Du Bois's writings, though how he does so is not made clear in the text. Later, he connects his abandonment of Lynne to a return to his racial roots. His artistic efforts are large images of black women with oversized breasts. While creating these Black Madonnas, he is living in New York with a young white woman from Alabama. Yet he cannot sustain the actual black woman in his life, Meridian, as an object of desire or as an actual person. When he returns to her three years after marrying Lynne, he claims that he should have married her instead. But she is no longer impressed by his words or superior tone. When he makes his claim, she insists that it is because it has now become fashionable to be associated with black women, not white ones. Then she turns his denial against him:

> "Because I'm black?"
> "Because you're *you*, damn it! The woman I should have married and didn't!"
> "Should have *loved*, and didn't," she murmured.
> And Truman sank back staring, as if at a lifeboat receding in the distance. (138)

While Truman makes the narcissistic error of equating personal desire with political agenda and is repeatedly shocked by his self-delusion, both

Meridian and Lynne link the personal and political in different ways.[2] Both of them are damaged by Truman's arrogance, but they also suffer because of their complex motivations for and responses to social activism. For Lynne, who grows up in a privileged northern Jewish environment that was both protected and standardized, the South and especially the black folk there represent vitality and creativity.

Lynne's need to escape that northern life is not a desire to become southern herself; she never in the course of the novel loses the individualistic, secular assertiveness that she brought with her from the North. Rather, she wishes to exploit the geographic, racial Other to satisfy her personal and cultural lack in a variation of what George Frederickson has called "romantic racialism" (97–129). Her Jewishness is part of her sensibility as well. She grows up in a post-Holocaust world that suppresses the knowledge of suffering so that children like her can develop in a state of carefully maintained innocence. She responds by seeking out suffering, but suffering that has been reified: "Mississippi—after the disappearance of the three civil rights workers in 1964—began to beckon her. For two years she thought of nothing else. If Mississippi is the worst place in America for black people, it stood to reason, she thought, that the Art that was their lives would flourish best there" (130). The South for her, then, is a living museum. Denied the narrative of her own people's great horror, in part because it is too real to be subjected to aesthetic control, she turns to a parallel experience that has both immediacy and distance.

The problem with Lynne's approach is her refusal to accept the humanity of those she has constructed as art objects. She cannot grasp the ambivalence created by her own whiteness, which produces a volatile mix of desire and hostility. She fails to understand the effect her presence has on both blacks and whites in the South. Tommy Odds blames her for the loss of his arm in an act of racial violence; by being with a group of black men, she endangered them. Through a conversation with Odds, Truman is able to understand the attitudes of blacks toward Lynne: "To them she was a route to Death, pure and simple. They felt her power over them in their bones; their mothers had feared her even before they were born. Watching their fear of her, though, he saw a strange thing: They did not even see her as a human being, but as some kind of large, mysterious doll. A thing of movies and television, of billboards and car and soap commercials. They liked her hair, not because it was especially pretty, but because it was long. To them, *length* was beauty" (137).

In an important reversal, Lynne, as the white woman, is herself made into an object, but a dangerous, taboo one. The fact that she is northern and Jewish does not change this attitude. In the South, White Woman is a category nearly overwhelming in ideological, social, and erotic significance. The white woman who aligns herself with blacks is seen as a race traitor and whore by whites, who read her association with an "inferior," "promiscuous" race as the lowest form of profanation. Blacks, regardless of their individual views of her, retain a clear perception of her symbolic power in southern society. Her motives *must* be questioned because affiliation with her is deeply problematic. At the same time, her significance (and danger) can make her a powerful object of desire, less in the sexual than in the political sense. A sexual attack on her is an attack on the basis of white supremacy. It is simultaneously an act of revenge and rebellion, though in one sense it reinforces racism by accepting the premise of contamination. To have a white woman is to "ruin" her for white men.

Thus Tommy Odds's rape of Lynne expresses his personal rage and allows him to engage in a political act. He can vent his hostility toward whites without committing a suicidal attack on the white men who shot him. But the assault on her is a strangely safe act. She is already viewed as racially promiscuous by the white community simply by being where she is; attacking her will not affect their views in the least. Moreover, he is reasonably certain that she will not seek justice: "She wished she could go to the police, but she was more afraid of them than she was of Tommy Odds, because they would attack young black men in the community indiscriminately and the people she wanted most to see protected would suffer" (162). The very motives and circumstances that necessitated the movement generally and Lynne's participation specifically make it impossible for her to seek justice. The very power of her whiteness precludes her resistance to sexual violence. Moreover, her aestheticist view of black life holds even during the assault:

> She lay . . . thinking of his feelings, his hardships, of the way he was black and belonged to people who lived without hope; she thought about the loss of his arm. She felt her own guilt. . . . She did not any longer resist but tried instead to think of Tommy Odds as he was when he was her friend and near the end her arms stole around his neck, and before he left she told him she forgave him and she kissed his slick rounded stump that was the color of baked liver, and he smiled at her from far away, she did not know him. (159)

As Elliott Butler-Evans has noted: "If the novel's racial politics demands that it explore Tommy Odds's behavior within the context of racial oppression, it is also committed to investigating Lynne's status as victim. That issue is somewhat ambiguously presented through the graphic detail of the rape coupled with Lynne's commitment to the 'correct' political attitude, even at the expense of her own welfare" (122).

Rape is transmuted into a permissible effect of black suffering and white penance for that suffering. Lynne denies him the humanity of being responsible for an act of violence. Her embrace of him turns assault into fulfilled desire, apparently for both of them. He can both satisfy his sexual need for the white woman and express his hostility toward the white world; she can be the sacrifice that links her to black suffering. By kissing his stump, which approximates the phallus, she submits to black (male) authority and thus escapes the guilt associated with her whiteness. At the same time, she can sustain her image of black experience in something like its purity.

Significantly, neither Truman nor Meridian wants to hear her story, in part because they, too, wish to construct a version of the folk that serves their private purposes while permitting them to interpret themselves as benefactors. Meridian is the most extreme example of this. Her responses to the world are shaped in part by guilt, first the guilt of having "stolen" something from her mother and, second, the guilt of having abandoned her son to pursue her education. Hers is the dilemma of the modern woman: how is it possible to live an individually meaningful life in a world that still demands loyalty to traditional roles? What she has "stolen" from her mother, simply by being her child, is independence and individuality. She exacerbates the problem by giving up her own child; she in effect discredits the sacrifice made by her mother (cf. Callahan 159; Daly 254–55).

This conflict about maternity inspires Meridian's commitment to the civil rights movement. She seeks, in effect, the social equivalent of her mother's sacrifice. She takes in and identifies with the outcasts in the college community. She has an abortion when Truman loses his interest in her, but she never tells him. She offers to die for the movement but is uncertain of her willingness to kill. When she is rejected by her revolutionary friends for her ambivalence, she chooses to return to the rural South, even though that form of activism has become passé. During all this time, her health is fragile, and she consistently enters catatonic states after her public challenges to authority. In this sense, her repudiation of her mother's life in truth reenacts its sacrificial quality.

Her work with the folk has a healing effect on her over time. In her encounters with them, there is little evidence of ethical or political principles being transmitted in either direction. The people are particularly empowered by her actions. She sees herself as doing *for* them: "They *appreciate* it when somebody volunteers to suffer" (25). They are consistently shown to be simply good people who must be led. Even the transformative religious service near the conclusion of the novel reveals a largely passive people. After the grieving father has spoken his ritual three words—"My son died"—on the anniversary of the young activist's death, Meridian has an insight into the congregation's response to his call: "The people in the church. . . . were saying, 'we are slow to awaken to the notion that we are only as other women and men, and even slower to move in anger, but we are gathering ourselves to fight for and protect what your son fought for on behalf of us. If you will let us weave your story and your son's life into what we already know—into the songs, the sermons, the 'brother and sister'—we will soon be so angry we cannot help but move'" (199).

Meridian's voicing of their feelings itself suggests the text's limited faith in the power of the folk. She, though an outsider, must speak for them. Moreover, it is the expression of a desire to be fulfilled at some future point, not the planning of an action in the present (cf. Hall). In fact, implicit in the statement is justification for inaction: "if your son should come again," they could act; but, of course, resurrection is not to be expected. The weaving of narrative must precede any movement into the social realm. It is Meridian's insight into her own situation, not that of the congregation, that is the focus of narrative attention. *She* now understands the circumstances under which she could take a life. She claims spiritual maternity by asserting that she could kill to save the boy and others like him. Her role is that of nurturer, protector, and culture-bearer. The revolutionaries do the fighting, and Meridian provides the music that makes sense of the struggle and that saves the soul of the people. "When they stop to wash off the blood and find their throats too choked with the smell of murdered flesh to sing, I will come forward and sing from memory songs they will need once more to hear" (201). The people themselves have no role in this tremendous effort on their behalf. They are kept outside of history, an object of contemplation and a source of inspiration for the fighters and artists of the revolution. For Meridian, in slight contrast to Lynne, it is not the folk but the souls of black folk that are Art (cf. Hall 104).

Given her understanding and commitment in this passage, it is significant that Meridian is absent herself from the end of the novel. Her efforts for the people and her overcoming of maternal guilt by interpreting those efforts as maternal have healed her. And having been healed, she walks away. She leaves Truman to take over guiding the people and in the process healing himself. This transition suggests that what happens to the individual is more important than the community or society. Meridian has been the guide, not so much for the folk as for those modern individuals—Truman, Lynne, Anne-Marion—who are no longer part of the community and who suffer as a result. Once the self-healing occurs, there is no longer a responsibility to the people. Social action is a form of therapy; community improvement is merely a means to a private end.

The furthest remove from community comes in "Advancing Luna—and Ida B. Wells." The story develops the logic of the rape of Lynne depicted in *Meridian*. The narrator is a young black woman who spent a brief time one summer doing voter registration work. It was here that she met Luna, who had come to Georgia for the same purpose. They work together until the narrator takes advantage of a fellowship opportunity to visit Africa. Later, they meet again in New York, and it is on this occasion that Luna describes the rape.

Almost no attention is paid in the story to civil rights activities. In fact, the narrator comments that the effort "seems not only minor, but irrelevant" (88). The focus of this part of the story is on the narrator's smugness and world-weariness. She describes the extent to which she takes for granted the efforts on behalf of the students by the local people, including the danger to which their assistance subjects them. The movement becomes simply the occasion to explore the politics of rape and race. Implicit in this analysis, however, is the view, similar to that established in *Meridian*, that the movement is more interesting in terms of what it reveals about young activists and about ideology than what it says about its effects on black southerners. As in the previous work, the folk are not delineated in any depth; they are simply there in their saintly being—patient, courageous, understanding.

Unlike them, the modern young volunteers must deal with larger moral and political issues. When the rape is first described to the narrator, she immediately turns to critical commentary on the sexual politics of Eldridge Cleaver and LeRoi Jones, both of whom she attacks for advocating the rape of white women. When Luna tells of her attack and the narrator asks why she had not screamed, the white woman responds, "You know why" (92). This comment leads into the narrator's imaginary conversation with Ida B. Wells, the turn-of-the-century antilynching activist. Wells consistently urged blacks to protect their sons, fathers, and husbands against accusations of sexual assault because such accusations endangered not only individuals but entire communities. Just as Lynne had done, Luna chooses protection of blacks over punishment of her assailant. In this instance, though, the narrator is more interested in her own conflicts and in the ideological implications of the assault than in the emotional and psychological states of either victim or victimizer (cf. McKay). In fact, the narrative effectively diminishes both of these figures. Luna is consistently described as childlike, while Freddie Pye seems almost bestial in his unattractiveness and inarticulateness. Such reduction allows the argument with Wells over the writer's need to depict reality as she finds it, regardless of the social or racial consequences. "'No matter what you think you know, no matter what you feel about it, say nothing. And to your dying breath!' Which, to my mind, is virtually useless advice to give a writer" (94). The literary rights of the individual must supersede whatever consequences might develop for the community. Just as the narrator walked away from activism to pursue her private agenda, so here she ignores history to enable self-expression.

Having rejected the sexist aspects of black nationalism and the suppressions of Wells, the narrator now turns on Luna: "And yet the rape, the knowledge of the rape, out in the open, admitted, pondered over, was now between us. (And I began to think that perhaps—whether Luna had been raped or not—it had always been so; that her power over my life was exactly the power *her word on rape* had over the lives of black men, over *all* black men, whether they were guilty or not, and therefore over my whole people)" (95).

The question of power takes priority over the question of rape; Luna in this passage is not a distinct character but White Woman, though it is precisely her racial power that she resists using. The narrator refuses to engage the complexity of a situation that positions Luna closer to Ida B. Wells (and implicitly to "my whole people") than the narrator herself. Not surprisingly, the two women grow apart, though not before Freddie Pye appears in their apartment coming out of Luna's bedroom one morning. We also learn that the narrator goes back to the South because of "the need to return, to try to understand, and write about, the people I'd merely lived with before" (97). She does not describe the impact of the return, choosing instead to end the story proper at this point.

In a metafictional move, Walker offers several appendices to the narrative that attempt to specify its ideological significance. One addition locates the existing ending in the context of current reality, "a society in which lynching is still reserved, at least subconsciously, as a means of social control" (98). But this "unresolved" conclusion cannot support the narrator's vision of what the society ought to be and so, after a brief comment that again deprecates Luna's efforts at racial understanding ("A very straight, clear-eyed, coolly observant young woman with no talent for existing outside her own skin" [99]), she offers "Imaginary Knowledge," an alternative ending. In this version, she depicts Freddie and Luna engaging in a night-long conversation about their lives and the rape. Importantly, she focuses on Freddie's coming to the North as an "exhibit" of what southern oppression had done to black men. When he has done his part at a fund-raiser, he is abandoned by both his black and white sponsors, who clearly want nothing to do with his real life. After Freddie has described this situation, this ending stops with the comment that it would now be Luna's turn to talk and that she needed to understand the rape and her response to it. But this conversation is never presented, though in some sense it would seem to be the key to the story.

Instead of granting voice to Freddie and Luna about their central experience, the narrator turns to a "Postscript" that undermines what has just been offered. In Cuba, the narrator tells the story, but her listener objects that she has been unable to imagine true evil. He speculates that Freddie was a government agent paid to disrupt the civil rights movement by acts of sexual violence. Though the narrator seeks to qualify this scenario, she clearly is attracted by it. By positioning it as the actual conclusion to the narrative, she grants it considerable authority. In this sense, what began as an attempt to understand a crucial aspect of the sexual-racial dynamic of the South and the movement becomes a political commentary far removed from its beginnings. The narrator is ultimately concerned with the ideological underpinnings of her story rather than with the people and experiences of the South. Freddie Pye, as an emblem of the southern folk, is cast either as the Pathetic Victim of southern oppression and northern exploitation or as the Dark Villain, much like the black beast of racist imagination. He is, in other words, Art.

In "The Black Writer and the Southern Experience," Walker says, "In large measure, black Southern writers owe their clarity of vision to parents who refused to diminish themselves as human beings by succumbing to racism" (19). Ironically, what we see in her fiction of the civil rights movement is a focus on the individual, especially the modern individual, alienated from the folk in some way, whether through media, representation, education, guilt, or artistic impulse. The attraction to the people is consistently motivated by some private need, and when that need is met, the folk become irrelevant. Black southern life is primarily an aesthetic idea and ideal by which to measure those who are doing the truly important work in life, struggling for virtue and justice within modern consciousness. Unlike Ernest Gaines, who also writes of the South and the movement of the mid-twentieth century, as an artist Alice Walker is not particularly interested in the complexities of southern people or the social movements of the region. Rather, she sees them as a means to explore current issues of gender and power. She generates sympathy or antipathy about them depending on the requirements of ideology and modern character development. Like her character Lynne, Walker as author sees black folk as Art; unlike that character, however, she does not acknowledge her aesthetic hegemony.

Notes

1. For other interpretations of Walker's views on the South and civil rights, see Butler (two articles), Daly, Donaldson, Ensslen, Hall, and Manvi.
2. On interracial friendships in *Meridian*, see Jones and Porter.

Works Cited

Butler, Robert James. "Alice Walker's Vision of the South in *The Third Life of Grange Copeland*." *African-American Review* 27.2 (1993): 195–204.

———. "Visions of Southern Life and Religion in O'Connor's *Wise Blood* and Walker's

The Third Life of Grange Copeland." *College Language Association Journal* 36.4 (1993): 349–70.

Butler-Evans, Elliott. "History and Genealogy in Walker's *The Third Life of Grange Copeland* and *Meridian.*" *Alice Walker: Critical Perspectives Past and Present.* Ed. Henry Louis Gates Jr. and K.A. Appiah. New York: Amistad, 1993. 105–25.

Callahan, John F. "The Hoop of Language: Politics and the Restoration of Voice in *Meridian.*" *Alice Walker: Modern Critical Views.* Ed. Harold Bloom. New York: Chelsea House, 1989. 153–84.

Daly, Brenda O. "Teaching Alice Walker's *Meridian*: Civil Rights According to Mothers." *Narrating Mothers: Theorizing Maternal Subjectivites.* Ed. Brenda O. Daly and Maureen T. Reddy. Knoxville: U of Tennessee P, 1991. 239–57.

Donaldson, Susan. "Alice Walker's *Meridian*, Feminism, and the 'Movement.'" *Women's Studies* 16.3–4 (1989): 317–30.

Ensslen, Klaus. "Collective Experience and Individual Responsibility: Alice Walker's *The Third Life of Grange Copeland.*" *The Afro-American Novel Since 1960.* Ed. Peter Bruck and Wolfgang Karrer. Amsterdam: Gruner, 1982. 189–218.

Frederickson, George M. *The Black Image in the White Mind: The Debate on Afro-American Character and Destiny, 1817–1914.* New York: Harper, 1971.

Hall, Christine. "Art, Action and the Ancestors: Alice Walker's *Meridian* in Its Context." *Black Women's Writing.* Ed. Gina Wisker. New York: St. Martin's, 1993. 96–110.

Jones, Suzanne W. "Dismantling Stereotypes: Interracial Friendships in *Meridian* and *A Mother and Two Daughters.*" *The Female Tradition in Southern Literature.* Ed. Carol S. Manning. Urbana: U of Illinois P, 1993. 140–57.

Manvi, Meera. "The Second Reconstruction and the Southern Writer: Alice Walker and William Kelley." *Literature and Politics in Twentieth Century America.* Ed. J. L. Plakkoottam and Prashant K. Sinha.Hyderabad: American Studies Research Centre, 1993. 92–98.

McKay, Nellie Y. "Alice Walker's 'Advancing Luna—and Ida B. Wells': A Struggle Toward Sisterhood." *Rape and Representation.* Ed. Lynn A. Higgins and Brenda R. Silver. New York: Columbia UP, 1991. 248–60.

Porter, Nancy. "Women's Interracial Friendships and Visions of Community in *Meridian, The Salt Eaters, Civil Wars,* and *Dessa Rose.*" *Tradition and the Talents of Women.* Ed. Florence Howe. Urbana: U of Illinois P, 1991. 251–67.

Walker, Alice. "Advancing Luna—and Ida B. Wells." *You Can't Keep a Good Woman Down.* New York: Harcourt Brace Jovanovich, 1981. 85–104.

———. "The Black Writer and the Southern Experience." *In Search of Our Mothers Gardens.* New York: Harcourt Brace Jovanovich, 1983. 16–21.

———. *Meridian.* New York: Harcourt Brace Jovanovich, 1976.

———. *The Third Life of Grange Copeland.* New York: Harcourt Brace Jovanovich, 1970.

"Trouble" in Muskhogean County

The Social History of a Southern Community in the Fiction of Raymond Andrews

Jeffrey J. Folks

Born of sharecropper parents in east central Georgia near the small town of Appalachee, Raymond Andrews (1934–1991) experienced the agrarian poverty and intensely segregated society of the rural South during the 1940s and 1950s. Although the biographical details of Andrews's life roughly parallel those of several of his male and female protagonists, the larger-than-life characters of his fiction are clearly imaginative creations, not merely the recording of figures from the author's experience. The fictional settings, knowledge of farm and small-town life, realistic depiction of work and domestic routine, and, most important, the intricate sense of racial relations in the pre–civil rights South, however, are drawn from the everyday experience of ordinary people whom Andrews knew intimately. Perhaps no other recent writer has described as bluntly and realistically the system of racial repression in the rural South before the civil rights era.

In the course of his brief career, Raymond Andrews published a cycle of four novels detailing the modern social history of the fictional Muskhogean County, Georgia. The first and best known of Andrews's novels, *Appalachee Red*, published in 1978, was followed by three sequels: *Rosiebelle Lee Wildcat Tennessee* (1980), *Baby Sweet's* (1983), and the posthumously published *99 Years and a Dark Day*. Andrews's other books are *Jessie and Jesus and Cousin Andrew* (1994) and *The Last Radio Baby: A Memoir* (1990). In the Appalachee series, Andrews traced the social history of his home county in Georgia over a period of some forty years from the 1940s through the 1970s.

Centering his social history on a particular group of residents of the town of Appalachee, Georgia, eighty-four miles northeast of Atlanta, Andrews positions race relations over the period from World War I until the early 1960s against the larger panorama of American history with references to figures such as Franklin D. Roosevelt, Joe Louis, Jackie Robinson, and John F. Kennedy. For the black population of Appalachee, these and other historical figures assumed legendary status and served as the basis of hope for a future of improved racial relations and new opportunities. Indeed, Andrews locates his fiction within a national history in which a modern politics of race was emerging as a crucial political issue. Within the larger national history, the social history of Appalachee can be viewed as a significant case study of race relations in a southern community resistant to change: the predominantly black town of Appalachee and its neighboring but all-white community of Yankee Town, four miles to the northeast, with which it shares a painful history of slavery, war, and racial conflict. For Andrews's people, the "Great Wall," the earthen railroad embankment that separates sections of town along class lines, is another topographical marker for the deeply repressive psychological condition of the town, a condition that for years only humor can make bearable. The almost absolute separation of black and white communities in the southern small town and the enforcement of an apartheid code of relationships are recognized as a way of life until they are challenged in the 1960s by Blue Thompson.

"'Trouble' to southern blacks had always meant something to do with the white man, or even worse, the Man himself," Andrews writes (*Appalachee Red* 102). The relationship between modern-day black and white residents of Appalachee, part of a long history of social repression and distrust, is shaped by the town's still-vivid recollection of slavery and Reconstruction. Throughout this history, white males in particular have resorted to violence to force black males and females into subservient roles, and during the period that Andrews chronicles, the most threatening stance that a black male can adopt toward this socially repressive structure is, in the eyes of whites, one of "disrespect." The frequent violence and ubiquitous threat of violence of white males toward black men, women, and children—and the various responses toward this violence on the part of the black community—are among the most dramatic episodes in Andrews's fiction. The consequent limitations of this unequal system, with the restrictions of economic and cultural exclusion that it imposes, form a bitter reality beneath the benign surface of humor, folk legendry, and popular amusements with which most members of the African American population fill their lives. The harsh reality of this subject is not ameliorated but grimly underscored by Andrews's often humorous voice and satiric commentary.

Underlying the satire is Andrews's realistic appraisal of the impact of racial inequality on the ordinary aspects of everyday life. The emphasis on work, food, clothing, property, conflict, jealousy, pleasure, and bodily function, as well as on common psychological needs and fears, is tied to Andrews's conception of narrative as a social history of ordinary existence. These universal needs and emotions, in their stress on the elemental level of experience, link the narrative to the theme of racial repression but also point toward elements of life not determined by economics: the human participation in social relationships that is conducted in spite of economic limitations.

By using a single building, the ironically named "White House," as the central locale of *Appalachee Red*, Andrews provides artistic shape to a novel that might otherwise seem unfocused, so concerned is the work with the broad canvas of decades of racial history. The house that John Morgan agrees to build for his mistress, Little Bit Thompson, becomes the scene of legendary events that are always subject to the influence of racial pressures. The epic domestic struggles between Little Bit and her husband, Big Man Thompson, after his release from state prison, are precipitated by Thompson's jealousy of white males and are followed by the sale of the White House to Samuel Wallace, proprietor of Sam's Cafe, and later by the cafe's transformation, under "Appalachee Red" Thompson and his mistress, Baby Sweet Jackson, into a center of gambling and illegal liquor distribution (as well as the venue for the finest barbecue in Muskhogean County).

Other than the cafe, which is much more than a mere "eating place" and actually serves as the main social center for much of the town, a few other establishments serve as gathering places. Known as "the Alley," the small black business district of Appalachee barely covers two run-down blocks. A competing pool hall draws the high school crowd, the county poorhouse shelters elderly indigents, and Blackshear's, the black funeral parlor, finds its front porch chairs occupied all day by elderly women.

The interweaving of several family stories, based on the interconnected lives of the Thompson, Morgan, Jackson, and Wallace families, offers further dimension to a broadly conceived social history. As various newcomers enter the story, their lives are soon interconnected with those of the town's leading personalities. In his saga of race relations, Andrews follows a sizable cast of characters through several generations; the author narrates his history from the remove of decades, thus opening the history to patient analysis and authorial commentary.

Members of the local community accumulate and pass down a great deal of shared knowledge. Nicknames, which are used for almost everyone in the county, become not just labels of affection or derision, knitting the black community's residents closer together, but labels of character that are difficult to shake. Names such as "Big Man" Thompson or "the Snake" Odell Jackson reflect the black neighborhood's perspective, at least the perspective of those "beyond the Wall," in succinct and exclusive language, the full meaning of which is not easily grasped by outsiders. The effect of this local speech is to create social cohesion that strengthens black identity in the town. Through its shared language, the local community can acknowledge its bonds and refine its communal ethic. In many other ways nicknaming and local idiom create opportunities for the recognition of shared experience, alluding to intimate shared knowledge of past and present conditions and events while protecting this experience from the examination of outsiders, especially from representatives of authority such as "the Man."

Colorful speech and tale-telling are important amusements in Appalachee County, as Alan Cheuse noted in his description of *Rosiebelle Lee Wildcat Tennessee* as "folk saga" with its stretching of the oral tale to the boundaries of believability. Speech idioms in their own way lend a local interpretation to events that they are used to relate. The limited vocabulary of Odell Jackson (the Snake) is frequently punctuated by a common expression suggesting a certain incestuous behavior, but the nuances that he is able to draw from that one word are remarkable. In a similar fashion, local idiom is used to describe the battle between Big Man Thompson and then Chief of Police "Boots" White, as Big Man's initial victory and his subsequent death enter permanently into the legendry of Muskhogean County. As the narrator describes it, "in the spring of '36, the meat was laid out" between Big Man and Boots.

The communal knowledge shared by Appalachee's black citizens includes many episodes of racial conflict, but confrontations in this society are not restricted to racial divisions. Social class divisions are notable within the black community itself. Significantly, black middle-class residents also live *within* the "Wall" that divides Appalachee along class lines and exhibit their own prejudices toward those blacks who reside on the other side. Baby Sweet attempts unsuccessfully to ingratiate herself with the middle-class blacks who attend Wesley Methodist in Light Town, rather than continue to attend Dark Town's Bethel Baptist. When she encounters the prejudice of Appalachee's light-skinned African Americans, many of whom hold professional positions in the community, Baby Sweet begins lightening her own skin with an acidic mixture, until Red forces her to consider the damage she is doing to her health and to her social identity.

In Muskhogean County the divisions between men and women are nearly as great as those between race and class. As a rule, Andrews presents women characters from the point of view of a male narrator whose idea of sexuality emphasizes their physical allure and sensuality but who is not unaware of a parallel quality of romantic love. Baby Sweet Jackson's first encounter with a "real man" depicts her as completely in the power of Red ("the Great Massager"), yet her relationship with Red evolves into one that claims the deepest loyalty and respect on both sides, while never dismissing the importance of their physical bond. In their first night together, Red is described as "introducing her . . . body and, more important, her mind to a way of love she had never before suspected existed" (142). By contrast, Roxanne Morgan's crush on Red (carried out from her father's upstairs window with a pair of high-powered binoculars) is immature and voyeuristic.

Andrews's narrator takes for granted that men and women hold different attitudes toward the most basic aspects of existence, even including birth and death, and the narrator is never reluctant to highlight such assumed gender distinctions. Humorously, the "Death Watchers" at Blackshear's, the black funeral parlor that doubles as a social center for elderly women, are described as waiting for Little Bit or anyone else to die and celebrating the rituals of death with perhaps too much observance of their own continuing survival: "These Death Watchers were all women, who themselves—unlike men, who don't understand life, much less death, so that they fear one and shun the other—being the bringers of life, were more easily able to fit death into the mystical pattern forming their existence" (243). As the female Death Watchers are subjected to Andrews's tongue-in-cheek satire, his narrative mocks their condescension toward male "ignorance" of life and death as well as the women's self-assurance in their role as the "bringers of life." As they oversee the rituals of birth and death and as they command authority in the domestic realm, Andrews's black women assume a matriarchal role that, in the view of some black males, represents a threatening form of control. In Andrews's depiction of the community, this sort of rivalry is rarely excluded from the relationships of black women and men.

For males, physical force and size, as well as cleverness and sheer bravery, are the object of pride in their own gender, as well as a necessary means of survival. The town admires Big Man Thompson, the "King," and after his death at the barrel of Boots's revolver, his dominant role is taken over by Little Bit's son Red. Following the mysterious "illness" and sudden death of Sam Wallace, whom the town believes to have been poisoned by Red's liquor, Sam is buried suspiciously in a hurried funeral, leaving behind a suspect will naming his "cousin" Red (a will undoubtedly signed by the newly literate Baby Sweet). Taking over the White House, Red first draws customers with the fabulous barbecue cooked by Baby Sweet, then expands his business to include gambling and bootlegging operations based on an alliance with Boots White, his father's killer. The godlike Red rarely leaves the upstairs office and gambling room above the cafe, but he controls events by the aura of his presence alone. His shiny black pointed-toed shoes are all that some ever see of him, but they are enough to beget terror in men, giddiness in women, and respect in all. Lesser males attempt to compete with Red's authority, but they inevitably fail: the Bird or "Blade King" (Arzell Johnson) fails so miserably that he leaves town and his sycophantic follower the Snake (Odell Jackson, Baby Sweet's older brother) crosses over and aligns himself with Red.

Andrews's use of summary narration from the point of view of a godlike omniscient author, not unlike Henry Fielding's technique in *Tom Jones*, frees the author to draw a broad canvas and to comment satirically on the behavior of his characters. After the manner of the tall tale, for example, the narrator describes how Clyde "Boots" White, after his election to county sheriff, is presented with a suit of western clothing by Red and is immediately renamed "Cowboy Boots" by the black townspeople. With a drier wit, Andrews narrates how the county's white churchgoers tolerated illegal whiskey but not gambling, which "to these believers entailed much more, involving the nucleus of America's morality . . . money" (225). Co-opting these righteous objectors, Red opens his gambling room for their exclusive use on Monday nights, a practice that came to be known as the "White Nights."

Not just the narrative voice and omniscient technique, but the events constituting the novel's plot encode the human distortions originating in a socially repressive system. In its most overt form, the repression practiced by whites is carried out by the Ku Klux Klan. After Big Man, at the cost of his life, stands up to Chief White and his widow Little Bit avenges his killing by cutting the Chief's eye, Little Bit's family is burned out by the Klan, who kill three members of her family during the attack. Klan activity is especially frequent outside the relative shelter of the town of Appalachee and among rural residents.

Another form of repression has always been the "right," exercised by outright rape or by various other kinds of violence and intimidation, that some white men have claimed in their sexual relations with black women. One result of these forced relationships is the birth of children of mixed racial parentage. During the historical period covered in *Appalachee Red*, the children of these black-white relationships suffer exclusion from both ethnic communities. Big Man's fury toward Little Bit for giving birth to John Morgan's son is only partially deflected by her having sent the child north to live with her sister Cora. Similarly, Baby Sweet aborts the child of Boots White, presumably in response to Red's insistence. To an equal extent, the children of interracial affairs are shunned by whites, particularly by fathers such as John Morgan, who refuses to acknowledge Red as his son.

Still another aspect of the repressive social structure that Andrews records is the way in which, as Blue Thompson claims, the victimized at times accept the roles of the repressed, adopting undignified postures in relation to the demands of their repressors and even deflecting their sense of victimization onto others in their own community, especially onto those who are perceived to be different in other respects. For example, the difficulties encountered by Darling Pullman, the young homosexual who becomes cook at Red's, are only compounded by his local academic distinction in having completed high school and by his dislike for conventional "male" pursuits of farming and fighting. For the Snake, slapping Darling for acting "sissy" is ironically termed the "He-Man's Burden." At first Baby Sweet's confused reaction to Darling mirrors the community's dismissal of "the Sissy": "she reached the frightening conclusion that he acted in many instances even more feminine than she did herself!" In time Baby Sweet, if not the community at large, comes to accept Darling for the person he is: "a friend whom she very much liked" (162). Nor is Baby Sweet the only woman who comes to appreciate Darling: Mary Mae Mapp's futile crush results in large part from her sensible attraction to that rarity—a man who knew how to cook and clean.

In response to their repressive condition, black people in Appalachee turn to storytelling and legendry as ways to preserve their dignity and to maintain a sense of integrity as a community. Several dramatic moments in the life of the community achieve truly epic proportion, such as the return from World War II of Little Bit Thompson's and John Morgan's son, later known as Appalachee Red, and his passionate meeting with the "Black Peach," Baby Sweet Jackson (daughter of Poor Boy Jackson, who is overseer of the county's largest peach farm). Tale-telling soon elevates important events and people to legendary stature, with men like Big Man Thompson, facing down white antagonists such as Boots White, taking on the aura of Homeric heroes. Women also rise to the level of goddesslike or heroic figures. Little Bit and Baby Sweet possess widely admired qualities of toughness and sensuality, respectively. Baby Sweet's Saturday afternoon walks downtown, timed to coincide with the influx of farmers from the county, suggest a comparison with Helen of Troy in terms of the extraordinary admiration she draws from all virile males. Even the children of such heroes and heroines find their lives partially controlled by the legendary status of dead parents, from whom the children gain not merely automatic respect but also the onus of "greatness." Such is the case with Big Man's son Blue after he goes to work at the White House: the clientele "immediately began looking upon him with that certain manner of respect which is reserved only for those sons of gods" (181). After he fully appreciates the significance of his father's deeds in standing up to "the Man," Blue Thompson is driven to fulfill his father's mission in bringing equal dignity and freedom to the black citizens of Muskhogean County.

Although Blue Thompson is the first black citizen of Appalachee who overtly tries to challenge the system of segregation, Red's whole plan of gaining and displaying economic power, and before him Big Man Thompson's resistance to "the Man," are significant if less overt challenges to the status quo. In sending his half-brother Blue to a northern college on condition that he never return to live in the South, Red is carrying out what he believes to be a subversion of the system, but it is a subversion only of an indirect and nonconfrontational sort, for it does little to challenge the southern racial system per se. Blue's return to Appalachee ten years later, after his disillusioning discovery of racism in the North—at the University of Michigan as well as in the Chicago work world—begins a period of more direct resistance. Through a generational saga that includes Big Man Thompson, Appalachee Red, and Blue Thompson, Andrews is able to record a painfully slow and difficult process toward racial unity in the South, and by structuring his narrative around these three figures, Andrews also stresses the continuity of their resistance.

Ultimately, of course, it is not only the African American population that suffers as a result of the repressive social system. At the conclusion of the novel, the town's whites, now fearful of blacks in their newly acquired political power, live "imprisoned" in their middle-class homes. The amassed guilt and emerging fear of the white townspeople find expression not only in violence toward others but in various neurotic idiosyncrasies. The everyday life of the county operates as a colonized structure within which whites act out the anxiety tied to their own relative impoverishment. Boots White is an example of the monstrous distortion of human character in such a system. With something like the quality of Sterne's *Tristram Shandy*, Boots's mental world involves strange mechanisms centering on an infantile need for dominance and a neurotic dependence on the symbols of power: the badge, the pistol, and his own whiteness.

In some ways, however, Appalachee Red seems as much an automaton as Boots: both are wounded men trying to prove something to others. In America in the 1950s, the Cadillac possesses a symbolic power of which Red must be fully aware before driving his newly purchased model from Atlanta to Appalachee, thereby not only igniting jealousy toward him personally but bringing into the open the repressed white resentment of his economic success. Red's purchase of the only Cadillac in Muskhogean County brings a swift reaction from the county's whites, who begin "regarding him as some mythical monster from another world" (215). In this and other such episodes, Andrews shows people, black and white, brutalized by an economic colonization that affects every aspect of life but which cannot entirely crush their humanity. That the "Kiddy," the Cadillac purchased by Red, sets off shock waves of admiration and jealousy among black and white residents, respectively, is evidence of the economic deprivation of all in Muskhogean County. Just as Boots White is twisted by a compulsively domineering personality, Appalachee Red himself seems motivated by barely conscious drives of egotism and self-assertion related to his birth and early childhood. His obsession with returning to Appalachee and achieving business success (and publicly flaunting his success through such status symbols as the Cadillac) arises from anger at his father's refusal to acknowledge him and toward the entire town's silent endorsement of this refusal. Appalachee Red's business success is motivated in no small measure by his desire to prove himself in the face of humiliations and restrictions by white townspeople, including Sheriff Clyde "Boots" White. Indeed, the cessation, or at least interruption, of business at Red's Cafe occurs after Red's murder of Sheriff White on November 22, 1963 (the date of a far more eventful political assassination) and of Red's subsequence disappearance from town.

For many other characters, Andrews suggests that their lives, lacking the opportunities available to most Americans at the time, are subject to the law of whim and accident. For Arzell "the Bird" Johnson, the chance event of being visited and rejected by a major league recruiter at the unfortunate moment of his drunken celebration of having pitched a successful double-header victory determines the rest of his embittered life. Creating his own "field of dreams," the Bird starts his own local baseball team in Appalachee after his retirement from minor league ball. In Arzell Johnson's unfortunate tale, however, Andrews suggests how limited the opportunities were for everyone in his community: failing his single "try-out" for the major league—an unannounced try-out of which he was only too late made aware—the Bird spends the rest of his life obsessed with his failure and convinced of his unworthiness.

The wise humanity of Andrews's narrative follows the emotions and lives of a wide range of characters in their need for love, prestige, respect, and acceptance, as well as in their idiosyncrasies of individual character, of dominance and submission, violence and passivity, pride and self-loathing. The omniscient point of view of his novels reflects Andrews's fundamental values, his love and wonder at human beings in their variety, his openness to experience, his realistic and satirical view, especially toward human pretension, and his warm acceptance of people at all levels of society. Andrews's satiric wit is often directed at the provinciality of the small-town South and indeed at that of his own local community. On her first trip to Atlanta, in the summer of 1950, the twenty-year-old Baby Sweet marveled at the sights along the route: "Going up, both she and Odell had enjoyed their first train ride, which on that scenic trip took them past or through such way-out exotic spots and tourist attractions as Madison, Rutledge, Social Circle, Covington, Conyers, Lithonia, Stone Mountain—Georgia's answer to Everest—and Decatur, worlds of faraway places she had at one time given up all hope of ever experiencing" (193). Presumably Andrews sees the "greater society" of Atlanta as only a larger-scale site of folly than he is able to portray in Appalachee, Georgia. His satire is capable of suggesting many objects at once, as his humorous skepticism encompasses everything in its sight. As Thomas J. Davis wrote of Andrews's book *The Last Radio Baby: A Memoir*, "Andrews musters a parade of regional color that reveals the substance and shape of rural kinship and community. Sketches of family, friends, relatives, and local characters dominate the episodic glimpses of southern black folk mores and wisdom" (92).

The climax of *Appalachee Red*, in which Red, after shooting Boots, escapes town in the company of Roxanne Morgan, his half-sister, may seem to offer a weak ending to this volume, but the plot is taken up in Andrews's sequel novel, *Baby Sweet's*, which picks up the social history of Appalachee in the spring of 1966. Overall not as successful as Andrews's first novel, *Baby Sweet's* does contain the marvelous set piece of Lea Prickard's autobiographical history as told to Baby Sweet, including the framed tale of her mother's love for Sugar Boy, son of Rosiebelle Lee Wildcat Tennessee. At the conclusion of *Baby Sweet's* the death of John Morgan Sr., atop Lea in the upstairs bedroom of the White House-turned-brothel, quite literally puts to rest the cycle of sexual and economic exploitation in the Appalachee series of novels.

Raymond Andrews's highly original novels offer something nearly unique in recent American fiction: an affectionate, realistic, witty record of southern rural and small-town African American experience. At the time of his death, he was working on a novel entitled *99 Years and a Dark Day*. It is difficult to say what direction his further work would have taken, but in his cycle of Appalachee novels Andrews demonstrated a unique talent in presenting the realities of small-town southern life from the omniscient point of view of a narrator entirely aware of the town's larger historical and cultural situation. For those readers willing to enter the depths of feeling and knowledge beneath the surface of his novels, the fiction of Raymond Andrews will offer a broader understanding of the South's troubled racial past, and of the complex relationships of power, status, and privilege that exist within all human societies.

Works Cited

Andrews, Raymond. *Appalachee Red*. New York: Dial, 1978.

———. *Baby Sweet's*. New York: Dial, 1983.

———. *Jessie and Jesus and Cousin Andrew*. Atlanta: Peachtree, 1994.

———. *The Last Radio Baby: A Memoir*. Atlanta: Peachtree, 1990.

———. *Rosiebelle Lee Wildcat Tennessee*. New York: Doubleday, 1980.

Cheuse, Alan. "American Grotesques." *The New York Times Book Review,* 17 Aug. 1980: 11, 15.

Davis, Thomas J. "Review of *The Last Radio Baby: A Memoir*." *Library Journal* 115, no. 17 (15 Oct. 1990): 92.

"Raymond Andrews." *Contemporary Authors* (New Revision Series) 15 (1985): 31–32.

"The Politics of THEY"

Dorothy Allison's BASTARD OUT OF CAROLINA as Critique of Class, Gender, and Sexual Ideologies

Moira P. Baker

"We were the *they* everyone talks about—the ungrateful poor," asserts Dorothy Allison, referring to her childhood experiences in Greenville, South Carolina ("Question" 13). Her work, she writes, represents "the condensed and reinvented experience of a cross-eyed working-class lesbian . . . who has made the decision to live . . . on the page . . . for me and mine" ("Preface" 12). In the stories collected in *Trash* and in her stunning first novel, *Bastard Out of Carolina,* she offers an uncompromising vision of the ugliness and injustice of poverty. Incandescent with grief, rage, and pride, her fiction also affirms the complex subjectivity of persons who must endure the contempt of a society that affords them one of two mythologized positions: "the truly worthy poor" or "white trash." In "A Question of Class," Allison exposes how the middle-class mythology of the noble poor—those "hard-working, ragged but clean, and intrinsically honorable" persons—encouraged her family to destroy themselves because they did not fit this myth (18). In *Bastard Out of Carolina,* Allison critiques not only two of the most damaging bourgeois myths about so-called white trash—their characteristic illegitimacy and incest—but also the ideology of motherhood underpinning a sex/gender system that cuts across social classes.[1] Central to her critique is her conception of a lesbian subjectivity forged in resistance to the economic and sexual systems whose ideological interests these myths serve.

As Roland Barthes suggests, the production and dissemination of bourgeois ideology require a process of mythmaking that distorts and appropriates objects by emptying them of their history and then investing them with new meanings. The new meanings constitute a mystification that naturalizes a concept. This mystification obscures causality and contingency in order to legitimize the bourgeois order, making its values seem natural, eternally given, ahistorical, and inevitable.[2] Dominant discourses of social class mystify poverty by erasing the historical and economic conditions that produce, indeed require, it in advanced capitalism. These discourses then replace history with a cultural myth: that anyone who is willing to work hard will rise out of poverty and that anyone who cannot rise out of poverty is either unwilling to do so—lazy—or naturally incapable of any human development—trashy.

Allison analyzes how bourgeois ideology conceals the actual material conditions of families like her own. Her own family, she writes, "were the bad poor: men who drank and couldn't keep a job; women, invariably pregnant before marriage. . . . We were not noble, not grateful, not even hopeful. We knew ourselves despised" ("Question" 18). In her essays and fiction, Allison deconstructs self-serving bourgeois mythologies about poverty; she interrogates what she calls "the politics of *they*" grounded in socially constructed categories of class, race, gender, and sexual orientation. Though produced by heteropatriarchal bourgeois culture, such categories purport to derive from nature and claim to describe the innate, inevitable, immutable essence of devalued or stigmatized groups. In fact, these categories serve to rationalize and justify the domination of one group by another. Discussing her project, Allison posits as central her examination of the myriad ways in which a politics of marginalization pervades contemporary society: "Most of all I have tried to understand the politics of *they*, why human beings fear and stigmatize the different while secretly dreading that they might be one of the different themselves. . . . All the other categories by which we categorize and dismiss each other—need to be excavated from the inside" ("Question" 35). Rejecting bourgeois notions of social class, *Bastard Out of Carolina* excavates "from the inside" the material conditions of those whom society stigmatizes as "white trash."

In the first several pages of the novel, Allison deconstructs the category of class by demonstrating that the dichotomous and hierarchical terms it rests upon to distinguish the privileged from the lower classes—industrious/lazy, legitimate/illegitimate, respectable/shameful, civilized/uncivilized—are arbitrary, self-serving, and reversible. As the novel opens, Allison's narrator, Ruth Anne "Bone" Boatwright, recounts her illegitimate birth to her fifteen-year-old mother, Anney Boatwright, and her mother's annual humiliating attempts to get her child a birth certificate without "Illegitimate" stamped across the bottom (4). In Bone's narration of Anney's quest for a new birth certificate without the dehumanizing stamp, Allison indicates that the category "white trash" is an ideological construct—one of the enabling myths of a bourgeois society that relies on the exploited labor of the class it stigmatizes to secure its own wealth: "Mama hated to be called trash, hated the memory of every day she'd ever spent bent over other people's peanuts and strawberry plants while they stood tall and looked at her like she was a rock on the ground" (3–4). Allison reverses the qualities associated with the privileged class—

hardworking, honest, civil—and those associated with the underclass—lazy, shiftless, uncivilized. In Allison's analysis, Anney's employers appear inhumane, unjust, and uncivil as they objectify her body stooped in labor for their benefit; she appears hardworking and purposeful while they appear lazy and self-indulgent in their exploitation of her work. Thus the qualities ascribed to the underclass and the elite cannot embody metaphysical essences constituting the nature of each class since the allegedly defining qualities of each are interchangeable. Allison implies that rather than innate, "natural" attributes of each class, these characteristics are arbitrarily assigned signifiers of class distinction that serve the interests of the economically privileged. In "A Question of Class," Allison suggests that the horror of class prejudice, racism, sexism, and homophobia is that they persuade people that their security "depends on the oppression of others, that for some to have good lives there must be others whose lives are truncated and brutal" (35).

Allison does not merely demonstrate the anguish that this zero-sum ethics and its corollary, the "politics of *they*," cause members of a subordinated class: on the political level she analyzes how prejudices are the grease lubricating state apparatuses as they grind out ever more intricate hierarchical relationships and stamp individuals with their ideological imprint; and on the psychological, she examines the interior mechanisms of class prejudice. "Certified a bastard by the state of Carolina" (3), Bone has effectively been relegated by the state to the category "white trash," that is, positioned in a class system. The state exercises its power even in the most intimate matters of sexuality, marriage, and birth to maintain a class system. The concepts of the patriarchal nuclear family and of legitimacy or illegitimacy thus afford mechanisms not only for the regulation of sexuality but for the perpetuation of a class system; illegitimacy is not a moral blight endemic to the lower classes but a conceptual tool for regulating them.

As Anney makes her annual pilgrimage to the county courthouse in her futile attempts to erase the stigma of illegitimacy from her daughter's birth certificate, the psychological mechanisms that maintain the class system are apparent in the behavior of the clerks conducting the state's business. The male clerk takes enormous pleasure as he exercises power to establish "truth" and to categorize Bone as "illegitimate" and Anney, therefore, as sexually promiscuous:[3] "'Well, little lady,' he said. . . . She could see some of the women clerks standing in the doorway, their faces almost as flushed as her own but their eyes bright with an entirely different emotion. . . . 'The facts have been established' . . . The women in the doorway shook their heads and pursed their lips. One mouthed to the other, 'Some people'" (4–5). Though they occupy a marginal position in the office, the women feel no empathy for another beleaguered woman; instead, they are inflamed—with moral indignation? Or pleasure? Like the male clerk, they take delight in Anney's humiliation and in their power over her. Subjects produced by hierarchical class and sex/gender systems, the male and female clerks reproduce those systems not only in their concepts of themselves and of those labeled "different" but also in their work.

Allison's representation of the psychological mechanisms of class prejudice suggests a homology with racial prejudice. Afro-Caribbean theorist Frantz Fanon has distinguished what he calls a "manicheism delirium" (183) characteristic of racist thinking as it creates an *"imago"* of the black as absolutely different—as "The Other," who is dangerously sexual, morally slack, and bestial, not fully human (169–70). Postcolonial theorist Abdul R. Janmohamed, drawing on Fanon, argues that when confronted with the complex and incomprehensible alterity of the racially different, at least one type of European colonialist thinking seizes upon a "manichean allegory" that posits the native as absolute evil by projecting onto him or her all the darker motives and desires that the colonizer refuses to acknowledge in him or herself.[4] Psychologically this "manichean allegory" assures the colonizer of his or her own moral rectitude; it produces "'surplus morality,' which is further invested in the denigration of the native in a self-sustaining cycle" (23).[5]

In the novel Allison demonstrates how the construct "white trash" creates not a racial but a class-defined Other, the effect of a psychological process of projection similar to the one Fanon and Janmohamed describe in the mind of the colonizer. Most of the upper classes in Greenville County accumulate "surplus morality" from their projected fantasy about the Boatwrights. In the series of courthouse scenes in which Anney seeks the new birth certificate, we see how the surplus morality that the community gathers to itself through its denigration of the Boatwrights turns the clerks ever more savagely upon Anney. Finally, a lawyer, whom Anney has retained to help her, says with a "grin that had no humor in it at all, 'By now, they look forward to you coming in'" (9). As with racial prejudice in a colonial situation, the "manicheism delirium" that attends class prejudice in Allison's fictional world is a psychological sickness that pervades a whole society and infects the state apparatuses and their functionaries.

Allison's novel intervenes in dominant discourses concerning social class, gender, and sexuality not only to expose their self-interested political and psychological mechanisms but also to explore whether the human subject might resist their ideological pressure, and if so, how. To elucidate Allison's portrayal of her characters' resistance to ideology, I would like to turn briefly to some contemporary theory on subjectivity and agency. In his influential essay "Ideology and Ideological State Apparatuses," Louis Althusser theorizes that individuals acquire subjectivity only when interpellated by ideology, which "hails" them by a name that they accept.[6] The act of naming at once creates subjects and subjects them to the ideology within which they recognize themselves. Problematizing Althusser's concept of the subject, Paul Smith suggests that the interpellation of individuals is never final because they emerge out of a shifting intersection of interpellations that call them to a number of conflicting subject-positions. The contradictions and disturbances among these subject-positions allow for agency and resistance to ideological pressure (xxxv). Allison's novel demonstrates how working-class women are often called by a variety of discourses to contradictory subject-positions and how, out of the contradictions, an individual may begin to exert agency, resisting the powerful, debasing interpellations of the state that would "hail" one into the position of "white trash" or "bastard."

By the end of the novel, Allison suggests that the private, oppositional discourse spoken among the Boatwright kinswomen empowers Bone to resist interpellation by a bourgeois, patriarchal state. Working in an almost subterranean, matrilineal network on the margins of patriarchy and capitalism, these women enable Bone to resist subjection to mutually reinforcing class and gender ideologies that define her as trash because she is both poor and a woman. We see inklings of the potentially subversive workings of this network in Granny's derisive comments about the irrelevance of the state's document conferring "legitimacy" upon a child. By the time Granny is through with it, the state's stamp of "illegitimate" appears in all its naked glory as an ideologically interested fiction. When Anney's sister, Alma, leaves her husband, Wade, because of his philandering while she is pregnant, we see how important the private discourse spoken among the Boatwright women is to Bone's developing sense of herself; ultimately, her position as a Boatwright woman—kin to strong, independent women like Granny and Aunt Raylene—is one factor that allows her to survive the abuse she eventually endures once her mother marries.

Unfortunately, Anney and most of her sisters have so internalized patriarchal norms that the discourse they speak among themselves cannot counteract the powerful interpellative effects of the surrounding society's discourses on femininity, sexuality, and the family that bombard them from every quarter, telling them that their life is incomplete without a male lover, that their ultimate validation comes from bearing children to their husbands, and that they are nothing without a man no matter how much income they bring home to support their children. Though they share a woman-centered kinship network on the margins of society, the grid of heteropatriarchy is superimposed on their lives. Their powerful "woman-talk" points out the contradictions in patriarchal ideology that represents women as passive, helpless, and dependent yet expects them to bear children, take full responsibility for raising them, keep house, hold down a job, and "stand by your man" when he is beat up, drunk, in jail, down and out, or out of work. Awareness of the gaps and fissures in patriarchal ideology creates spaces in which women exert some agency, as when Alma leaves Wade. But it does not always enable the women to resist the ideological pressures that urge conformity to patriarchal gender norms; neither does it help them to cope with the crushing economic burdens that drive them back to the men who hold them in contempt. Alma, after all, must return to Wade when the demands of raising her obstreperous sons and ailing infant become more than she can handle alone. Without a man in their lives, most of the Boatwright women feel worthless. To that extent their interpellation as female subjects in a heteropatriarchal state has been effective.

Only Raylene Boatwright, Bone's lesbian aunt, who refuses to work for the factory system or for anyone else, resists becoming a subject in, and being subjected to, capitalist and heteropatriarchal ideologies though she cannot entirely escape them. Allison's critiques of class and gender ideologies intersect and reinforce each other in her portrayal of Raylene, who represents a subject-position in radical conflict with the one to which Bone's other aunts and mother seem irresistibly pulled back. She does not merely speak an oppositional discourse; she embodies it in her own living. I do not mean to imply that Allison constructs a utopian lesbian site or a conception of lesbian subjectivity essentially outside dominant binary categories of gender and sexuality, beyond culture and discourse, or outside the mechanisms of power. As Annamarie Jagose suggests in *Lesbian Utopics,* such transcendent, utopian conceptions underpin some instances of contemporary lesbian theory and fiction that depend on an inside/outside, heterosexual/queer dichotomy. But they "may be entirely complicit with the oppressive categories they are intended to exceed" because they, too, essentialize the lesbian subject, freeze her into a single "nature" to which every lesbian must conform (7).

Rather than offer a lesbian space outside of dominant discourses and beyond the sex/gender system entirely, where the binary gender categories of male and female do not exist, Allison suggests that the lesbian subject is crosshatched by dominant gender discourses and engages in what Judith Butler calls a "radical invention, albeit one that employs and deploys culturally existent and culturally imaginable conventions" (139). Far from offering a utopian fantasy of transcendence in which the subject escapes the sex/gender system, Allison's text may be seen, in Butler's terms, as working toward the "dissolution of binary restrictions through the *proliferation* of genders" (136), a move that suggests possibilities beyond the conventional opposed roles of "male" and "female." Raylene is both maternal and tough-talking; she is as

likely to wear a black serge skirt as a pair of overalls; she cans her own pre-
serves and spits out of the side of her mouth; her porch and yard swarm with
children yet she has no desire to bear children of her own. Allison does not
envision a stable lesbian essence beyond the categories of gender; rather her
notion of lesbian subjectivity has no universal essence; it is multiple, shifting,
and seemingly contradictory. Raylene's "performance" of gender improvises
its own script by drawing on available cultural norms for both female and
male identity, embracing qualities that the sex/gender system assigns to both
genders.

Raylene's place overlooking the Greenville River affords Bone a space
in which oppositional discourse reverberates, calling into question dominant
ideologies. A marriage resister and fugitive from the injustices of a workplace
that has worn her brothers out, Raylene manages to maintain her household
by scavenging for trash that floats down the river, marketing it by the road-
side, and earning "steady money by selling her home-canned vegetables and
fruit" (18). Raylene transforms into a locus of resistance the domestic space
that entraps her sisters; the labor that goes uncompensated in traditional patriarchal households provides her enough income to live as she wants. Operating in the informal economic sector outside the state's regulated structures,
Raylene consistently makes the rent on the place she has called home for
most of her adult life, while her married sisters are displaced from one house
to another, bill collectors and eviction notices hounding them from the homes
they struggle to hold together.

From her lesbian space of resistance, Raylene quite pointedly redefines
gender, class, and sexual ideologies for herself and for Bone, who begins spend-
ing her afternoons at Raylene's place when her stepfather's emotional rages
and physical abusiveness are exacerbated by his failures at work and his father's
intensifying scorn. In the crucial chapter in which Anney tells Bone to stay
with Raylene after school, it is clear from their violent masturbatory fantasies
that both Bone and her younger sister, Reese, are being sexually molested by
their stepfather, Daddy Glen. Though Anney is not aware of the sexual abuse,
the reader infers it from the children's masturbation and their accompanying
fantasies of entrapment and escape, their means of coping with the abuse by
reclaiming their own sexuality and pleasure. Before this chapter, Glen has
subjected Bone to vicious beatings, ostensibly to discipline her for misbehav-
ing, while Anney stands helplessly by. Earlier in the novel, grunting, sweating,
and masturbating against Bone's terrified body, Daddy Glen molested the seven-
year-old, his wrist bone ground into her flesh, the delicate petals of her child's
vulvae crushed down and forced open. Consumed by shame and self-loathing,
afraid of hurting her mother, Bone conceals this sexual abuse and all Glen's
subsequent sexual violations as he disciplines her while Anney is at work (113).

By the time Bone arrives on Raylene's front porch, having (mis)recognized herself in dominant discourses concerning social class and gender, she has accepted the position of a soiled, culpable, "trashy" girl whose life will amount to nothing. Almost immediately Raylene calls into question society's discourses on social class, femininity, and romantic love that have fashioned Bone's subjectivity. "Trash rises," Raylene jokes. "Out here where no one can mess with it trash rises all the time" (180). At Raylene's place, Bone is fearless and masterful, her former hopelessness challenged by Raylene's affirmation of her capacity to make a difference in the world: "I'm counting on you to get out there and do things, girl. Make people nervous and make your old aunt glad" (182).

Raylene offers a critical perspective on the country music Bone adores, reserving her greatest contempt for lugubrious ballads that bemoan faithless lovers and include "a little spoken part during the chorus: 'Terrible maudlin shit,' she'd declare" (183). The maudlin variety of country music is a highly effective working apparatus of heteropatriarchal ideology, one that tells a woman her worth comes from being loved and remaining faithful even to a "faded love" that leaves her nothing but passivity and obsessive "sweet dreams."[7] Unlike Bone's mother, Raylene has not fallen into the trap of "romantic thralldom," which, according to Rachel Blau DuPlessis, is one of many "socially learned" patterns or "scripts" that are "central and recurrent in our culture" (67). DuPlessis suggests that every culture has social conventions that function as "scripts"; she examines three such scripts operating in narrative structures and subjects as well as in human social institutions and practices: heterosexual romance, romantic thralldom, and a telos in marriage (2–3). Like DuPlessis, Allison is concerned with the ways in which culture mandates certain gender norms and sexual practices while proscribing others. DuPlessis defines romantic thralldom as "an all-encompassing . . . love between apparent unequals. . . . While those enthralled feel it completes and even transforms them, dependency rules" (67). Refusing to perform the cultural scripts of heterosexual romance and romantic thralldom, Raylene is the only person Bone knows who always seems "comfortable with herself" and is "completely satisfied with her own company" (182, 179).

Under Raylene's guidance, Bone confronts the inevitable and justified, though misplaced, anger and destructive self-loathing that are developing not only because of her experience of abuse but also because of the class hatred she has internalized from the surrounding culture. When Bone runs away from Anney to stay with Raylene after Glen's physical violence becomes family knowledge, she is seething with a potentially healthy but presently corrosive and inward-turning anger. She challenges Raylene: "How am I supposed to know anything at all? I'm just another ignorant Boatwright . . . another piece of trash barely knows enough to wipe her ass or spit away from the wind. Just like you and Mama and Alma and everybody" (258). Bone's despondent and angry outburst at Raylene suggests not only her need for love and acceptance but also her introjection of dominant class and gender ideologies: "Hellfire. We an't like nobody else in the world. . . . Other people don't go beating on each other all the time. . . . They don't move out alone to the edge of town without a husband, . . . run around all the time in overalls, and sell junk by the side of the road!" (258).

Urging Bone to see beneath the prejudices that oppress them as working-class women, Raylene counsels: "People are the same. . . . Everybody just does the best they can. . . . You think about it, and you'll see that the biggest part of why I live the way I do is that out here I can do just about anything I damn well please" (258–59). Raylene cautions Bone to refuse the position most often accorded women in the dominant culture's sex/gender system, that of passive female victim; to exert agency in shaping her own life, however limited her means or circumscribed her circumstances; and to redirect her anger away from herself and the women in her family toward the sources of abuse and suffering in her life. Only then can Bone's self-destructive anger be transformed into a force that enables her to refuse the subject-position of victimized girl-child, occupying instead the positions of survivor of sexual abuse and resister, like her Aunt Raylene, of the compulsory heteropatriarchal family structure.

Ultimately, Bone—whose emerging identity is forged in the crucible of conflicting discourses about what it means to be a woman, to be poor, to be a Boatwright—exerts agency by asserting her own worth no matter how poor or abused she may be: she refuses to return to a violent patriarchal household, even if it means leaving her mother and choosing a home with her lesbian aunt as surrogate mother. Bone resists, in other words, the interpellation that her mother and other aunts accept. Together on the margins of hegemonic institutions, Bone and Raylene carve out a space in the fissures and cracks, and there they preserve the oppositional discourse of Boatwright women that is muffled or silenced in the mainstream. Raylene cautions Bone: "I like my life the way it is, little girl. . . . You better think hard, Ruth Ann, about what you want and who you're mad at. You better think hard" (263).

Anney's desperate quest for a patronymic to legitimize her child suggests how effectively she, in contrast to Raylene, has been interpellated into bourgeois heteropatriarchal ideology and subjected to it and how effectively her actions are molded by the scripts of heterosexual romance and romantic thralldom. Her quest results in her marriage to Glen Waddell, whose family is comfortably middle class, upwardly mobile, ashamed of him for his failure to succeed at anything, and thoroughly contemptuous of the Boatwrights. Ironically, the marriage intended to protect Bone from class prejudice associated with illegitimacy exposes her to emotional, physical, and sexual abuse at the hands of her stepfather. Allison explodes the myth of incest as characteristic of the underclass and traces its taproot to the unequal power relations of patriarchy itself. The novel suggests that incest originates in the "traffic in women" that establishes kinship relations.

In describing Anney's introduction to Glen by her well-meaning but thoroughly proprietary brother, Earle, Allison emphasizes Anney's desire for a conventional patriarchal nuclear family that will shield her children from the contempt they have already met in Greenville County. Allison's careful staging of the scene also emphasizes ominously how little power Annie will have to protect herself or her children in this relationship, for Annie appears as an object of exchange in a transaction between two men. Allison associates the incest that follows Anney's marriage not with Anney's class status but with her position in an unequal power relation, and she associates that unequal relation not with social class but with the structures that undergird patriarchy itself and the practices that sustain it.

The scene in which Anney meets Glen is a curious one, indeed. Though Earle brings Glen to the restaurant where Annie works to show her off, he gets "hot-angry" when Glen leers at Anney's body, his sense of male entitlement momentarily offended even though he intends to set Glen up with his sister. Glen's attraction to Anney is intensified by his hatred of his father, his damaged sense of himself as a man, his preoccupation with his own projected fantasy of "the notorious and dangerous Black Earle Boatwright," and his desire for a bond with Earle: "Glen Waddell wanted Earle Boatwright to like him. . . . He would marry Black Earle's baby sister, marry the whole Boatwright legend, shame his daddy and shock his brothers" (12–13).

I contend that we can make the fullest sense of this scene in view of Claude Lévi-Strauss's theory of the fundamental structural principles of kinship relationships and Gayle Rubin's brilliant feminist critique of his thinking. Like Rubin, Allison offers a critical perspective on patriarchal systems of kinship based on "the exchange of women" that Lévi-Strauss posited in *The Elementary Structure of Kinship* as the normative origin of social organization in all cultures, whether "primitive" (as the anthropologists say) or contemporary. At the same time, Allison also interrogates the myth that incest is a common occurrence in low-income families and something to which the upper class is, for the most part, immune. Allison suggests that Anney's class status is not a determining factor in the abuse of her daughter. Rather the power differential between men and women in conventional marriages based on the exchange of women encourages abuses of paternal authority that can, in extreme cases, result in incestuous abuse.

Drawing on Marcel Mauss's "Essai sur le don," which examined the theory of reciprocal gift-giving as the basis for social exchange in primitive cultures, Lévi-Strauss distinguished women as the most important gift to be given, marriage as the most basic form of exchange, and the incest taboo as a safeguard to ensure exogamous exchanges.[8] The metaphors Lévi-Strauss seizes upon are revealing: women must be "given" in marriage and men have a "right" to the daughter and sister of other men; marriage is constituted by an "exchange" between two groups of men rather than between a man and a woman; women are "objects of exchange" rather than partners.

Allison's novel plays out the disastrous consequences of this system of sexual exchange and the patriarchal kinship system it produces, a system that relegates women to a relatively less powerful position and requires the suppression of feminocentric systems of kinship like the one we see among the Boatwright women. Her analysis hews closely to Rubin's critique of the theory that the origins of culture are prescriptively invested in the "traffic in women." Rubin examines theoretically, and Allison fictionally, the destructiveness of a sex/gender system in which "women do not have full rights to themselves" (Rubin 177), a system that Rubin argues cuts across social classes and cultures.

Though valuing Lévi-Strauss's work because it illuminates "what would otherwise be poorly perceived parts of the deep structures of sex oppression" (198), Rubin faults him for failing to see the implications of his own thinking: for failing to see that the "exchange of women" is a systematic social apparatus responsible for the oppression of women and for positing this exchange as a cultural necessity rather than criticizing it as a socially constructed and mutable system. Rubin finds in the "traffic in women" not the origins of culture but the "ultimate locus of women's oppression" (175). Calling for nothing less than "a revolution in kinship," she advocates a rearrangement of the social machinery that has produced the sex/gender system characteristic of most Western capitalist societies in order to "liberate human sexual life from the archaic relationships which deform it" (199, 200).

Allison elucidates some of the same "deep structures of sex oppression" that Rubin critiques and reaches some of the same radical conclusions as does Rubin about the need to reconstitute kinship relationships and eliminate obligatory heterosexuality if we are to shape a society in which women and children are safe. Allison stresses not only that the "exchange of women" is a locus of women's oppression; she reveals, further, its fundamental *ineffectiveness* as a system of social organization. In the novel, the exchange of Anney between Glen and Earle does not preserve the incest taboo, the supposed "supreme rule of the gift," for it rather encourages the man who has been given one woman as a gift to consider any woman, even his daughter or step-daughter, as his own property, a sexual object to be taken and not given. Allison suggests that any system positioning women as sexual objects over which men have proprietary rights may invite, rather than discourage, breaches of the "supreme rule" prohibiting incest, just as Anney's marriage to Glen opens the way for his sexual abuse of her daughter. Thus she attributes incest not to lower socioeconomic class status but to a sex/gender system that produces male subjects who assume ownership rights over women and female subjects who internalize the culture's discourses that shape femininity, sexuality, and the family.

Anney and Glen's courtship is shot through with troubling emotions: his regressive infantile dependency needs and violent possessiveness beneath a veneer of romantic ardor, her need for romantic love and a father to legitimize her child. The emotional extortion beneath Glen's lachrymose, slobbering proposal of marriage betrays not only the dominance and submission that DuPlessis claims are implicit in the cultural script of romantic thralldom but also the dangerous privilege of male entitlement to women and children that Rubin critiques in Western, capitalist sex/gender systems: "Oh Anney. . . . I can't wait no more. . . . And your girls, Anney. Oh, God! I love them. . . . You're mine, all of you, mine. . . . Don't say no, Anney, don't do that to me!" (36) When Anney says she'll think about it, Glen pounds his fist on the car and screams: "Goddam . . . Goddam Anney! . . . I knew you'd say yes. Oh, what I'm gonna do, Anney! . . . You an't never even imagined!" (36). Indeed she hadn't.

For her part, Anney desires a father for her child to erase the stigma that bourgeois culture attaches to illegitimacy (13, 15). Allison emphasizes the complexities of Anney's desires, shaped not only by class ideology but also by the ideology of love, mapped out in the cultural scripts of heterosexual romance, romantic thralldom, and a telos of marriage that DuPlessis notes. Though all of Anney's family have misgivings about Glen, they acquiesce when Alma invokes sentimental illusions of romantic love: "But Anney loves Glen. . . . She needs him, needs him like a starving woman needs meat between her teeth" (41). Anney's sense that her children might find security and happiness only in a conventional nuclear family and that she might find only in that same institution someone to love her with a love as strong as hers for her children is oddly out of sync with the experience of love and nurturance her two girls find in Anney's extended family—a complex kinship network of strong and capable aunts, numerous cousins, and an indomitable matriarchal grandmother.

In contrast to this feminocentric, non-nuclear family, the male-dominated nuclear family that Bone enters when her mother marries Glen is a site of verbal and physical violence, obsessive male jealousy of Anney's attention toward her children, and escalating sexual molestation culminating in Bone's rape by her stepfather. I suggest that Allison's use of such incendiary material does not flirt dangerously with demeaning class stereotypes, as Randall Kenan suggests in his review of the novel. Nor does it function solely as a paradoxical defusing of stereotypes that enhances the humanity of Allison's characters, as David Reynolds argues in his otherwise fine study of working-class literature. Allison offers horrific scenes of abuse and incestuous rape not only to defuse stereotypes about the working class but also to expose the secret violence against children hidden in the bosom of those bourgeois patriarchal families in which the authoritarian rule of males is given full sway. Modern Western society has both recognized and tried to conceal this violence for one hundred years—since Freud's repudiation of his "Seduction Theory."

In this theory, Freud hypothesized that the cause of his patients' hysterical symptoms was their repressed experience of incestuous abuse, usually by their fathers or other close family members ("Aetiology" 208). Based on his patients' testimony, Freud constructed his "Seduction Theory" of the origin of neurosis, which he delivered in a lecture to the Vienna Society for Psychiatry and Neurology on 21 May 1896. In a letter to his colleague Wilhelm Fliess, Freud angrily protested that his lecture was given "an icy reception by the asses" in the Viennese psychiatric establishment.[9] The Viennese psychiatric establishment aggressively ignored Freud's theory, and clients avoided consulting him.[10] Not surprisingly, he soon reversed his position, writing to Fliess that he had rejected his original theory because "in all cases, the *father,* not excluding my own, had to be accused of being perverse . . . whereas surely such widespread perversions against children are not very probable" (*Letters* 264). And this Freud concluded despite the compelling contradictory clinical evidence gathered from almost every one of his hysterical patients and from his observations in the Paris Morgue.[11] As Christine Froula argues, "Freud turned away from the seduction theory not because it lacked explanatory power but because he was unable to come to terms with what he was the first to discover: the crucial role played in neurosis by the abuse of paternal power" (118). He simply could not accept what all the evidence suggested: that sexual abuse by fathers or other family members was, indeed, "very probable."

Recent studies of sexual abuse, such as Judith Herman's *Father-Daughter Incest* (1981), David Finkelhor's *Sexually Victimized Children* (1979), and Diana Russell's *The Secret Trauma: Incest in the Lives of Girls and Women* (1986), all suggest that the incidence of incest and other forms of childhood sexual abuse is alarmingly high in our society.[12] In 1990, Finkelhor used a national

survey of 1,481 adult females and 1,145 adult males to examine the prevalence of childhood sexual abuse. He found that 27 percent of the women
surveyed and 16 percent of the men had experienced sexual victimization
("Sexual Abuse" 21).[13] Using much more thorough questioning about sexually exploitative experiences, Diana Russell's random sample of 933 adult
women indicates that 38 percent of the subjects experienced some form of
sexual abuse before the age of eighteen and 28 percent before the age of fourteen ("Incidence" 137).[14]

Reading Allison's fiction in the context of Freud's repudiation of his
seduction theory and in the light of recent statistics on the cross-cultural
incidence and prevalence of child abuse suggests at least one stark conclusion. The myth of the slack-moraled, oversexed, incest-ridden "white trash"
family could well be one mechanism whereby a bourgeois patriarchal culture
projects its darkest fantasy of the ultimate paternal power and control onto
an "other," thereby distancing itself from its own desires and occluding the
reality of abuse that pervades all social classes. The so-called white trash family functions as the scapegoat for the incest and abuse that are endemic to the
authoritarian household in which paternal rule goes unquestioned and un-
checked. By projecting incest onto a class-defined "other," the dominant culture does not have to confront it in itself.

Rejecting the self-serving mythology of the depraved, abusive "white
trash" family, Allison posits the origin of incestuous abuse in the upper-middle-
class Waddell family. A resolutely patriarchal family, the Waddells have so
damaged their own son that he turns his rage and regressive dependency
needs upon the Boatwright women in an attempt to compensate for his own
sense of emasculation. In Allison's fiction, incest is not a defining characteristic of poor white southerners, nor is it an inevitable phenomenon in that
class; rather, the conditions that breed it occur in the most "typical" bourgeois family and are exacerbated by the expectations that both patriarchy and
capitalism lay upon the male as he struggles to forge a secure identity. In fact,
when Bone's Boatwright uncles learn of Glen's physical abuse of her, they are
clearly appalled that a man would beat a child bloody. "Shit!" Uncle Nevil, a
man of few words, exclaims when Raylene shows him the angry welts and
weeping scabs on Bone's thighs (246). The uncles—Nevil, Beau, and Earle—
beat the tar out of Glen, sending him to the hospital and giving him a permanent limp to remind him of what a whipping feels like.

Allison, quite significantly, does not suggest that they do this merely
because Glen has violated their sense of male entitlement over their family's
sexual property, though proprietary they certainly are at times. Whatever problems the uncles have in dealing with their wives, they dote upon children.
Allison's depiction of their solicitude toward children is all the more signifi-

cant in view of the hard exteriors they have to present to a world that heaps abuse on them because of their social class.[15] In one of the more haunting moments of the narrative, Uncle Nevil comes to Bone after Glen rapes her and she is living with Raylene. Bone narrates their conversation: "Nevil . . . stood silently in front of me. He touched my bruised chin with one outstretched finger, traced my hairline, and leaned forward to kiss my left cheekbone with dry chapped lips. . . . 'I promise,' he said. . . . I knew what he meant, and I smiled" (304).

Despite the violence in the lives of these uncles, they are not characters with whom the abuse of a child sits well. After the workweek is over, they may get liquored up and bust a best friend's jaw, as Earle does; they will surely go to jail for it, as he does. They are often not concerned with their wives' emotional and sexual needs. Yet Allison's complex representation of their material circumstances suggests that they are emotionally drained themselves by a constant grind of work that never quite gets the bills paid. Forced to live amid undeniable economic injustices and seething with anger because of it, they seek releases from their circumstances in fighting or liquor, and they do not begin to acknowledge, let alone respond to, their wives' needs. When his wife leaves him because of his infidelities, Uncle Earle seeks out the sexual attentions of much younger women, who do not remind him of his own failures and insecurities. Allison does not make excuses for these behaviors; rather, she contextualizes them in the material realities of economic oppression. Whatever else the uncles do, they do not beat children bloody.

It would be possible to argue simply on the basis of that narrative fact, I suppose, that Allison is idealizing her own class, mythologizing them in just the way that she says is debilitating. In view of the whole novel, however, it would be quite difficult to support the position that Allison presents a romanticized view of the Boatwright males because their violence, drunkenness, and infidelities punctuate the narrative. It is more persuasive to argue that her location of the origin of sexual abuse in the Waddell family rather than in the Boatwright family is a strategic intervention in the discourses about social class that associate incest with poverty. I am not arguing that by rejecting the myth of the incestuous poor Allison implies that the middle class is responsible for most abuse or that the poor are immune to it; rather, I contend that by challenging conventional prejudices about incest and poverty, she suggests that incest pervades society, not just the one social class with which it is stereotypically associated.

Glen's successful businessman father constantly taunts him because he is a failure while his brothers are successful professionals, whose conspicuous consumption Glen yearns to emulate. Glen's father practices what psychologist and therapist Alice Miller calls a "poisonous pedagogy" that constantly humiliates and shames a child or beats the child under the guise of a "spanking for your own good," so that he or she will "know his/her own place." Though widely acceptable, such pedagogy, she argues, has both domestic and political consequences: it creates children who may grow into tyrannical and physically abusive parents, and it may account for the widespread acceptance of violence in society (vii-xii, 142–89).

The effects of his father's "poisonous pedagogy" on Glen's masculine identity are devastating. Whenever Glen brings his family to his father's house, he dare not leave "before his father [has] delivered his lecture on all the things Glen had done wrong in his long life of failure and disappointment" (99). Glen's reactions to his father suggest two things: the atmosphere of shame that bleeds into terror in an oppressive authoritarian household and its continuing traumatic effects on the victim. When he is around his father, Glen breaks out into a sweat and watches his father's face nervously, pulling on his pants "like a little boy" and dropping his head if anyone asks him a question (99).

When Bone's Aunt Ruth asks her whether Glen has ever molested her, Bone cannot speak the truth, but she remembers: "Mama thought that keeping me . . . away from Daddy Glen was the answer, that loving him and making him feel strong and important would fix everything in time. But . . . every time his Daddy spoke harshly to him, every time he couldn't pay the bills, every time Mama was too tired to flatter or tease him out of his moods, Daddy Glen's eyes would turn to me, and my blood would turn to ice" (233). Glen turns abusive when his failure in a capitalist system and his father's continuing emotional tyranny reopen old wounds, which he feels can be stanched only by letting the blood of his own stepchild. Like Miller, Allison discloses the roots of violence and the monstrous proportions to which it can grow in the hidden and acceptable cruelties visited upon children by the child-rearing practices of typical families. And so the cycle of paternal abuse continues generationally: the trauma visited upon the shamed and terrorized child is revisited upon his or her own children.

In addition to challenging the myth that poverty is the provenance of incest, Allison critiques deeply ingrained patriarchal ideas of motherhood, insisting that the power vested in motherhood in heteropatriarchal households is an illusion that frequently guarantees women's failure. She deflates the cherished myth of the blissful nuclear family as the most healthy and "natural" site for raising children. As Janet Jacobs contends, feminist theorists of child abuse see it as a consequence of patriarchal family arrangements that produce female dependence and powerlessness and maintain male control over women and children ("Reassessing" 500). Feminist theorists such as Nancy Chodorow,

Dorothy Dinnerstein, and Adrienne Rich have urged a reexamination of the traditional patriarchal family and its institution of motherhood, arguing that the process of mothering is not simply a biological or natural imperative but rather a culturally determined political institution that reproduces not only the species but also male dominance. As Dinnerstein so tartly puts it, the "female monopoly of early child care" (33) perpetuates a sex/gender system in which women are expected to be all-powerful in the domestic sphere because that is their "natural" realm; they are defined by their maternal functions and are judged by their success or failure as mothers. Although the *experience* of motherhood confers upon women a sense of their own power through the biological fact of parturition, in fact, as Rich argues, women have relatively little social power within the *institution* of motherhood since their reproductive power remains under male control (13).

Regardless of the affective power Anney Boatwright exerts in the lives of her daughters, as the wife of Glen Waddell she is powerless to save them. In "A Question of Class," Allison writes that one story haunted her until she understood how to tell it: "the complicated, painful story of how my mama had, and had not, saved me" (34). This is the story she tells in *Bastard Out of Carolina.* Allison lucidly elaborates the impossible expectations placed not only on damaged men like Glen but also on the mother in the traditional patriarchal family. She critiques patriarchal family norms and power relations founded on the sexual division of labor and the conception of the two spheres, the public and the private, representing the male and female domains. As pathological as it is, Allison suggests that Anney and Glen's marriage represents merely an exaggeration of patriarchal norms, not a departure from them. Because a woman's primary and defining function in patriarchy is motherhood, she is expected to be the sole nurturer of everyone, including her husband, if need be. She is to meet the needs of her children and her husband, making a haven for him in the domestic realm and bolstering him up so that he can return to the more important work in the productive sector. Given this ideology, a woman whose husband is in a regressive state of infantile dependence, as is Glen, almost certainly will fail in her role as nurturer.

In the novel, the institution of motherhood compels Bone's aunts to define themselves entirely in terms of their reproductive and nurturing functions: "Ruth, Raylene, Alma, and even Mama . . . seemed old, worn-down, and slow, *born to mother,* nurse, and clean up after the men" (23; emphasis added). None of the aunts, except Raylene, questions a system in which women define themselves by their capacity to nurture and their responsibility to mother even grown men. Bone notices how these gender arrangements infantilize men and boys: "My aunts treated my uncles like overgrown boys—rambunctious teenagers whose antics were more to be joked about than worried over" (23). Dinnerstein argues that the institution of motherhood as we know it "gives us boys who will grow reliably into childish men" (81).

In an unbearably poignant moment, Aunt Ruth tries to create a space in which a deeply troubled Bone can talk about why she would say, "Daddy Glen hates me" (122). Bone refuses to speak, but Ruth continues: "Glen don't like you much. He's jealous. . . . There's a way he's just a little boy himself, wanting more of your mama than you, wanting to be her baby more than her husband. And that an't so rare. . . . Men . . . are just like little boys climbing up on titty whenever they can" (123). Ruth and all the Boatwright women understand that their maternal powers are jealously guarded and circumscribed by men, who are themselves trapped in an infantile state. Allison suggests that the institutionalized practices of mothering create these dynamics and encourage paternal abuse. Significantly, Ruth's next utterance implies that the abuse of children is one logical outcome of the not "so rare" appropriation of women's nurturing capacity in the interest of adult male needs: "Bone, has Daddy Glen ever . . . well . . . touched you? . . . Down here, honey. Has he ever hurt you down there?" (124).

"Born to mother" and interpellated into the ideologies of heterosexual romance and romantic thralldom, Anney is drawn into an ever more destructive relationship with Glen precisely because he is in such dire need of the mothering and nurturance he never received as a child. Narratively, Allison erases Glen's own mother almost entirely, suggesting the maternal paralysis and passivity that attend paternal domination. In a conversation with Ruth, who warns her of Glen's jealousy of Bone, Anney protests: "Anybody can see how Glen got bent, what his daddy's done to him. . . . All Glen really needs is to know himself loved, to get out from under his daddy's meanness" (132). Anney has interjected the myth of the all-powerful mother whose love can heal all wounds.[16] Anney feels compelled to play the role Glen's mother never could in a household where masculine authority was absolute. In fact, his vulnerability and seeming need for her maternal love if he is to become a man ineluctably draw Anney to Glen. Through Anney's plight, Allison suggests that the ideology of motherhood, with its emphasis on the power of female nurturance, can put women into a double bind: they are asked to meet the needs of both children and husbands and yet these needs may be in conflict if the husband has unmet dependency needs. Merely nurturing her children, Anney unwittingly incites Glen's jealousy, exacerbates his insatiable needs, and deepens his hatred of Bone, whom he sees as a rival for Anney's love.

As Janet Jacobs argues, the incestuous father often turns to his daughters to satisfy the needs that the wife cannot fulfill. No one can. When this occurs, the mother is blamed by both the child and society for not fulfilling her role as nurturer and protector of her children ("Victimized Daughters"

133–35, 137).[17] Jacobs contends that the most important recent studies of incest reveal that the mother becomes the focus for "feelings of anger, hatred, and betrayal on the part of the daughters who were abused by their fathers" ("Reassessing" 501–2). Furthermore, and more disturbingly, she asserts that existing theories of sexual abuse and therapeutic models for recovery incorporate a "strong bias toward mother blame" (502), which freezes the victim of abuse in a state of rage against her mother and severs permanently the bond between mother and daughter. Contemporary family dysfunction approaches to sexual abuse and psychotherapy thus "support the notion that the mother is in some way responsible for the acts of the father, a view that is consistent with cultural norms that justify male violence by blaming the female victim for the actions of the aggressor" (502).

Jacobs submits that anger at the mother is an important stage in the process of emerging from childhood sexual abuse as a survivor because it helps the victim separate from the mother, whose sense of helplessness the child often internalizes ("Reassessing" 500). Moreover, focusing anger on the mother allows the victim to externalize the anger that she so frequently turns inward as she directs "hatred and aggression against [herself]" (512). Remaining in this stage of mother-blame, however, though it offers a strategy for psychological survival, causes conflicts in the victim's own gender identity and a devaluation not only of the mother but of women in general (513). Jacobs contends that once the anger at the mother is expressed and validated, a feminist perspective on the incest can help the victim move beyond anger at the mother to a "less distorted perception of the mother's role in her victimization" and an appropriate focusing of the anger on the perpetrator (512). Allison interrogates the bias toward mother-blame in dominant theories of sexual abuse, family pathology, and psychotherapy. She exposes mother-blame as another myth of patriarchal ideology. And she rejects it. In its stead, she textualizes a process for emerging from the experience of paternal sexual abuse as a female survivor who understands, richly and empathetically, the position of her mother and the ultimate responsibility of her father in the abusive household. For the sake of narrative compression, she distills into thirty pages and a matter of only a few fictional days a process that can take years, decades, or a lifetime to complete, if ever.

In the rape scene and its emotionally devastating aftermath, when Anney leaves Bone with Aunt Raylene so she can care for the man who has raped her daughter, Allison pulls the reader through the experience of an exhausting and bewildering range of contradictory emotions: horror, numbness, rage, resentful blaming of the mother, anguish for her impossible position, and a painful recognition that blame is an utterly inadequate response to the sufferings of this mother and her child. The rape itself is excruciating reading, as a child is violated in unspeakable ways. Allison speaks the unspeakable, articulating with precision and sharp detail the emotional and physical savagery of the act, the verbal and sexual specifics of an assault intended to overwhelm and damage not only this twelve-year-old child's blossoming female sexuality but her sense of her own worth as a human being.

Limp from exertion and detumescent, Glen lies draped over the brutalized child when Anney happens upon the scene. Her reaction is immediate and fierce as she beats Glen off Bone's body, calls him "monster," and tries to protect and calm Bone, covering up the child's nakedness as best she can, clasping her to herself, and soothing her with her repeated whisper, "Baby, baby" (287–88). When Anney tries to get Bone to the car, Glen begins sobbing "like a child," and Anney slaps, then punches him "full on" in the face as he whines her name "like a little boy" (288). As Anney struggles to get the driver's door open, her prostrate child pleading "Mama" to her from the passenger side, Glen threatens suicide in a whisper: "Kill me, Anney. Go on. I can't live without you. I won't. Kill me! Kill me!" (290). Punctuating each blow with the cry, "Kill me," Glen repeatedly slams his bloody head into the closed car door. As Anney grabs his head to block the impact, Bone pleads, "Mama," and Glen whispers, "Kill me, Anney" (290), the emotional extortion of his marriage proposal having come full circle.

Allison clarifies the impossible and conflicting demands laid upon mothers in heteropatriarchy by placing her character in the situation of having to choose between her battered child and the emotionally damaged husband whom she has loved as a vulnerable child because the institution of mothering and the ideology of motherhood have conditioned her to do so. No matter what she does, in her own eyes, Anney fails. The easy response for a reader is simply to write this character off as a failure and to despise her, as Bone initially does, because she leaves her child. Bone reacts with instant rage and hatred of her mother: "I hated her now for the way she held him, the way she stood there crying over him" (291). But the superb rendering not only of a child's brutalization but also a mother's anguished position between an abused child and a disturbed, desperately needy husband, whose nurturing she has been acculturated to take responsibility for, throws the reader into a conflict-ridden position not unlike Anney's.

Bone's rage is salutary because it prevents her from blaming and despising herself for the abuse, as we have seen her do earlier in the narrative. But as Raylene speaks to Bone, who is convalescing at her house after Anney abandons her at the hospital, the text nudges the reader beyond an initial response of rage at the mother to a fuller understanding of Anney's position. Raylene tries to get Bone to see how wrong it was for Glen to put Anney in the position of having to choose between her child and her lover. Without denying Anney's responsibility, Raylene urges Bone to remember that her mother loves her and will suffer forever for her failure to protect her child.

In the wrenching scene in which Anney returns to give Bone a new birth certificate without "illegitimate" stamped on the bottom and to assure her that she loves her, Bone's growing awareness of her mother's difficult life moves her toward forgiveness: "Maybe it wasn't her fault. It wasn't mine. . . . Maybe it was like Raylene said, the way the world goes" (307). When Bone notices the unstamped certificate, she begins to reflect on her mother's failure in the context of her whole life: its deferred dreams, its terrors, its unmet needs, its shame. Bone asks, "Who had Mama been, what had she wanted to be or do before I was born? . . . What would I be like when I was fifteen, twenty, thirty? Would I be as strong as she had been, as hungry for love, as desperate, determined, and ashamed?" (309). By refusing to go with her mother, choosing instead to live with her Aunt Raylene in a safe space out by the river where "trash rises," Bone takes her first step toward survival. She directs her anger not inward, nor outward toward her mother, but toward her abuser. Though Bone holds her mother responsible for her choice to stay with Glen, she places full responsibility for her sexual abuse squarely on Glen's shoulders. Allison represents the abused child as taking her first steps toward survival in a way that liberates her from both self-loathing and rage against her mother.

Allison rejects myths about incest and about those "white trash" families who are allegedly haunted by it. Further, she offers a feminist analysis of paternal sexual abuse in place of an essentializing myth that at once posits incest as the exclusive domain of the underclass and lays the blame for its incidence on the mother. In "A Question of Class," Allison writes: "I grew up poor, hated, the victim of physical, emotional, and sexual violence, and I know that suffering does not ennoble. It destroys. To resist destruction, self-hatred, or lifelong hopelessness, we have to . . . refuse lying myths and easy moralities, to see ourselves as human, flawed, and extraordinary. All of us— extraordinary" (36). By rejecting bourgeois myths about "white-trash" illegitimacy and incest, by exposing the injustices of an economic system whose interests those myths legitimize, and by critiquing some of our society's most cherished institutions—the heterosexual family and its institution of motherhood—Allison lets us see the Boatwrights and persons of their social class not as subhuman trash but as human, flawed, and extraordinary.

Notes

1. I predicate my analysis on Gayle Rubin's theoretical position that every society is organized by a sex/gender system (168). Rubin repeatedly stresses that a sex/gender system is socially constructed and subject to historical change (166).

2. Barthes contends that bourgeois ideology requires and produces cultural myths that veil social or cultural processes in order to give the appearance of the natural and inevitable to phenomena that are socially, culturally, and historically produced (117–74). The fundamental principle of myth is that "it transforms history into nature. . . . Myth has the task of giving an historical intention a natural justification, and making contingency appear eternal" (140, 155).

3. In "The Subject and Power," Foucault elaborates his conceptual model for analyzing the operations of power in the constitution and regulation of human subjects. In *The History of Sexuality*, Foucault analyzes Western discourses of sexuality and their implications for the constitution and government of the subject. Foucault examines how power permeates discourses, gaining access to the "forms of desire" as it "penetrates and controls everyday pleasure" and "wrap[s] the sexual body in its embrace" (11, 44). In "The Subject and Power" he delineates a technique of power that "categorizes the individual, marks him by his own individuality, attaches him to his own identity. . . . It is a form of power which makes individuals subjects" (781). In *The History of Sexuality*, he explains the pleasure derived by those employing this technique of power (45).

4. Janmohamed describes the colonialist's psychological process as follows: "The native, who is considered too degraded and inhuman to be credited with any specific subjectivity, is cast as no more than a recipient of the negative elements of the self that the European projects onto him" (20).

5. Janmohamed's description of the psychological benefits of the "manichean allegory" clarifies the unquestioned sense of moral superiority as well as the gratuitous cruelty of Allison's upper-class characters (23).

6. Althusser suggests that all ideology constructs individuals as subjects:

> *All ideology has the function (which defines it) of constituting concrete individuals as subjects. . . .* I shall then suggest that ideology "acts" or "functions" in such a way that it "recruits" subjects among the individuals (it recruits them all) by that very precise operation which I have called *interpellation* or hailing, and which can be imagined along the lines of the most commonplace everyday police (or other) hailing: "Hey, you there!" . . . The hailed individual will turn round. By this mere one-hundred-and-eighty-degree physical conversion, he becomes a *subject*. Why? Because he has recognized that the hail was "really" addressed to him, and that "it was *really him* who was hailed" (and not someone else). (160, 162–63)

7. Allison also examines the subversive potential of country music, inevitable because of the contradictory positions to which women are called in patriarchal ideology (*Bastard* 256).

8. Lévi-Strauss writes: "The prohibition on the sexual use of a daughter or a sister compels them to be given in marriage to another man, and at the same time it establishes a right to the daughter or sister of this other man" (51). The exchange is

established not between a man and a woman but between two groups of men, the woman figuring "only as one of the objects in the exchange, not as one of the partners" (115). Perhaps most tellingly, Lévi-Strauss argues that the incest taboo, the "supreme rule of the gift," is more a rule "obliging the mother, sister, or daughter be given to others" than a rule prohibiting marriage to her (481).

9. The fierceness of Freud's conviction about his theory is striking as is the psychoanalytic community's snubbing of his work. Fully persuaded of the legitimacy and importance of his findings, he published an expanded version of the lecture in his 1896 essay "The Aetiology of Hysteria," a piece written "in defiance of [his] colleagues" (*Letters* 190). Contrary to accepted practice, Freud's colleagues refused to publish in the weekly journal *Wiener Klinische Wochenschrift* the abstract of his lecture and an account of the ensuing discussion (Masson 6–9).

10. Freud confessed to Fliess: "I am as isolated as you would wish me to be" (*Letters* 185). Though Freud claimed to be bearing the contempt of his colleagues "with equanimity," the fact that his "consulting room [was] empty" and no new clients had sought him out for weeks was "more troublesome" to him (*Letters* 185).

11. For a fascinating but controversial account of Freud's recantation of his "Seduction Theory," see Jeffrey Masson's *The Assault on Truth*.

12. In Finkelhor's nonrepresentative sample of 796 college students, 19 percent of the women surveyed and 9 percent of the men reported childhood experiences of sexual victimization (*Sexually Victimized Children* 53). In a later study using a representative sample of 521 adults, Finkelhor found that 15 percent of the women and 5 percent of the men reported experiences of sexual abuse as children ("How Widespread," par. 21).

13. Some of Finkelhor's additional findings are also pertinent to Allison's examination of sexual abuse. Males were more likely to be abused by strangers, females by family members. Both males and females reported that most of their abuse was perpetrated by men ("Sexual Abuse" 21).

14. Sixteen percent of Russell's subjects experienced intrafamilial sexual abuse before the age of eighteen and 12 percent before the age of fourteen; 31 percent of the subjects experienced extrafamilial sexual abuse before the age of eighteen and 20 percent before the age of fourteen. The 38 percent figure resulted when both categories of sexual abuse were combined, and the number was adjusted to account for overlap between the two categories since some subjects experienced both kinds of abuse ("Incidence" 137).

15. In her recent autobiographical piece, Allison writes: "Two or three things I know for sure, and one of them is that no one is as hard as my uncles had to pretend to be" (*Two* 32). The Boatwright uncles are similarly compelled to conceal their vulnerabilities beneath a granitic facade.

16. For a discussion of the destructiveness of this myth, particularly on the mother-daughter bond in cases of incest, see Regen 17–21.

17. I am grateful to Harriet Mauck Regen for pointing out the importance of Jacobs's work to a reading of Allison.

Works Cited

Allison, Dorothy. *Bastard Out of Carolina*. New York: Dutton, 1992.

———. "Preface: Deciding to Live." *Trash*. Ithaca: Firebrand, 1988. 7–12.

———. "A Question of Class." *Skin: Talking About Sex, Class and Literature*. Ithaca: Firebrand, 1994. 13–36.

———. *Two or Three Things I Know for Sure*. New York: Dutton, 1995.

Althusser, Louis. "Ideology and Ideological State Apparatuses." *Lenin and Philosophy, and Other Essays*. Trans. Ben Brewster. New York: Monthly Review, 1971. 127–86.

Barthes, Roland. "Myth Today." *Mythologies*. Trans. Annette Lavers. Toronto: Paladin, 1973. 117–74.

Butler, Judith. "Variations on Sex and Gender: Beauvoir, Wittig and Foucault." *Feminism as Critique*. Ed. Seyla Benhabib and Drucilla Cornell. Minneapolis: U of Minnesota P, 1987. 128–42.

Chodorow, Nancy. *The Reproduction of Mothering: Psychoanalysis and the Sociology of Gender.* Berkeley: U of California P, 1978.

Dinnerstein, Dorothy. *The Mermaid and the Minotaur: Sexual Arrangements and Human Malaise*. New York: Harper Colophon, 1976.

DuPlessis, Rachel Blau. *Writing beyond the Ending: Narrative Strategies of Twentieth-Century Women Writers*. Bloomington: Indiana UP, 1985.

Fanon, Frantz. *Black Skin, White Masks*. Trans. Charles Lam Markmann. New York: Grove, 1967.

Finkelhor, David. "How Widespread Is Child Sexual Abuse?" *Children Today* July-Aug. 1984: 27 pars. Online. Info Trac. Expanded Academic Backfile. A3328948. 30 Aug. 1997.

———. *Sexually Victimized Children*. New York: Free Press, 1979.

Finkelhor, David, et al. "Sexual Abuse in a National Survey of Adult Men and Women: Prevalence, Characteristics, and Risk Factors." *Child Abuse and Neglect* 14.1 (1990): 19–28.

Foucault, Michel. *The History of Sexuality*. Trans. Robert Hurley. Vol. 1. New York: Vintage, 1978.

———. "The Subject and Power." *Critical Inquiry* 8.4 (1982): 777–95.

Freud, Sigmund. "The Aetiology of Hysteria." *The Standard Edition of the Complete Psychological Works of Sigmund Freud*. Trans. and ed. James Strachey. Vol. 3. London: Hogarth, 1962. 189–221.

———. *The Complete Letters of Sigmund Freud to Wilhelm Fliess, 1887–1904*. Trans. and ed. Jeffrey Moussaieff Masson. Cambridge, Mass.: Harvard UP, 1985.

Froula, Christine. "The Daughter's Seduction: Sexual Violence and Literary History." *Daughters and Fathers*. Ed. Lynda E. Bosse and Betty S. Flowers. Baltimore: Johns Hopkins UP, 1989. 111–35.

Herman, Judith, with Lisa Hirschman. *Father-Daughter Incest*. Cambridge, Mass.: Harvard UP, 1981.

Jacobs, Janet Liebman. "Reassessing Mother Blame in Incest." *Signs* 15.3 (1990): 500–514.

———. "Victimized Daughters: Sexual Violence and the Empathic Female Self." *Signs* 19.1 (1993): 126–45.

Jagose, Annamarie. *Lesbian Utopics*. New York: Routledge, 1994.

Janmohamed, Abdul R. "The Economy of Manichean Allegory." *The Post-Colonial Studies Reader*. Ed. Bill Ashcroft, Gareth Griffith, and Helen Tiffin. New York: Routledge, 1995. 18–23.

Kenan, Randall. "Sorrow's Child." Rev. of *Bastard Out of Carolina,* by Dorothy Allison. *The Nation* 20 Dec. 1993: 815–16.

Lévi-Strauss, Claude. *The Elementary Structure of Kinship*. 1949. Trans. James Harle Bell, John Richard von Sturmer, and Rodney Needham. Ed. Rodney Needham. Rev. ed. Boston: Beacon, 1969.

Masson, Jeffrey Moussaieff. *The Assault on Truth: Freud's Suppression of the Seduction Theory*. New York: Farrar, Straus and Giroux, 1984.

Mauss, Marcel. "Essai sur le don: Forme et raison de l'echange dans les societes archaiques." *Annee Sociologique* n.s. 1 (1925): 30–186.

Miller, Alice. *For Your Own Good: Hidden Cruelty in Child-Rearing and the Roots of Violence*. Trans. Hildegarde Hannum and Hunter Hannum. New York: Farrar, Straus and Giroux, 1983.

Regen, Harriet Mauck. "Undoing the Damage: Dorothy Allison's Vision of Motherhood and Family." M.A. thesis. Radford U, 1996.

Reynolds, David. "White Trash in Your Face: The Literary Descent of Dorothy Allison." *Appalachian Journal* 20.4 (1993): 356–72.

Rich, Adrienne. *Of Woman Born: Motherhood as Experience and Institution*. 10th ed. New York: Norton, 1986.

Rubin, Gayle. "The Traffic in Women: Notes on the 'Political Economy' of Sex." *Toward an Anthropology of Women*. Ed. Rayna R. Reiter. New York: Monthly Review, 1975. 157–210.

Russell, Diana E.H. "The Incidence and Prevalence of Intrafamilial and Extrafamilial Sexual Abuse of Female Children." *Child Abuse and Neglect* 7.2 (1983): 133–46.

———. *The Secret Trauma: Incest in the Lives of Girls and Women*. New York: Basic, 1986.

Smith, Paul. *Discerning the Subject*. Minneapolis: U of Minnesota P, 1988.

Transcendence in the House of the Dead

The Subversive Gaze of A LESSON BEFORE DYING

John Lowe

> Under a government which imprisons any unjustly, the true place for a
> just man is also a prison.
>
> Henry David Thoreau

> The Hebrews produced the image of Job. Only the Greeks could have
> imagined Prometheus, but the Hebrews were more pitiless, and their hero
> more true to life.
>
> Antonio Gramsci

A Lesson Before Dying, a masterpiece many readers have yet to discover, concerns several stories, but all of them revolve around a black man awaiting his execution on death row, a burning metaphor of southern history that remains relevant today; unfortunately, this "scene of inscription" that inspired Gaines's narrative also speaks for America as a whole, in a postmodern age when more black men are in prison than in college. As a prosperous nation edges closer to an unthinkable apartheid, we would do well to ponder the significance of this narrative, its semiotics, and its relevance to the world we wish to shape in the new century.

One might miss these reverberations on a first reading; the story, after all, is set in 1948. The narrator, Grant Wiggins, teaches in a barely funded rural Louisiana school; he hates living there, hates teaching, and seems to hate his students. Although the story quickly moves beyond Grant to focus on the aforementioned prisoner, Jefferson, a parallel between their lives emerges quickly: both live imprisoned lives, one that seems hopeless (Grant), another that will inexorably—and quickly—lead to death (Jefferson).

I asked Ernest Gaines why he decided to set the book in 1948 rather than 1988, as he had originally planned: it had always seemed to me that he has never been interested in merely glossing history, but rather wants history to speak to our own time. He replied that the story had some dimensions in the earlier period it would not have had in 1988: that in our age, attorneys would fight some of the battles the book's characters have to wage on their own. Further, 1948 registers as a kind of annus mirabilus for Gaines personally, as he left Louisiana that year to live with his mother and stepfather in California, a move that he credits as a kind of salvation. Interestingly, a year or so before, a young man had bent sent to the electric chair twice because the chair had malfunctioned the first time. Gaines read about the story and became intrigued with the powerful icon of the portable electric chair that was used at the time. Finally, Gaines wanted the story to relate powerfully to the rural black schoolchildren of the time, who got to go to school for only five and a half to six months, in rather rudimentary conditions. Anyone familiar with Gaines's biography, or better, who has visited Cherie quarters in Oscar where Gaines grew up, knows that the building that serves as both church and school in *Lesson* is the very one Gaines attended himself, so the powerful pull of personal narrative must have directed him to relocate *Lesson* in the earlier time as well. Still, Gaines did agree that "the whole thing comes back to probably help us—I should hope so" (Lowe 307).

My own reading is that Gaines saw that setting the story in a period when racial feeling was far more virulent and exposed than it is now would uncover issues that have been muffled in our own age, despite the statistics that tell us that an old story continues in horrifying new fashion. Gaines agreed that the racial situation in America has not completely changed; he disclosed that the little powder-faced white woman who is rude to Grant when he picks up Jefferson's radio is based on a woman in New Roads, Louisiana, who turned away when Gaines asked her to recommend a coffee shop: "She looked at me and just turned away from me and spoke to Schlondorff [the director of the film of *A Gathering of Old Men*], who was standing aside. So it's the same sort of thing" (Lowe 310).

On another occasion, however, Gaines gave yet another reason for setting the story when he did, as he was intent on using his memories of bitter black schoolteachers. "Grant's a pretty angry person. All Grant wants to do is leave. We're talking about the forties, too, remember . . . all he could do as an educated black man was to teach . . . I suppose we have produced as many good teachers, percentage-wise, as anyone else has produced in this country, with much more feeling for their students. But many blacks who would have preferred some other position than just being a schoolteacher, may have been poor schoolteachers because they were forced—that was the only thing they could go into—they did it, but they hated it" (Lowe 308).

Gaines also said that Grant must spend as much time in the prison as in the schoolhouse, implying not only symmetry but overlap. This overlap has meaning today as well. I have already spoken about the appalling numbers of black men in the nation's prisons. As I write, the black underclass continues to grow, despite the nation's prosperity, and more children are going to bed hungry and poorly educated. Public schools continue to deteriorate and, indeed, in many ways could be thought of as virtual prisons. Newt Gingrich a few years ago extended the concept of institutions as storage bins for problems when he suggested a new building program of orphanages. Thus the embarrassing spectacle of the black underclass (the larger group of white poor conveniently gets left out of many discussions of poverty) is to be incarcerated, first in orphanages, then in substandard, dangerous, prisonlike schools, and then in prisons themselves. Surveillance, work, isolation, and punishment are hallmarks of all three "houses of correction." In *Discipline and Punish*, Michel Foucault lists a number of goals that prisons are supposed to accomplish and also accounts for the rationale behind them. As he notes, "How could the prison not be immediately accepted when, by locking up, retraining and rendering docile, it merely reproduces, with a little more emphasis, all the mechanisms that are to be found in the social body? The prison is like a rather disciplined barracks, *a strict school*, a dark workshop, but not qualitatively different. This double foundation—juridico-economic on the one hand, technico-disciplinary on the other—made the prison seem the most immediate and civilized form of all penalties" (233; emphasis added): especially, one might add, in a racist-capitalist society, where "civilization" all too often means confinement and concealment of the poor.

By listing Foucault's "prison goals" one sees this overlap between the "strict school" that Grant, working under white supervisors, runs and the prison: 1. "The first principle was isolation"—ranked rows/cells; silence in both. 2. Work (lessons, work around the schoolroom/prison work) is defined, with isolation, as an agent of carceral transformation; it is to instill the ideals of order and regularity and forces subjects to conform to a central and shaping power. Work is seen as the agent that takes the student/prisoner and transforms him or her into a machine. The student/prisoner is both "the cog and the product." For as Foucault asserts, "What then, is the use of penal labour? Not profit; nor even the formation of a useful skill; but the constitution of a power relation, an empty economic form, a schema of individual submission" (243). Where the school and prison differ is in the "modulation of the penalty," Foucault's third principle. The modern equivalent would be parole, which modifies the offender's original penalty because he has been deemed reformed and can be returned into society.

Grant, reflecting on his own harsh days in this same school under the cruel regime of the mulatto teacher Matthew Antoine, mourns his peers who were "released into society" after they had "served time" in a school that taught them they were worthless and doomed. "Bill, Jerry, Claudee, Smitty, Snowball—all the others. They had chopped wood here too; then they were gone. Gone to the fields, to the small towns, to the cities—where they died. There was always news coming back to the quarter about someone who had been killed or sent to prison for killing someone else" (62).

The affinity between Grant and Jefferson is signaled early on as we see how the white power structure regards Grant with deep suspicion; he has, after all, broken away from the circle of surveillance, and worse, during that time, has acquired an education, which is tacitly understood to mean mastery of techniques of resistance. As long as he can be confined, however, to the narrowly tolerated and barely nourished black school, a school necessarily inscribed within the black church (an institution, with its white God and "servants obey your masters" Bible, felt to be helpful for social control—at least up to the civil rights movement), Grant can be tolerated as a necessary evil; but his activities on behalf of Jefferson immediately arouse suspicion and resistance among the powers on the plantation and in the prison.

Despite these travails, Grant's life is made somewhat bearable through his affair with his fellow teacher Vivian Baptiste. Like Grant, she too feels entrapped by her circumstances; she dares not leave the area because of her angry estranged husband, who has threatened to take her children. Ironically, because Grant loves Vivian, it is chiefly she who keeps him in his "cage" at the school. Moreover, Grant in some ways still labors under the matriarchy: he lives with his Tante Lou, who is in her seventies. Miss Emma Glenn, Jefferson's godmother, also past seventy, is her best friend. The two old women, operating in tandem, use sheer force, will, and burning looks to get Grant to do their will, which is to make Jefferson walk to his death with dignity, rather than to wallow in fear and self-pity, like the "hog" the defense attorney says he is.

The defense attorney's statement to the jury attempts to build upon the prosecutor's assertion that Jefferson killed the old Cajun store owner, Gropé, drank, and stole the money, thereby proving "the kind of animal he really was" (6). According to the defense, Jefferson was merely in the wrong place at the wrong time: "Look at this—this—this boy. I almost said man, but I can't say man. Oh, sure, he has reached the age of twenty-one, when we, civilized men, consider the male species has reached manhood, but would you call this—this—this a man? No, not I. I would call it a boy and a fool. . . . No, gentlemen, this skull here holds no plans. What you see here is a thing that acts on command. A thing to hold the handle of a plow, a thing to load your bales of cotton. . . . What justice would there be to take this life? . . .

Why, I would just as soon put a hog in the electric chair as this" (8). What the defense attorney attempts to do here, of course, is employ metaphysical condensation. As Toni Morrison attests, "Collapsing persons into animals prevents human contact and exchange; equating speech with grunts or other animal sounds closes off the possibility of communication" (68). Additionally, as Herman Beavers has acutely noted, the defense attorney's strategy is to persuade the jury to read Jefferson anew, to view him with "new eyes" in a "new social gaze" (175).

The reference Jefferson's lawyer makes to the shape of his client's skull rehearses a long discourse derived from racist scientific treatises that still circulate about the supposed inferiority of African bodies and minds (*The Bell Curve* is only the most recent of these studies). Because this and other observations form a seamless argument of reduction and displacement, the implications of the defense attorney's speech reverberate throughout the rest of the novel. The transfer of personal pronouns into "it" and "this"; the reduction from man to boy and then further to fool finds a parallel in nature, that of "cornered animals," "Deepest jungle of darkest Africa," and finally, in a further reduction yet (for African animals may indeed by powerful and fear-inducing), to "hog," which is understood to also be a "thing." More important, perhaps, the sweeping configuration of white gazes, somewhat like a ring of white spotlights centering on the accused, initiate the thematic of discipline as centered on separation, categorization, surveillance, and control.

The white courtroom, however, has its counterforce in the presence of Miss Emma and Tante Lou, who are present but not described. In the next chapter, when they confront Grant with his mission, they are, however, and we are meant retrospectively to see them this way in the courtroom scene too: "They sat there like boulders, their bodies, their minds immovable" (15). The wash of white gazes, white words, has swirled about them and they have not been moved, and through their stoic and heroic power, they will an agent of transformation and resistance out of Grant, and interestingly, partly through a silent *black* gaze that has the power to command. The women's wisdom may further be seen in their shrewd manipulation of the white folk, whose help they need to reach Jefferson. They confine themselves to essentials: speaking to Pichot, Miss Emma says "The law got him, Mr. Henri . . . and they go'n kill him. But let them kill a man" (22). "The law got him" registers one way with Mr. Henri and another with us as readers. It has the same effect as what old black Molly Beauchamp tells Gavin Stephens about her imprisoned grandson in the story *Go Down, Moses*—"Pharaoh got him."

Miss Emma's replication of this speech and indeed the entire courtroom sequence becomes reduced to four words: "Called him a hog" (12). Her charge to Grant similarly employs economy: "I don't want them to kill no hog. . . . I want a man to go to that chair, on his own two feet. . . . You the teacher" (13).

Yet Grant is not accorded much respect for his ostensibly higher status by the white patriarch on the plantation. The prisonlike quarters is dominated, as it was during slavery, by the "big house," not accidentally the colloquial name in modern times for the prison. Henri Pichot, the contemporary version of "ole massa," lives in the gray antebellum manse and has no children. His long white hair, his general ineffectiveness, speaks to a Compson-like decline in the family. Still, he maintains strict control over the quarters and relies on informers to extend his gaze. The link between this center of surveillance and control with that of the jail is signified by the fact that Pichot's brother-in-law is the sheriff, Sam Guidry; his wife owes much to Miss Emma, who raised her, and this stereotypical but common situation becomes useful for Jefferson's cause.

Similarly, Grant uses the principle of strict surveillance in his classroom and has students act as his lieutenants when he is not present. In the quarters, hard by the big house, in the school, in the cell, the position of constantly being watched creates a disciplined and subjected person. Periodically, this position is reinforced through the device of the examination. *A Lesson* is punctuated regularly with such moments, many of them involving Grant, who must "pass" inspection from his white superiors; the interrogations he endures in Pichot's kitchen, in the sheriff's office, and during the white school inspector's visit offer ample evidence of the kind of "examination" all African Americans had to face in the pre–civil rights South. Perhaps the most vivid example of this may be seen in Richard Wright's unforgettable *Black Boy*, when Richard loses his job at the optical company through a rigged interrogation/examination he undergoes from his bigoted white co-workers.

Foucault calls such moments the ceremony of objectification: as such, it offers an opportunity for dominant culture to exercise its privilege in performance. In yet another variant of the examination, the school and prison, with endless documents and classifications for the students/inmates, "capture and fix" them. Particularly in the latter institution, written description of the inmate, which begins with the legal category of criminal he or she inhabits, places the person under a growing and increasingly restrictive written definition of personhood. As Foucault notes, this development in categorization radically restricted the possibilities of individuality, as one became grouped with others and described through the words and terms of the oppressor. "The chronicle of a man, the account of his life, his historiography, written as he lived out his life formed part of the rituals of his power. The disciplinary methods reversed this relation, lowered the threshold of describable individuality and made of this description a means of control and a method of domination" (191). Thus the brilliance of the device of Jefferson's death row diary, which inverts this method, restoring his individuality, voice, and also offering security, for the sheriff, knowing Jefferson is engaged in this activity, fears the journal's power, sensing it could be used to annul his own official record of his prisoner's identity and daily life in the cell.

The plantation house as site of "slave labor" may be seen in the fact that Miss Emma was the cook there for many years, and Grant had worked for the owners, too. The current yardman, Farrell Jarreau, is in his late fifties and has known Grant all his life; since the latter's university days, however, Farrell takes his hat off before him, and calls him Professor. The internally created hierarchy of the quarters increasingly is revealed as a mechanism for an alternative social sphere and as a strategy, therefore, of resistance. Since Grant clearly has been elevated within this realm already, he has virtually no choice but to be its champion in the community's campaign to infiltrate and then subvert the operations of the book's various "prisons."

The quarters/big house configuration echoes that of early factories, where huge walls were erected to maximize concentration of labor, to protect materials and tools, but above all, to control the labor force, which is accomplished through order and constant surveillance (Foucault 142). The labor force must be divided within this concentration, too: no large gatherings are to be encouraged, and each individual is to have his or her own space. It is a commonplace to speak of the black church as the major locus for communal gatherings, social organization, and site of resistance; Gaines underlines and deepens the point since the church, locus of Grant's school, is the only communal gathering place permitted on the quarters. Although it constricts him early on in the book, his acceptance of his mission there at the end, through the agency of Jefferson's transcendent and sacrificial death, transforms the concept of the school as individual straitjacket into dynamic center for communal unity, development, and revolution, the opposite of the individual cells in the prison.

The prison, similarly, must be transformed into a nurturing, communal space if Jefferson is to die with dignity and thereby unify, inspire, and instruct the children in particular and the people in general, in the quarters and in the larger black community. This seemingly impossible mission is accomplished gradually and somewhat magically by the narrative, as it inches forward from the initial gifts of home-cooked food to the final scene in the cell, where the schoolchildren visit Jefferson en masse with Grant. To make the transformation transcendent, the initial squalor must be established dramatically. As Grant enters the jail, so do we, seeing it through his eyes. He is coldly searched; then the prisoners extend their hands though the bars, asking for cigarettes or money. Grant sees repellent things: "a toilet without seat or toilet paper; a washbowl, brownish from residue and grim . . . barred window, which looked out onto a sycamore tree. . . . We were standing, because there was no place to sit" (72). Jefferson's brutalization is seen in his indifference: "don't matter . . . when they go'n do it?" but also in his crazed perception that Grant is the one "Go'n jeck that switch" (74).

More disturbing still is the manner in which Jefferson subsequently "performs" this script, actually making sounds like a hog and "rooting" at food on the floor to repel Grant. This self-loathing results from the assembled white gaze, first in the theater of the white courtroom and subsequently in the scornful watchfulness of the deputies. All these factors fill out our initial survey/surveillance of the penal space.

Gaston Bachelard's oft-cited *Poetics of Space* has little to offer this study in that he is concerned primarily with positive images of what he calls "felicitous space," hardly that of the prison, but we might gain some insight into Gaines's method by remembering some moments when Bachelard notes exceptions to his argument. He states that all really inhabited space creates in some way the idea of home. Clearly, a prison is meant to unmake the domestic, to isolate, disorient, to punish; Bachelard states: "An entire past comes to dwell in a new house. The old saying: 'We bring our *lares* with us' has many variations . . . after we are in the new house, when memories of other places we have lived in come back to us, we travel to the land of Motionless Childhood, motionless the way all immemorial things are. We comfort ourselves by reliving memories of protection" (6). These theories are contradicted in Jefferson's case, however, and not just because of the structure around him. The retreat into the identity of a "hog" is actually in keeping with the nature of his circumstances, for he is in a "pen" fattening up for the "kill," as a thing, a commodity on which society will "feed," in the classic sense of the scapegoat (indeed, a pig was often the sacrificial animal). Once the community infiltrates the prison walls, however, expressing their newfound love and admiration for Jefferson, he indeed does begin to reflect back over his past. But by contrast to Bachelard's paradigm, Jefferson has had a history of rejection and marginalization even *within* the black community—he has indeed brought his own *lares* with him, but they are negative and pain-inducing, and this is manifest in his final interview with Grant. He thanks his former teacher for showing him the way to die with dignity but also tells him, "Y'all axe a lot, Mr. Wiggins. . . . Who ever car'd my cross, Mr. Wiggins? My mama? My daddy? They dropped me when I wasn't nothing. Still don't know where they at . . . I went in the field when I was six, driving that old water cart. I done pulled that cotton sack, I done cut cane, load cane, swung that ax, chop ditch banks, since I was six. . . . Yes, I'm youman, Mr. Wiggins. But nobody didn't know that 'fore now. Cuss for nothing. Beat for nothing. Work for nothing.

Grinned to get by. Everybody thought that's how it was s'pose to be. You too, Mr. Wiggins. You never thought I was nothing else. I didn't neither" (224). These are hardly the "Motionless Childhood" memories Bachelard describes, but they are, nevertheless, memories that indeed humanize and strengthen Jefferson, as he sees the change in people's perceptions of him because of his situation, and he does indeed remember his Job-like childhood, which prefigures his Promethean present. Further, this is a devastating moment for Grant, for it damns his teaching up to his experience with Jefferson in a way even the scenes we have been privy to in his current schoolroom have not.

These dramatic events at the end of the book bring me to a consideration of the force of Antonio Gramsci's remarks that began this essay. For Gaines has enfolded in both Grant and Jefferson initial personifications of Job and subsequent transformations into Prometheus. Literacy is understood in this community, as it always was in the slave narratives, as the tool one needed for all the necessary tasks of the hero: education, empowerment, revolution, and finally, spiritual transcendence. The black teacher, constantly suspect in the white community because of his potential for insurrectionary leadership, always contains the potential for Promethean donation, but also for that figure's torments. Chained to the rock of the Jim Crow system in a rural hamlet, Grant is tormented daily by the endless and demeaning rituals and modes of white southern patriarchy, be it on the plantation, in the town, or, especially, in the prison. The bitterness he feels, however, becomes destructive to his mission; hating his life, he also hates his students. As he states to Miss Emma early on, "I teach what the white folks around here tell me to teach—reading, writing, and 'rithmetic. They never told me how to keep a black boy out of a liquor store" (13). As this passage indicates, his "fire" has become muffled, internalized, destructive; it is up to Jefferson, the "new Prometheus," although nearly illiterate, to demonstrate though his diary the power of language, self-expression, and communal forms of knowing and thereby to inspire Grant to redirect his passion into the truths that will empower his students.

I need not rehearse here the powerful role literacy has played in the quest for freedom and identity for all peoples, but particularly in classic texts of the African American experience. Frederick Douglass's first great moment of illumination comes when he realizes the power of literacy: "From that moment, I understood the pathway from slavery to freedom" (49). Again, freedom can mean many things; as Gaines told me, the diary was Jefferson's acceptance and expression of his humanity. Although I cannot do so here, it would be interesting to examine the long line of such scenes in African American literature, which lead, perhaps most famously in our own time before

Lesson, to the great transformation of Malcolm Little to Malcolm X via a prison library and the writings of Elijah Muhammad.

Literacy is no panacea, however; as Douglass himself stated, his growing knowledge of the depth of his degradation, acquired through reading, torments him: "The more I read, the more I was led to abhor and detest my enslaver . . . that very discontent which Master Hugh had predicted would follow my learning to read had already come, to torment and sting my soul to unutterable anguish. As I writhed under it, I would at times feel that learning to read had been a curse rather than a blessing . . . I envied my fellow-slaves for their stupidity. I have often wished myself a beast. . . . Any thing, no matter what, to get rid of thinking" (55). This passage from the nineteenth century helps us see the source of Grant's bitterness and Jefferson's willingness to become a "hog"—a beast—to escape the torment of contemplating his execution. Again, early on in the book, Jefferson thus represents Job, the man of sorrows; practicing literacy, however, Jefferson then becomes, initially at least, a suffering Prometheus, passing on the "torch" of the "book" to Grant, who in turn abandons his Job-like passivity, accepting his role as agent of cultural exchange, signed by his actual figurative transmission of the book/ "book" to his students.

All these stages, however—including those to follow after the book's conclusion—unfold under a baleful, often punitive, patriarchal gaze, in the actual prison and in the prison-seeming church/school; the latter is dramatized at one point through the visit of a white school official. Job/Promethean torment comes in the form of the patriarchal gaze. As Foucault has noted, the exercise of discipline requires a mechanism of surveillance, one that employs its methods of seeing simultaneously to create modes of power (170–71). This system must be understood in its significance by the observed, and Gaines's narrative makes it clear how the white power structure has built such a system on the plantation, in the town, and in the prison. All public spaces become, in effect, variations on the "prison" in their closely monitored and regulated dimensions.

Presumably, the ancient racial code of the South, constitutive of another community of the dominant and the oppressed, may be characterized in a similar fashion, as *A Lesson Before Dying* amply demonstrates, in its endless inventory of patriarchal, legal, penal, servile, and subversive gazes. It behooves us to think about this aspect of Gaines's "lesson," in that this gaze has become a regular, public feature of contemporary life. Virtually every evening our local news programs feature images of young black men spread-eagled against police cars, standing silently in a courtroom hearing a sentence pronounced, marching in ranks in prison yards. Karla Holloway has asked what the intent of such a camera is as it pans a child being taken in for a "voluntary" interview with the sheriff. She concludes: "There is no text for this event, only the image, which in the United States we have learned to file away as the public prejudices of our culture direct us to do. We create a file of anticipation that black youth, especially and specifically black male youth, fit a stereotype of criminal activity and generalized lawlessness. The camera's intent is to solidify the imagery and the expectation of a national text that criminalizes black youth. Consequently, it suppresses even the reporter's voice-over" (152). For me, such a scene is not just an image but a communal gaze, a gaze of surveillance, categorization, and locking away. The "voluntary" interview is part of a ritual of examination that all too often takes the form of a subtle and ritualistic torture. Because Gaines's novel, set in 1948, presents these issues unobscured by our contemporary modes of obfuscation, it helps us to read our present situation and helps us think twice about our seemingly passive look that is actually a participatory act of surveillance, judgment, and filing away of human beings.

And yet the gaze outward can bespeak defiance as well; on another occasion Gaines spoke about regrets people have about failure: "That moment when he took an insult and dropped his eyes, lowered his eyes. . . . If I could make up for that" (Lowe 271). As this essay will demonstrate, the gaze takes many forms in this novel; most involve the mechanism of power, which can be positive or harmful. As Gaines has stated: "There's also silence from a glance, a look gives as much meaning as a word or a line. It's when you've lived in that community and the community is very old—you don't have to speak a word. . . . You understand when these older women, whether they're black or white, look at you in a certain way or *don't* look at you in a certain way. . . . Grant slams that door hard when he's taking off to Pichot's house, and he gives a whole feeling, emotion just by not seeing his aunt look at him, but knowing that she's looking at him, and at what part of his body she's looking at the back of his head, the side of his face! . . . When you're part of the community, when there's even the slightest movement of the hand or a mere look, or *not* looking—it can mean so much" (Lowe 310–11).

As Grant and Jefferson renegotiate their relationship, Jefferson becomes armed against white interpretations of his being, learning to send his own gaze inward and outward; consequently, the cell becomes transformed: instead of "cell" of separation, confinement, punishment, it is opened up to become the scene of instruction. The relentless "gaze" of surveillance in this novel becomes transformed as well, into a sense of shame and revelation. The white men who come into Jefferson's cell shortly before the execution have made a bet that he will die terrified, debased. Their anxiety over the wager forces them to examine him in a new way—the gaze now becomes exploratory, not for sauciness, surliness, or outright insurrection but for hitherto unsuspected virtues. Ultimately, at least for the sheriff and Paul, the gaze leads to shame and revelation, total inversion of the penal surveyance.

It would be far too extreme to suggest such a total transformation in *A Lesson Before Dying's* white characters, but at least Paul—and perhaps the sheriff, too—have been the recipients of a deeply revelatory "lesson," taught by a lowly, virtually illiterate waterboy, one they doubtless continue to believe is a murderer and a thief. This, too, becomes part of the lesson, one that transcends race, for Gaines operates against the dictates of class as well, particularly in terms of the equation between stupidity and peasant. He everywhere demonstrates Gramsci's point, namely that "there is no human activity from which every form of intellectual participation can be excluded: *homo faber* cannot be separated from *homo sapiens*. Each man, finally, outside his professional activity, carries on some form of intellectual activity, that is, he is a 'philosopher,' an artist, a man of taste, he participates in a particular conception of the world, has a conscious line of moral conduct, and therefore contributes to sustain a conception of the world or to modify it, that is, to bring into being new modes of thought" (9).

This aspect of Jefferson's portrayal is certainly meant to combat its obverse, the relegation of prisoners to animals/objects. In Jerome Washington's prison stories, based on real experiences, a guard tells an inmate, "You're my hoss and I'm your boss." The text focuses on the prisoner later after years of physical and mental abuse: "Now he just wanders sort of aimlessly around the yard and sometimes he sits in the sun. Once in a while he mutters, 'I ain't nobody's hoss'" (qtd. in Franklin, *Prison Writing* xii). This attempt to transform a man into a beast, paralleling Jefferson's portrayal as a hog, has further ramifications. Hosses and hogs, as chattel, are "things," and we would do well to remember that the original subtitle of *Uncle Tom's Cabin* was "The Man Who Was a Thing." Similarly, Frederick Douglass, sent to the harsh disciplinary prison farm of Thomas Covey, a slave breaker, reports: "Mr. Covey succeeded in breaking me. I was broken in body, soul, and spirit. My natural elasticity was crushed, my intellect languished, the disposition to read departed, the cheerful spark that lingered about my eye died; the dark night of slavery closed in upon me; and behold a man transformed into a brute." Later, however, before describing how he rallied and in fact fought and defeated Covey, Douglass tells us, "You have seen how a man was made into a slave; you shall see how a slave was made into a man" (75, 77). We might note here Paulo Friere's classic formulation that the oppressed must find life-affirming humanization not just in having more food but by ceasing to be "things," by fighting as men. "This is a radical requirement. They cannot enter the struggle as objects in order *later* to become men." How is this to be accomplished? For Friere, only through a humanizing pedagogy in which the leaders set up a continuing dialogue with the oppressed. The method of instruction must express the consciousness of the students themselves (55–56). This eventuates in Friere's teaching of a pedagogy designed to lead to the *mutual humanization* of the teacher and the student. The relation becomes one of partners, and in fact, this is precisely the evolution of Grant's relation to Jefferson. By the end of the novel, Grant has helped Jefferson transcend the limits of the cell and his terrorized soul, but in a kind of symbiosis, Jefferson has transcended Grant's model to become a true hero, "the one" who can take on "the cross" for the community. Indeed, in his last interview with Jefferson in the cell, Grant refers to him as his "partner" (219). When I was discussing this relationship with Gaines, he told me his intention for the diary: "I thought that the diary would elevate it. . . . I needed something to get into Jefferson's mind, to show you who this was, and what was going to happen. Who this simple little waterboy, or cottonpicker, or whatever he was, was; it had to be clear he was the savior of Grant, so Grant could save the children" (Lowe 301).

The tension in the book comes from many sources, but one of the most structurally important ones is Grant's Jonah-like unwillingness to "go in(to) the belly of the beast," to use famous prison writer Jack Henry Abbot's terminology, and at least part of his animus, we later feel, is in his initial scorn for Jefferson. This is somewhat obscured at the beginning of Grant's sequence of visits to the jail, however, by various demeaning encounters he has with authority figures in both the white and black communities. Although Jefferson has real walls pressing in on him, Grant has metaphysical walls that seem to menace him more each day. His classroom, situated in the hamlet's church, in many ways is perceived by him as prison/torture chamber, thus paralleling Jefferson's realm. Ironically, however, although Grant feels himself an inmate, as teacher/authority figure who hates his students, he becomes a replication of the white master, even inflicting physical punishment along with psychologically wounding sarcasm. The thematic of surveillance finds expression in his own stance but then is inverted when a white supervisor comes to inspect the school. Although the scene in some ways offers comic technique, on a deeper level it disturbingly replicates slave-day practices, as Grant indicates: as the superintendent, Dr. Joseph Morgan, inspects the students' teeth, "he would have the poor children spreading out their lips as far as they could while he peered into their mouths. At the university I had read about slave masters who had done the same when buying new slaves, and I had heard of cattlemen doing it when purchasing horses and cattle" (56).

Grant always has, however, a negative example in his own race to keep him from "running"; this is his old teacher Matthew Antoine, who had predicted that most of his male students would "die violently, and those who did not would be brought down to the level of beasts. . . . He hated himself for the mixture of his blood [he is mulatto] and the cowardice of his being, and he hated us for daily reminding him of it" (62). One of the things that Antoine clearly does *not* impart to his students emerges from Jefferson's diary: namely, the potential of language and writing for developing not only a sense of identity and discovery but also of uniqueness and worth. Gaines once told me a story about a conversation he had with two clerks in a hardware store in Lafayette, where he teaches. One, who recognized him, introduced him to the other as an important writer. The second clerk, a young African American, responded, "If he's so important, what's he doing here?" For Gaines, this indicated that she saw herself as not important and the university there as not important. "What I'm always trying to do is show how this place and these people *are* important. They may think they're insignificant, but the great stories have been written about people who constantly question their significance. . . . I've always been an admirer of writers . . . who pick up people who seem insignificant and look at their essence" (Lowe 299).

To understand this concept, which leads to the "expansion" of Jefferson's cell, we need to peruse one of the novel's key early scenes, which takes place in Pichot's kitchen. Grant, Miss Emma, and Tante Lou, who seek permission to visit Jefferson, are kept waiting there for hours while the white folks eat. When the stuffed white men saunter in to discuss whether Grant can visit Jefferson, their gazes dictate the performance of an old script. None of the blacks are asked to sit. At one point Grant knows he's in trouble for using "doesn't" instead of "don't" and recognizes a trap when the sheriff asks who's right about letting him see Jefferson, he (the sheriff) or his wife, Pichot's sister. When Grant, Solomon-like, replies, "I make it a habit never to get into family business, Mr. Guidry," the sheriff responds, "You're smart . . . maybe you're just a little too smart for your own good" (49). These scenes in the kitchen are in effect *torture* scenes, the site of interrogation, and as such find their parallel at the jail when Grant is played with by the white jailers. Throughout the novel, the white gaze is meant to be corrective as well. When Grant slips up and asks for Paul at the jail, rather than "Mr. Paul," he is immediately corrected: "He stood there eyeing me until he felt that I understood" (188).

Grant provides us with a summary of past events set in Pichot's kitchen and links them to the events he must endure at the jail: "Everything you sent me to school for, you're stripping me of it . . . the humiliation I had to go through, going into that man's kitchen. The hours I had to wait while they ate and drank and socialized before they would even see me. Now going up to that jail. To watch them put their dirty hands on that food. To search my body each time as if I'm some kind of common criminal. Maybe today they'll want to look into my mouth, or my nostrils, or make me strip. Anything to humiliate me" (79). This complex union of kitchen, food, jail, and torture requires unpacking. Regarding the kitchen, Elaine Scarry has noted that "the unmaking of civilization inevitably requires a return to and mutilation of the domestic, the ground of all making" (45). Richard Wright, William Faulkner, and many other writers have played on this thematic by placing horrific scenes of torment in kitchens. The "unmaking" of the black world can find an antidote only in formulas for "remaking," and thus the importance of the food lines from the old black women's kitchens to the jail cells, and not just that of Jefferson. By the end of the novel, when the community visits Jefferson en masse and shares a meal with him, the jail cell has become domesticated, inverted, transformed. Further, we should remember that this is one of many adjoining cells, and the regeneration of one could perhaps in biological symbolism lead to that of many. The visits to the jail take on a new quality after Miss Emma decides not to go. Grant resists again, objecting that Jefferson's "no kin," echoing Cain's cry, "am I my brother's keeper," but also denying the communal in favor of his wounded individuality. By contrast, Grant inadvertently, through his sarcastic humor, shows us the opposite of this approach by observing that the bag of food that Miss Emma sends in her stead: "There was enough to feed everybody in the jail" (79). This reference suggests how what Grant represents—literacy, the community, African American culture—could indeed, like Christ's loaves and fishes, feed the multitudes.

Regarding the significations on torture, the system of reference becomes more complexly entangled with variants of the "gaze," when Grant finds Miss Emma, Tante Lou, and the elderly Reverend Ambrose waiting for him in his aunt's kitchen. "'Folks been sitting here hours, waiting for you.' . . . She looked at me the way an inquisitor must have glared at his poor victims. The only reason she didn't put me on the rack was that she didn't have one" (98–99). Later, during a church service, Grant hears the songs from the church, which, we remember, is also the constricting schoolhouse. Miss Eloise's Termination Song, "Were You There When They Crucified My Lord?," which he has heard all his life, is like torture, and he knows others will take it up and go on for hours: "It was impossible to do anything but listen to it or leave" (102).

The torture motif finds extension when the three old women arrive in the kitchen to find Vivian there: "they were not glad to know her" (112) because she is a light-skinned denizen of Free LaCove. Grant's aunt gives Vivian a real grilling, says she's heard folks there don't like dark people, inquires about her religion; because her own color-struck relatives have played out this scene against her dark estranged husband and have scorned her own dark children, Vivian murmurs, "Well, I see that mine are not the only ones" [who have color bias] (115) .

The thematic of torture expands further when Jefferson finally begins some bitter exchanges with Grant in the cell. He accuses him of "vexing" him and makes disparaging remarks about Vivian. Grant's interrogations by the sheriff and the deputies continue relentlessly, and it becomes plain that he, too, has been under surveillance when in Jefferson's cell: "I know you haven't done a thing yet. Boys on the block tell me . . . I doubt if you ever will" (134).

These remarks are inspired by the debate over whether to grant the old women's request to let them have a meal with Jefferson in the dayroom rather than in his cell, a message they submit indirectly through the sheriff's wife, pressuring her with their long record of service to the family. The sheriff, who comically can't deal with "women . . . always coming up with something new," nevertheless intones with menace, "This ain't no school, and it ain't no picnic ground" (134). These remarks, however, prepare us for the transformation of the prison, for it indeed *is* a school, a scene of instruction, and it becomes a "picnic ground" as eventually the entire community sends representatives to communal meals with Jefferson. The traditional picnic ground for rural African Americans has been the area around the church, which in this book is also the school, so the telescoping/transforming of space accomplished in the novel's complex symbolism melds prison/school/church, collapsing metaphysical walls of separation, thereby annihilating the key mission of penal incarceration. Moreover, Grant's interrogation by the sheriff on this point takes place in the presence of the same group of white men who were in Pichot's kitchen in the earlier scene, thereby pulling the spaces in closer configuration through repetition of both cast and suggestions of inspection, interrogation, humiliation, in short, of torture.

Religion's greatest scene of torture, of course, is Calvary, and Gaines employs several Christic references as the novel builds to a powerful climax. The children at the school are preparing a Christmas pageant, and Jefferson remarks, "It's Christmas? . . . That's when He was born, or that's when He died? . . . That's right . . . Easter when they nailed Him to the cross. And He never said a mumbling word" (138–39). This exchange, however, links his looming execution with the school pageant, which is described in loving detail. Here the constriction of Grant's cruel classroom becomes utterly transformed with the help of sheets, cheap decorations, makeshift costumes. Gaines/ Grant carefully names all those who are there, giving them individuality and warmth. The ensuing writing seems truly masterful. Grant, ever critical, mocks the humble pageant, yet the wealth of detail he gives makes us admire the scene despite the attitude of our narrator. The scene culminates in Grant's failure to see the deep comfort that the community receives from repetitive forms of behavior: "I was not happy. I had heard the same carols all my life, seen the same little play, with the same mistakes in grammar. The minister had offered the same prayer . . . same old clothes. . . . Next year it would be the same, and the year after . . . where were they changing? I looked back at the people. . . . I was not with them. I stood alone" (151).

Grant's association with Jefferson as a man locked into his own world of individual pain without thought of others is brought forward powerfully through Reverend Ambrose's prayer: "He asked God to visit the jail cells all over the land and especially in Bayonne. . . . No matter how educated a man was (he meant me, though he didn't call my name), he, too, was locked in a cold, dark cell of ignorance if he did not know God in the pardon of his sins" (146). The original scene of instruction (the school), here serving as a church, yet still a school, again becomes enfolded with the space of the cell through Reverend Ambrose's simple sermon, which also makes the point of the soul as a constrictive cell.

The key revelation in the novel comes after the community receives news of the date fixed for Jefferson's execution. As Grant tells Vivian: "I don't know if Miss Emma ever had anybody in her past that she could be proud of . . . but she wants that now, and she wants it from him. . . . What she wants is for him, Jefferson, and me to change everything that has been going on for three hundred years. She wants it to happen so in case she ever gets out of her bed again, she can go to that little church there in the quarter and say proudly, 'You see, I told you—I told you he was a man'" (166–67).

Jefferson's slow ascent from his despair into "standing" is partially gauged by his ability to joke and by his request for a radio. As Gaines has stated elsewhere, once a character becomes more human, she or he becomes more humorous. The fact that the community of "sinners"—mostly folk from the jook where Grant and Vivian go to have a quiet beer—takes up a collection for it brings another part of the broader community into configuration with Jefferson. Although Gaines does not develop music's role in Jefferson's awakening identity as fully as he might, we should remember that the diary he eventually composes, his legacy to the children and the community, had a powerful counterpart historically in the magnificent blues songs that grew out of the African American prison population. "Penal Farm Blues," "My Home Is a Prison," and "'lectric Chair Blues" are some of those titles (Franklin, *Prison Writing* 7).

Jefferson's final conversion, which leads to his diary, comes in a powerful scene that summons forth Grant's most eloquent rhetorical effects. With Reverend Ambrose and the two old women, Grant comes to the dayroom to share a gumbo. When Jefferson refuses to eat, Grant walks him around the room privately, tells him what a hero is, and reveals that he, Jefferson, is Grant's hero, that by standing and dying with dignity he can give direction to him; he can, in fact, revitalize myth for the entire community. The spatial expansion of the cell, the mobility, the circling around the vital center of communal life symbolized by the Reverend, the two devout matriarchs and the steaming bowl of gumbo (profoundly Afrocentric, but also French/Creole in origin, and yet embraced by all in this culture) configure the scene as epiphanic, as does the language employed. Jefferson's tears, however, are his only response before he joins the others at the table and eats. There are several levels of reference here, typologically. In a sense, Grant is the John the Baptist to Jefferson, the savior. In this baptism of inspiring words and communal gumbo, Jefferson not only rejoins the community but finds the nourishment he needs to stand and walk. Significantly, his silence here sets the stage for the incandescent revelation of his diary, which is prefigured in his last interview in the cell with Grant.

That diary in *all* its implications lies outside the scope of this essay. But some aspects deserve mention here. First, it must be reckoned as one of the most powerful pieces of writing in American literature, on a par with the "whiteness of the whale" chapter in *Moby-Dick*, or Beloved's communal memory of the Middle Passage. Everything in the novel leads up to it; everything after is really "amen." Writing the diary gives Jefferson a way of consolidating the memories that the visits of the community have inspired in him with his resultant new conceptions of himself, now that he knows he is part of a culture, indeed a kind of keystone—albeit perhaps a temporary one—of that culture. Writing himself also gives him a measure of security in his final days, for the sheriff, fearful that he will indict him for prior harsh treatment, waxes solicitous, his gaze no longer baleful but actually apprehensive.

Appropriately, after the revelation of the diary, Gaines takes the narrative in some ways away from Grant and lets many other characters—some of them new to the tale but all part of the community—describe the day of the execution. The sequence of writing focuses on their views—their gaze—at the electric chair. White people, black people react in varying ways, some with nervous jokes, others with feigned sarcasm, but many with fascinated horror. One of the jokes follows the ancient tradition of gallows humor: "A man said it did look gruesome, and that's why they called it Gruesome Gerty. The man told the woman that whoever sat in Gruesome Gerty's lap when she was hot never sat down again" (241).

The actual execution, modeled on the historic story of the traveling electric chair I referred to earlier, takes place in the basement of the courthouse. Faulkner once described his fictional Yoknapatawpha County courthouse as "above all, the courthouse: the center, the focus, the hub, sitting looming in the center of the county's circumference like a single cloud . . . musing, brooding, symbolic and ponderable, tall as cloud, solid as rock, dominating all: protector of the weak, judiciate and curb of the passions and lusts, repository and guardian of the aspirations and hopes" (35). By locating the execution in the basement, Gaines indicates the sorry true foundation of white law, which inverts Faulkner's values into a compendium of oppression, a spectacle of raw power, with the chair a magnet for the public gaze and a source of diverse reactions reminiscent of the doubloon chapter in *Moby-Dick*.

The dual endings of the book—the end of Jefferson's diary, the end of Grant's narration—are parallel in their settings, which express both men's release from the prison of self. The diary ends with Jefferson spiritually leaving his cell through his appreciation of the dawning day: "I jus wash my face/ day breakin/sun comin up/the bird in the tre soun like a blu bird/sky blu blu mr wigin/good by mr wigin tell them im strong tell them im a man good by mr wigin im gon ax paul if he can bring you this/sincely jefferson" (234). Similarly, when Jefferson's moment of execution is imminent, Grant has his pupils kneel, but he cannot stay in the restricted space of the church/school with them—he wanders outdoors, oblivious to all until a flitting yellow and black butterfly lights on a grassy hill and makes Grant aware of the vista; somehow this event, where space opens up for Grant, coincides with his knowledge that Jefferson has just died. He stands (always a significant verb in Gaines), stretches, and notices "the river, so tranquil, its water as blue as the sky," images, as in Jefferson's reverie, of purity and immensity (252).

This scene is soon followed by Paul's arrival to give Grant the diary. The former plays a key role in the novel, for he is a source of information for Grant and us regarding Jefferson's daily life. As Foucault states, the life of the prisoner is strictly regulated, in every way. Paul describes the times and types of meals prisoners eat, the allotted time in the dayroom, one shower a week, haircuts, and so on. But Paul's own "conversion" also contributes to the mildly hopeful tone of the final section.

In a moving sequence, Paul "testifies" as a "witness" to Jefferson's heroic courage. Truly, Paul Bonin—Paul the good—has been transformed, too, expressing not only his wish to be Grant's friend but also his willingness to return some day and testify to the children as well. Interestingly, another famous prisoner, Malcolm X, remembers how he read, over and over, while in prison, how Paul on the road to Damascus, upon hearing the voice of Christ, was so smitten that he was knocked off his horse, in a daze. "I do not now, and I did not then, liken myself to Paul. But I do understand his experience . . . truth can be quickly received, or received at all, only by the sinner who knows and admits that he is guilty of having sinned much. Stated another way: only guilt admitted accepts truth" (163). The biblical Paul, née Saul, was of course a tax collector—a hated public official—and found redemption, leading to his role as the principal evangelist of Christ's doctrine. Gaines himself comments on his Paul, stating that at the novel's end, he "has been changed, and he is going to make some points—at least I hope so" (Lowe 307).

A final word on the diary: Christ was originally remembered, according to legend, not by the Gospels, which were still oral, but by his shroud, a "text" that continues to have meaning for pilgrims to Turin. African American culture has been an oral culture for much of its history, and Gaines easily could have had Jefferson deliver a noble piece of oratory rather than his halting diary—certainly this is what Wright did in *Native Son*, after taking Bigger off the stage for pages in favor of the platitudes of his white lawyer, Max.

Gaines, however, has said that Jefferson was virtually incapable of expressing his inner thoughts in speech—"oh, he gave Grant some answers—those answers were from him, yes, but they were not his way of speaking all of his true self, and he could do that when he was alone" (Lowe 301), that is, writing the diary. But we must also remember, as Walter Ong remarks, that "an oration might be as substantial and lengthy as a major narrative, or a part of a narrative that would be delivered at one sitting, but an oration is not durable: it is not normally repeated. It addresses itself to a particular situation and, in the total absence of writing, disappears from the human scene for good with the situation itself" (141).

The first sentence of *A Lesson Before Dying* reads, "I was not there, yet I was there." Grant is telling us he was not there when Jefferson's sentence was pronounced, but the sentence aptly speaks as well to the community's relation to Jefferson throughout. They were not there when fate involved him in a criminal script that is interpreted wrongly and against him; they were not there in the cell with him, yet all of them identify with him in his position as pariah and scapegoat. As Etheridge Knight says in his magnificent poem "The Idea of Ancestry," as he peruses the photos of his family pasted on the walls of his prison cell, "I am all of them, they are all of me, I am me, they are thee, and I have no sons to float in the space between." It is Ernest Gaines's achievement to illustrate this principle in the amplitude of prose, as Jefferson's importance to the community emerges in a way that it never did in his unconfined state. The poetry of his heroism unites the community, inspires an act of resistance, and lifts their hearts. Surely the same is true for all readers of this deeply moving novel, who leave it knowing "they are all of them, they are all of me." This book is a hymn to the indomitable spirit of man and a simultaneous indictment of man's paradoxical lust for power and cruelty. More particularly, however, it concerns the African American community's changing same, its ability to fashion dignity and even glory out of debased circumstances, inhumane treatment, and the constrictions of every kind of confinement, prisons of the body and the spirit alike. Gaines has stated, and this book illustrates, that "this is the responsibility of man; taking responsibility for the whole, all humanity, is what I think manliness is. It seems that too many of the whites are afraid to take that kind of responsibility, and so many of the blacks have been denied that kind of responsibility, and refuse to accept it because of their long denial. I hope I'm not only speaking for blacks; you use the tools that you have, and because I am African American and most of my characters are, I put the situation there. But I could do the same with white characters" (Lowe 321). Jefferson truly is, as he says, "youman," as he faces death; he is ours, he is "you," he is "man." In unfolding these parables, *A Lesson Before Dying* becomes a deeply instructive book for the ages to come, in its indelible presentation of the resilience of man's spirit.

Works Cited

Bachelard, Gaston. *The Poetics of Space*. New York: Beacon, 1994.

Beavers, Herman. *Wrestling Angels into Song: The Fictions of Ernest J. Gaines and James Alan McPherson*. Philadelphia: U of Pennsylvania P, 1995.

Douglass, Frederick. *The Narrative of Frederick Douglass, An American Slave*. 1845. New York: Signet, 1968.

Faulkner, William. *Requiem for a Nun*. 1951. New York: Vintage, 1975.

Foucault, Michel. *Discipline and Punish: The Birth of the Prison*. Trans. Alan Sheridan. New York: Pantheon, 1977.

Franklin, H. Bruce. *Prison Literature in America: The Victim as Criminal and Artist*. Expanded ed. New York: Oxford UP, 1989.

———, ed. *Prison Writing in 20th-Century America*. New York: Penguin, 1998.

Friere, Paulo. *Pedagogy of the Oppressed*. Trans. Myra Bergman Ramos. New York: Continuum, 1983.

Gaines, Ernest J. *A Lesson Before Dying*. New York: Vintage, 1994.

Gramsci, Antonio. *The Prison Notebooks*. Ed. and trans. Quintin Hoare and Geoffrey Nowell Smith. New York: International Publishers, 1971.

Holloway, Karla. *Codes of Conduct: Race, Ethics, and the Color of Our Character*. New Brunswick: Rutgers UP, 1995.

Knight, Etheridge. "The Idea of Ancestry." *The Norton Anthology of African American Literature*. Ed. Henry Louis Gates Jr., Nellie Y. McKay, et al. New York: Norton, 1997. 1867–68.

Lowe, John, ed. *Conversations with Ernest Gaines*. Jackson: UP of Mississippi, 1995.

Morrison, Toni. *Playing in the Dark: Whiteness and the Literary Imagination*. Cambridge, Mass.: Harvard UP, 1992.

Ong, Walter. *Orality and Literacy: The Technologizing of the Word*. London: Methuen, 1982.

Scarry, Elaine. *The Body in Pain: The Making and Unmaking of the World*. New York: Oxford UP, 1985.

X, Malcolm. *The Autobiography of Malcolm X*. Told to Alex Haley. 1964. New York: Ballantine, 1973.

Walker Percy's Lancelot Lamar

Defending the Hollow Core

Julius Raper

One of the faults from the great catalogue of complaints Lancelot Lamar in Walker Percy's 1977 novel *Lancelot* lodges against modern culture in general and the contemporary South in particular is that the age lacks a sense of evil as a "living malignant force" for which "no explanation" exists (52). In so doing, Lancelot, wittingly or not, places himself in distinguished southern company, for an insistence on the way evil or sin marks southern identity threads through influential statements about the region from *I'll Take My Stand: The South and the Agrarian Tradition, by Twelve Southerners*[1] to *The Burden of Southern History*, C. Vann Woodward's 1961 collection of essays that rank guilt with defeat and localism as traits distinguishing the region's culture. The present essay argues, however, that Lancelot's statement about evil is a central strand in the rope that Percy gives his unreliable narrator to hang himself and that the novel itself forgoes whatever benefits one derives from embracing the metaphysical view of evil in favor of greater goods to be gained from explaining, to whatever degree possible, the specific evils that Lamar himself commits.

Having established Lamar's chief marring to date of the order of things, such as it is, in the opening reference to the fire at Belle Isle and to the accompanying deaths (50), the author allows his protagonist to fill the novel with reasons for his acts of rage and to map the revolution, crusade even, he plots as his future. There can be no doubt that Lamar sees his murders in the tradition of creative violence, though he traces that tradition well beyond Richard Wright and Jean-Paul Sartre, back to acts of violence that include the rebellion of the American Confederacy, the revolt carried out in the 1770s by the original federation of American states, the protests of the Reformation, as well as to the much older medieval crusades that European Christian kingdoms conducted against the Muslim powers, a tradition of violence that continues at present among Lancelot's less-reputable "cousins," the hermit survivalists and militiamen who still inspire headlines. Although Percy gives Lamar free rein to provide motives for the events through which he first achieves a new sense of himself and allows him to project his creation of a new culture, many critics agree that his self-justifications belong to the dramatic ironies of the novel.[2] Consequently, rather than offering sufficient justifications, his explanations extend the southern tradition of evasive idealism and high-minded violence that our writers since Mark Twain and Ellen Glasgow have identified as central to southern ways of thinking.

Only by constantly reading between Lamar's lines to double- and triple-think his account do we arrive at truer motives for his deeds, including a way, not of explaining away evil (as Robert Coles following Lamar feared [Coles 227–28]) but of comprehending it. The goal here is to understand Lamar's excesses without resorting to the fatalistic alibi that posits an absolute metaphysical "Iago" whose powers this contemporary Othello proves impotent to resist and whose existence—desperate faith indeed—would somehow prove the existence of Go(o)d—as though shadow creates light as surely as light (or idealism, especially evasive idealism) creates shadow.

Second-guessing Lamar has become a booster industry of southern studies, as well it should be. For Percy has deliberately suppressed the presence of the psychiatrist-priest known now as Father John—a.k.a. Harry Hotspur, Prince Hal, Northumberland, Percival, Parsifal, and Pussy (9–10)—so completely that, given Lamar's breaks from reality, we cannot be sure Father John, in truth, is there. In fact, whereas other characters, excepting Lamar, speak in quotation marks, the presence called Father John speaks, when compulsive Lamar finally gives him room to talk at all, in italics, a type style we generally associate, at least in southern fiction since Faulkner (if not in Western culture since Freud's *The Interpretation of Dreams*), with a shift to another level of personal consciousness.

To insist on John/Percival's reality is an unnecessary and desperate act, it seems, since he is chiefly an Iserian gap or blank in the novel, an obvious invitation to participate with the author in creating a brilliant reader-active text that, given the passion and range of responses to its episodes, is finally the novel that individual readers have enough insight and imagination to create. The strategy of the fiction finally resembles that of an unfinished dialectical process, one in which Lamar presents himself as the antithesis refuting the thesis of postmodern southern culture. The clash between antithesis and thesis generates a not-yet-visible new synthesis that must be supplied by a not-quite-visible John/Percival, a.k.a. the reader, who is addressed from the first words, "Come into my cell" (3).

Aside from the limited actions, including personal transformations, that Lamar *imputes* to Father John and that a number of critics including John Edward Hardy have catalogued (173–74), John/Percival remains largely a reader's invention. His status, therefore, resembles that which other individuals assume in one's dreams or in therapy sessions: the entity who appears in such contexts refers to a factual being, but his or her representation *in* the dream or session is what vitally matters. The entity therefore is a selfobject, one both self and other. In relation to *Lancelot*, John/Percival exists as a selfobject first in Lamar's reverie and second in the significance assigned him by readers of the novel. Often the latter John/Percival greatly overshadows the former, for when critics, from Robert Coles in 1978 to the contribution in 1996 by Lewis A. Lawson, write about *Lancelot* they tend, in the language of Lawson's own confession, to grow a bit obsessive (ix) and to write with a charge of energy that generates a type of (often helpful) criticism bordering on free associations. This variable response seems to have been what Percy desired by leaving the elements of the book in so volatile dramatic a state, rather like the best of Hemingway in some short stories or *The Sun Also Rises*.

In the dramatic ironies thus created, Percy has corrected the excessively didactic quality of his earlier novels, especially *Love in the Ruins*. Eliminating statements of final intent, chiefly by leaving John/Percival in his shadowy state, inasmuch as it leaves blanks allowing the reader to enter the story, creates a free space in which the author may, as Coles believes Percy desired, find out "what others believe" (229). That is the way Percy's dialectic works here: first to identify a cultural crisis of some urgency, though not as dire as Lamar makes it out to be; next to put forth Lamar's apocalyptic and therefore unconvincing solution; and finally to offer in the sketchiest way possible a synthesizing alternative, chiefly Father John's modest mode of preaching, communion, and forgiveness that Lamar seems to scorn for its smallness of ambition even as he imputes it to John (256).

In their eagerness to fill in Father John and other dramatic gaps that Percy leaves in his treatment of Lamar's grand scheme, critics have touched effectively on almost every element of the novel, certainly on those that interest me here, chiefly Lamar's violence, narcissism, grandiosity, shame, and early family life. What remains unclear, however, is, in Hardy's words, the "chronology of the development, or disintegration, of [Lamar's] mental life," and that is the gap this essay seeks to fill. Hardy chiefly has in mind Lamar's disintegration in the recent past, which begins with his discovery that Siobhan is not his biological daughter, but Hardy concedes that the process, including Lamar's metaphysical speculations and his identification with Lancelot du Lac, may have been "well advanced *before* he blew up the house" (155).

Although Percy's drama focuses on events in the recent past, the author draws on his own psychiatric interests beginning at the time he was a medical student (Allen xviii) to provide a background that includes key moments in Lamar's psychological development. Dividing that process into phases, we can turn to Lawson for a view of Lamar's final crusade as his schizophrenic "delusion of grandeur" (222), to Hardy for a sense of Lamar's aristocratic arrogance and family embarrassment (149–56), and to Allen for a portrait of the protagonist's oedipal conflicts (118–25). What we seek is a vision that brings these stages of disintegration together as an ongoing process, one in which we can comprehend other dimensions of Lamar's life, including elements that remain outside the explanatory power that these approaches taken separately possess.

To do so, we can build on a suggestion in *Violence: Our Deadly Epidemic and Its Causes*, published in 1996; this study is the psychiatrist James Gilligan's moving plea that we cease regarding our too common episodes of violence as "morality plays" separating the good individuals from the evil, or as "dramas of pathos" focused on victims of certain forces over which no human has control. We would do better, Gilligan argues, to view them the way we do the struggles of Captain Ahab or Joe Christmas, to take them as tragedies not only of the victims but for the victimizers. This change in focus would permit us not to exonerate felons in our prisons, and Lancelot Lamar is a felon, but to begin to understand the *causes* of their violence; such knowledge would, in turn, bring changes that could enable us to survive a disease that, given modern weaponry, could destroy us not only in families, or across regions like the South, but around the globe (6–9, 24, 30). Gilligan views contemporary violence as a contagion that spreads not through microorganisms but through teaching by example, a process beginning in the family and continuing in the schools, in the legal and political systems, and in various other instruments of socialization (272–73, note 12).

While Gilligan arrives at his impassioned position through his years of working with the criminally insane, his approach dovetails with the metapsychology I use in this essay, that borrowed from Heinz Kohut's Self Psychology. Whereas Kohut speaks of deficits caused by distant or intrusive parents, our primary selfobjects, Gilligan cites numerous examples of parental rejection, abandonment, assault, insult, humiliation, and other abuses leading to a feeling of inner numbness, deadness, emptiness, insufficient self-love, various emotional pains that felons in prison report they have tried to vanquish with acts of rape, murder, and self-mutilation (39, 45, 48). Gilligan characterizes such destructive parental behaviors as "soul *murder*," but both Kohut and he speak often of *shame*. The two concepts, murder and shame, converge in Gilligan's use of the double-edged word "mort-ification" (43, 49). Kohut, in asserting that *oedipal* pathology may have an underlying *self*-pathology of depression and narcissistic rage (*How* 5), concurs, we may assume, with Gilligan's reminder that Oedipus, long before he murdered his father and incested his mother, suffered the severe abuse of having a stake driven through his foot and of surviving parental abandonment on a hill where he was expected to die (Gilligan 50). With Kohut and Gilligan joined, we have at our disposal a persuasive approach that possesses sufficient explanatory powers to integrate the various scenarios Percy uses in creating Lamar's life story.

Percy does not give much evidence that Lamar as a child experienced physical violence from his parents, but he takes time to mention Lamar's abandonment by Maury Lamar, his father, who, like a number of southern literary fathers (his name echoes that of Caroline Compson's brother, his behavior that of her husband), withdrew into solitude and "poesy dreams" of the past: reveries, in Maury's case, of Lee and an idealized Anglican-Episcopal culture. Lamar's mother, Lily, also often turned up missing, whenever she, as many critics note, was "out for joyrides" with a character called Uncle Harry, who in fact was her distant cousin (Percy 55, 96, 215). When she was not absent, she acted far too intrusive in a "nervous joking aggressive" way, one seemingly good-natured but still likely to mortify, to use Gilligan's verb, a young boy. She had the habit of "getting" little Lance by coming at him "with her sharp little fist boring away into [his] ribs"; this behavior goes "past joking" (215). Hers is a boring or poking gesture resembling an act the mature Lamar sees his father-in-law, Tex Reilly, perform with little Siobhan; Reilly's gesture causes Lamar to wonder whether old Tex is "fooling with" the child (54–55). This association tells us at least as much about Lamar and his mother as it does about Tex and his granddaughter: it suggests that in his suspicion of Tex, Lance may project one of his own memories and reminds us that Lily was a powerfully sexed woman—lovely and delicate as a dove, Aphrodite's bird—likely as capable of carelessly eroticizing her son as of committing adultery with Harry Wills, her adultery being the conclusion Lamar employs his hallucinated "Lady of the Camellias" to reach (212).

That Lily also sent her son upstairs "to swipe some of [her husband's] pocket money from his sock drawer" reveals a good deal more about the household in which Lamar grew up than at first it may seem to show. It multiplies the double-barreled shame of the family, the crooked father with ten thousand dollars in kickbacks in his drawer and the mother out cavorting with Harry Wills. Lily's request here points to an intrafamilial warfare that apparently lurked behind the facade of good spirits and cavalier acquiescence to adultery mother and father constructed before their son and the world (41–42, 106). For are we to imagine that Lily did not know what her son would find under the pocket change, that she did not turn to that drawer regularly to finance her outings? Certainly his discovery in that place would strengthen her position in whatever sub-rosa tug-of-war went on between a husband and wife so oddly yoked together. This probable motive for her delegating to her son the pilfering of pocket change, a motive detected between the lines, adds to our understanding that Lamar grew up in an atmosphere of parental indifference, intrusiveness, probable abandonment, and deadly hostility, all sugarcoated by his mother's high spirits and his father's aristocratic complacency.

Lamar passes such qualities off as part of the mores of his parents' time and place. Added, however, to the obviously shaming transgressions of his father and mother, to the kickbacks and adultery, they indicate that Belle Isle was a facade long before Margot restored it—Belle Reve indeed—"to a splendor it had never known" (117). This remark, perhaps the keenest line in the novel, skewers the South's need throughout the extended postbellum century to (re)construct a seldom-existing antebellum aristocracy (cf. Hardy 158–63). As the book shows, such pretenses weakened Lamar's early development by undermining his hold on reality. Aside from the ministrations of Suellen, his family's long-standing black servant (55), the place where Lamar has spent most of his life has since done little to fill the vast gaps in what Kohut would term his core self. Although Belle Isle has become a movie-set South sufficiently attractive to appear on the Azalea Trail tour, the house has been a respectable shell covering a hollow or diseased core all Lamar's life. Little wonder then he feels most comfortable in the pigeonnier (or "dovecot," in association with his mother) since the droppings left by its namesakes and former residents appropriately signify the hidden core of the place where he grew up (17–18, 82).

Given the gap between his childhood's reality and its appearances, Lamar falls naturally into a lifelong pattern of compensating and repressive public successes. We do not learn a great deal about his adolescence, chiefly what he reports as part of his fantasy about his Lady of the Camellias. He sees her as the type of "voluptuous forty-year-old woman [who] attracted a [cheerfully obscene] fifteen-year-old youth" relaxing after playing football and who with her sauntering walk could inspire such boys, including adolescent Lamar, to query one another, "How would you like some of that?" (211). Although typical of young male sexual fantasies, the question implicitly degrades its feminine subject while automatically inflating the boy who presumes, rightly or wrongly, that he can triumph with a woman old enough to be his mother. Even if her designation as Lady of the Camellias did not echo Lily's name and Percy did not have her finally dream-evolve into Lamar's sword-proffering (phallic) mother, this hallucination would still provide a clear example of the way self-pathology, or deficits in the core self creating shame, lead (as in Lamar's case) to the oedipal delusions that empower postpuberty boys to imagine taking their father's place (225–26), if only in playing-field fantasies.

Lamar needs such empowerment to displace not Maury Lamar but Harry Wills, his mother's lover, who, in Lance's imagination at least, is his biological father. Wills seems given to a sort of Noah complex in that he sets out to rescue Lily from her seemingly sexless marriage (considering Maury's "own limitations") and goes on to expose his "large button [his genital] over a great veined ball" to his probable son. The heavy smoke and "genital musk" of their encounter seem to embarrass both males, threatening a flood of inappropriate intimacy that Wills dispels with an explosion of masculine bravado: "Have a drink! Goddamn . . . !" (212–14).

A more important oedipal conflict established in the football fantasy is that Lamar at fifteen has dealt with the incest taboo much the way Eugene Gant and other southern male protagonists have. He has split off the mother of sexual desires from his (abundantly sexed) mother, whom he sees as neither beautiful nor good-looking "but rather as too pale," so that the repressed mother of desires can return to him disguised as any of "forty women in that parish of a certain age" who possessed "full figures and a certain reputation from the past" (210, 214). It is a split that will follow him through his first marriage to virginal Lucy Cobb, his lady of light who dies of *leukemia*, the (too) white disease. The same disjunction will haunt him through his final splitting of all his fateful fairy women, his incarnations of Morgana le Fay, into corrupt Margot and "reenvirgined" Anna, each a product of his overcompensating imagination, though in opposite directions.

During the years that come between his confusing childhood and the locker-room encounter with Harry Wills, or with either of his wives, Lamar covers over his deficits and shames with a series of triumphs that vary in value. At one end of this continuum falls his ambivalent relationship with John/Percival, whose frail, gracile, feminine appearance foreshadows Lamar's interest in Margot's combination of voluptuousness and boyishness, much as one of his companion's nicknames, Harry, likely adds unconsciously to his locker-room embarrassment with his mother's naked "Uncle Harry." Although Lamar insists at least three times that, other than his holding the college friend's skinny arm a lot, the two of them "never touched each other," he nonetheless senses they may have been "too close." At a preconscious level he probably knows what their sharing "a whore between" them "in a motel bed in Jackson, Mississippi," implied: that the one-night ménage à trois allowed them a sexual intimacy forbidden by their conscious values. In more recent times he indicates his displeasure with signs of his son's own homosexuality by characterizing him as a "scared little prick [hiding from assertive contemporary women] with other scared little pricks"; he similarly reacts to the video of his daughter Lucy passively accepting the gentle sexual "assaults" of Raine and Dana by likening their bodies on the bed to a "rough swastika" and recalling the only time he ever killed a crow, by shooting it through the head (177, 192–93). In his college days, however, his own three-way arrangement clearly aggrandized his sense of personal power, for he now refers (guiltily) to the medium of sexual exchange between John/Percival and himself as "the poor whore [simultaneously assaulted] between us" (74, 94), language betraying the swastika-like superiority he then sought.

At the other end of the continuum of Lamar's compensations occurs the string of successes in college. He was a Big Man on Campus, "debater . . . all-S.E.C. halfback, Rhodes scholar, even 'smart' . . . [and] Golden Gloves." While these accomplishments clearly allow him to ignore for a time the emotional wounds left by his childhood, his pain survives in his failure to embrace his triumphs wholeheartedly. The underlying low self-esteem shows through in the way he downgrades his all-conference status to "second-string," his Phi Beta Kappa rank to "a sort of second-echelon," and his boxing rank to "runner-up" (14–15). He struggles mightily, accomplishes a good deal, yet always ends feeling second-rate, haunted by his shame-filled childhood. No matter what want of value he now attaches to these achievements in college, he believes he reached "the peak of his life" there (14–15). Unable to find satisfaction in himself, he must struggle again and again, and likely a shade more desperately each time around. He must keep striving because such achievements provide his major defense against the emotional pain of his past.

In his first marriage, to Lucy Cobb, Lamar, as we have noted, proves an overachiever, a suitor too dazzled by the "Limelight" playing on their car radio and by the sunlight flashing from Lucy's smooth legs as she dances across the tennis courts dotting the more mannered and socially higher Highlands in the Carolinas (12, 82). As spouse, he aspires to love her, but Lucy disappears into the white cloud of leukemia.

So, too, does the high professional idealism of his 1960s liberalism disappear, though it vanishes at the opposite end of the spectrum. This is the phase during which his heroic efforts on behalf of African Americans arose from ambiguous personal motives. On the one hand, Lamar was convinced the blacks struggling for civil rights "were right." On the other, he was bored and "wanted to be unpopular with the whites." His desire to be unpopular betrays the aristocratic luxury in which he indulges by feeling superior, an attitude that an ordinary tradesman or hired worker, who has daily to please others, could not afford to reveal. His desire to court conflict in order to transcend boredom reveals both the degree of the boredom and the depth of the hollowness leading to his boredom. It also demonstrates the increasing desperation of his need to cover over his inner emptiness. In the late 1960s, when radical young blacks led by H. Rap Brown and Stokely Carmichael unleash their anger against Roy Wilkins and M.L. King for electing to work for reform with white liberals (Manchester 1066–70), they confuse Lamar in his liberal stance and open him up to the ambivalence underlying his position, thereby gradually robbing him of his certitude (Percy 58–59). With the cessation of his "happy strife" for civil rights, he tumbles into a dark, drunken depression (Percy 60).

Before he reaches this nadir, however, he experiences a new excitement and, we can infer, suffers abandonment by it. For if Siobhan was conceived in July 1968, Margot entered Lamar's life before he became disillusioned in the 1970s with the services he performed as a civil rights attorney (31). Thus his marital and professional deflations overlap. Of the two, the defection by Margot opens the older wounds and drops him into a darker hole of depression. For defending civil rights offers him the excitement of conflict, whereas loving Margot brings the ecstasy of the divine.

For example, when Lamar asks John/Percival what is wrong with him, "Are you in love?" he is asking a question with metaphysical significance (6). For by the time Lamar met Margot, his emptiness was so great that he felt compelled to seek a religious solution. Whereas Lucy flooded him with the light of idealism, Margot brings the passion of the transcendent. Later Lamar will distinguish his metaphysics from John/Percival's by asserting that while the latter's "absolute and infinite" is God, his own is "loving a woman" (128–29). Although Lamar now looks back on the intense sexuality of the 1960s and 1970s as a perversion that justifies his purifying crusade, he earlier saw it as the royal road to divine ecstasy. When that road led him to the temple hidden in "the warm cottoned-off place between [Margot's] legs" (81), he was celebrating a communion he shared with many of his contemporaries in a decade when the press declared the God of the churches dead but the scientists of desire, chiefly Masters and Johnson, discovered a long-repressed infinity in the female ability to sustain orgasms (Manchester 1108–9).

The position Lamar attempts to explain to his friend was, according to poet, publisher, and anthologist A. Poulin Jr., a mainstay of poems written by many of Lamar's distinguished contemporaries. In the afterword to his influential anthology, *Contemporary American Poetry*, Poulin gives Lamar's brand of faith an elegance it lacks coming from the lips of a wife-murderer. Poulin writes:

> Since an explicit or implicit belief in the death of God necessarily posits the end of belief in a supernatural life or life force, it simultaneously necessitates a greater understanding of what is ostensibly the most powerful manifestation of the human life force, sexuality. In the past, the spiritual and cultural heritage of the West has been such that the traditional affirmation of the supernatural life force has been at the expense of the natural life force. . . . [The]

contemporary poets' celebration of sexuality may well be equivalent to a celebration of the god within . . . thereby suggesting a . . .
measure of the sacred. (702)

If Poulin's statement accurately reflects what Lamar means when he accuses
John/Percival of embracing "the wrong absolutes and infinities" and of joining a church that rules "out one absolute so you have to look for another,"
we can begin to assess the profundity of Lamar's need for Margot (Percy
128–29).

For Margot the marriage was a business arrangement, the exchange of
her wealth for his social standing; she tried to restore Lamar, much like his
house, to what in fact would be a parody of all the stereotypes of southern
men foisted on the popular imagination by histories and Hollywood (73,
81–82, 120), thus inflating his compensatory false self to the grand facade
of an epic movie. For him, on the other side, their marriage was a religious
commitment.

If his seeking divinity in another human at first seems an exceedingly
desperate act of faith, let us recall that Lamar in this effort belongs to a tradition that finds expression in America in the essays of Ralph Waldo Emerson
and especially in the poems of his follower Walt Whitman, a tradition that in
our century flows through D.H. Lawrence, the "priest of love," to all the disciples of Whitman and Lawrence. The latter would include several of the
poets discussed by Poulin. Although this tradition does not possess a church,
it does include many priests, for whom publishing houses and reading ven-
ues serve as ad hoc temples. Consequently, as a sign of his times, Lamar's
sentiments here cannot be taken lightly.

Nor can we take lightly, from his point of view, the significance of Margot's
defections with Merlin and Jacoby. Lamar's turning to Margot as his incarna-
tion of divinity constitutes his penultimate defense against his shame and the
abandonment depression of his childhood, which in turn underlie all the
activities he recollects in his cell. For Lamar behaves in the manner that Kohut
ascribes to individuals fallen prey to borderline states included among the
self disturbances. Such men and women manage more or less effectively to
cover over "permanent or protracted breakup, enfeeblement, or serious distortion of the self" by developing seemingly strong "defensive structures"
(*Restoration* 192). Kohut describes such sufferers as possessing "covertly psychotic personality organizations" because the nuclear or core self is basically
"hollow," a state they conceal with their "well-developed peripheral layer of
defensive structures" (*How* 8). Whatever forces, including analysis itself, in-
terfere with this vulnerable shell of defenses can cause such personalities to
implode, to collapse, to fall from their usual state of significant public achieve-

ments into the psychological chaos hitherto concealed within them. Such people consequently stand at the border that separates individuals with temporary narcissistic disorders from those suffering from permanent or protracted psychotic disorders (Kohut, *Restoration* 192–93). As part of their project of staving off chaos, they may aspire to and achieve greatness, but chaos still may follow on the heels of their greatest success.

In Lamar's case, Lawson has classified his pathological behavior as schizophrenia, a full-blown psychosis (208–24). Viewing him, however, the way we do here, as a borderline who collapses, emphasizes the development of his total life, not only the excesses of his recent activities. His recent psychotic performance goes back to his earliest years with Lily, Maury, and Harry. In an important sense, he has been holding his violence off since the start, with his collegiate sexual experiments and triumphs, his idealistic first marriage, his civil rights work, and most recently the urgent passion he brings to the marriage with Margot.

When Margot in her final fragment of dialogue says to her husband, "That's what you never knew. With you I had to be either—or—but never a—uh—woman. . . . I'm dying" (245), we cannot go wrong by filling in her blanks thus: "I had to be either a *virgin* or *whore*." For Lamar clearly has inherited what Freud considered a dominant tendency in the psyche of Western men, the mind-set we noted in Lamar's playing-field fantasy that splits the image of the feminine (or the mother) along strictly sexual and moral lines. But other words to fill Margot's blanks need be considered. Margot has just spilled out certain memories of her childhood, especially her poverty and her habit of walking to her Texas town carrying her good shoes in a paper bag so that she could change into them at the bridge before entering town. "I'm nothing," she begins, as though confessing that she has given her life to the desperate struggle to live down the social cipher that made up her childhood, an effort mirroring Lamar's own struggles. Following this possibility, her final disjunction would read: "With you I had to be either *everything* or *nothing* but never a—uh—woman."

Because Margot's little vanity with the shoes echoes that of Lena Grove in *Light in August*, Percy's intertextual move reminds us that readers often fill Lena—who if not a cipher is a relatively small number—with very large meanings, including that which assigns her the role of the Virgin Mary in the symbol system Faulkner based on the crucifixion story. As "everything" or the Virgin Mary—who is in modern Greek the *Panagia*, literally "All-hallowed" but containing the suggestion "All-earth"—Margot initially becomes what she originally was for Lamar, his divinity; she turns, however, into what her name suggests: the Mar-got(t), the marplot or disfigurer of Lamar's divinity (since *Gott* is German for God) in the desperate paradise he seeks through his second marriage. Percy underscores this aspect of Margot's name by echoing her marring powers in Lamar's commonly ignored, if not repressed, surname. Seen in this light, her final words to Lamar would have been: "I had to be either *God* or *the Devil* but never *a real* woman." Either way we fill her significant blanks, in Lamar's swings between the light of idealism and the darkness of depression: she "had to be either *white* or *black* but never *the grey of a woman.*"

Lamar's options are absolute ones, and have been since the fall of both his parents cast him violently from the necessary Eden of childhood, a paradise that was never "good enough," in D.W. Winnicott's[3] phrase, to produce in him the inward security that would allow Lamar to feel "good enough" to enjoy the ordinary successes of his life. In his recent collapse into narcissistic rage, although he has committed acts of murder while destroying the Lamar house and the family it publicly represented, he seems to feel justified, when he feels anything, in doing what he has done. In this he resembles most murderers, who believe their crimes have justifying causes (Gilligan 11–12). As he sees his behavior, he has simply fallen into the familiar trap of a man who senses he must defend the sanctity of his home by avenging himself as a dishonored husband. It is a common tragedy of justice-ridden men, as old at least as the Trojan War. Whether or not the most recent irritation of Lamar's old narcissistic wounds is based on a typo (or I-O blood type), he produces additional evidence more substantial than Desdemona's kerchief to support his suspicions regarding Margot, evidence sufficient in his mind to support the cold rage of his campaign to destroy her and her fellow deceivers. As with Othello, however, we as audience to his tragedy know that, no matter how justified he may feel, his vengeful acts are excessive ones, out of scale, grandiose. Divorce, certainly. A personal holocaust? Let's be reasonable. But reason, of course, is the faculty least operative when borderlines such as Lamar finally implode into the utter chaos that is narcissistic rage. Such victim-murderers are as likely to destroy themselves as their targeted enemies, for they see no clear difference, no border separating self from other. They were never given the care necessary to construct such boundaries for the self.

The rages, however, of individuals involved in the tragic struggle to defend a central self too wounded to sustain itself are usually not permanent. The defenses may again restore the facade of social achievement, even when these protective behaviors have to leap to a higher level of overcompensation. In his own mind, having escaped extended punishment for his private acts of violence, Lamar as his account ends is prepared to expand his already inflated campaign into a nationwide, perhaps global, crusade of self-justified and righteous violence. Others, including Lawson, have already described the psychotic dimensions of this crusade. Clearly it constitutes the most extreme and violent, not to mention most grandiose, of all his compensating defenses. Just as clearly, it is part of our southern tradition to identify one's culture with that of medieval knights—Lancelot, Percival, Ivanhoe, and so forth—and to lose all awareness of the border separating reality and metaphor, fact and desire, when one begins the ensuing crusades of violence that follow. Certainly it helps in such crusades to persuade the innocent ones, the Parsifals, "the Innocent Fools," to come along, for they, whether internal to one's self or external, will provide the sanction of good conscience, the ultimate defense that justifies the rages of a self as damaged as Lamar's.

If *you* were Percival, as finally you are, and Lancelot asked you, "Is there anything you wish to tell me before I leave?" (257)—knowing what you know now, what would you say? This is the problem Percy has left us, his readers and our age, to resolve.

Notes

1. See, for example, Tate 159, 165.
2. See, for example, Allen 105–6, 128.
3. D.W. Winnicott (1896–1971) was a leading British object-relations psychoanalyst who, in his work with children uprooted by World War II, developed the concepts of "transitional objects" and "transitional spaces."

Works Cited

Allen, William Rodney. *Walker Percy: A Southern Wayfarer.* Jackson: UP of Mississippi, 1986.

Coles, Robert. *Walker Percy: An American Search.* Boston: Little, Brown, 1978.

Gilligan, James. *Violence: Our Deadly Epidemic and Its Causes.* New York: G.P. Putnam's Sons, 1996.

Hardy, John Edward. *The Fiction of Walker Percy.* Urbana: U of Illinois P, 1987.

Kohut, Heinz. *How Does Analysis Cure?* Ed. Arnold Goldberg. Chicago: U of Chicago P, 1984.

———. *The Restoration of the Self.* New York: International Universities Press, 1977.

Lawson, Lewis A. *Still Following Percy.* Jackson: UP of Mississippi, 1996.

Manchester, William. *The Glory and the Dream: A Narrative History of America, 1932–72.* Toronto: Bantam, 1975.

Percy, Walker. *Lancelot.* New York: Farrar, Straus and Giroux, 1977.

Poulin, A. Jr. "Contemporary American Poetry: The Radical Tradition." *Contemporary American Poetry.* Boston: Houghton Mifflin, 1985. 701–2.

Tate, Allen. "Remarks on the Southern Religion." *I'll Take My Stand: The South and the Agrarian Tradition, by Twelve Southerners.* 1930. New York: Harper & Row, 1962. 155–75.

Regeneration Through Nonviolence

Frederick Barthelme and the West

Robert H. Brinkmeyer Jr.

For all the talk about a southern sense of place, a large number of contempo-rary southern writers have lately been roaming far afield from the old homeplace. Significantly and somewhat surprisingly, in lighting out to new territories, many of these writers have not been heading, as one might expect, to the North (where southerners have for generations looked longingly for escape), but instead have been heading west, a geographical turning that marks an important shift in the history of southern literature. In contrast to the enormous appeal of the West in the American (that is, nonsouthern) literary imagination, southern writers have historically found little of worth in the West. Southern writing about the West typically has emphasized less the American dream of possibility and freedom—the "regeneration through vio-lence" that Richard Slotkin has found embedded in the American experi-ence—than the southern knowledge of the impossibility and irresponsibility of that dream, focusing on the cultural destruction wrought by the frontier impulse (Caroline Gordon's *Green Centuries*, for example), the misguided belief that one can step free from history and the past by going west (Katherine Anne Porter's "Pale Horse, Pale Rider," Eudora Welty's *The Golden Apples*, Robert Penn Warren's *All the King's Men*), and the harsh reality behind the western dream of endless possibility (Mark Twain's *Roughing It*). All in all, southern literature for 150 years or so has had very little interest in and very little good to say about the West.

Until lately, that is. Beginning with Doris Betts's *Heading West* (1983) and carrying up to the present day, an ever-increasing number of southern writers are writing about the West and particularly southerners' experiences there. Southern authors who have written about the West, either about con-temporary life or about the days of settlement, include Cormac McCarthy, Barry Hannah, Barbara Kingsolver, Richard Ford, Rick Bass, Clyde Edgerton,

Chris Offutt, James Lee Burke, Madison Smartt Bell, Tim Gautreaux, Dorothy Allison, and Frederick Barthelme.

As surprising as it is that so many southern authors are writing about the West, it's just as surprising, if not more so, that one particular writer has looked westward—Frederick Barthelme. From his first collection of stories, *Moon Deluxe* (1981), up through his novel *Bob the Gambler* (1997), Barthelme has written almost exclusively about the glitzy and kitschy cities and suburbs of the Mississippi Gulf Coast, a world of high-rises, shopping malls, and now casinos. Barthelme characteristically focuses on the everyday lives of everyday suburban people, their small victories and their small defeats, their efforts to experience the wonder they hope still exists in their otherwise humdrum lives. The pull west is rarely in Barthelme's fiction except metaphorically—that is, in the urge to cut loose and start anew. Characters may want to, and at times do, walk away from marriages, jobs, or relationships, but these unburdenings rarely involve picking up and moving to the West. Cutting loose usually means moving across town.

But things are quite otherwise in *Painted Desert* (1995), a novel wherein several characters set off from the Mississippi Gulf Coast on a quest for vigilante justice—a journey that takes them into the heart of the desert Southwest. This is utterly new fictional territory for Barthelme. The confluence of his primarily postmodern—urban and suburban—imaginative vision with the vast spaces of the desert engenders a rich and wondrous novel, one that draws from and revises the legends undergirding the mythic West. *Painted Desert*, the sequel to *The Brothers*, is best read with its companion novel, as that work goes a long way in exploring the suburban world from which Del and Jen, the protagonists of both novels, flee in the later novel.

The Brothers follows the meeting and developing relationship of Del, a forty-four-year-old divorcee, and Jen, a free-spirited woman twenty years his younger. Like most relationships in Barthelme's fiction, Del and Jen's is strained and fractious, with much going on in their emotional lives that they don't understand and can't control. What they do have going for them is their quirkiness. Somewhat disconnected from the middle-class culture that they inhabit, they frequently act with refreshing and enriching spontaneity. For Del, Jen represents the possibility of mystery and wonder in his lackluster life, and in this she can be understood as a manifestation of the lure of the legendary West—of newness, freshness, possibility. Like Eudora Welty's King MacLain and her other golden characters, Jen seems wondrously aglow, her hair, as Del describes it at one point, "a shower of lake light, her whole bearing a suggestion of things still very much possible, the time to do all those things written in absent flaws, in perfect skin, in sympathetic years" (*Brothers* 48). As Del says at another point, Jen appears to be "from another world, not one Del knew, but one where the rules, the ways, were all new" (*Brothers* 132).

Maintaining the capacity to experience wonder and surprise is crucial for Del. Significantly, Del does not think about fleeing west looking for renewal; he's content to find joy and possibility in the world about him. While the lure of the West, of starting over in a world of endless possibility, still lurks for some characters in Barthelme's postmodern world, by and large it seems merely stuff of fanciful dreams. Del's brother Bud, for instance, in a fit of enthusiastic hopefulness, picks up and goes to California, hoping to break into the movie business and begin a new life. But within a few weeks, he's back in Biloxi and into his old routines; his only explanation for his return is that things didn't work out. Del's ex-wife, Karen, likewise finds the West a disappointment. After their divorce, she moves to Oregon to start over; there she discovers that the West is so overrun with people who have so given themselves to the idea of independence and liberation that they have, ironically, lost their individuality. "I think there's something seriously wrong," she writes to Del. "The Body Snatchers have made more progress than we know. These beings are too eager, too simple. What's most frightening is that they can make the world just what they want it to be simply by believing in it together" (*Brothers* 89).

Unlike Karen, Del heads east rather than west after their divorce, moving from Houston to Biloxi. He feels no need to bolt west; as he says later in *Painted Desert*, California has always seemed to him merely an upscale mall. More significant, for Del imaginative wonder has nothing to do with geography; it's a matter instead of noticing and embracing the mysteries of everyday life. The locus of imaginative wonder and possibility can be anywhere, from the glistening asphalt of a parking lot to an industrial dump to looming storm clouds. And so, no matter what he's doing—walking the beach, eating at a restaurant, strolling through a park—Del is always noticing things, always on the lookout for that detail that transfigures the everyday into the luminous. Stunned at one point by what he sees as the beauty inside and outside a shopping mall, Del notes that "nobody sees how gorgeous this is or knows why." Most people, he adds, rather than observing the dazzling details of the mall, "come here looking for Odor-Eaters" (*Brothers* 177, 178). At another time, watching a line of incoming storm clouds, Del describes a wondrous transformation of the world: "[The clouds] transform everything instantly. It's like suddenly you're in a different world and the junk of your life slides away and you're left with this rapture, this swoon of well-being and rightness. You get the world in its amazing balance" (*Brothers* 176). Such moments of transfiguration are what Del always seeks. He and Jen both know that the capacity to see the wondrous in the apparently inconsequential keeps one imaginatively alive and vital; that's why they work so hard to nurture their imaginative visions, striving to discover the miraculous in what most people see as numbing and dull.

Losing this capacity for wonder, the capability to see the world "in its amazing balance," is perhaps the gravest threat to Del's happiness. Certainly this threat is always at hand; what appears at the moment as fresh and inspiriting always threatens to become, over time, mundane and stultifying. Del fears this might happen with his relationship with Jen, as he has already seen it happen in his failed marriage with Karen, a marriage that Del characterizes as one that slowly lost its freshness. Moreover, almost every day he confronts the quiet desperation of his brother Bud and his wife, Margaret, a couple whose marriage survives apparently only by inertia and the deadening comfort of routine. Telling Del that she and Bud will never get divorced, Margaret goes on to characterize her marriage: "You get sick and tired of everything—every breath, gesture, nasal note in the voice—but you get over it, and after a while it's like having a big pet around, a dog, a giant monkey lizard" (*Brothers* 83). There's also plenty of evidence for Del to fear that he and Jen might be headed in the same direction. At one point, much to Del's obvious dismay, Jen voices her frustration and boredom with sex, saying, "I don't know what happened to the old days when people felt things for each other, touched each other, cared for each other—I had better sex in high school than I've had since" (*Brothers* 154). In that same conversation, she happily imagines a marriage with Del as being easy and depthless. "And we won't have any peculiar or difficult thoughts, either, you've got to promise me that, so it'll be even easier," she says. "It'll be like *I Married CNN*" (*Brothers* 153).

Jen's mention of CNN is particularly significant, since in Barthelme's fictional world the media's packaging of experience plays a crucial role in postmodern culture's commodification of life, a process that saps imaginative vision and vitality. Jen is particularly sensitive to the media's manipulation of experience. She describes her own deadening of sexual desire after seeing on the screen representations of her favorite sexual techniques: "That film stuff ruins it for me, disauthenticates it. . . . Before it was great, but sooner or later somebody notices and puts it in a movie, and that gets on TV, and then it creeps back into our lives as the TV version of the real thing it really was before" (*Brothers* 50). Jen's posting of flyers all over town describing grotesque real-life stories is her attempt to unpack the media's packaging of experience. Her flyers present events simply and directly, as close to real life as possible, and she wants people to respond to them viscerally and passionately. "They're grotesque enough so there's no disguising what goes on in them," she says of her stories. "It's like all the cartoony plot stuff in books and movies—it makes them easy to follow, easy to understand. You don't get lost, and you don't have to worry about what things mean all the time" (*Brothers* 127). As she says later in *Painted Desert*, she hopes her posters will make people feel "a little more human," a little less selfish and self-centered, in the face of "the routine clubbing, shooting, paralyzing and punishing and pain-inflicting crap we get every day on the television" (*Painted* 46).

If Jen uses her stories to resist postmodern culture's packaging and commodification of experience, Bud takes a different, more postmodern approach to dealing with the problem: he deliberately embraces and takes joy in the packaging of self and identity. At the end of the novel, he has Del wrap him up with sheets, and then, completely draped and appearing like "an enormous Q-Tip" (*Brothers* 262), he walks repeatedly back and forth across Del's balcony, by all appearances a mindless automaton. But Bud's actions are anything but mindless; by casting himself as a mummy, a modern-day reincarnation of Wells's invisible man, Bud makes visible the general mummification of everyone by the cultural forces of postmodern society. Bud's strategy at coping with the diminishment of self contrasts sharply with Del's and Jen's: he appropriates and takes joy in the cultural forces meant to destroy joy; they resist the destructive forces by keeping the capacity for joy and wonder alive in their everyday life.

By the time we pick up their story three years later in *Painted Desert*, however, Del and Jen seem to be losing their battle against imaginative deadening, their capacity for wonder now sorely diminished. The controlling power of the media, and particularly that of television, pervades everywhere; and clearly Del and Jen have fallen under its sway. They always seem to be watching TV—at home, at restaurants, on errands (they carry a miniature set), everywhere they go. Del even likes to go to sleep with the TV on. The flexing light, he says, makes the room feel occupied; it's as if images on the screen have more presence than the body itself. Whereas Del and Jen once had found the potentiality of wonder all about them, they now seem to find it only on the television screen, particularly during TV spectacles—car wrecks, hurricanes, murders, the O.J. Simpson freeway chase. Unless framed within the TV screen, life for them goes mostly unobserved and unnoticed. It's safer that way, as Del observes in a conversation with his brother about having little desire to see Dealey Plaza since he's already seen it on TV and in photographs. "I can probably live without the real experience," he says. "I find as I get older, Bud, that there are many real experiences I can live without" (*Painted* 41). Under the media's sway, Del and Jen seem to be fast becoming replicas of Bud wrapped in his sheets (without his deliberateness and joy), their once hopeful lives now papered over by the mundane and the routine, a debilitating process that Del characterizes at one point as the weighing down of life by "the growing pile of tiny failures and missed opportunities, things dismissed for one reason or another" (*Painted* 94). At another point, he describes himself as imprisoned by a system of authoritarian control, victimized by "the tyranny of class, of gender, of sexual preference, of unrehabilitated language. If it's not one thing, it's another, for us. We're in trouble every which way we turn. We can't move. We're sealed in. We're locked out" (*Painted* 80).

Ironically, it's something they witness on TV—a news special on violence in America that has footage of the Los Angeles riots after the Rodney King verdict—that jolts Del and Jen from their stultifying complacency and toward a commitment to break out of their packaged lives. They suddenly feel the need to act, to do something in real life rather than merely to observe things on TV. Jen tells Del that she gets "the feeling we've been living wrong. We've kind of been hiding out, and we need to get out a little more. All this world is going on out here and we watch it on television, but these people are living it" (*Painted* 29). Del reacts similarly, characterizing the riots as "*The Year of Living Dangerously* in real life," adding that he identifies with the rioters' frustration and desire to lash out. "They were," he says, "as desperate as the rest of us for something to happen, something big, something significant" (*Painted* 22).

Del and Jen now vow to live dangerously themselves, to make something big and riotous occur in their lives: they decide to be vigilantes, modern-day gunslingers (though they never buy any guns) to clean up the streets of Los Angeles. "It's important for us to take a stand," Jen says at one point, echoing the lines of previous hard-line reformers from the South. "We need to demonstrate that certain behavior is not acceptable in our civilization" (*Painted* 37). "We've got to do something," she says a bit later. "You've got to do something or else you're just part of the shit, part of the fucking landscape. I don't want to be that anymore" (*Painted* 47–48). She now embraces "the idea of stepping out of the shadows. Do that and you're empowering yourselves. You're demanding to be heard" (*Painted* 75).

With Jen's father, Mike, and her friend Penny in tow, Del and Jen head west on their violent quest, passing through Texas and out into the desert Southwest. By the time the four hit the desert, the trip to deliver retribution has begun to evolve into something else—a journey to discover the mystery lurking in the self and the world. The desert, the landscape where searchers for thousands of years have gone to wrestle with elemental questions, begins to work its effect on the travelers. They begin to drift, swerving off the beeline to Los Angeles, becoming more interested in the sights than in vengeance. On the surface, the journey evolves into something close to a sightseeing expedition, but it's clear that something profound is going on amid all the detours, that the travelers are growing in mind and spirit.

What most strikes Del and Jen is the unmediated beauty of the wide-open western landscape, particularly when a view catches them unaware.[1] They're stunned. Although they assimilate some of what they see to their previous experience, as when Del notes that the colors of the desert resemble "prewashed J. Crew blues and grays and reds" (*Painted* 211), much of what they see defies description in familiar terms. "There was nothing to compare it with," Del says of a view of the Canyon de Muerto, "so nothing prepared you for what it was like to stand on the edge of the canyon and see sunlight playing on rocks jutting out of the cliff faces" (*Painted* 208). Such moments of defamiliarization, of experiencing unmediated nature, revitalize Del and Jen. The world now appears wondrously transfigured. Seeing Canyon de Chelly, Del says, "redefined the world, made it more wonderful than we thought—it was like seeing sky for the first time. Standing on the ridge overlooking the canyon, I had that sense of wonder at the color, the space, the scale, the farmland on the canyon floor, the great power of the sheered rock—the Red Sea parted in stone" (*Painted* 209).

Significantly, even the tourist spots and the culturally appropriated places now start to dazzle Del and Jen. When Del early on expresses some disappointment about the constructed presentation of Carlsbad Caverns ("It was a little Walt Disneyed," he says [*Painted* 144]), Jen responds that "it's fake-looking, staged, but it's still great. If it was natural, it would be wonderful because it was natural. As it is, it's wonderful because you can still sort of imagine what it would be like if it were natural, plus it's so weird the way those people set it up—the way it was lit, and the way it was organized and arranged, and the way the paths went. It was like earth taxidermy" (*Painted* 144). Soon Del will also be enjoying what we might call the cultural taxidermy, all the kitschy tourist spots and funky hotels and restaurants. In their newly rejuvenated eyes, not merely the breathtaking views of unmediated landscape but the whole West has become an awe-inspiring spectacle.

Previously startled from their everyday lives by the violence of the Los Angeles riots, Del and Jen are now utterly shaken from their violent intentions by their responses to the West's beauty. Commenting on why they decide to call off their vigilante action, Jen says that it's because "the world is so gorgeous that we can't stop ourselves from going around and looking at it. The reason is that putting one foot in the Painted Desert is more satisfying, more fulfilling, more rich and human and decent, than all the vengeance in the world. This country is making us into saints, making us feel like saints, and that's worth everything" (*Painted* 226).

Del and Jen now recognize the terrifying narrow-mindedness and senselessness underpinning vigilante thinking, precisely the thinking that undergirds that of Durrell Dobson, an e-mail correspondent of Jen's who pleads with her to join him in a terrorist campaign against modern society. Dobson represents the extreme to which Del and Jen might go were they to carry out their original plans. He wants to cleanse the earth of the sources of evil, starting with politicians and television commentators—and he's willing to kill to do it. After writing to Jen that it is now time to act, he adds: "I am ready to kill and maim and damage and wound and dismember and eviscerate, to do what is necessary to bring about the change that is required" (*Painted* 192–93).

Dobson's apparent sniper attack in Las Vegas not only highlights the madness of his vision but also, by contrast, Del's and Jen's regeneration through nonviolence—regeneration through the constructive power of the imagination rather than the destructive power of violent retribution. As they journey through the West, Del and Jen move from embracing violence to embracing forgiveness and generosity—the same virtues that Jen had hoped her flyers would instill in her readers. Their model for action shifts, from another point of view, from Dobson to Lopez, the victim of a brutal beating during the L.A. riots who subsequently, Del and Jen learn, forgives his attacker and calls for a return to normalcy. Lopez's hope for decency and humane values mirrors Del and Jen's revised plans. "Maybe we should just go back to Biloxi," Jen tells Del at one point. "Hunker down. Take it one day at a time. Do what we can" (*Painted* 159). Rather than raging at the tyranny of postmodern life, seeking radical ways to fix things with violence and vigilantism, they now see, as they once had during the early days of their relationship, the value of making do in the everyday and of celebrating the wonder and beauty of the world about them. Jen's comments on tourists, about whom she and Del were once so scornful, underscores their reconfigured lives and their return to the ordinary:

> These people are all lovely and sweet. They've come out of their holes for a little bit. It's a pleasure to be among them, to be one of them, to be like them. Because all they want out of their trips is a little bit of first-order experience, a little bit of contact with the ground, a little reminder of the wonder of things. And that's what they get out here. That's what we're getting, too, because once you're out here, all the easy ways you use to understand the world no longer work, and you're left with a mountain or a sea or a river or a canyon. Suddenly, blowing a hole in Damian Williams's face seems like a small idea. Almost every idea seems small and you can't imagine why we spend our time the way we do. Why we sit in our little houses complaining about people doing things wrong, sit there having our little precious thoughts, clinging to our ideas and opinions and arguing for our "beliefs." (*Painted* 227)

In the novel's last scene, Del and Jen are driving happily off into the desert, having decided to get married and to return home—as Jen puts it, she wants to be "regular married. Just like everybody" (*Painted* 242). Gone is the TV—or at least almost. In a gesture echoing the novel's opening, Del reaches out to turn on his miniature TV, but Jen stops him, telling him to try the radio instead. She wants to hear some dance music, some western swing, rather than to watch the TV news. She wants, in other words, to be an active participant in the dance of life rather than merely a passive observer of information. They're ready to go home again, renewed and reinvigorated.

In terms of cultural legend, Del and Jen's journey out and back both invokes the classic American dream of western independence and then reconfigures it along less violent and more humane lines. Their flight west echoes the western hero's desire to leave behind a world fast becoming standardized and mechanized, the desire to be free from the web of culture and to be able to create oneself through action and ordeal. That's the dream of the West, the dream of living in space rather than place. But Del and Jen's decision to give up their violent quest and to return home signals both their imaginative rebirth and their revisioning of the western dream of freedom and possibility. The isolated and alienated heroes, hoping to take the law into their own hands and to find a space to stand outside cultural constraints, in the end become tourists. In *West of Everything: The Inner Life of Westerns*, Jane Tompkins writes that Westerns embody a spirit of hard-nosed seriousness, "the opposite of a recreational spirit" (13). But *Painted Desert* suggests that recreation is serious business, that in a postmodern world of commodification and control, recreation is a means for re-creation. The West for Barthelme is not a place to which one flees to escape culture but a place that one visits to reintegrate oneself back into culture. Barthelme's West thus embodies a geography of hope and possibility; but that hope and possibility come not through finding a place for deed and action but through finding a place for renewing imaginative vision by one's encounter with the world's beauty. Once that renewal occurs, once the geography of the West becomes the geography of the mind, the anywhere of postmodern society becomes somewhere, a place to come home to.

Note

1. Lurking throughout *Painted Desert* is the work of Walker Percy, particularly his essay "The Loss of the Creature" and his novels *The Last Gentleman* and *Lancelot*. Most relevant are Percy's ideas from "The Loss of the Creature" about modern people's loss of individual sovereignty due to their being merely consumers of experience. Percy discusses various ways for recovering sovereignty, including what he calls the

"dialectic of sightseeing." Barthelme works most of Percy's stratagems for recovery into *Painted Desert*, particularly in the journey west and the encounters with tourists and landscape. *Painted Desert* also echoes *Lancelot*, particularly in Del's and Jen's sudden reawakenings from deadening everydayness and their subsequent desire to lash out at a modern culture's failings; Durrell Dobson, too, bears a striking resemblance to Lancelot Lamar. Finally, one can't help noticing the similarity of endings between *Painted Desert* and *The Last Gentleman*, with the two sets of questers last seen rocketing off into the desert.

Works Cited

Barthelme, Frederick. *The Brothers*. New York: Viking, 1993.

————. *Painted Desert*. New York: Viking, 1995.

Tompkins, Jane. *West of Everything: The Inner Life of Westerns*. New York: Oxford UP, 1992.

Making Peace with the (M)other

Barbara Bennett

Southern fiction is rife with family conflicts, breaks, and reconciliations, and much attention has been given to specific types of relationships—father-son, mother-son, father-daughter, and mother-daughter. In fiction written before the 1970s, however, the mother-daughter connection is much less pronounced, perhaps because the coming of age of a young woman is generally marked by psychological changes rather than the concrete acts—a sexual experience or a hunting triumph—that more often mark the adult initiation of a young man, as in the fiction written by William Faulkner or Thomas Wolfe. Further, when a young woman is involved in the main action of the novel, the focus tends to be on the father-daughter relationship.

Very often in pre-1970 fiction, the mother figure is simply missing. Harper Lee's *To Kill a Mockingbird* (1960) offers such an example, as does *The Member of the Wedding* (1946) by Carson McCullers. In both these novels, the young female protagonists are motherless, lacking a proper white southern lady as a role model. As a result, they become tomboyish, resisting female dress and behavior. As Carol Pearson and Katherine Pope point out in their study *The Female Hero in American Literature*, for girls, leaving childhood is complicated by several things: first, American culture, especially in the South, does not foster independence and autonomy for females as it does for males. Second, young girls have "internalized the myth of female inferiority." Finally, a female, even more than a male, needs approval and fears that by demanding autonomy she will displease her parents (105). Perhaps, too, girls recognize unconsciously that the cultural power in the South belongs to white men—not to invisible females of any color—and so they resist adolescent movement toward southern womanhood and the inevitable acquiescence to what Lucinda MacKethan calls "the cage of southern patriarchy" (10). This attitude toward women, of course, can be traced to the antebellum South, when men "expected to remain patriarchs 'eternally' and who thus held tenaciously to ideals for women that kept them in their subservient place" (MacKethan 8). Behavior expectations for southern women—with descriptions that include such words as "leisure, passivity, dependence, sexual purity, submission, ignorance" (Jones 28)—persisted into the twentieth century, despite progress for women in other regions; but contemporary daughters in both fiction and life are resisting this condition, which Margaret Ripley Wolfe describes as being "shackled to pedestals" (2).

In Eudora Welty's *The Optimist's Daughter* (1969), the protagonist, Laurel McKelva Hand, initially senses that the power of the patriarchy is available only by association with men: through her father and through her husband. Laurel is a good example of the emerging female protagonist who comes to a new awareness of her own strength—foreshadowing the female heroes of the next decade. As Pearson and Pope argue, this new breed of female hero masters her world "by understanding it, not by dominating, controlling or owning the world or other people" (5), as male protagonists generally do. As Helen Hurt Tiegreen notes, Laurel chooses to "examine and control" her memories of her father "rather than to be controlled by them" (607), freeing her to be an independent being rather than, as the title suggests, just being someone's daughter, refuting the southern traditional belief that a woman's value is perceived in her relationship to a man.

Perhaps the pre-1970 author who deals most often with the mother-daughter relationship is Flannery O'Connor, whose own conflict with her mother, Regina, is reflected in her stories. As in many aspects of her work, O'Connor was the precursor to contemporary female authors in her examination of the traditional mother at odds with the modern, educated, southern daughter. And while at least six of O'Connor's thirty-one stories include a mother-daughter conflict, she was never able to resolve these issues completely—either in her work or in her life. It was simply too early for the South—and the women in it. The significance of mothers and daughters in O'Connor's work, though, is in her exploration of what happens to women who do not fit the traditional, submissive role dictated by the southern culture of her era. As Louise Westling notes, O'Connor's stories are full of "sour, deformed daughters and self-righteous mothers" (511). Remnants of O'Connor's daughters can be seen in many contemporary works by southern women writers who create female characters who cannot survive and thrive under the "oppressively restrictive southern values of their mothers" (Seidel, "Gail Godwin" 290). As a result, this conflict drives many fictional mothers and daughters apart.

The conflict between child and mother and the inevitable separation from the mother is nothing new and has been a part of the male and female heroic quest since ancient times. The search for the father figure—the person who will initiate the youngster into adulthood—requires first the rejection (or even the slaying) of the mother image. As Joseph Campbell describes this process for males, the mythic hero must reject the status quo and the traditionally held cultural beliefs—represented by mother and home—before he can discover truth and his own potential and reconcile with the powerful father. For female heroes, the importance of the father is equally significant because it is typically "the hero's father who first indicates to her what her identity in the patriarchal world will be" (Pearson 121). Unlike the male heroes, however, a female is limited in her access to power, realizing that she will eventually be relegated to a powerless position in the dominant culture—and become, ironically, the figure she herself rejected at the beginning of her quest for adulthood.

In contemporary southern fiction, the relationship becomes more complex because of the image of the southern lady so persistent in southern culture. Because mothers are "the main purveyors of information about southern culture" and are "advocates who attempt to teach their daughters to conform to that culture," as Kathryn Lee Seidel explains, southern daughters "must reject these mores and hence reject in some measure the women who represent them" in order to become "autonomous women of action" ("Gail Godwin" 287). Although this process has always been evident in southern literature—and perhaps missing mothers in Lee's and McCullers's and Welty's works are the result of authors trying to avoid this painful and aesthetically unpleasant rejection—the pattern seems to be changing in southern fiction by women since 1970, a time when the women's movement began to change opinions and expectations for women everywhere. Rejection of the mother is only one step in the developmental process for female protagonists. The most important step is the eventual reunion with the Mother—who is no longer the Other. Recognizing this fact often comes as a result of a series of awakenings, during which the adolescent or young woman experiences disappointment and even tragedy. When life fails to live up to fairy-tale expectations, a young woman senses that perhaps her mother—while seeming to choose a life so different from her daughter's—had at one time faced similar realizations about the limitations of her life.

In addition to accepting what she first perceives as her mother's weaknesses, a young woman often comes to terms with her father's shortcomings as well. And humanizing both the villain/mother and the hero/father allows the daughter to incorporate their strengths as well as their weaknesses in the creation of a whole adult self. And unlike earlier southern women protagonists—such as Edna Pontillier in Kate Chopin's *The Awakening*—contemporary protagonists have awarenesses that lead to hopefulness instead of hopelessness because they are no longer entrenched in a culture that will not allow them to make use of their newly found self-knowledge and self-confidence. Perhaps by analyzing three contemporary novels by southern women—Jill McCorkle's *Ferris Beach* (1990), Tina McElroy Ansa's *Ugly Ways* (1993), and Josephine Humphreys's *Rich in Love* (1987)—we can better see this pattern with its variations, as well as see how relationships between fictional mothers and daughters in southern literature are changing.

At first glance, McCorkle's novel *Ferris Beach* seems to follow most closely the classic pattern seen in earlier works—that is, rejection of mother and quest for adulthood by identifying with male figures, since the female protagonist, young Kate Burns, seems to identify with her father and reject her mother. In fact, however, McCorkle's novel is a female quest for the mother, not the father. Although her mother is alive and active in the novel, Kate has rejected her mother, a woman whose name defines her daughter's image of her: "My mother's name, Cleva, was tightlipped with teeth clenched on the long *e* . . ." (4). Ironically, Cleva is a Yankee, and while southern-born mothers often pass on information about southern culture and female behavior in the South without realizing the limitations it places on modern young women who may desire more than "the ethic of self-sacrifice and denial" that Seidel claims southern mothers "so often embody" (*Southern Belle* 168), Cleva sets out deliberately to initiate her daughter into southern traditions by demanding that she participate in such groups as the Children of the Confederacy.

Regardless of Cleva's attempts, Kate rejects Cleva both as a mother and a faux southerner, as do many contemporary female protagonists who practice a form of self-orphaning to separate themselves from parental figures. As Joan Schultz has observed, this is especially significant to southern females because by rejecting their family names and identities, "they signal themselves as resisting, refusing, or rejecting the kind of family identity, family roles, and family ties with the past or the present considered so vital to the Southern way of life" (92). And by rejecting only the mother figure, as Kate does—who is not southern but is one of the South's leading proponents—she specifically dismisses the ideals her mother so much wants her to adopt. As Kate begins her quest for what she believes is a more "suitable" mother figure, she chooses three females—all southern by birth but all on the margins of southern society. Nonetheless, to the naive Kate, these women represent idealized female status and behavior as she understands it at her young age. In the end, however, Kate watches all three topple off the unsteady pedestals she has constructed for them, leaving her to replace them with the more stable and real mother she initially rejects.

The first mother figure is Mo Rhodes, the mother of her best friend, Misty. Mo moves into the neighborhood and immediately begins to challenge the accepted norms for southern women. She wears pink toenail polish and dangling earrings, paints her house electric blue, and turns her front yard into a Japanese rock garden. Despite her unconventional behavior, the community eventually accepts her eccentricity because it does not threaten them in any substantial way. Kate is drawn to Mo's individuality and wishes secretly that Mo would adopt her. She idealizes Mo to the point of blindness, much like the game she played as a child, blindfolding herself and wandering around her room in "Helen Keller simulation" (1). When she finally learns the truth about Mo—that she is not the ideal mother and has been having an affair with a family friend for years—Kate is stunned but still resistant to the truth. And when Mo is killed in a car wreck while running away with her lover, it seems a fitting ending to Kate's shattered image of womanhood. In retrospect, Kate claims there were so many times she "felt so homesick, only to discover that what [she] was missing was Mo" (168). What she is missing, however, is not the flesh-and-blood Mo but the idea of Mo as the ideal mother.

The second figure idealized by Kate is connected to her growing sexuality. Perry Loomis, a girl in Kate's class, is poor and culturally deprived but beautiful and therefore desired by all the young boys. Kate admits that most girls despise Perry for her beauty and popularity with boys but that she "couldn't help but envy her; it was almost like having a crush, so taken with this person's appearance, so much wishing [she] could claim it as [her] own" (113). The illusion of Perry's perfection is destroyed when Kate becomes the unwilling witness to the gang rape of Perry by neighborhood boys. When she tries to sleep that night, Kate sees "Perry's eyes wide and frightened, her face frozen in silent terror . . . and those breasts that were the subject of all the adolescent boys' dreams of womanhood and sexiness, just those of a young girl, pale blue veins underlining pale white skin, breast bone as fragile as that of a chicken ripped and torn apart" (177). Because Kate is just beginning to recognize her own sexual longings, this scene has particular significance for her. As a formative experience, Kate learns that sex and love are not always connected, that beauty can be a curse as well as an advantage, and perhaps most important, Kate realizes her physical fragility as a woman in a man's world. Over this scene, McCorkle hangs a "fairy tale moon," a significant symbol in many of her works. The moon as romance, the moon as female, and especially the moon as illusion's partner hangs in sharp contrast to the scene it illuminates.

Kate's third mother figure is ironically named Angela, her father's younger sister, who lives in Ferris Beach. Both Angela and Ferris Beach attain icon status when Kate is only five years old—when her father takes her to visit Angela secretly because Cleva so much disapproves of her. It is a powerful memory for Kate, first because it involves deceiving her mother (something she will reenact during her first sexual experience later in the novel) and because it is on this day that Kate embodies in Angela and Ferris Beach all that she admires and desires:

It was that very day that I attached to Angela everything beautiful and lively and good; she was the easy flow of words and music, the waves crashing on Ferris Beach as I spun around and around because I couldn't take in enough of the air and sea gulls as they swooped and whined. Angela was energy, the eternal movement of the world, the blood in my veins and the wind in the bare winter branches that creaked and cried out in the night like tired ghosts in search of a home. She was the answer to a prayer and I thought about that day at Ferris Beach often, re-creating every word and every movement before I fell asleep. (5)

Such romantic language indicates the depth of Kate's illusions. By age five she has established unreal expectations about love, romance, and marriage that she will have to replace as each one is shattered.

Although she learns that Angela is irresponsible, promiscuous, and immature, the first memory of Angela and Ferris Beach sustains Kate's illusions, and it is not until one of the final scenes in the novel that she faces the truth about both the woman and the place. Angry with her mother, who has just discovered Kate in bed with her boyfriend, Kate runs away and stays overnight with Angela in Ferris Beach. Kate finally tells Angela she wishes she were her daughter. (In one scene, in an attempt to redefine herself as Not-Cleva's-Daughter, Kate imagines herself as the Little Match Girl, rescued by Angela—who was herself orphaned at birth—believing and hoping she is Angela's "love child.") After reminding Kate that orphanhood is *her* story and not Kate's, Angela tells her the truth about the ideal mother: "'We all want a fairy tale, Kitty,' she whispered. 'Nobody wants the truth. But sooner or later you learn that there are no fairy tales; there *is* no glamorous mother hidden on a faraway island, no prince on a white horse, no treasure chest full of jewels.' She kissed me quickly on the top of the head. 'That's the real story and the truth is that I'm sorry that's the truth'" (270–71). Reminiscent of the fairy-tale moon, Angela's imagery clearly marks the moment when Kate sees through her own illusions. Even her feelings about Ferris Beach—that it is a place with "huge Ferris wheels and strings of blinking lights, and cotton candy whipped and spun around a paper cone" (15)—have been replaced after the unexpected death of her father. She realizes it is only a place with bait-and-tackle shops, trailer parks, and a pier.

If the novel ended with the destruction of her illusions and she entered adulthood alone and unsustained by hope, McCorkle would have written a bleak novel indeed. But the rejection of the mother and the shattering of childhood illusions are only two steps toward the completion of Kate's adult identity. The final step includes the acceptance of the true mother, with both her strengths and weaknesses. After Kate loses the two strong male figures in her life—her father and her boyfriend Merle—and after she loses all three of her female role models, Kate has no one except her mother, Cleva. But desperation and loneliness are not what help Kate accept her mother again; it is the realization that her mother is not what she believed before—in the same way that she learned Mo, Perry, and Angela were not.

In Kate's first description of her parents, she says, "My parents never looked like they went together to me, even in the wedding photo that was permanently placed on our living room mantel. I expected the real spouses to step in from the wings on either side" (2). Judging her parents' marriage on appearances alone is one of the mistakes that leads Kate to her misconceptions about love in general. Believing that her parents did not belong together, Kate believes they did not love each other, but after witnessing her mother's emotional breakdown after her father's death, Kate finally asks her mother the question she always assumed she knew the answer to: "You really did love him, didn't you?" (277). And although McCorkle resists the fairy-tale ending with mother and daughter apologizing, hugging, and agreeing, Kate does experience an important awareness: "That I *was* my mother's daughter" (276). No longer an orphan, Kate has discovered her real maternal roots.

The rejection of the mother figure in Tina McElroy Ansa's novel *Ugly Ways* is much more severe in nature, but the mother who is rejected is much more difficult and demanding of her three daughters. She is an excellent example of the evolution of the maternal image in contemporary literature from stereotype to real woman. As Mickey Pearlman points out, "The mother as currently depicted in American literature by women has moved from sainted marginality (as icon) to vicious caricature (a destroyer), to the puzzling figure" (2). Ironically named Mudear Lovejoy, Ansa's matriarch sees herself as icon, her daughters see her as vicious destroyer, and the reader, with the best perspective, sees her certainly as puzzling and perhaps therefore more realistic. Mudear is an eccentric, all-powerful woman who decides when her children are young that she has had enough of the traditional oppressions so many wives and mothers endure. She gradually pulls away into her own world, never leaving the house, refusing to do any of the housework or child rearing, tending only her garden—and then only in the middle of the night. Significantly, she rejects her husband, children, and position in the community before any of them have a chance to reject her.

Eccentric characters are nothing new in southern literature, but Ansa has transcended stereotypes with this character. In the early years of her marriage, Mudear is emotionally and physically abused by a husband who does only what he believes a black man at the head of a family should do: demand complete control and punish disobedience. Rather than fight back against both a man and a subculture that are much more powerful than she, Mudear chooses to withdraw into passive aggression. She subtly undermines her husband's authority, making jokes at his expense, calling him "Mr. Bastard" behind his back, ignoring food on the stove until it becomes "an okra holocaust," and gradually giving up control of the household to her young daughters. Rather than just running away and deserting her three young girls, she makes a decision: she says, "*I decided to stay in body. But to leave in spirit and let my spirit free*" (106).

A heartless rejection of her offspring? Perhaps, but not necessarily so. If the genders were reversed, that is, if the father had removed himself emotionally and psychologically from the family, leaving everyone else to keep things going, most readers would be more accepting. In fact, in retrospect, the father, Ernest, admits before Mudear changes and withdraws, "I was so full of myself then . . . so sure about how things should be, so sure about always being right, that I guess I was. . . . He stopped thinking for a while, struck by the weight of what he was about to say to himself. I guess, he thought slowly, I guess I was like Mudear" (96). What is so shocking and perhaps unforgivable to the readers is that the one rejecting home and family is the mother.

Regardless of the moral issue in what Mudear does, the fact remains that her daughters perceive that their mother has rejected them by refusing to participate in their upbringing, and so they, in turn, reject her. They accomplish this in several interesting ways. First, they turn to each other rather than to her when they have problems and need nurturing. Ansa writes that "all three had felt at one time or another that the sound of them laughing together was their only line to sanity and safety" against their mother and against the community that has labeled them the "crazy Lovejoy sisters" (192). Second, they reject all that represents motherhood to them: they make an adolescent vow "that they would never get pregnant and have children" (142), and feeling that Mudear took better care of her garden than she did of her children, they fill their homes only with fake plants and flowers. Finally, around their mother they construct a mythical image that separates her, objectifies her, and dehumanizes her; at various times in the novel, her daughters compare Mudear to the goddess Yemaya, Giya, Pandora, and Medea.

By making Mudear bigger than life and seeing her as "some kind of powerful goddess who can strike [them] mute or dead for some minor transgression" (257), the daughters try to rationalize the lack of maternal love in their home and excuse themselves from dealing with a power they believe is too strong to overcome. But Ansa's choices of mythological references speak more about the daughters' feelings than they can articulate themselves: Yemaya is the Yoruba goddess of the womb and Giya is the mother goddess of earth, both certainly maternal images. Pandora, whose curiosity caused her to open Epimetheus's box, releasing a multitude of plagues on humanity, is the purveyor of knowledge as well as vice for the world. Much like Eve, Pandora indeed caused problems, but she also gave the world hope and the possibility of growth through experience. By comparing Mudear to Pandora, Ansa suggests that Mudear should not be dismissed as a villain so quickly, that her actions have had positive as well as negative effects on the daughters. Medea, perhaps the ultimate archetype of an enraged feminist, kills her own children rather than leave them with her unfaithful husband, Jason, punishing him by denying him a lineage. While this is undeniably a brutal act, Medea's actions could be seen as protecting her children's innocence and purity and as expressing her love for them, which, Jason admits, is evident in the fact that she takes their corpses along with her when she flees in her dragon-drawn chariot. René Girard, author of *Violence and the Sacred*, theorizes that Medea's human sacrifice is necessary "to stem this rising tide" of murder and violence "and redirect violence into 'proper' channels" (10). In short, Medea's children are sacrificed in a religious act of a kind, and heartless though the act seems, good comes from bad in that a balance is restored.

Regardless of any feminist revisioning of *Medea*, though, perhaps most important, these references are Ansa's way of signaling to readers that we cannot completely trust the criticism Mudear's daughters heap upon their mother. In addition, Ansa includes Mudear's own voice in the novel—posthumously, since the novel begins with the three sisters reuniting at their mother's funeral, a significant time in her daughters' lives because, as various scholars have pointed out, very often "only the mother's death can free her daughter from anger so that she can see her mother less subjectively" (Werlock 175–76). By allowing Mudear to tell her own story in her own voice, Ansa forces the reader to recognize that for a woman like Mudear, there are few choices in life. Rather than remain the victim of an abusive marriage, Mudear uses withdrawal as her only outlet and escape. Her anger is undeniable, but it is an anger aimed not just at her own situation but also at the southern and black patriarchal society that dominates and subjugates women like her. Rather than supporting that structure by submitting to it, she tries to teach her daughters to be strong and independent, to transcend barriers for the black southern woman. Her daughters believe she has abandoned them when in fact she has forced all three of them to succeed. She says, *"I didn't coddle 'em and cuddle 'em to death the way some mothers do. I pushed 'em out there to find out what they was best in. That's how you learn things, by getting on out there and living. They found their strengths by the best way anybody could: by living them"* (37). The growth, then, for the Lovejoy sisters, comes when they realize the good their mother has done, when they let go of the anger at her and appreciate her legacy of strength, and when they accept both her positive and negative impacts on their lives.

Although the sisters believe they are nothing like their mother, Ansa's descriptions prove otherwise. Emily, for example, toys with the same "edge of the ravine, the chasm between sanity and insanity," which resembles her mother's eccentricity and near lunacy. Emily fails to see her own withdrawal as similar to Mudear's escape from an existence that is both lonely and debilitating; Mudear could be speaking when Emily asks herself, "What I got to 'come on back' to reality for? . . . Even the edge of insanity felt safe to her compared to the chaos and loneliness she saw in her own life" (224). The most interesting comparison between mother and child, however, concerns the youngest daughter, Annie Ruth. Throughout the novel and in keeping with the mythological references, Mudear is compared to a cat. In ancient Egypt, the cat was revered as sacred, mysterious, and almost godlike partly because it seemed so unknowable, much like the daughters' image of Mudear. Annie Ruth remembers Mudear telling them about a strange encounter she had with a cat; the cat seemed drawn to Mudear, who was almost hypnotized by the purring and singing of this supernatural and somewhat sinister cat. The connection between mother and cat continues when Annie Ruth comes home for the funeral and goes into her mother's bathroom. She claims she "could almost see Mudear floating around the room spraying her Essence of Mudear all over the place. Like a cat" (134). It is no wonder, then, that Annie Ruth develops cat hallucinations, "cat sightings" that begin when Annie Ruth hears of Mudear's illness and approaching death. She sees "suspicious, sneaky, vicious, filthy" cats at home, at work, and even on the airplane on her way to the funeral. It is easy to conclude that Annie Ruth identifies similar characteristics in cats and in her mother, a contradiction of love and hate.

Much like her sisters Emily and Betty, Annie Ruth is drawn to her mother and her mother's behavior despite her anger about her childhood; she claims that even thousands of miles away, she still drags Mudear "around like a dead stanking corpse tied to my leg, like some cat rubbing up against my leg" (256). When she goes to her mother's viewing, Annie Ruth dresses in "a black cotton knit cat suit," and to enter the funeral home, she has to move through a "barrage of cats" that seem to be "prowling around the entrance to the building" (241). Once inside, Ansa describes Annie Ruth as struggling "like a kitten" and "claw[ing]" at the funeral director until she draws blood with her nails (262). Much like the cat in the childhood memory, Mudear is the target of both love and fear, and as Annie Ruth finally admits, she "feared and hated and admired and cursed" her mother (241).

It is also Annie Ruth who first breaks the vow the three sisters made as teenagers by coming to her mother's funeral pregnant. When her sisters try to talk her into an abortion, she refuses. Deciding to have a child might be a way to let go of her anger at Mudear and move forward, to make peace with the past. Part of that release includes giving up the stereotype of the Ideal Mother, just as Kate has to do in *Ferris Beach*. Admitting and rejecting unreal expectations frees these daughters to love their mothers as they are. As Emily says, "It's like as long as we all keep talking and thinking like every black mother in the world is this great wonderful self-sacrificing matriarch . . . it's like as long as we don't think about our mothers as anything but these huge black breasts oozing chocolate milk on demand, we keep all our demons in check" (232). As this conversation continues, the sisters realize their mother did give them needed advice and knowledge, just in a stripped-down manner: "She just give you what you needed, you know, that little piece of wisdom without any of the flavoring to make it taste better" (235).

There are other signs that the sisters are coming to accept their mother and her life's decisions as a precursor to moving on with their own lives. In the penultimate chapter, which takes place at the funeral home, the three sisters find themselves, having accidentally dumped Mudear's body out of the coffin into their own laps—a reversal of the standard mother-child position—conversing with their deceased mother, pouring out all their frustration and anger. In a scene of catharsis the sisters free themselves from the past, pledging to "work on happy and peaceful and appreciative and joyful," hoping to "move on" (270). Finally in the scene, they include their mother in a shared ritual, introduced in the first few pages of the novel. Whenever the sisters reunite, they play a sort of "game," revealing to each other terrible things they have done, a ritual that has the effect of reconnecting the sisters by creating a fresh bond of intimacy and trust. In the funeral home scene, the sisters play this game again, but this time, and for the first time ever, they include Mudear by speaking directly to her. Symbolically, they are letting her into their lives, showing her that they finally trust and love her.

Fittingly, Ansa gives the final word to Mudear. The last chapter is hers, as she reflects on her daughters' confessions as well as on the funeral itself. While it seems fair to be optimistic about the sisters' futures, Mudear reminds us that "*getting mad is just the first step*" (276), suggesting that her daughters are just beginning to be the kind of women she hoped they would be, and like McCorkle's novel, which resists giving us a completely happy ending, *Ugly Ways* ends only with hope and the potential for growth, begun with the reunion and acceptance of the mother.

As in Ansa's novel, the shattering of stereotypes is also a major factor in Josephine Humphreys's 1987 novel *Rich in Love*. At first glance, this novel seems to revert to the father/daughter/missing mother pattern found in earlier southern novels, but it has interesting twists. Similar to Ansa's novel, Humphreys's story includes a reversal of roles—a mother's rejection of home and family as she runs away to "start a second life" (18). This is not the first time the mother, Helen, has rejected the traditional southern family; as the book progresses, Humphreys reveals Helen's earlier attempt to reject her daughter Lucy. Already saddled with the responsibility of one daughter, Helen decides to abort her next pregnancy, but she is carrying twins, and the doctor unknowingly removes only one fetus, leaving Lucy—when she finds out years later—with "the strange sensation of incompleteness and loneliness" and with the sense that her mother "seemed aloof" (51).

Having already been rejected once, Lucy at age seventeen reacts to her mother's new abandonment with intense resistance, partly in the form of role reversal. Lucy assumes the role of mother, thereby pinning the role of rebellious child on Helen. She holds fiercely to tradition: she finds her knowledge of Latin "useful," and she clings to history, finding security and value in the "artifacts" of their household that her mother defines as "creeping clutter" (60–61). On the phone she berates her mother for running away, asking naively, "Is this something feminist . . . or is it something real?" (26). After informing the reader that her "one personality trait" is "vigilance," Lucy labels her mother with the somewhat more childish term *"nonchalant"* (5, 16). She begins to cook and clean for her father, attempting to protect him from the effects of Helen's abandonment, to the extent of rewriting her mother's farewell message—passionless in tone and practically written on a word processor—as a handwritten, sentimental note claiming that Helen felt "absolutely *adrift*," confused, and regretful (18). In one comic confrontation, Lucy even warns Helen, in a very motherish tone, "Don't fall on that screwdriver. . . . You'll put your eye out" (208). Lucy's love for her parents even sounds much more like parents' love for their children: "It was the kind of love that tuckered me out while returning no great reward" (77).

But perhaps the most destructive maternal characteristic Lucy assumes, in the worst stereotype of motherhood, is her fear of change, of risk, and of disruption in the order she has come to view as security since stereotypically it is the mother figure who symbolizes home as a haven from the outside world. Paralleling the breakdown of the family and its traditions in the novel is the destruction of the Old South and a replacement with an ostentatious and artificial New South with names like "Seagull Shores" and "Gator Pond Estates," names, Lucy critically observes, chosen as "memorials to what had been bulldozed into oblivion" (6). Like the developers who threaten tradition and stasis, Helen clearly seems unbothered by the chaos her decision creates and the structure she disrupts, a common characteristic of contemporary female heroes as opposed to earlier generations of women in fiction who defend home, family, and order. As Regina Barreca argues, today's fiction by women is often characterized not by "the perpetuation of the familiar but from its destruction" depending on "surprises, disruptions, reversals, disunity and disharmony" (19). Many contemporary female characters, like Helen, especially southern ones, do not mind disruption simply for the reason that patriarchal structure has rarely placed them in a position that has been satisfactory in the past; they prefer disorder over an order that subordinates them. The ironic difference in Humphreys's novel is that the perpetrator of change and chaos is the older mother rather than the younger daughter, who would be the most likely proponent for change.

Lucy, like earlier and generally older fictional women, equates stasis with contentment, order with happiness, and her need for control and structure results from her fear of change and of loss of control. Rather than adjusting to disorder, Lucy continues to maintain the illusion of order by, in a way, becoming her mother. She can ignore her lack of control over major events such as her mother's departure by taking control over minor things like household chores and taking care of her father as well as by assuming the role her mother has abandoned, as is evident in her description of the power she feels running the household: "I owned the house, this hour of the morning. If I wanted to I could burn it down and everything in it, or I could fix breakfast. It was a moment of power and charity every morning, when I made the decision to cook" (57).

As the novel progresses, Lucy learns to give up control and become more childlike by depending on others, starting with small things like cooking and moving on to bigger ones like divorce. Like traditional mothers, Lucy spends most of her energy trying to protect others, believing, like the best stereotype of the southern matriarch, that only she has the power to hold the family together. She resists disruption and change, and during a brief reunion when Helen returns to help with the difficult birth of Lucy's sister's baby, Lucy tenaciously attempts to reunite her parents, refusing to give her father the car keys so he can visit his new love interest, Vera. But after hiding the keys, Lucy goes to bed and dreams of a lawn mower bulldozing her beautiful countryside, hearing the words, "*And you will stop . . . and you will be as if you never were*" (255). Waking, she realizes she does not want to be left out of the progress of the world or her family, does not want to be left behind.

Awake, she still hears the mower from her dream and glances out the window in time to see her father riding "in the direction of Vera Oxendine's house" on "his Snapper lawn mower" (255). Finally, Lucy is forced to accept that both her parents must make their own choices and she cannot control the present or the future. At the end of the novel, she knows she can make plans only for herself, remarking, "But who knows what will happen? We'll have to wait and see" (255–61). Accepting her parents as fallible rather than trying to force them to fit her idealistic mold, Lucy begins to move toward a real adulthood for herself. Significantly, Lucy has accepted the chaos created by her mother's leaving as well as what she perceives as her mother's weaknesses. She is also working toward an understanding that being a mother does not mean being static. She has given up trying to control her father's choices, recognizing his own ability to choose what is best for him. And by relinquishing her role as parent, Lucy is given license to be a daughter again.

Although Lucy has achieved growth, Humphreys, like Ansa and McCorkle, resists the happy ending of traditional novels that typically reinstates the hierarchical structure. The disruption in Humphreys's family continues beyond the final page as Lucy's parents pursue their new lives with no guarantees that those lives will be any better than the one they shared. Typical of contemporary women's fiction, Humphreys celebrates female experience and choice, allowing Helen to abandon the rules and to disrupt the patriarchal structure, establishing new definitions of the southern family. True, no promises are made for her happiness—only possibilities—but even a chance for a more fulfilling life was very often unavailable to earlier generations of fictional mothers who chose to explore their own individuality, especially when it was at odds with southern ideals for women. Helen Odom will not need to walk into the water as Edna Pontellier does in *The Awakening*. Helen has a choice, and Lucy's growth comes from allowing her the freedom to choose.

The changes in southern mother-daughter relationships are significant ones. The variety of roles available for women in the real world is growing, and this growth is certainly reflected in the literature of the time. The thread that runs through these three novels, and through the majority of today's southern novels by women, is the reconciliation and acceptance of the old traditions with new choices, represented by the changing image of the southern mother. Coming to terms with the differences from and similarities to her mother is crucial before a daughter can move toward her adult potential. In contrast to the contemporary male protagonists, who, Carol Pearson and Katherine Pope point out, are "usually anti-heroes in a hopeless and meaningless world," female protagonists "are increasingly hopeful, sloughing off the victim role to reveal their true, powerful, and heroic identities" (13). Part of this process includes reconciliation with parents, very often the father but nearly always the mother. By acknowledging the weaknesses but also recognizing the strengths of southern traditions and the role of women within that structure—symbolized by the southern mother—a young southern female protagonist is in a better position to reject the qualities that may limit her growth but also to integrate those positive traits that will contribute to a complete adult being.

Works Cited

Ansa, Tina McElroy. *Ugly Ways*. New York: Harcourt, 1993.

Barreca, Regina. *Untamed and Unabashed: Essays on Women and Humor in British Literature*. Detroit: Wayne State UP, 1994.

Girard, René. *Violence and the Sacred*. 1975. Trans. Patrick Gregory. Baltimore: Johns Hopkins UP, 1977.

Humphreys, Josephine. *Rich in Love*. 1987. New York: Penguin, 1988.

Jones, Anne Goodwyn. *Tomorrow Is Another Day: The Woman Writer in the South, 1859–1936*. Baton Rouge: Louisiana State UP, 1981.

MacKethan, Lucinda H. *Daughters of Time: Creating Woman's Voice in Southern Story*. Athens: U of Georgia P, 1990.

McCorkle, Jill. *Ferris Beach*. 1990. New York: Fawcett Crest, 1991.

Pearlman, Mickey, ed. *Mother Puzzles: Daughters and Mothers in Contemporary American Literature*. New York: Greenwood, 1989.

Pearson, Carol, and Katherine Pope. *The Female Hero in American Literature*. New York: Bowker, 1981.

Schultz, Joan. "Orphaning as Resistance." *The Female Tradition in Southern Literature: Essays on Southern Women Writers*. Ed. Carol S. Manning. Urbana: U of Illinois P, 1993. 89–109.

Seidel, Kathryn Lee. "Gail Godwin and Ellen Glasgow: Southern Mothers and Daughters." *Tulsa Studies in Women's Literature* 10.2 (1991): 287–94.

———. *The Southern Belle in the American Novel*. Tampa: U of South Florida P, 1985.

Tiegreen, Helen Hurt. "Mothers, Daughters, and One Writer's Revisions." *Mississippi Quarterly* 39.4 (1986): 605–26.

Werlock, Abby H.P. "A Profusion of Women's Voices: Mothers and Daughters Redefining the Myths." *Mother Puzzles: Daughters and Mothers in Contemporary American Literature*. Ed. Mickey Pearlman. New York: Greenwood, 1989. 171–84.

Westling, Louise. "Flannery O'Connor's Mothers and Daughters." *Twentieth Century Literature* 24 (1978): 510–22.

Wolfe, Margaret Ripley. *Daughters of Canaan: A Saga of Southern Women*. Lexington: UP of Kentucky, 1995.

Toward Healing the Split

Lee Smith's FANCY STRUT *and* BLACK MOUNTAIN BREAKDOWN

Linda J. Byrd

In virtually all of Lee Smith's novels, a female protagonist struggles in search of her identity. In the canon of her novels, Smith treats female experience progressively, revealing in her early novels the limited possibilities for women and employing in her later novels ennobling images of women. Just as Nancy Friday, in her psychological study *My Mother/My Self*, poses a choice for women between sexuality and motherhood, Smith, in her early novels, disallows the coexistence of sexuality and motherhood as qualities within one character. Monica Neighbors of *Fancy Strut* (1973) and Crystal Spangler of *Black Mountain Breakdown* (1980), like the protagonists of Smith's first two novels, *The Last Day the Dogbushes Bloomed* (1968) and *Something in the Wind* (1971), suffer from a split identity based on their acceptance of an inherent incompatibility between sexuality and motherhood. All four novels are similar in that Smith takes the perspective of the daughter, not the mother, thus linking her early fiction to the psychological studies of both Friday and Dorothy Dinnerstein. At this point in her writing, Smith saw the possibilities for women's lives as limited by social and cultural constructions, and her fiction reflects this vision.

Fancy Strut breaks from the first-person point of view of the first two novels as the author begins narrative experimentation and in effect offers an enlarged view of women's positions within a community. The story is told by a shifting, third-person omniscient narrator, with each chapter related from a different character's point of view. In the novel, all the members of the community of Speed, Alabama, effectively "strut their stuff," struggling to conform to rigid conventional codes, thus eradicating the possibility for any individuality or even imagination. *Fancy Strut*, indeed, presents a dark view of the possibilities for females as the women in town play out their allotted roles in this patriarchal society. Although not to the same degree, these female characters experience similar struggles with sexuality, violence, maternity, and religion as did the protagonists of Smith's first two novels. Monica Neighbors, arguably the leading protagonist, since nine of the novel's thirty-eight chapters are divulged from her vantage point, comes closest to continuing the development of female identity Smith began in *The Last Day the Dogbushes Bloomed* and *Something in the Wind.*

Monica, the young wife of the respected and wealthy newspaper editor Manly Neighbors, suffers from a split identity not unlike that of Brooke Kincaid (*Something in the Wind*). A sexual creature, Monica is drawn to natural, growing things, particularly roses (consistently representative of female sexuality in Smith's work). Married only three years, Monica already experiences restlessness, at first trying to use her overflowing energy in a socially acceptable way by repeatedly redecorating a new home. Anne Goodwyn Jones writes that Monica cannot deal with any person or problem directly: "She is too distant from her own sexuality and aggression to do anything direct" (127). For three years Monica has been a model wife, or so it seems, but suddenly she feels on the verge of madness; everything feels artificial. Like Brooke, Monica has split into a public self and a private self, refusing even to attempt to integrate the two. While presenting the outward appearance of a happy housewife, she secretly harbors fantasies of sexual degradation. Even though Manly has made it clear that he wants children, she shudders at the thought of pregnancy. When Caroline Pettit shares with Monica her feelings about being pregnant, Monica perceives Caroline's comments as inappropriate, feeling that she neither possesses common interests with pregnant women or mothers nor desires any.

Monica suffers from the separation between mind and body that earlier Smith protagonists battled. Her sexuality is revealed when Smith explains that the summer before Monica married Manly, while on a trip to Europe, she had casual sexual intercourse with several Italians and one Swede, "just to prove . . . she could do it" (33). Away from the restraints of southern society, Monica had enjoyed the purely physical connection with strangers. Upon returning home, however, she is plagued by guilt and feels extremely grateful to Manly for marrying her and rescuing her from her sexual vagaries. Never attempting to integrate her European experience and reconcile her sexuality with her role in southern society, Monica marries a fatherly man whom she perceives as a "teddy bear" (184), someone to save her from what Dorothy Hill calls "the burden of self-exploration." As Hill points out, Monica hopes to remain comfortable and safe by "liv[ing] out a cardboard caricature of life modeled on an image manufactured by women's magazines" (37). Since her lifestyle demands that she have a lovely home and a full-time maid, she does, even though she despises the meddling housekeeper. Feeling like an "impostor" (*Fancy Strut* 32), married under false pretenses, Monica secretly revolts against Manly's "goddamn Boy Scout" (34) ways by driving too fast without a seat belt while imagining meetings with a fantasy lover.

Although Manly is a perfect husband in all outward respects, he reifies the mind/body split. Monica desperately wants to be needed by her husband, but Manly, with his overactive rational mind and undeveloped sexuality, thinks he has no problem he cannot logically solve by merely analyzing it. He loves Monica, but he doesn't need her sexually or in any other way, and he is puzzled when she gets that "distant look in her eye" (180). He resolves that women are not meant to be understood anyway, but rather they are to be "reverenced and protected" (179), perfectly articulating the age-old southern practice of placing women on pedestals to be admired but not touched. Manly's inability to understand his wife is captured when he notices Monica daydreaming and thinks: "What did she have to daydream about? What could she be thinking of that was not real and present and accounted for?" (179–80). The obvious irony is that she dreams of driving to a sleazy motel to meet a lover with whom her sexuality is unrestrained, even secretly harboring the "wild hope" that Manly will "burst through that door [their home] . . . and rip off her Tanner dress so violently that the buttons would sound like bullets as they hit the wall, and throw her down upon the floor . . . she wishe[s] he would strip her and set her up on the coffee table and make her do terrible things" (185). But Manly only stands and stares at his wife, wondering what's for supper. Dorothy Hill describes Manly as one of Smith's "willfully benign men . . . self-consciously desexed and self-castrated, cut off from their sexuality and aggressiveness" (38), a man who, through his own acceptance of the dichotomy between mind and body, contributes to his wife's bifurcated view.

When Monica encounters Buck Fire, an out-of-work actor and the pageant manager, the conflict between her mind and body begins. Monica and Buck literally collide on the stairs of the pageant headquarters, and even at this first meeting, Buck grasps her buttocks for a "quick feel." Buck, also a sexual being (as his name suggests), thinks there's "no risk in screwing the married," planning to "love-'em-and-leave-'em panting" (36). After Monica's first brush with Buck, having felt her sexuality emerge, she is uncomfortable and desires the safety and assurance of her husband, so she rushes home to Manly. She still thinks she can suppress her sexuality as long as she is away from Buck Fire, but soon, no longer able to keep her mind separate from her body, she begins to fantasize about him. Monica's thoughts reflect her confused feelings: "She realized that she was real in her daydreams, and real in her house with Manly. But not here. She was not at all real in this plane" with Buck (140).

These feelings of confusion about her true nature are similar to Brooke's in that Brooke considers one of her selves to be real and the other to be fake. With Brooke, however, it is the "real" self that is sexual, whereas Monica believes she can express her sexuality only in her daydreams. Monica's sexuality emerges with increasing intensity as her affair with Buck progresses. Very soon after their first sexual encounter, Monica perceives that there is no longer a dream lover, but rather a battle within her between Manly and Buck, a contest between the two sides of herself. With no hint of integration, Monica allows her mind to struggle against her body in a battle that ensures defeat for her either way. As she lives out her fantasy of an illicit love affair, Monica's need is satisfied by Buck, rather than by the ironically named Manly. Monica thinks with satisfaction she'll go straight to hell, having given in to the desires of the flesh, but then she decides she doesn't believe hell exists anyway.

Smith's depiction of Buck Fire is rife with religious connotations. In a personal interview, Smith explained her feeling that sexual passion has some of the same power as religious passion; therefore, a character often searches for spiritual intensity in a sexual relationship because both sexual and religious ecstasy take a person "totally outside yourself" (Personal Communication). Often after a sexual experience, a female character feels "born again"; by expressing her sexuality, she has reclaimed her body. When Buck walks around, in and out of a patch of sunlight, "it had seemed to Monica that he was not only illumined but transfigured," and her sexual experience with him will in fact be both illuminating and transformative for her. Buck's association with divinity is implied when his hair is described as glowing "a thousand colors in the sun . . . from palest yellow to brightest red to black," and his "astonishing gold shirt" reflects the sunlight and "sho[ots] it back in rays," evoking the image of Christ with a glowing halo. When Monica first sees Buck, she describes him as possessing a "new and startling dimension . . . unlike any man she had ever known. . . . Like a damn Annunciation" (42). Smith's diction here clearly implies Buck's association with Christ; his arrival in Monica's life signals the opportunity for sacred union, or salvation. Observing Buck, Monica says, "Oh Jesus" (44); then later, she thinks "Oh Christ," when she sees his bare chest (217). Establishing his close connection with Monica, Smith describes Buck's hand as "almost exactly the same size" as Monica's (218). Monica and Buck are the first of many couples in Smith's works who are described as being the same physical size, suggesting their equality in relationships that are nonsacrificial. Neither Monica nor Buck dominates; rather, they divinely complement each other in their mutual enjoyment of sexuality.

Smith's interest in language and in women's need for expression in a patriarchal society most strongly emerges in *Fancy Strut* with the portraiture of Monica. Having been silenced for so long, her voice is not heard or acknowledged by anyone. Monica's daydreams of illicit sex usually involve no conversation; she imagines "no words spoken . . . just the fierce crush of their violent embrace" (33). Monica finds the English language inadequate to express these feelings. She even admits at one point in the novel that she doesn't actually enjoy talking; patriarchal language cannot convey her feelings. Effectively separating her mind from her body, she rediscovers sexual pleasure. The mind, where language originates, seems to be a world away from the body that can feel and express the sensuality of certain experiences.

A protagonist whom patriarchal religion leaves unfulfilled, Monica, in search of selfhood, makes the conscious decision to wallow in what she believes to be the degradation represented by her sexual relationship with Buck. Ironically, Buck Fire, the carefree ladies' man, has fallen in love with Monica. Unable to integrate her sexuality into her life with Manly, Monica believes she must choose either Buck and the physical pleasure he provides or Manly and the stability and boundaries he represents. Even though the affair with Buck transforms Monica's understanding of her own sexuality, at the end she chooses what Anne Goodwyn Jones calls the "permanence and guilt" of her relationship with Manly (127). Monica decides that perhaps she has successfully lived out a fantasy that will now disappear. The affair quickly seems distant and once more doesn't seem to exist in Monica's "real" life. At the end, with neither fantasy lover nor real one, she feels "worn out and empty and suddenly brittle and just a little bit old" (*Fancy Strut* 335). She does, however, try to express her sexual passion with Manly, but he doesn't understand. The futility Monica feels about being misunderstood and her final resignation to it are illustrated in a vision she has of Manly finding a note inside a bottle that has washed up on the shore: "It was as though Manly had found her, picked her up off a beach someplace where she had drifted, and dusted her off and kept her carefully among his most prized possessions. But he couldn't read the note" (335–36). So, unlike Buck, who realizes that Monica is not a possession, Manly owns Monica as he would a treasure, all the while unable to "read" or understand her sexual nature and desire for passion.

With no hope of ever expressing her sexuality with her husband, Monica chooses the community-validated path that has been so disgusting to her earlier; she tells Manly that she's ready to have a baby, making the choice posed by Nancy Friday between sexuality and motherhood. Ironically, earlier in the novel, just after Monica has met Buck Fire but before their affair, she makes an unconscious connection between sexuality and motherhood when, bursting with pent-up sexual frustration, she admits that she feels "pregnant" with things "building up and preparing to explode." At this time she sees motherhood as a grim alternative. Concerning pregnancy, she thinks: "After it happened to you, you really had only two choices: you liked it or acted like you liked it, or else you hated it, in which case your husband would hate you and you would hate yourself and probably go crazy" (207). So Monica sees pregnancy and motherhood as totally separate and apart from sexuality, and in choosing to remain with Manly, to suppress her sexuality and become a mother, she has opted for an unfulfilled life but for one that she believes to be secure.

Crystal Spangler, of Smith's next novel, *Black Mountain Breakdown*, shares Monica's fascination with, and attraction to, sexual aggression, and like Monica, she is also willing to settle for an unfulfilling life, one without the passion she so desires. In this novel, Smith creates a protagonist who epitomizes the passive female torn between society's conflicting values. Originally a short story titled "Paralyzed: A True Story" and told from the unsympathetic point of view of Agnes McClanahan, *Black Mountain Breakdown* tells the story not only of a young girl's stunted maturation process but also of a changing community. Smith said that one of her aims in writing the novel was to "capture the way it was growing up in that time and place," to show the change in this semi-rural mining section of Appalachia between the 1950s and 1970s ("Interview" [Arnold] 243–45). The novel is set in rural western Virginia in a small town named Black Rock, a town loosely based on Smith's memories of Grundy, the town where she grew up. With a tragic tone, Smith couples the third-person point of view with present verb tense to achieve what Lucinda MacKethan calls "a tension between closeness and distance crucial to both mystery and meaning in the novel" (11). So, although Crystal does not tell her own story, the omniscient narrator's present verb tense creates a striking sense of immediacy.

Crystal's experience echoes those of Smith's earlier protagonists, but Crystal is, by Smith's admission, a more extreme case than the lost female characters in the earlier novels. Katherine Kearns describes Crystal as a total contradiction, a symbol for "the missing half to every man's desires, to every woman's anxieties, and whatever she seems to become is through the infusion of others' meanings" (183).

Crystal's name describes her nature perfectly. Feeling herself to be totally transparent, she must stand beside or opposite something to gain any substance at all. Often posing in front of a mirror, she gazes at herself and imagines different identities. Crystal cannot settle on one image but constantly changes identities as she searches for her selfhood. Smiling at everyone in order to gain easy popularity, Crystal becomes what people want her to be, not retaining enough individuality even to adopt her own unique handwriting. As light reflects from a crystal, she deflects all individuality away from herself and onto those around her. Only when people are pleased with her and noticing her does she feel at all alive. The sole ninth grader chosen for cheerleader, Crystal quickly attracts the attention of the high school boys and begins to define herself through them: "It's only when she's with boys that she feels pretty, or popular, or fun. In the way they talk to her and act around her, Crystal can see what they think of her, and then that's the way she is" (140). Dorothy Hill argues that "no world could be more split" than Crystal's; there is no connection between the outside and the inside (41).

Crystal does, however, start to feel a connection between her two worlds when she begins dating Mack Stiltner, the high school dropout with a bad reputation. Mack represents the sexual, physical aspect of love as he awakens the erogenous aspect of Crystal, who says she would rather be with Mack than anyone else since only then can she be her true self. Following her breakup with Mack, she experiences religious salvation at a local revival, but she admits that her relationship with Mack seemed to have more connection to real life than her salvation. Crystal's communion with Mack, in fact, serves as a type of salvation for her since she says she can "be herself" (98) with him; he houses the potential to "save" her from her own passivity. The divine nature of their mutual sexuality is more "real" to Crystal than experiencing salvation in the imposed patriarchal religion that denies women both physical pleasure and a voice. Without Mack, she resumes imagining other selves, what it would be like to be a bag boy at a hotel or a frail woman at a beauty pageant. Even after her eventual marriage to Roger Lee Combs, Crystal "makes up other selves"—a businesswoman, a mother "dressing children . . . plaiting pigtails, tying strings of saddle oxfords . . . frying bacon, wiping tears" (221). But Crystal, basing her feelings on the wishes of others rather than on her own, perceives actual motherhood as an impossibility for herself, afraid that Roger might not love her anymore if she changes herself in any way. So although she can imagine herself fulfilling the role of a mother, Crystal is caught in the same trap as other Smith protagonists who believe, as Nancy Friday would argue, that they must make a choice between sexuality and motherhood, that they cannot possess both qualities.

Similar to several of Smith's earlier female characters, Crystal's sexuality is likewise connected to her love of nature and her acute senses. As Crystal wraps Christmas ornaments for storage, her hands are described as "mov[ing] silently like birds" (60), reminiscent of the Queen's fluttering movements in Smith's first novel, *The Last Day the Dogbushes Bloomed*. On her first date with Mack, Crystal's senses are awakened not only by Mack's presence but also by the sweet outdoor smells and the warm wind blowing across her face. Later, when Crystal goes swimming after having been cooped up inside reading the Bible for days, the colors of the mountains and the sky excite her and stir her sensory perceptions. Her senses are heightened even as she sunbathes, loving the sensation of the hot cement burning her body through the towel and the rough, scratchy feeling when she moves.

Crystal's elevated sense of touch is clear throughout the novel in her continuous interest in textures and patterns. Part of her "crystal-ness" seems related not only to her receptivity to other people but also her sensitivity to sensory stimuli. As a child, she fingers her father's bathrobe hem and the lace on the armchair in the parlor as he reads poetry to her. The first scene of the novel describes Crystal tracing the raised lettering on a Mason jar with which she plans to capture fireflies. Later, at the old homeplace at Dry Fork, she traces with her fingers the carved initials of her father on a windowsill and fingers Uncle Devere's flannel shirts that are hanging in the closet.

Crystal's sensuality serves as a source of contention between her and her mother. Lucinda MacKethan defends Lorene Spangler's lack of understanding and sensitivity to her daughter Crystal as a "survival mechanism" in coping with a reclusive, emphysematic husband and two disappointing sons (8), but her callousness toward her husband, Grant, and her manipulation of Crystal demonstrate a self-centeredness and artificiality common to mothers in Smith's earlier novels. Totally unconnected with nature or the senses, Lorene has difficulty understanding Crystal's desire to stay outside at night catching fireflies and enjoying the outdoors. Lorene insists that her daughter start rolling her hair at age twelve, herself proud to be rolled up "in pink plastic curlers with snap-on tops" (*Black Mountain* 12), the epitome of artificiality. Lorene's primary concern lies with appearance, and even at almost fifty years old, "still a blond, strong woman, running to fat maybe . . . she keeps herself up, wears heels when she goes to town" (13). Although Lorene considers her husband a fool and a bad influence on Crystal, she ignores this and anything else she doesn't like, consoling herself by spouting off empty platitudes. Lorene calls Crystal the "child of her old age, the joy of her heart" (14) and centers her whole life around this beautiful, perfect little girl; however, she is satisfied only when Crystal conforms to her expectations. Lorene wants to shape Crystal into her version of the perfect woman—a beauty, a trophy, a prize, reminiscent of *Fancy Strut*, where Manly saw Monica as a treasure.

Lorene plans for Crystal to go to a fine school, marry a doctor, and "be somebody" (14). And she begins "seeing to that" by rushing Crystal into adulthood before the girl is ready. The summer before Crystal starts high school, Lorene and her sister Neva, a hairdresser, put Crystal through the grueling process of having her hair frosted. When Crystal protests, insisting she wants to play in the sprinkler outside with Babe and then begins to cry because of the physical pain she is experiencing, Lorene offers her daughter a tissue and says, "Honey, don't you want to look real cute for high school?" Crystal wails, "I don't care. . . . I don't care if I look cute or not, I don't care, I don't care!" (42). Throughout the entire beauty ritual, Lorene and Neva engage in a private conversation, completely ignoring Crystal's questions, particularly when they pertain to Crystal's father and his illness.

Lorene's callousness toward her sick husband and her lack of insight into her daughter are apparent on several occasions when she tells her husband he should be ashamed of himself for reading "The Spider and the Fly" to Crystal since Lorene perceives Crystal's "intense emotion" (17) at hearing the poem as distress and accuses Grant of upsetting the girl. But Grant knows his daughter in a deeper sense; he can also "read" her emotions as he reads poetry to her, observing that language makes Crystal "wholly alive" (17). Grant and Crystal's connection is rooted in language, in shared stories and poetry, and Crystal craves literature and language, sensing in her father a link not only to the past but also to another sensual human being.

Grant Spangler serves as Crystal's connection to the mysterious world of fantasy, poetry, and language, and her fascination with stories, both true and made-up, ties her to Smith's earlier female protagonists in their common desire for a voice of their own and a language in which to express themselves. Grant captures his young daughter's imagination with tales of the past and romantic stories. As Grant's health deteriorates, he increasingly craves the company of his daughter, "rasping on in his hoarse voice, telling Crystal all the old stories he knows" (64). Even though Grant is slowly dying, Crystal won't allow herself to believe it and finds within his darkened parlor, where he has secluded himself, a warm and protective environment, a retreat into the symbolic womb of the cave where she receives nourishing words. As father and daughter share a love for language in the cavelike parlor, Crystal experiences regeneration, thriving on the words her father provides and discovering a voice with which to express her innermost feelings.

This regeneration is short-lived, however, because the double tragedy Crystal suffers at age fourteen damages and forever changes her. The memory of Crystal's rape at Dry Fork by her Uncle Devere submerges into her subconscious mind almost immediately after it occurs, not to resurface until sixteen years later. Crystal is silenced by the assault, robbed of the language to express her pain. The nightmare that has just occurred is soon followed by another even more painful one when Crystal returns home the next morning to discover her father dead. Crystal feels "the whole world fall away from her by degrees until nothing at all is left" (70), once more robbed of a voice since her father was her source of, and inspiration for, language. As her aunt attempts to silence Crystal, shouting: "You shut up that hollering, now. That's not the way to act . . . you're acting so wild" (74–75), Crystal clings to her father's body, begging, "Don't let them take him out of here" (77). Dorothy Hill notes that after the rape and then her father's death, Crystal's problem becomes "an absence of feeling; Crystal is separated from herself and from love" (46). Effectively silenced, she manages to attend the funeral without saying a word or shedding a tear, but she "feels as empty as light, somewhere outside herself" as she experiences mind/body separation, watching "herself walk up the aisle, then sit, then walk back out at the end" (*Black Mountain* 80). Despite her initial cool exterior, Crystal is consumed by rage when her family tries to move her from her father's grave. Once again, just as she remained by her father's side in the parlor, she feels paralyzed and refuses to leave the site. As they "pull at her arms," forcing her from her chair, Crystal finally finds enough voice to scream, expressing the pain that she alone seems to feel (83). Apparently, no one else is affected by her father's death. In fact, no one ever seems to think of Grant again after this day, no one except Crystal.

Mack Stiltner's presence in Crystal's life seems to fill a void left by the death of her father. As Crystal is drawn to Mack Stiltner, she seems for the first time "self-possessed" (86). Similar to the relationship between Brooke and Bentley, then Monica and Buck, Smith's interest in language and its inability to convey sexual feelings again surfaces in the relationship between Crystal and Mack when, after they make love, "they lie on the mattress all tangled up, not talking, and the fresh air from outside blows in across them as softly as breath" (99). No words are necessary between Crystal and Mack; they are soul mates. The only person who understands Crystal's desire to "have it all" (103), Mack admits his similar aspirations, then explains that the only difference between Crystal and himself is that he realizes the impossibility of this goal and Crystal doesn't. When Mack shares with Crystal a song he wrote about her "angel hair" and its sharpness, keeping him at a distance from her, Crystal becomes uncomfortable and confused, feeling "all lost inside" (101). Suddenly remembering the story her father told her about a rockslide in a mine, Crystal panics as she had earlier when she and Roger, while on a picnic, went into a cavelike mine. Once inside the mine, Crystal recalled the childhood experience of riding a pony "in and out of the mine" (53) when her father took her there with him on a business matter.

Nor Hall discusses the point of sexual awakening for a girl as a time when "spirituality and sensuality intermingle." During these pivotal moments in a girl's life, Hall argues, the girl finds herself drawn to babies and to horses, "to undomesticated libido" (56). Monica Neighbors, upon seeing Buck Fire for the first time, also remembers horseback riding at summer camp, calling this "the only experience which she had ever had in her life that was in any way analogous to her vision of Buck" (*Fancy Strut* 42). Both young women's memories are linked to their awakening sexuality.

Crystal's relationship with Mack and its concomitant intensity and exposure elicit from her a fear of the symbolic cave and rebirth. In Mack's song, Smith again mixes the sacred with the profane in her depiction of Crystal's divine, "angelic" qualities, which are simultaneously extremely dangerous. The words of the song demonstrate Mack's understanding and acceptance of

Crystal, but she is unable, or unwilling, to face self-knowledge and regeneration represented by the cave. In the ensuing argument between Mack and Crystal, he challenges her, in John Kalb's words, to "own for once her passion and desires instead of drifting in the sea of dreams and proddings of others" (24), but Crystal, extremely distraught, wishes for a minute that Mack were Roger, longing for the safety of a distant arrangement like the one she and Roger had. In his song, Crystal immediately recognizes Mack's ability to penetrate her soul while "all Roger ever did was give her rings" (*Black Mountain* 101). There was safety in Crystal's relationship with Roger because it did not threaten to disturb her carefully constructed exterior, but with Mack, the danger of exposure and penetration proves too great.

The communion between Mack and Crystal is suggested by Mack's blatant remark to Crystal: "We're two of a kind, baby, we're just alike, you and me." Uncomfortable with Mack's honesty, Crystal reacts with a gesture that serves once more to sever her mind from her body and keep her "safe." Mack asks Crystal to marry him and go to Nashville, where he will pursue his career in music, but Crystal cannot make any decision. Mack realizes that Crystal's unwillingness to risk suffering the pain of self-knowledge remains an impervious barrier between them. Perhaps it is Mack and his piercing song on which Crystal thinks back years later, long after Mack has gone to Nashville and become successful, when her older brother Jules, who is homosexual, calls in the middle of the night to tell her "something sad." Jules confesses: "The only kind of man I like is the kind you can't live with, the kind you pick up in a bar. . . . The kind I'm attracted to . . . is the kind I could never love" (193). Jules's words to his sister imply his own battle with the painful dichotomy between mind and body since he feels unable to express physical passion with someone he could also love spiritually. The phone call greatly disturbs Crystal, though she remains silent, never telling anyone about it; "it's as though Jules has reached down inside her and plucked one note on an antique musical instrument, and the echo goes on and on, a high painful keening note" (193–94). Jules's phone call serves as a painful reminder of the kind of love Crystal felt for Mack, with its offer of integration and regeneration.

The strong link between sexual passion and religious intensity apparent in many of Smith's novels surfaces in Crystal's experience of salvation at a local revival. For Crystal, her religious salvation becomes tied to the intense feelings she had for Mack, who is always associated with nature. As Crystal sits on the porch with Agnes and Jubal Thacker (the young Holiness preacher with whom she grew up), she wonders "if Jubal ever hears voices . . . [or] has seen God's face" (114). It is, in fact, fear of a metaphorical death (of her passivity) and the pain of rebirth and regeneration that the sweet, sacred union with Mack offered that halted her relationship with him. As Jubal talks about salvation, Crystal once again experiences those same sensations she felt with Mack: "the hair along [her] arms rises at the sound of Jubal's voice" (118), and her stomach feels queasy as she notices the sweet-smelling trumpet vine. In this setting, Smith interweaves the ingredients that have come to suggest strong and natural female sexuality: the power of language in Jubal's "soft . . . disembodied voice" (118), the sensation in Crystal's stomach, the sweet sensuality of nature, and the concept of death and rebirth in Crystal's thoughts. Crystal will continue to experience a strange feeling in her stomach on her way to the revival, and when she arrives, she is drawn physically into the ecstatic service. As the choir sings and Crystal, unsaved, considers her own death, she feels "fear shoot[ing] straight through the middle of her like a sweet sharp knife" (121). Smith's diction is important here; although "sweet" and "sharp" almost seem contradictory, they, in fact, capture the complexity of the sensation Crystal experiences as she is equally drawn to and terrified by the spirituality that envelops her. Smith explains the ecstatic religious conversion as a person's being "compelled and repelled in almost the same measure," adding: "I think that sort of giving over—it's sort of an identity question for me. If you are born again, who are you? If you are totally in the spirit, then where is your self? What happens to the self? And I find it absolutely terrifying: it's like annihilation, and it's just really scary" ("Interview" [Byrd] 97). But Crystal is not terrified because she finds comfort only when she is outside herself. In her salvation experience, in the giving of self in spirit as much as in flesh, she feels truly alive. Her sensuality is elevated as she detects "electricity . . . shooting straight into her head and all down her body, crackling in every nerve." With "a current arc[ing] through her body," she feels again "like she felt when she was with Mack—alive, fully alive and fully real, more than real" (126).

When Crystal attends Girls' State after her senior year of high school, she experiences an encounter with the divine that approaches the intensity of her earlier religious conversion and of her sexual passion with Mack. At camp, she awakens in the early morning hours "tingling from head to toe" (142). In a setting permeated with divine imagery, Crystal experiences the power of her own sexuality, her inner divinity. As "the air around her seems to move," Crystal notices the "sounds of breathing intensify" as the air appears to make "a swell, rising movement." Crystal's initial sensation is one of "disconnect[ion]," the way she had felt when her father died and again when Mack got too close to her. Then, she feels "oddly terrifyingly buoyant, borne up on the gray moving air and floating." Suddenly, "all the air has turned to wind . . . loud and roaring," and Crystal feels "the blood run[ning] like a creek in her veins." Just when she expects to "plummet down some awful immediate spiral," she feels suspended and watches the early morning light fill the room.

She hears a voice call her name, and "now Crystal can speak, and she does," asking "What?" (143–44). Following what she believes is the sound of a deep, sad, familiar man's voice, she rushes outside only to be disappointed at finding no one there. Unable to comprehend what has happened to her, Crystal tries to explain to Agnes "this vision" that she has decided was sent by God, but Agnes's response works to silence Crystal as Crystal "doesn't know what to say." With her heart beating "like thunder in her chest," she wishes she could feel "this much alive" forever (146–47). The only time Crystal can feel this life pumping through her veins, however, is when she is experiencing religious or sexual passion.

In her relationship with Jerold Kukafka, Crystal briefly finds the old spark that has been missing from her life since her experience at camp. She senses that her relationship with Jerold is for the present only and never considers a future with him. The important thing about Jerold is that he makes Crystal feel "so much alive" with the old passion. And Jerold, like Mack, tells Crystal that they are alike, but he also insists they are both "doomed" (188–89), which she refuses to believe, just as she had denied Mack's poignant observations about her. Thinking about Jerold after his suicide, Crystal recalls his instructions to her to "live," to "breathe" (188–89). Jerold's silence and mystery hold a magnetic attraction for Crystal, but she does not understand him or his suicide.

After a presumed nervous breakdown that lands Crystal in the hospital for a while, she is once more unable to find words to express her pain and begins searching for something with which to connect. While Crystal is visiting her aunts at Dry Fork, her mind whirls as she goes through the house, examining photographs, furniture, and clothes until she finds a dusty leather-covered journal hidden in an old box and suddenly realizes that "this journal—or something like it—is what she has been looking for" (202), something with which to reconnect to her lost past and provide much-needed continuity in her life. Crystal's search reflects Hall's observation that a woman's need to discover "the roots of her femininity" often materializes in her "choosing among or 'digging through' [her] grandmother's possessions," eventually choosing one item to keep that "link[s] her to her feminine ancestor" (200–201). Crystal had often asked her aunts about her grandmother, trying to learn every possible detail as she rummaged through the remnants of the past in search of some clue to her own identity. Now settling on the journal, Crystal believes she has found a thread with which she can stitch together the scattered pieces.

Crystal finds another passion to fill the void within herself when, encouraged by her old high school English teacher, she embarks on a teaching career. She has always loved language and literature, but until now she has taken jobs based on the convenience and approval of the man with whom she was involved at any given time. Once the creative spark is ignited within her by making a mobile for a baby gift, she begins to wonder "what else might be lurking down there, unrecognized all these years" (177). As a successful teacher, Crystal finds the words and the language truly to reach her students, even the ones who don't want to be affected, falling into "the rhythm of teaching" extremely well, "like there's a part of her which knows how to do it already" (189). With teaching, Crystal reconnects with her father and his love of language that drew her so close to him. Jones argues that for Crystal, teaching is a "third source of reality," one other than religion and sexuality (129). Her teaching gives Crystal another chance to feel complete, integrated, the way she felt with Mack, briefly during her religious conversion, then again with Jerold. Now in her twenties, as a teacher Crystal speaks with her own voice and demonstrates a strength of character previously absent, and even though several people encourage her to date men, she doesn't have the desire. For the first time in her life, Crystal seems to be truly self-possessed.

Just when it seems Crystal has discovered her own voice and a language of her own, her world is shattered by the reappearance of Roger Lee Combs. In "The Second 'Rape' of Crystal Spangler," John Kalb argues that the juxtaposition of Part I of the novel, in which Crystal is raped by Devere and then returns home to discover her dead father, and Part III, in which Crystal returns home from Dry Fork to have Roger tell her, "I'm not going to rape you" (*Black Mountain* 206), suggests the pattern of violation in Crystal's life. She again becomes a victim of assault, not physical this time but emotional. Roger, now married with twin daughters, insists on delivering Crystal from her present existence. Crystal tells him that she is happy and doesn't need to be rescued at all, but Roger argues that even though she thinks she's happy, she's really not; she needs a man, love, a home, children, and "a position in the community" (209), and all he's ever wanted in his life is to provide her with these things. Although Crystal puts up an argument, the temptation to return to passivity proves irresistible for Crystal (Jones 129), and Roger convinces her of her basic unhappiness and real need for a man. With Roger to take care of her, she won't be required to make any decisions, suffer any consequences, or feel any pain. Her weak constitution cannot stand up to Roger's entreaties; Crystal dismisses her newfound sense of wholeness and decides she must have a man in her life to feel complete.

Even as Crystal relinquishes her fledgling selfhood to Roger, who says he doesn't even care if she loves him now because she *will* love him eventually, "some part of her is screaming, or almost screaming, and then it breaks off and is still" (210), as her silent rebellion is squashed. Just as her screams were unheard at her father's death, she ignores the screams of her inner self now as a vital part of her is surrendered. Once more Crystal is violated, and her reaction here, although silenced, is reminiscent of her behavior when her father died and she could not stop screaming. Agreeing to quit the successful and satisfying teaching career that she loves in order to please Roger by going away with him, she slips into a role he has designed for her, much like Monica's acquiescence to Manly's desires at the end of *Fancy Strut*. Roger assures Crystal that she'll never have to work again, patronizing her by saying he'll take care of his "baby" (210–11). And again, to represent his love for her (or rather his ownership of her), he gives her a parting gift, a Valentine present—a gold ring with a dark red ruby. Although pleased, Crystal still begs Roger to stay and make love to her, longing for the intensity, the passion. Jones explains Crystal's situation, arguing that Crystal's "sense of her own reality that accompanies a feeling of inner sexual response, something she has never felt for Roger before, compels her now and makes her following *his* words inevitable" (130). A victim of her own sensuality, Crystal craves the touch of another human being. Roger, however, leaves her unsatisfied and hollow, just as their eventual marriage will do.

Now alone, Crystal stands in her bathroom holding up her hand while "the ruby flashes red in the mirror, red as blood in the mirror, holding secrets" (211) that will be revealed only when Crystal comes face-to-face with her passivity. Perhaps, as Hall insists, wounded women must seek healing "in the blood of the wound itself"; the void cannot be filled by "conjunction with the male, but rather by an internal conjunction, by an integration of its own parts, by a remembering or a putting back together" of a divided self (68). Crystal's perception of the ruby red ring as blood in the mirror identifies her wound, the source of her division, but she lacks the strength and volition to make the necessary journey to self-knowledge. Seeing Roger as "inevitable," Crystal allows the thought of him to "slide all over like body lotion, covering her, working in." Comforted by the sense of absorbing Roger's identity into her own "crystal-clear" one, she feels relieved to have somebody telling her what to do once more, but the comfort is factitious because Crystal goes to bed and "cries and cries as if her heart might break" (212). She seems partially aware of the loss of her selfhood, but she can't find the strength or the words to hold on to her newfound identity as a single, adult, career woman. At this point in her life and in her writing career, Smith sees no other options for Crystal but to follow the community-validated path of becoming a wife and losing her own struggling individuality.

After Crystal and Roger leave town and marry, Crystal's happiness is short-lived; the conflict within her is ceaseless even though she loves Roger just as he had said she would. One suspects, however, that Crystal's love is similar to Monica's, described as "love or something close enough" for Manly

(*Fancy Strut* 46). But Crystal believes she loves Roger so much that she can't become pregnant or otherwise change their relationship. She isn't ready to become a mother, and although she won't tell Roger, she doesn't think she'll ever be. The only time Crystal feels complete is when she and Roger are having sex, believing that "she has known his body so long, so well, that it's her body, in fact. Hers too" (219). None of the old intensity she felt with Mack or Jerold is there; Crystal has simply merged with Roger. Without him, she has no identity. Alone, she feels like only half a person, hollow and empty. She cries a great deal and often looks into mirrors, seeing no individual facial features, only "a glaze . . . come over her face" (218); it is crystal clear to her that she is no one without Roger.

Crystal understands her marriage to Roger as being inevitable, but she also understands that their marriage is more precarious than he realizes. Charmed by Crystal's lassitude and mysteriousness, Roger has provided every convenience to make his wife's existence totally effortless, completely unaware that to feel at all alive, Crystal requires stimulation and exertion. As Crystal sinks deeper and deeper into passivity, she draws more and more into herself, afraid to tell Roger about her feelings for fear of losing his love, the only thing that defines her. She spends a great deal of time thinking of Jerold and his talk of doom, still believing it to be ridiculous. And like Monica, who after her affair with Buck and her resolve to stay with Manly, feels old and brittle, Crystal begins to feel "sour and old, like a washcloth left for too long in the sink" (222). Her youth and passion are gradually disappearing, giving way to resignation and atrophy.

During Roger's political campaign for a congressional seat, Crystal agrees to go on a tour of a psychiatric hospital. It is during this tour that she confronts the repressed memory of her rape by her retarded uncle. At the hospital, Crystal wanders off alone and finds herself in a room with four large cribs in it. In one crib Crystal sees a "young man, hunched in the corner . . . struggl[ing] to hold up his wobbling oversized head . . . and control his face." As he reaches his hand through the bars toward Crystal, she is struck immobile by the face, which is described as "a moonface, white and smooth, a moonface like Devere's" (228). The face of the encephalitic patient immediately transports Crystal back to the rape she suffered when she was fourteen. Smith describes the pain Crystal felt during the rape as "traveling up her whole body into her shoulders and then pinpointing itself somewhere up at the very top of her head, like somebody driving in a nail up there" (229).

The imagery here suggests a crucifixion, in which Crystal is sacrificed at the hands of a mentally disturbed man. Her paralysis during and even after the rape is an early key to the problem of her passivity and an indication of the behavioral pattern that will follow. Never moving, she waits for the brutal rape to end, subconsciously connecting with her father and the past by occupying her mind with lines of poetry and imaginary ghosts until all she is aware of is "pressure and this nail in the top of her head" (230). By recalling lines from poems and stories read to her by her father to block out the pain of the rape, Crystal uses language as a tool for survival until the rape ends and the pain stops. And since "she can't breathe," language, though silent, is Crystal's salvation, her only means of sustenance, just as her father's words nourished her in the private world of their parlor. As her body is assaulted, she divorces her mind from her body and imaginatively travels elsewhere so she can endure the immediate physical abuse. The second mention of "the nail," the source of Crystal's pain, along with Crystal's name itself, strongly links Crystal to Christ and His suffering. When the rape ends, Crystal watches Devere calmly dress and leave; his eyes "don't seem to see her at all." By his calm, smooth face, Crystal sees that "he doesn't know. . . . He doesn't know anything about it" (230). Here again, Crystal's thoughts remind the reader of Christ's last plea to His Father in heaven while dying on the cross when He asks God to forgive His persecutors because "they know not what they do"; although she doesn't ask for Devere's exoneration, Crystal, as victim, realizes Devere does not know what he has done or the great pain that Crystal will suffer. Just as Crystal had been unable to move during and after the rape, and as she felt paralyzed at her dead father's side and again at his funeral, now her hand is glued to the hand of the mental patient in the hospital, and she sits beside his crib until she is forced to leave.

With the emergence of the memory of her rape, Crystal's capacity for language and integration is completely lost as she sinks into what will prove to be permanent passivity. Roger's assistant later tries to convince Roger to put Crystal into a hospital, but he explains that he won't have her committed, hoping she will make that decision herself. It is ironic that at this point Roger would expect Crystal to make any decision for herself. Earlier he had promised always to take care of her completely. Crystal is oblivious to the entire conversation, wanting only to watch out the window as the leaves fall from the trees and to read from the journal in which she has so often found solace. Her senses ever sharp, she immerses herself in nature and in a book that, for her, has come to represent the past. Roger, unable to understand Crystal's indifference and angered by her passivity, takes the journal from her and tosses it into the fireplace, thereby destroying, for Crystal, an important link to the past and to her father's family. Although Crystal weakly protests that she wants the book, she is unable to make even the slightest effort to retrieve it, her voice and her will rapidly deteriorating. Comforting Roger as he breaks into sobs and puts his head in her lap, Crystal knows there is nothing left between them and tells him, with the first words she has spoken since the episode at the hospital, that she wants to go home, back to her childhood home in Black Rock.

It is here that "Crystal paralyzes herself. She just stops moving. She stops talking, stops doing everything" (237). Smith's choice of the active rather than the passive voice here emphasizes Crystal's willful decision to be paralyzed; she is not a victim this time. She chooses silence over language. No medical explanation can be given for what has happened to her; the experts agree that it's all in her mind. Lying in bed all day every day looking out the window at the roses in full bloom and the green mountain, Crystal remains closely attuned to nature, but she lacks the ability, or the will, to participate in life anymore. On her frequent visits, Agnes reads to Crystal while Crystal stares out the window as "the seasons come and go and the colors change on the mountain" (240). For Crystal, there is nothing else. For her entire life, she has defined herself through other people, never finding a way to develop and grow on her own. Now she is paralyzed by the emptiness in her life. As Dorothy Hill points out, "she has tried every community-validated path to female identity and all end in paralysis" (49).

As sexual beings who have great difficulty expressing their sexuality in their respective community-validated roles, Monica and Crystal struggle with the same issues as Smith's earlier protagonists. At the end of *Fancy Strut,* Monica, however, has decided to try the role of motherhood that had so disgusted her earlier. She is willing to make the choice posed by Nancy Friday between sexuality and motherhood. We do not know how she will fare in her new role because the novel ends before she becomes pregnant; but all indications are that she will eventually again experience a great void in her life because of her inability to express her sexuality. Crystal, however, serves as the culmination of Smith's unintegrated female characters, her mind so completely severed from her body that she is consciously unable to choose between sexuality and motherhood. Crystal is by nature sensual and sexual, but she never mindfully makes a choice to be so. She does elect not to become a mother, but only for fear of changing her life and upsetting the established order. Crystal desperately needs sexual love to feel complete, and the risk of losing that is too much for her.

It is only in Smith's next novel, *Oral History* (1983), that she attempts to heal the split between sexuality and motherhood when she "writes her way out of patriarchy" (Hill 21), not in overthrowing patriarchy by fantasizing about parthenogenesis or supporting lesbianism, solutions offered by some feminists as ways to integrate the dichotomy, but by attributing mythic qualities to female characters. What Smith has done in her novels written after 1980 is to discover and vitalize what has been lost in our literature and in our lives: the mythic goddess. In her depiction of female characters who are both sexual and motherly, and in the description of their sexuality in religious terms, she offers a new vision of the sacred female that heals the split between sexuality and motherhood that society has long imposed on women.

Works Cited

Dinnerstein, Dorothy. *The Mermaid and the Minotaur*. New York: Harper & Row, 1976.

Friday, Nancy. *My Mother/My Self*. New York: Delacorte, 1977.

Hall, Nor. *The Moon and the Virgin: Reflections on the Archetypal Feminine*. New York: Harper & Row, 1980.

Hill, Dorothy. *Lee Smith*. New York: Twayne, 1992.

Jones, Anne Goodwyn. "The World of Lee Smith." *Southern Quarterly* 22.1 (1983): 115–39.

Kalb, John. "The Second 'Rape' of Crystal Spangler." *Southern Literary Journal* 21.1 (1988): 23–30.

Kearns, Katherine. "From Shadow to Substance: The Empowerment of the Artist Figure in Lee Smith's Fiction." *Writing the Woman Artist*. Ed. Suzanne W. Jones. Philadelphia: U of Pennsylvania P, 1991. 175–95.

MacKethan, Lucinda. "Artists and Beauticians: Balance in Lee Smith's Fiction." *Southern Literary Journal* 15.1 (1982): 3–14.

Smith, Lee. *Black Mountain Breakdown*. New York: Ballantine, 1980.

———. *Fancy Strut*. New York: Ballantine, 1973.

———. "An Interview with Lee Smith." By Edwin T. Arnold. *Appalachian Journal* 11.3 (1984): 240–54.

———. "An Interview with Lee Smith." By Linda J. Byrd. *Shenandoah* 47.2 (1997): 95–118.

———. *The Last Day the Dogbushes Bloomed*. Baton Rouge: Louisiana State UP, 1968.

———. Personal Communication with Linda J. Byrd. 1996.

———. *Something in the Wind*. New York: Harper and Row, 1971.

Stories Told by Their Survivors (and Other Sins of Memory)

Survivor Guilt in Kaye Gibbons's ELLEN FOSTER

Linda Watts

The year 1997 brought Kaye Gibbons, whose work had already earned numerous prizes and awards, at least two more public acknowledgments of her fiction. Both were destined to widen her readership and recognition. In November, Oprah Winfrey selected two Gibbons novels, *Ellen Foster* and *A Virtuous Woman*, as featured titles in her book club, and in December, a television movie based on *Ellen Foster* aired as part of the Hallmark Hall of Fame series. Amid this fanfare, Kaye Gibbons persisted in a manner so measured in voice and reverent to language as to appear self-effacing. There is something quiet, private, and reflective about both Gibbons's fiction and her way of talking about it. During a television appearance on the Oprah Winfrey program, Gibbons seemed almost confessional. Early in the segment, she confided that "I am Ellen Foster and I admit it." Along the way, she owned that Bertha, rather than Kaye, was her given name (after her grandmother). She drew the listener close in confidences, saying she writes "because I have to. . . . I'm compelled to" ("Interview").

The stories must be told, and Gibbons's stories have as a connecting thread the power of women's experience. Gibbons explains how Louis Rubin, her professor at Chapel Hill and subsequently her editor at Algonquin, "told me years ago that I would always write about women's burdens, and I have found that to be almost uniformly true. I write, in part, to discover what those burdens are and how a character's load can be lessened, her pain mitigated" ("On Tour" n.p.). In a media moment in which others might have fallen prey to self-promotion, she spoke with quiet gratitude for language and its redemption. Hers is a story of generations, and she honors those women who came before her—their narratives, their lives, their words, and their legacies—through her writing. Indeed, Kaye Gibbons opened a 1991 essay by sharing with her readers something that sounded a bit like a secret: "It started with my mother, this writing urge" ("My Mother" 52). If it is a secret, it is hardly one in which Gibbons need suppose herself a woman alone.

I probably shouldn't be telling you this. . . . With these words have commenced countless intimacies, confessions, self-discoveries, and recountings of trials endured. These are the words through which secrets unfold in halting words but hopeful moments; this is the whisper hum of memories traded among trusted women. For many, these spoken confidences help demarcate a community of women's speech. This hearth of sound warms girl children into womanhood, and its light guides their ancestral journeys, while at the same time issuing vital warnings and change-making lessons. In Toni Morrison's *Beloved*, this poignant legacy uniting women receives the name "rememory," perhaps for its temporal and generational power of recurrence. In one telling exchange with her daughter Denver, Morrison's Sethe speaks to this ongoing (and everlasting) meaning of a woman's memories, one in which words and images have taken on the very work of prayer.

> "What were you praying for, Ma'am?"
> "Not for anything. I don't pray anymore. I just talk."
> "What were you talking about?"
> "You won't understand, baby."
> "Yes, I will."
> "I was talking about time. It's so hard for me to believe in it. Some things go. Pass on. Some things just stay. I used to think it was my rememory. You know. Some things you forget. Other things you never do. But it's not. Places, places are still there. If a house burns down, it's gone, but the place—the picture of it—stays, and not just in my rememory, but out there, in the world. What I remember is a picture floating around out there outside my head. I mean, even if I don't think it, even if I die, the picture of what I did, or knew, or saw is still out there. Right in the place where it happened." (36)

Time does not simply pass (away); every time passes into every other. It is the pain of women's living and the sorrow of their dying that render things—places, images, and occasionally mere words—sacred, eternal. A daughter's story inheritance does not merely preserve, then, but rather continuously activates, makes ever alive and newly felt, her identity through matrilineal connection.

As Alice Walker's by now famous call to go "in search of our mothers' gardens" (231) suggests, the literal and symbolic implications of the cultural and literary mother-daughter dynamic can be transformed into an astonishing and energizing force in women's writing. Many contemporary women writers engage this tradition forthrightly, even joyously, in their work. In Tillie Olsen's *Yonnondio: From the Thirties*, it stirs in the mother-song little Mazie heard and the "fragile old remembered comfort [that] streamed from the stroking fingers into Mazie, gathered to some shy bliss that shone despairingly over suppurating hurt and want and fear and shamings—the Harm of years" (101). Its stirrings pervade the exchange of women's wisdom by characters in Ntozake Shange's *Sassafrass, Cypress, and Indigo*:

> EMERGENCY CARE OF WOUNDS THAT CANNOT BE SEEN
> Hold the victim gently. Rock in the manner of a quiet sea. Hum softly from your heart. Repeat the victim's name with love. Offer a brew of red sunflower to cleanse the victim's blood and spirit. Fasting and silence for a time refurbish the victim's awareness of her capacity to nourish and heal herself. New associations should be made with caution, more caring for herself. (50)

It stirs, too, throughout Paula Gunn Allen's vivid posing of the Laguna question, "Who Is Your Mother?," for beyond clan membership, one's response to this query "enables people to place you precisely within the universal web in your life, in each of its dimensions: cultural, spiritual, personal, and historical" (209). These are the testimonies of, and to, women's survival as a process that may never be considered complete. As long as there are stories to tell, hear, and retell, the cycle of discovery and healing thrives.

These matters of self-knowledge through mother tongues are also the primary terms in which Kaye Gibbons speaks of her own development as a fiction writer. Her stories, novels, and essays suggest that knowledge is not uncovered so much as it is recovered, in large part through contact with one's kindred spirits among (in this case, southern) women. In this spirit of shared confidences, the books of Kaye Gibbons, with their diary-like shape and heft, suggest keepsakes, confidential memories pressed in paper. Through their tributes to a legacy and lineage passed through language, these stories gather a reader in a close narrative embrace. So long as one listens, the auditor experiences a sense of connection, a twinning of consciousness. That link between teller and hearer can be quite intimate in its address, shape-shifting in its influence, and cleansing in its repetitions.

There is something profoundly healthful and affirming to an individual's own acts of narrative memory. Perhaps it is with this in mind that the neurologist Oliver Sacks, author of such best-selling medical narratives as *Awakenings* and *The Man Who Mistook His Wife for a Hat and Other Clinical Tales*, describes himself as "compelled to speak of tales and fables as well as cases" (xv). He, too, attests to the importance of the traditional pathographical

method in which the patient is subject rather than object by means of report-
age offering the kind of personal perspective only a literary narrative can
render. He writes convincingly of the relationship between identity formation and acts of narrative. It is dangerous for the patient if medicine deals
with disease yet labors heedless of its implication for the patient's personhood.
Indeed, Sacks devotes his own writings to the reconstruction of people's lives
rather than mere dissections of their problems. "To restore the human subject
at the centre—the suffering, afflicted, fighting human subject—we must
deepen a case history to a narrative or tale: only then do we have a 'who' as
well as a 'what,' a real person, a patient, in relation to disease—in relation to
the physical" (xii). It is a holistic approach, in which all circumstances, particularly those unique to the individual, bear detailed scrutiny and telling. In
this effort to understand patients in terms of all their relations, Sacks expresses his indebtedness not only to the traditions of medical narrative but
also to storytellers more generally, with their abilities to recount full and credible tales of human experience and, at times, human tragedy. As literary texts
invite us to reflect on the human condition—especially its distress, pain, confusion, and bereavement—they open for our inspection casebooks more ex-
tensive and varied than medical history has ever produced.

   Although it might be unwise to approach a literary text as if for purposes of diagnosis, we ought not pass too quickly over the psychological register of fiction. Literature often yields insights into psychological phenomena
and invites discussion in these psychodynamic (as well as other) terms. This
essay is an effort to analyze one novel, Kaye Gibbons's *Ellen Foster*, in terms of
its psychological domain. This close reading explores the title character's developing awareness of mortality and her experiences of survivor guilt as she
sustains the loss of three key adults to death before reaching her twelfth year
of life. In particular, in what ways does Ellen negotiate her own identity and
voice once (although perhaps not "once and for all") deprived of the sound
of her mother's voice?

   In his own exploration of survivors' responses to the death of an intimate other, the scholar Robert Jay Lifton, like Oliver Sacks, offers a narrative
approach to the phenomenon of survivor guilt. Although such reactions of
blame may be most conspicuous in survivors of such profound traumas as
torture, combat, and prison camps, guilt may also play a part in the responses
of any survivor of another's death. To understand the link between death and
survivor guilt, Lifton suggests one need only look to the origin of the word
"guilt":

   The image of a debt to the dead conveys the idea of something
   one owes, a duty, an obligation, a matter in which there is some

form of accountability. The etymological derivation of the word
guilt is apparently uncertain but it is thought to have some relationship to the idea of "debt" and the associated idea of obligation (from old English *scyld* and German *schuld* or "should"). There
are similar meanings in the different etymological derivation of the
word responsibility (from the Latin *respondere*, to respond), and
the ideas of answering to something and accountability loom large
in the history of the word's usage. (*Oxford English Dictionary*, quoted
in Lifton 144)

Survivors experience at least two different forms of guilt, as Lifton points out:
"moral guilt" and "psychological guilt." Moral guilt "involves a judgment of
wrong-doing, based upon ethical principles and made by an individual
(whether or not the transgressor himself), group, or community" (132). Psychological guilt, however, requires merely "an individual sense of badness or
evil, with a fear or expectation of punishment" (132).

It is this second definition of guilt that pervades the fiction of Kaye
Gibbons—guilt that originates in an internally generated sense of blame or
responsibility. In her critical essay on Katherine Anne Porter's Miranda stories, Gibbons alludes to the restorative power of "sensuous memory" in responding to painful experiences and awarenesses ("Planes" 79). In this same
spirit, characters in Gibbons's own fiction, during moments of sorrow, uncertainty, or guilt, search their memories for guidance and comfort. These recollections (and their narration) may be burdensome, but they may also hold
the salve for—or secret behind—present afflictions.

Nowhere is that comfort more welcome than in the lives of those who
have lost a family member. In each of five novels published by Gibbons, a
central character reckons with the emotions of memory and, in particular,
the guilt feelings of a survivor. In *Ellen Foster* (1987), the young title character outlives both her parents and a grandparent, then tells the tale of her own
emergence. In *A Virtuous Woman* (1989), it is Blinding Jack Ernest Stokes, a
widower who uses his words to beckon the spirit and voice of his beloved
wife, Ruby. *A Cure for Dreams* (1991) finds Marjorie Polly Randolph grap-
pling with the challenge of taking up the storyteller's mantle of her recently
passed mother. Gibbons's *Charms for the Easy Life* (1993) recalls the deeply
affecting memory of the narrator's midwife/healer grandmother. In *Sights
Unseen* (1995), a daughter comes to terms with the relationship with her
mentally ill mother. In all five of these works, those forced to confront yearning for a loved one must find a way to heal their hearts and resume their lives.
As the critic Linda Tate has noted, to the women of Gibbons's novels, language is like nourishment, a vital fuel for the regeneration of a woman and

her community. "Talking," observes Marjorie in *A Cure for Dreams*, "was my mother's life" (1). Memories and stories retold immortalize the ones we love, especially those lost to us. The narrative act also empowers the bereaved to order memories and summon them as needed throughout the grieving and healing process.

In this essay, I consider a text in which narrative strategies hint at levels of painful (and potentially immobilizing) awareness in the life of a young child. Ellen Foster, the title character of Gibbons's first novel, is a girl with a great many secrets in her life, most of them kept out of loyalty directed toward undeserving adults. A few are secrets she guards even from herself. Ellen Foster's autobiographical narrative is more than an amusement or a statement for the record; it is part of an ongoing effort to acquit herself of any wrongdoing. It is also her means to mark the beginning of a different life than the one she knew in a dysfunctional childhood home and subsequent residential placements. In many ways, it reads as if one were reviewing entries in the locked diary Ellen bought as her own present for the first Christmas after her mother's death.

Chief among Ellen's suppressed and damaging memories is her mother's death, an event in which the child has convinced herself she was implicated. After being tormented for years by Ellen's violent and alcoholic father, Ellen's mother swallows an overdose of heart medication. When this fact is discovered, Ellen's father forbids the girl to seek help, threatening to kill them both if she disobeys him. Ellen has little choice but to make her mother—and herself—as comfortable as possible given the circumstances. Ellen's mother dies beside her on the bed, and Ellen can never forgive herself for doing no more to help her. For the rest of her life, Ellen revisits this awful time in an effort to put her fears and regrets to rest. The novel's dual narrative, with its expertly situated flashbacks, makes the point that this past is very much a part of Ellen's lived present. Ellen's grief has transformed itself into guilt (with a bit of assistance from an accusatory grandmother), and so Ellen gives her still-new life over to remorse for an invented memory.

Although quite young and isolated, "old Ellen," as the prematurely worldly child refers to herself, recognizes early on that her home is in swirling chaos. She refers repeatedly to her pain in this disorderly and dangerous environment as "the spinning." As the story unfolds, Ellen perceives this feeling of uncontrolled movement as the force that destroyed her family and killed her parents. The child, at such times, portrays the trauma as almost occult in origin. Ellen describes her household as if it were a runaway roller coaster or a grotesque carnival whose master lost interest and suddenly forfeited control. If there is a God at work in this situation, Ellen fails to see how. As she paraphrases in her puzzlement, "the way the Lord moves is his business" (7). As a youngster at risk long after the death of her parents, Ellen must devise ways to understand her survival (while both her mother and her father "gave in" to destruction), restore her internal sense of order, and bring meaning to her own life.

Throughout the novel, there are symptoms that Ellen struggles mightily with this "burden of memory" (Gibbons, "Mother" 60). Her hands shake so much that at times she must hold them beneath her desk at school. More than anything, she dreads weekly sessions with a school-employed therapist, whose efforts on her behalf strike her as preposterous. Witness her impish recollection of an encounter with Rorschach ink blots. Ellen suspends her disbelief and cooperates with the therapist to a point but mostly out of deference to his training and his feelings. After all, she notes with no small bit of condescension, he did seem to put a good deal of energy into solving the riddle that was Ellen's past. His conclusions, however, tend toward the obvious: the child is nervous, afraid. Since the therapist is of little help, she prefers to heal herself through less clinical means.

Just what are the means by which Ellen seeks her recovery? Largely, Ellen dedicates herself to acts of control and containment. Through order, she strives to "walk away from the noise" (110). When left to her own devices, as Ellen usually is, she busies herself with meticulous organization of all manner of tasks. In much the way that another child might devote herself to preparing a Christmas list, Ellen composes her own wish lists: what she would like a home to be, what would make a proper family, what might be a suitable job, and the like. These lists openly defy Ellen's father's insistence that wishes are worthless.

When not involved in some activity, Ellen makes a conscious effort to crowd her mind with harmless thoughts so that threatening ones will find no place there.

> So I try to keep my head pretty full at all times. But as soon as a spare room opens up in there here comes somebody like my daddy settling in thinking he might make his self right at home.
> But I got my own ideas about what comes and goes through my head and I intend to think about what I please from now on. But I figure it will take a while to get that system down pat. (102)

Ellen strives to choose her mind's chain of associations, to direct her subconscious through the most conscious and deliberate means. The premise here is that the refusal of an unwelcome memory can neutralize its harmful effects. It is better to lavish attention on a list of topics to discuss with her friend Starletta than to give herself over to the haunting memories of an abusive household. It is safer to count coins than to find one's mind available to the work of mourning. Ellen finds herself caught between the nurturing memories and the ones that threaten to destroy her. In such circumstances, one has reason to cultivate certain mental distractions and comforting, if also small, rituals. For the time being, as when she discontinues sessions with the meddlesome school therapist, Ellen finds it safer not to talk about the past. As she says when she decides to discontinue "therapy":

> He will not be seeing me again. I might be confused sometimes in my head but it is not something you need to talk about. Before you can talk you have to line it all up in order and I had rather just let it swirl around until I am too tired to think.
>
> You just let the motion in your head wear you out. Never think about it. You just make a bigger mess that way. (89)

Too often, she has found people and events at odds with anything a reasonable child might expect. As a result, Ellen has learned to inhabit a realm of diminished expectations, when allowing herself any at all. In this way, her life seems like a novel, only one in which she is trapped—without agency—as a character in a story she has not written, left with no choice but "to see what would happen next" (72). She has not the luxury of play, but as a compensation, she develops a variety of academic interests. When looking through her microscope, painting "brooding oceans," and writing in her diary, Ellen's world is enlarged, and she is permitted to experience her own power of perception, one of her most life-sustaining and life-affirming gifts. Through these activities, she is reminded that she is worthwhile and that she can function creatively.

Ellen's imagination becomes her greatest torture, though, when she is forced to reside for a time with her "mama's mama," a woman so bitter about the loss of her daughter that she even blames little Ellen for the death. This woman cannot accept the knowledge of her daughter's life of abuse and her death by suicide and so blames everyone else in her daughter's household. Ellen's grandmother begins her reign of terror by placing Ellen in the room her mother occupied as a girl. This is Ellen's first clue that her grandmother means to punish Ellen for "killing" her daughter. The grandmother then puts the girl in the fields to perform labor so physically demanding that even the workers wonder aloud, "It must be a mighty bad debt you is out here working off" (64). It is indeed—a debt to the dead.

"I swear," vows her grandmother, "you will never stop paying for your part" (78). Ellen's grandmother can scarcely look at Ellen without seeing both the visage of her deceased daughter and the eyes of a son-in-law she holds responsible for her daughter's death. Consequently, no punishment will suffice. It is at this point in Ellen's troubled life that she comes closest to suffering her mother's tragic fate. Her grandmother's treatment of her is so harsh that Ellen fears she is becoming someone else, the person her "mama's mama" so detests—Ellen's father. This fear threatens to destroy Ellen. This is the closest she comes to harming herself, to surrendering to "the spinning," as she believes her mother did in taking her own life.

Perhaps only the physical deterioration of her grandmother spares Ellen this untimely end. When her grandmother becomes ill, it falls to young Ellen to care for her. This is a hauntingly familiar role for Ellen, as she has already cared for a mother with heart trouble. In characteristic tones of suspicion, though, Ellen's grandmother greets this care by warning Ellen that "you best take better care of me than you did of your mama" (73). Ellen must relive her mother's illness and endure still more accusations from her grandmother in the process. Still, Ellen makes a sincere effort to tend her grandmother, in part as an act of atonement toward her mother. In time, however, despite Ellen's vigil, her grandmother dies. In a curious way, this opportunity to reexperience her mother's illness and death allows Ellen to rid herself of a measure of guilt. Although she realizes that no amount of care can banish death, in this case or in any other, Ellen still worries that people will question her about the death: "But I did not kill her just like I did not kill my mama or my daddy. She died in spite of me" (79).

Ellen has long felt tremendous guilt concerning the loss of her mother, and her distress allows her to extend her feelings of guilt to the deaths of both her father and her grandmother. When news of her father's death reaches her, Ellen feels little emotion. "I had practiced it all so many times," she explains, "that all I wondered was if he had died one of the ways I had planned" (69). Still, at other moments in the narrative, she feels it necessary to offer a defense, saying "I did not kill my daddy. . . . All I did was wish him dead real hard every now and then" (1). When her grandmother passed away, Ellen felt not relief so much as the onset of another duty. When her "mama's mama" dies, Ellen does her very best to bargain with God.

> And even when she was so dead I could not help her anymore I made her like a present to Jesus so maybe he would take her. Take this one I got prettied up and mark it down by my name to balance against the one I held back from you before. But I do not trust this newly dead one and when you look at her face you in your wisdom and seeing will know that her smile is a trick for you. But please take her anyway. And be sure I get the credit for it and if you can please show me some way that you and me are even now. I do not think I want to go through this again. (92)

With this settling of divine accounts, Ellen begins to see beyond blame and guilt.

Why, though, had Ellen translated her grief into guilt? As much as Ellen missed her mother and grieved over her tragic death, she also harbored some resentment. As a small child, she faulted her mother for allowing Ellen's father into their lives. Why would she choose and remain with such a man? As Ellen reasons, "she could not help getting sick but nobody made her marry him" (3). Further, she was disappointed that her mother had endured his abuse. To Ellen's way of thinking, her mother had surrendered. It is extremely difficult, though, for a child to experience directly such forms of anger and resentment toward a parent, especially when the child is mourning that parent at the same time. It is much easier for a child to direct those emotions inward in guilt and self-contempt. Ellen also feels a kind of spiritual and social shame for her mother's death. As she listens to the preacher at her mother's funeral, Ellen grapples with the unforgiving words spoken about individuals who commit suicide. Ellen is the one left to deal with the stigma.

Most of all, however, and little recognized by Ellen, the child can never forgive her mother for leaving her behind. Her feelings of abandonment are immediate and have a great deal to do with Ellen's decision to rest beside her dead mother, keeping the woman for her own as long as possible. It is not merely that Ellen blames her mother for taking her own life but also that Ellen holds her mother responsible for leaving a child in the hands of an abusive, alcoholic father. Still, as a child of a long-suffering parent, Ellen cannot allow herself to feel or express anger toward her dead mother. This unnamed feeling nonetheless torments Ellen: "So I decided to spend the rest of my life making up for it. Whatever it was. Whatever I decided one day I actually did. One day if I ever sorted the good from the bad and the memories of what I wish was true" (78–79).

Until her mother, father, and grandmother are cast out of Ellen's area of responsibility, she has little choice but to mount a daily defense against the attempts of her family and other adults to activate guilt in an innocent child. Once Ellen forgives herself, as she does when she dresses her "mama's mama" for death (her act of acceptance of life's cycle into death), the child can begin to act and choose on her own behalf. She is able to recognize herself once again in her ideas and deeds: "I am not exactly a vision. But Lord I have good intentions that count" (61).

It is with this outlook that Ellen soon sets out to find a permanent home that meets the specifications on her carefully compiled list. After some research, she resolves to gain admittance to a home she has selected because she feels confident it will meet her needs. Ellen's needs, as she expresses them upon introducing herself to the woman she has chosen as her "new mama," are simply what is necessary for the development of most children: the need for love, security, and affirmation. As Ellen puts it before she accepts a place in the foster home: "Well I need to know if you are pretty healthy or if you have a disease or bad habits like drinking. Also are you generally friendly or do you have days when you act crazy or extra mean?" (119). The questions that Ellen poses when "interviewing" her new guardian reflect her memories of neglect and abuse at the hands of her biological parents, and particularly at the hands of her alcoholic and abusive father. With her foster mother, Ellen begins a new life, literally renaming herself ("Ellen Foster," since this is the home in the community where the foster children live). The new home has much to recommend it. Best of all, perhaps, Ellen notes, "Nobody has died or blamed me for anything worse than overwatering the terrarium" (121). Through it all, Ellen manages to preserve some sense of her own worth. She takes special pride in her own survival and, in particular, in her choice of a "new mama" and home. Ellen has reinvented herself, reconfigured her sense of family, and found a way both to remember and diverge from—live beyond—her mother's life story.

"That is why," notes Ellen, "I think I am somebody now" (95). Her healing is not complete, but Ellen realizes she knows ways to protect herself and ways to accept appropriate forms of support from others. Like other survivors featured in southern women's fiction, including Zora Neale Hurston's Janie (*Their Eyes Were Watching God*) and Alice Walker's Celie (*The Color Purple*), Ellen's is a story of her second birth, forged in a renewed consciousness of the distinct part she plays in writing a story of generations. Indeed, when Hurston's Janie returns, her old friend Pheoby greets her by declaring, "You looks like youse yo' own daughter" (14). Although this is in large part an acknowledgment of Janie's conspicuous vitality upon her return, the phrasing of Pheoby's compliment seems more than coincidental. In an important measure, daughters left behind must learn to mother themselves. Ellen Foster's second birth, like her first, finds her blanketed beside the language hearth of women's voices. Like Janie and Celie, after her mother's death, Ellen must learn to kindle flames others have tended before her. While Ellen, Janie, and Celie must grow up without the physical presence of their mothers, they need only remember Sethe's message to her own daughter: what a woman does, knows, sees, and *learns* can never vanish. And so these daughters dare to ask aloud of mothers now distant only in body, "Tell me about the years that made you," knowing (yet no longer fearing) all the while that these same years continue to make them (Gibbons, *Cure for Dreams* 1).

Works Cited

Allen, Paula Gunn. *The Sacred Hoop: Recovering the Feminine in American Indian Traditions*. Boston: Beacon, 1986.

Gibbons, Kaye. *A Cure for Dreams*. New York: Vintage, 1991.

———. *Ellen Foster*. New York: Vintage, 1987.

———. "Interview with Kaye Gibbons." Oprah Winfrey Show. Harpo Productions. 8 Dec. 1997.

———. "My Mother, Literature, and a Life Split Neatly into Two Halves." *The Writer on Her Work: New Essays in New Territory*. Vol. 2. Ed. Janet Sternburg. New York: Norton, 1991.

———. "On Tour: Kaye Gibbons" and "Kaye Gibbons." *Bookwire*. On-line.

———. "Planes of Language and Time: The Surfaces of the Miranda Stories." *Kenyon Review* 10 (1988): 74–79.

Hurston, Zora Neale. *Their Eyes Were Watching God*. Urbana: U of Illinois P, 1978.

Lifton, Robert Jay. *The Broken Connection: On Death and the Continuity of Life*. New York: Simon and Schuster, 1979.

Morrison, Toni. *Beloved*. New York: New American Library, 1987.

Olsen, Tillie. *Yonnondio: From the Thirties*. New York: Delta, 1974.

Sacks, Oliver. *The Man Who Mistook His Wife for a Hat and Other Clinical Tales*. New York: Summit, 1970.

Shange, Ntozake. *Sassafrass, Cypress and Indigo*. New York: St. Martin's, 1982.

Tate, Linda. *A Southern Weave of Women: Fiction of the Contemporary South*. Athens: U of Georgia P, 1994.

Walker, Alice. *In Search of Our Mothers' Gardens*. New York: Harcourt Brace Jovanovich, 1984.

James Lee Burke's Dave Robicheaux Novels

Frank W. Shelton

Fred Hobson has observed that a number of recent southern writers "immerse their characters in a world of popular or mass culture, and their characters' perception of place, family, community, and even myth are greatly conditioned by popular culture, television, movies, rock music, and so forth" (10). His emphasis is on writers, one of the most evident being Bobbie Ann Mason, who include references to popular culture in their works. A significant and heretofore unnoted phenomenon, however, is the use by numerous mainstream contemporary southern novelists of a particular narrative genre in popular culture—the detective or mystery story. Several writers have ventured into the form. The late John W. Corrington, in collaboration with his wife, Joyce, published a series of four mysteries set in New Orleans. John Ehle wrote *The Widow's Trial* (1989), a novel set in the North Carolina mountains that focuses on a murder trial. In 1985, William Hoffman published *Godfires*, another novel with a lawyer as protagonist set in Virginia, and, in 1998, returned to the suspense genre with *Tidewater Blood*. Michael Malone has published two mystery novels, *Uncivil Seasons* (1983) and *Time's Witness* (1989), set in Piedmont, North Carolina, with the same two policemen as protagonists. Finally T.R. Pearson has published *Cry Me a River* (1993), another novel with a policeman protagonist and a North Carolina setting.

The production of such fiction by southern writers is certainly not a new phenomenon. Edgar Allan Poe, the inventor of detective fiction, was a southerner and set one of his most famous detective stories, "The Gold Bug," near Charleston, South Carolina. William Faulkner's *Knight's Gambit* is a collection of detective stories, with lawyer Gavin Stevens in the role of detective. His *Intruder in the Dust* takes the form of a murder mystery, and it has been argued that *Absalom, Absalom!* is in essence a detective story. One of the most beloved southern novels, Harper Lee's *To Kill a Mockingbird*, centers on a courtroom. Although these instances are more or less isolated, the decision of a significant number of more recent serious novelists to write fiction employing the conventions of crime or detective fiction is especially noteworthy.

One reason for the growth of interest in this literary form is suggested by Hobson's remark quoted above. He refers to the fictional characters' immersion in popular culture, but it is also true that contemporary writers themselves cannot escape at least an awareness of that culture without cutting themselves off from the contemporary world. Also, since Dashiell Hammett and Raymond Chandler have been taken seriously by both readers and literary critics, detective fiction has achieved a certain cachet and is viewed as a potential vehicle for serious comment on society. Perhaps most important, however, because of its focus on the theme of order and disorder, the mystery form resonates with several contemporary southern writers as they consider the changes occurring in the South.

James Lee Burke is the focus of this essay for several reasons. Early in his career, he wrote five mainstream novels that at the time met with modest success but that have been republished in light of his larger success. From 1987, with the release of *The Neon Rain*, through 1998 with *Sunset Limited*, Burke has published ten novels featuring the police detective Dave Robicheaux. Burke has certainly devoted more energy to the mystery genre than the other writers mentioned. His mysteries have been highly regarded by fellow novelists (with favorable comments by Larry Brown, Joyce Carol Oates, Walker Percy, and others), and those stories have struck a chord in the reading public as well. Burke has been able to bridge what is often a chasm between "popular" and "literary" works. For example, his story "Texas City, 1947" was originally published in *Southern Review*, then included in the 1992 Algonquin volume *New Stories from the South*, and finally formed part of *A Stained White Radiance*, one novel in the Robicheaux series. In the series as a whole, Burke portrays the changes occurring in the South and, through a focus on the character of Robicheaux himself, traces how one man copes with those changes. While most of the novels concentrate on the contemporary South, two novels, *In the Electric Mist with Confederate Dead* and *Burning Angel*, explicitly explore the influence of southern history on the southern condition. In important ways, the Robicheaux novels include and adapt some of the central themes of modern southern literature.

Burke has said, "The books are mysteries about the psychology of David Robicheaux" (Stroby 40). Thus they are not plot-driven, as are many mysteries, but character-driven, and the ten novels can in essence be seen as one, focusing on Robicheaux's character. Robicheaux is not the typical hero of mystery fiction. An English major in college, Dave has a distinctly contemplative, poetic, and mournful strain to his nature. Moody and complex, he engages in serious inner struggles, particularly with alcohol and his memories of Vietnam, especially in the first half of the series. Sober for four years before the first novel, in the early novels he occasionally succumbs to alcohol and even in the late ones continues to attend meetings of Alcoholics Anonymous. In fact, we see him on occasion visiting priests and therapists to discuss his problems.

Dave is haunted by memories that evoke both his personal past and the region's past. As a policeman he is forced to live in the contemporary world, but his roots are in the southern past, a simpler, rural way of life that he would like to preserve. Obsessed with time and mortality, he is a poet of southern place and mourns the passing of a way of life, even while desperately seeking to preserve it.

The novels contrast the contemporary urban South (New Orleans) with the rural South of Dave's past. A Cajun raised near New Iberia, he is first encountered in *The Neon Rain* as a New Orleans police detective living impermanently on a houseboat on Lake Ponchartrain. At the end of that novel, he resigns from the New Orleans Police Department and moves back to the house near New Iberia in which he was raised, joins the local police department, and runs a bait shop on the bayou near his house. At the end of *The Neon Rain*, Dave poetically describes his return as he and his wife "watched yesterday steal upon us—the black people in straw hats, cane-fishing for goggle-eyed perch, the smoke drifting out through the trees from barbecue fires, the crowds of college-age kids at fish fries and crab-boils in the city park, the red leaves that tumbled out of the sky and settled like a whisper on the bayou's surface. It was the Louisiana I had grown up in, a place that never seemed to change, where it was never a treason to go with the cycle of things and let the season have its way" (281). In particular, the house to which he returns, and which is described in detail in every novel, evokes his roots and the permanence of the past and represents the essence of what Dave seeks to defend: "Our house had been built of cypress and oak by my father, a trapper and derrick man, during the Depression, each beam and log notched and drilled and pegged, and the wood had hardened and grown dark with rainwater and smoke from stubble burning in the cane fields, and today a ball peen hammer would bounce off its exterior and ring in your palm" (*Burning Angel* 23). In most of the novels, Dave travels back and forth between New Iberia and New Orleans. The city is the scene of crime, mob activity, and disorder, but Dave hopes New Iberia, and particularly his house, will be the site of stability, order, and meaning. Of course, the novels reveal that the criminals do not remain in New Orleans, that New Iberia is not as pure as Dave would like it to be. In fact, Dave's house itself is at times invaded by criminals.

The novels compellingly evoke the myth of the rural southern past, embedded in the blue-collar Cajun world in which can be found the pride and independence so important to Dave. He contends that the appeal of the myth transcends class: "No matter how educated a southerner is, or how liberal or intellectual he might consider himself to be, I don't believe you will meet many of my generation who do not still revere, although perhaps in a secret way, all the old southern myths that we've supposedly put aside as members of the New South" (*Radiance* 265). These myths are of both history and community. Dave's long-deceased father, whom he remembers and mourns in every novel, embodies those myths. Though uneducated and a heavy-drinking brawler, "inside he had a gentle heart, a strong sense of right and wrong, and a tragic sense about the cruelty and violence that the world sometimes imposes upon the innocent" (*Prisoners* 215). His father's simplicity and honesty are beacons for Dave as he attempts to make his way in the complex modern world. To honor his father, on each anniversary of his death, Dave spreads flowers on the site in the Gulf where he perished in the explosion of an oil derrick.

Yet the novels do not simply romanticize the southern past. While Dave loves the myths and believes they are important, he also knows that they can obscure the racism, violence, and ignorance that were also a part of the southern past. So, along with his memories of barbecues, dances, and baseball games come memories of "the boys who went nigger-knocking in the little black community of Sunset, who shot people of color with BB guns and marbles fired from slingshots, who threw M-80s onto the galleries of their pitiful homes" (*Radiance* 65). The presence in *A Stained White Radiance* of a David Duke–like politician with a large following suggests that racial prejudice is alive and well. In fact, *Burning Angel* is an exploration of the historical origins and contemporary manifestations of that prejudice. Thus the novels embody a complicated vision—both nostalgia for and criticism of the southern past.

Dave frequently uses the term "New South" to describe the contemporary South, where commercialism, exploitation, and criminality are encroaching on a traditional way of life. His anger is aroused by the oil and chemical companies, the developers, and the Mafia, who "took everything that was best from the Cajun world in which I had grown up, treated it cynically and with contempt, and left us with oil sludge in the oyster beds, Levittown, and the abiding knowledge that we had done virtually nothing to stop them" (*Radiance* 31). But it is not simply that the supposedly innocent rural South is prey to urbanites, nor simply that, as Dave indicates, rural residents allow such changes to occur. These people are actually complicit in the changes, as in, for example, *In the Electric Mist with Confederate Dead*, where respectable New Iberians welcome the movie company to town, even though they know of its connections with the Mafia. They are willing to sell out their values for commercial gain and economic advantage. That novel also reveals that town leaders were being bribed by criminals even during the time Dave idealizes in his memory. Dave feels particular anger at the contemporary representatives of the southern aristocracy, like the Bertrand family in *Burning Angel* and the LaRose family in *Cadillac Jukebox*. Much of that anger originates in the class resentment of the blue-collar worker for the aristocrat. Dave typically has much more sympathy for the lower-class individual who is exploited or turns to crime than for the aristocrat who gets involved behind the scenes. In essence, Burke suggests that the threat to the rural way of life is not simply external—it is internal as well. Or, as he pithily puts it, "Judas Iscariot was us" (*Jam* 366). Joyce Carol Oates contends that the Robicheaux novels portray the archetypal drama of "our expulsion from the Garden of Eden, and our ignorant complicity in our fate" (5). The rural South may have indeed been a paradise, but the seeds of its destruction lay within.

Dave is a typical modern southern literary figure in his obsession with history, time, and mortality, both as they apply to the South and as they affect him personally. In *Burning Angel* Dave visits a priest who tells him, "I can absolve sins but I can't set either one of us free from the nature of time" (244). Aspiring to permanence and perfection, Dave is tortured by his losses and failures. Long before the beginning of the series, he alienated and lost his first wife through his drinking and his violence. In the first novel, *The Neon Rain*, he meets and marries Annie. In *Heaven's Prisoners* she is murdered in their home by criminals involved in a case Dave is working on. Throughout the following novel, *Black Cherry Blues*, he is haunted by her memory and his own guilt. In the next novel, *A Morning for Flamingos*, he again encounters Bootsie, his sweetheart from his college years whom he had driven away but whose loss he had always mourned. They marry, and he thinks they have recaptured the beauty and radiance of the past. Dave believes that "my Higher Power had given me back Bootsie when I had lost all claim to her, had undone my youthful mistakes for me, and had made that wonderful summer of 1957 as immediate and tangible and ongoing as the four o'clocks that bloomed nightly under the moon on Bayou Teche" (*Radiance* 75). But fate plays a trick on them. Not only are they older, but just as he thinks he has regained the past, they learn she has lupus. While the disease remains in remission to date, its shadow is always there, reminding them of their mortality.

Dave continues to have an uncertain attitude toward that mortality. He knows he should accept it but cannot do so consistently. For example, at the end of *A Morning for Flamingos* he summarizes what he has learned: "I've grown old enough to put away vain and foolish concerns about mortality, and to stop imposing the false measures of calendars and clocks upon my life, or, for that matter, upon eternity" (319). In the very next novel, however, tortured by the threat of Bootsie's lupus, he says, "I wanted a lock on the future;

I wanted our marriage to be above the governance of mortality and chance" (*Radiance* 186). Thus he remains haunted by the specter of impermanence, change, and death.

Dave's obsession with mortality is linked to his experiences in Vietnam, memories of which haunt him through the first half of the series and still surface occasionally. It is notable that numerous characters who appear in the series, good and bad alike, had experiences in Vietnam. Burke seems to suggest that the chaos in Vietnam is a necessary backdrop to the drama of change in the South played out in the novels. Dave was himself wounded twice in Vietnam, and he sometimes dreams of those woundings and the fear he felt in the war. His experiences there exposed him to a world of insane violence, and he carries with him a burden of guilt because he remembers being concerned only with his own survival, not the fate of his men. He holds himself to high standards and cannot forgive himself when he falls short. A frequent motif in the novels—most vivid in the murder of his wife, Annie—is Dave's guilt whenever the innocent are hurt as a consequence, however indirect, of his actions.

After he marries Bootsie, he puts some of his demons to rest. But the early novels hint that those demons are of deeper origin than Vietnam. In *Black Cherry Blues*, Dave notes that his first bout of extreme terror and guilt occurred when he was ten. And it was his black depressions in his teenage years that ended his earlier relationship with Bootsie. In later novels, memories surface that portray the childhood origin of his problems. It is as if, comforted by his marriage to Bootsie, he can now allow himself to remember. In *Dixie City Jam*, the memories are most fully described. He recalls at age seven seeing his mother in bed with a gambler; subsequently the gambler confronted and threatened him. Dave remembers the "sense of visceral revulsion and personal shame and violation" he felt when the gambler "made me an accomplice in the sexual degradation of my mother." He now understands his feelings: "Because as the object of someone else's perverse sexual obsession, you feel not only that you are alone, and I mean absolutely alone, but that there is something defective in you that either attracts or warrants the bent attentions of your persecutor" (191–92). The betrayal is not only of Dave's own innocence but also of his father, who is an extremely important figure in his life. These memories, only recently revealed, help account for Dave's inner conflicts and why memory is such a crucial but complicated thing to him. Memory evokes the rural past, but it also brings back Vietnam and aspects of his family life he still has difficulty coming to terms with.

Dave's inner conflicts result in a tendency toward violence, which the novels portray as a complex phenomenon. Dave usually fights against those tendencies. When he must engage in violence (frequently when his home and family are threatened), he does not do so easily or readily, and the results bother him. He remembers, for example, the faces and circumstances of everyone he has had to kill, and his violent nature is but one more reason for Dave to feel guilt. In fact, Cletus Purcel, Dave's former New Orleans police partner who is currently a private detective, functions as a double for Dave. They are close friends, but Clete is a very violent man, with none of Dave's moral compunctions. Clete often contends that in his violence, he simply acts out what Dave wants to do, that Dave secretly loves what Clete calls the "full-tilt boogie rock 'n' roll" (*Radiance* 59). Clete will not let Dave get too soft,[1] and in fact Dave admits that he is drawn to violence "in the same way that some people are fascinated by the protean shape and texture of fire, to the extent that they need to slide their hands through its caress" (*Jam* 72). He sees his proclivity to violence as evidence that "that simian creature we descend from was alive and well in my breast" (*Rain* 100). Thus Burke adds his voice to those of the many other southern writers who focus on the topic of violence. He considers Dave's violence to be a darker side of the southern myth, what Dave calls "our dark fascination with man's iniquity" (*Rain* 71). These novels treat violence in a way uncharacteristic of most crime novels. Though the plot of each novel is resolved by violence, that violence is far from cathartic. Rather, it is a disturbing manifestation of man's fallen nature.

Because of Dave's innate decency yet conflicted nature, he has a great deal of sympathy for others, particularly those who have had a difficult time. He comments, "The people closest to me have always been marked by a peculiar difference in their makeup. They're the walking wounded, the ones to whom a psychological injury was done that they will never be able to define" (*Radiance* 280). Dave's adopted daughter Alafair, present since the second novel, when Dave rescued her from a plane that crashed in the Gulf, often comes into danger in the novels, and she represents an innocence that Dave most wants to preserve. The origin of the title of *A Morning for Flamingos* indicates how fragile and easily wounded such innocence can be. Kim, a stripper, tells Dave what happened to her as a child. One day her father took her with him to tend the flamingos at Hialeah Racetrack. When she did not behave, he began beating her. A horse trainer appeared to rescue her. "He drove me down to Crandon Park to see the flamingos. He said my father wouldn't hurt me anymore, not as long as he was around. Then he bought me some ice cream and parked the car in some palmettos and sat me in his lap. Then he unbuttoned my blouse. I've always thought of it as my morning for flamingos" (146). Because of the damage he himself has suffered, Dave is drawn to and feels particular sympathy for such people. Nothing makes him angrier than an attack on innocence.

In *Sunset Limited*, Burke continues his exploration of the innocent and unprotected members of southern society. The novel circles around the crucifixion-death of labor leader Jack Flynn forty years earlier, the crucifixion imagery suggesting that Jesus was also a radical egalitarian who challenged the rich. The novel includes as well several instances of white men sexually exploiting black women through the last 150 years. All these events are tied to the Terrebonne family, another of those aristocratic families in Burke's fiction that are implicated in evil. Dave remarks at one point, "Jack Flynn's death was at the center of our current problems because we had never dealt with our past" (132). By the end of the novel, Flynn's murder is solved, though Archer Terrebonne will not be punished. The damage really occurs to members of the next generation, who carry the scars of the past, a past that does not die. The title of the novel refers to the name of the train that Dave's mother, full of dreams, takes when she leaves his father to go to Los Angeles with her lover. She soon returns, her dreams gone. Dave declares, "History books are written by and about the Terrebonnes of this world, not jarheads up the Mekong or people who die in oil-well blowouts or illiterate Cajun women who believe the locomotive whistle on the Sunset Limited calls for them" (280). Yet it is those very people for whom Dave continues to feel sympathy and to speak.

The Robicheaux series as a whole is engaged in a portrayal of Dave and his past and the development of the South over time. An interesting change has occurred in the later novels. It appears that, as Dave's marriage to Bootsie has somewhat stabilized his personal life and he is not quite as beset by inner turmoil, the series has taken a turn toward the social and historical. Three novels have evoked specific historical periods: the Civil War in *In the Electric Mist with Confederate Dead*, the Nazi era and World War II in *Dixie City Jam*, and the period of slavery in *Burning Angel*. The first and last of these are notable instances of how specific eras of southern history are shown to relate to the contemporary South.

In the Electric Mist with Confederate Dead can be read as a consideration of the connection between the southern past, especially the Civil War, and the present. Whether drug-induced, a result of being struck by lightning, a simple fantasy, or an actual occurrence, Dave is visited periodically by Confederate general John Bell Hood, who encourages him in his pursuit of justice and defense of the innocent. Telling him the war is never over, Hood urges Dave to persist in the cause, to pursue the *"quixotic vision"* of southerners. Asserting that *"venal and evil men are destroying the world you were born in"* (162), he emphasizes Dave's responsibility to continue the honorable southern fight. Through the device of Hood's appearance, Burke suggests parallels between the Civil War and the Vietnam War of Dave's experience, parallels noted in a general way by Owen Gilman in *Vietnam and the Southern Imagination*: "Often southerners have found in the Vietnam War provocative echoes of fundamental issues that came to the surface in the Civil War" (21). While the Confederate soldiers stand for honor, courage, and the effort to preserve a traditional way of life, Burke does not ignore the negative in the southern past, just as one cannot ignore the negative in the experience in Vietnam. Hood says: "*Oh, we were always honorable—Robert Lee, Jackson, Albert Sidney Johnston, A.P. Hill—but we served venal men and a vile enterprise. How many lives would have been spared had we not lent ourselves to the defense of a repellant cause like slavery?*" (*Mist* 315). The cause in Vietnam may also have been vile and repellent, but as in the Civil War there were individual acts of honor and courage. In the novel Dave acts honorably, as did the Confederate dead; though he suspects that his cause will not ultimately prevail, he continues to make the effort. In *Mist* he prevails once again—at least for a while—and the Mafia-backed movie company is driven from New Iberia. Yet as long as we welcome evil, as long as it appeals to something venal within us, the triumph will be only temporary.

The novel concludes with Dave and his family on vacation in Los Angeles, the seat of Hollywood and the movies, "the end point of the American dream . . . a city of illusion," where "black kids along palm-tree-lined streets in Watts hunted each other with automatic weapons" (342–43). But Burke does not end with this vision of the dream being undercut by fact. Rather, Dave then links the Spanish conquistadors with the Confederate soldiers "wending their way in and out of history—gallant, Arthurian, their canister-ripped colors unfurled in the roiling smoke, the fatal light in their faces a reminder that the contest is never quite over, the field never quite ours" (344). Thus the fight to preserve the dream will continue.

In its treatment of the legacy of the South's "vile enterprise," slavery, *Burning Angel* can be seen as an elaboration on the ideas in *Mist* and a corrective to the tendency to romanticize southern history. Of course Dave has always been sensitive to racial matters and includes blacks in his general sympathy for the dispossessed. Early in *Mist*, Dave remembers an incident in 1957 when he saw the summary execution of a black prisoner in a marsh. He tried to tell anyone who would listen about it but met only indifference. He comments now, "At age nineteen I did not want to accept the possibility that a man's murder could be treated with the social significance of a hangnail that had been snipped off someone's finger" (11). Too, the presence of Batist, the black man who helps him run his bait shop and who has worked for his family for decades, is significant. They are very close, with a mutual loyalty and devotion that transcends racial lines to become familial.

Burning Angel is the Robicheaux novel that most fully focuses on race relations. Its epigraph is taken from Solomon Northup's autobiography, *Twelve Years a Slave*, and it begins with a situation familiar to readers of Ernest

Gaines—the dispossession of blacks whose families have lived on a plantation for generations, with the family cemetery being dug up in the name of
progress. In this novel, the modern world and the criminal element intrude
on New Iberia as Moleen Bertrand, the plantation owner and descendant of
southern aristocrats, evicts the blacks so that a Mafia-controlled waste incin-
erator can be built on and pollute the land. Slavery is much on Dave's mind in
this novel: he dreams of a slave auction, and he finds a slave's leg iron in his
truck. He has long disliked Moleen, partly because of his general resentment
of aristocrats but more basically because of a conflict of values. Moleen tells
Dave: "Take the scales off your eyes. We don't serve flags or nations anymore.
It's all business today. The ethos of Robert E. Lee is as dead as the world we
grew up in." Thus speaks the modern New Southerner, for whom the South is
merely an arena for business and for whom memory is irrelevant. Dave's response is succinct but telling: "Speak for yourself" (232). For, although he
calls the plantation in all its historical resonance "our original sin" (215),
Dave attempts to keep the best of traditional values alive.

He does so by defending the dispossessed—the blacks being displaced—
and by combating big business and the Mob. But in the process he also learns
about people. In another plot element that could have come out of Gaines,
Ruthie Jean Fontenot, one of the blacks being evicted, and Moleen have had
a long-standing love affair. Dave initially sees that affair as but another instance of racial exploitation, but through discovering that indeed they love
each other, Dave gains some humility and realizes that such love can exist
beyond racial barriers and beyond exploitation. The South's sin was to deny
the humanity of an entire group of people. But at the end Dave takes flowers
to the place where Ruthie Jean and Moleen, now both dead, began their affair,
where "they had reenacted that old Southern black-white confession of need
and dependence that, in its peculiar way, was a recognition of the simple
biological fact of our brotherhood" (339). Thus Burke suggests that all
southerners experience a common history that cannot in the end be denied.

Cadillac Jukebox does not explore the southern past to the extent of
Mist and *Angel*, but its plot is based on the murder of a black civil rights
worker twenty-eight years before by Aaron Crown, a poor white—a clear
echo of Byron de la Beckwith's murder of Medgar Evers. The new governor,
Buford LaRose, scion of an old southern family and now an apostle of the
New South, has brought Crown to justice. The novel reveals that LaRose, too,
like Moleen Bertrand, has become implicated in criminal activity. Dave is
again tormented by his past, this time by a long-ago and short-lived affair
with Buford's wife. Dave helps bring down LaRose, and the novel's title evokes
the past that is so important but so ambiguous to Dave. The jukebox in the
bait shop is a working replica of a 1950s Wurlitzer filled with 45 rpm records

from the 1940s and 1950s, each one a "Cadillac." Dave initially will not play the records, in fact cuts the cord of the jukebox, because "their voices and music were out of another era, one that we thought would never end. But it did, incrementally, in ways that seemed inconsequential at the time, like the unexpected arrival at the front gate of a sun-browned oil lease man in khaki work clothes who seemed little different from the rest of us" (163). Here, Dave does not want to face the fact that the South has changed, but the end of the novel finds him dancing with Bootsie to the songs, "like giving yourself over to the world of play and non-reason that takes you outside of time" (297). In contrast, the new governor of Louisiana, "a practical-minded businessman, was not given to brooding over past events and letting them encumber his vision of the future" (295–96). Thus the practical man of the present and the future is juxtaposed with Dave, who finally cannot abandon his romantic love of the past.

The reflection on history is a crucial element in the Robicheaux series. *Burning Angel* ends with a meditation on the nearness of past and present.

> And if you should ever doubt the proximity of the past, I thought to myself, you only had to look over your shoulder at the rain slanting on the fields, like now, the smoke rising in wet plumes out of the stubble, the mist blowing off the lake, and you can see and hear with the clarity of a dream the columns marching four abreast out of the trees, barefoot, emaciated as scarecrows, their perforated, sun-faded colors popping above them in the wind, their officers cantering their horses in the field, everyone dressing it up now, the clatter of muskets shifting in unison to the right shoulder, yes, just a careless wink of the eye, just that quick, and you're among them, wending your way with liege lord and serf and angel, in step with the great armies of the dead. (339–40)

Compare this with Dave's perspective on the past in the first novel of the series, *The Neon Rain*: "It's the only measure of identity we have" (155). So, from that beginning point through the Confederate soldiers of *Mist* and *Angel*, to the songs on the Cadillac jukebox, to the scars that do not fade away in *Sunset Limited*, the past has been a constant presence in the novels. James Lee Burke is in the honorable tradition of southern writers whose works, in Allen Tate's formulation, are conscious of the past in the present. Dave puts his own twist to this idea in *Angel*: "I've often subscribed to the notion that history is not sequential; that all people, from all of history, live out their lives simultaneously, in different dimensions perhaps, occupying the same pieces of geography, unseen by one another, as if we are all part of one spiritual conception" (38). In the Robicheaux series, Burke explores change in the South, but it is change presented in the context of history. These novels vividly illustrate the continuing applicability of C. Hugh Holman's contention of twenty years ago: "The past has been and still is an inescapable element of the southern mind . . . as a pattern which can—if anything can—point us to the future" (101). Dave's inner conflicts arise from the ambiguous nature of his own past and from his attempt to apply traditional values associated with the past to the present. While his success is provisional, his attempt is honorable.

Note

1. Rob Carney contends that Purcel plays such a prominent role in *Dixie City Jam* to counterbalance Dave's increasing softness.

Works Cited

Burke, James Lee. *Black Cherry Blues*. New York: Avon, 1990.
———. *Burning Angel*. New York: Hyperion, 1995.
———. *Cadillac Jukebox*. New York: Hyperion, 1996.
———. *Dixie City Jam*. New York: Hyperion, 1994.
———. *Heaven's Prisoners*. New York: Henry Holt, 1988.
———. *In the Electric Mist with Confederate Dead*. New York: Hyperion, 1993.
———. *A Morning for Flamingos*. Boston: Little, Brown, 1990.
———. *The Neon Rain*. New York: Henry Holt, 1987.
———. *A Stained White Radiance*. New York: Hyperion, 1992.
———. *Sunset Limited*. New York: Doubleday, 1998.
Carney, Rob. "Clete Purcel to the Rampaging Rescue: Looking for the Hard-Boiled Tradition in James Lee Burke's *Dixie City Jam*." *Southern Quarterly* 34.4 (1996): 121–30.
Gilman, Owen W. Jr. *Vietnam and the Southern Imagination*. Jackson: UP of Mississippi, 1992.
Hobson, Fred. *The Southern Writer in the Postmodern World*. Athens: U of Georgia P, 1991.
Holman, C. Hugh. *The Immoderate Past: The Southern Writer and History*. Athens: U of Georgia P, 1977.
Oates, Joyce Carol. "Hard-Boiled in the Big Easy." *Washington Post Book World* 5 Apr. 1992: 5.
Stroby, W.C. "Hanging Tough with James Lee Burke." *Writer's Digest* (Jan. 1993): 38–40.

The Physical Hunger for the Spiritual

Southern Religious Experience in the Plays of Horton Foote

Gerald C. Wood

Unlike most southern writers, Horton Foote has been successful in more than one medium. Originally an actor, Foote first wrote plays in the late 1930s. Inspired by the direction of Mary Hunter and the enthusiastic support of Agnes DeMille, his off-Broadway work received positive reviews. Quickly shifting his allegiance from acting to playwrighting, Foote refined his skills and style during the 1940s, including a five-year sabbatical in Washington, D.C., at the end of that decade. By the beginning of the 1950s he returned to New York to write for both live television and theater. In the mid-1950s, with the release of his screen adaptation *Storm Fear*, he was credited with film writing as well.

Success in the three media—theater, television, and film—did not immediately spread Foote's reputation outside New York, however. On stage his southern stories, set in coastal southeast Texas, were sometimes considered literal, lacking the universal resonance of major art. Similarly, his television work, despite the support of creative producers such as Fred Coe and talented directors such as Arthur Penn, remained obscure until it was rediscovered by a later generation of critics and historians. Even when Foote won an Academy Award in 1962 for his adaptation of Harper Lee's *To Kill a Mockingbird*, Hollywood tried to pigeonhole him as a translator of more established southern writers. By then his understated, dedramatized plays had become unfashionable among the liberationist dramas of the Vietnam era. Out of step with the contemporary stage, nearly invisible on television, and frustrated in Hollywood, Foote's various successes seemed to neutralize one another.

But Foote remained steadfast in pursuit of his individual approach to drama, often supported by his work for independent film and public television. Then, in the mid-1970s, following the death of his parents, and at the age of sixty, Foote began his most ambitious project, the nine-play cycle *The*

Orphans' Home.[1] While revising and producing that series, he also wrote *Tender Mercies*, for which he won his second Academy Award for the best original screenplay of 1983. Subsequently, for the first time, his many successes for theater, television, and film began to serve one another. Film versions of plays from *The Orphans' Home* have been produced for public television and national film audiences. *The Habitation of Dragons, Old Man*, and *Alone* have been released for cable television; his adaptation of John Steinbeck's *Of Mice and Men* was directed by Gary Sinise in 1992; and he was chosen by the Signature Theatre Company in 1994–1995 for its annual series on contemporary American playwrights. Foote won the Pulitzer Prize for Drama in 1995 for the production of *The Young Man from Atlanta* in that series.

Although Foote's fifty years of dramatic work has gained relatively little scholarly attention, critics have agreed that he is inspired by his Texas homeplace. Following the lead of early interpreters like Mary Hunter and Stark Young, critics have emphasized that Foote's plays are fictional portraits of his family and other citizens of Wharton, Texas. Samuel Freedman's seminal work in *The New York Times Magazine* clarified the personal and regional quality of Foote's work, which other reviewers have compared with the writing of William Faulkner, Flannery O'Connor, and Katherine Anne Porter. No matter which medium he writes for, Foote, like these other southern writers, uses specific place material for general, even mythic ends.

But the southern tradition in Foote's writing can sometimes be overinterpreted. For example, his plays—whether for theater, television, or film—are sometimes placed in the Southern Gothic tradition (Watson 200, 211). Such linking of Foote's writing with that of Erskine Caldwell and Lillian Hellman, for example, is based on a few outrageous episodes in Harrison, Foote's fictional Texas town: in *The Roads to Home*, rumors are spread from Harrison to Houston that a Baptist preacher has run off with another man. Repeatedly, in plays like *The One-Armed Man* and *The Dancers*, wealthy men and women impose their wills on the less fortunate; everything from inheritance to physical attractiveness becomes a weapon for controlling the disadvantaged. And in *Valentine's Day*, George Tyler, driven insane by an obsessive attachment to his cousin, finally commits suicide on the main street of Harrison.

But the appearance of such extreme characters and actions in Foote's plays is not sufficient evidence that his writing is Southern Gothic. That tradition, admitting little sympathy for its characters, sensationalizes the eccentricities of the region, which it judges by a social/political standard of equality and justice. Such distancing in the writing of Erskine Caldwell or Lillian Hellman is rarely present in Foote's dramas; rather, his sympathy extends to even the most disoriented and violent characters. Silly and irritating as they may be, his characters are never grotesque. They express the primitive need of Foote's lonely individuals to find meaning and identity in the face of the mutability of the human condition. A humanist who believes all individuals have their own good reasons, Foote asks his audiences to empathize with, rather than judge, all kinds of experience, including the religious, in his plays.

To understand Foote's unique vision, readers and audiences need to recognize that his writing, though often historical and place-specific, is neither nostalgic nor sentimental. As he has explained in his preface to his collection of teleplays, *Harrison, Texas,* the primary drama in the lives of his characters, though they remain only partially conscious of the issue, is the struggle to accept the realities of their personal past and face death ("Preface" viii). Consequently, as the writer has declared in several interviews, the implicit subject of all his work is courage.[2] Foote writes, he says, to discover why some people are strong enough to become responsible for their lives while others are not.

One consequence of this focus on courage is a tolerance for, and sometimes even a sympathy with, the southern religious experience often ridiculed by other writers. Take, for example, Mrs. Coons in *Lily Dale.* At the beginning of the play, she accosts Horace on the train from Harrison to Houston. A busybody, she wants to examine his religion, the quality of his prayer life, the condition of his immortal soul. She is irritating and comical for both Foote's protagonist and the audience. Rightly ignoring her, Horace continues his journey to the big city, where, unfortunately, he meets with hostility from his stepfather, rejection by his mother, and bloodless competition from his sister. His despair and anger eventually throw him into a feverish delirium that threatens his physical and emotional life.

Horace then boards the return train to Harrison, where he once again encounters Mrs. Coons. This time, having experienced the disconnection and disorder of his broken life, she reappears to him, and to the audience, as a more sympathetic person, who, despite her aggressiveness and her own kinds of self-absorption, can offer comfort to Horace. While he largely ignores her insistence, as a Baptist, that he be baptized, he impulsively asks her to pray for "me and my sister and my mother" (203). He further insists that she pray immediately, not perfunctorily on some later prayer list. She begins angrily and abstractly, asking God's mercy on the whole "train filled with miserable sinners" (204). But Horace's genuine need leads her toward more authentic feelings. With Horace's sister singing her composition "Lily Dale" in the background, Mrs. Coons prays: "Father, I've been asked to remember in my prayers this young man, Horace, and his dear mother, Corella, and his dear sister, Lily Dale. Father of mercy, Father of goodness, Father of forgiveness . . ." (204). In the mouth of an evangelical, even somewhat obnoxious woman, Horace finds a release from pain and, more important, an image of forgiveness that will return peace to his life.

Like Flannery O'Connor, Foote uses imposing religious figures like Mrs. Coons for ends unimagined by the characters. But there is a crucial difference. In O'Connor's case, religious fanaticism highlights the failure of human efforts, the gap between natural evil and God's call to love. Employing her characters as the unwitting agents of God's will and design, O'Connor demonstrates the necessity of divine grace and mercy in response to the chaos of the world. While Foote's texts similarly explore realities unknown to their subjects, the playwright admits, and even celebrates, the power of personal choice and freedom. Consequently, though his religious activists can be just as ignorant and inflexible as O'Connor's, they serve an imaginary world that is more open-ended and finally more mysterious than O'Connor's.

Both writers believe the drama of human existence results from the struggle between divine order and human chaos. But Flannery O'Connor's resolution is predicated on the radical otherness of God and mankind's submission to the divine plan. In her stories, the physical world is essentially witless; it must be saved from itself by the intervention of the spiritual. Foote's view is more existential, insisting on the power and joys of human will. Consequently, he focuses less on particular beliefs than on the capacity of all belief to strengthen his characters. As Foote himself has explained: "You know, a lot of difficulty comes to people in their lives, and you have to ask yourself, What gets them through it? And if you are at all honest, you have to say that you may or may not understand it, but you have to witness to the fact that their religion must sustain them a great deal" ("Going Home" 30).

But his dramatization of southern religious life is not uncritical. While Foote values all belief as a source of order and courage, the subtexts of his plays express his critique of Calvinistic religion's vision of an angry, punitive God. In *1918*, for example, Mrs. Vaughn tells the story of her husband's encounter with such a religious tradition at the funeral of their infant daughter: "When we lost our second child your papa was sitting in the living room by her little coffin. Mrs. Coon Ferguson came into the room and said, 'Mr. Vaughn, did you ever think the death of this child was a judgement on you for not joining the church?' And his face flushed crimson, but he just said very quietly, 'No, Mrs. Ferguson, I never did'" (151). *The Orphans' Home* is, by the writer's own definition, a moral and social history of a particular time and place in American history. But happiness and peace are impossible in any epoch, the cycle implies, when people become the fearful disciples of a vindictive God. It is unimaginable to Mr. Vaughn, and to the playwright who wrote his quiet but assured response to the woman's hostile question, that God would take pleasure in punishing his creations.

At the center of the nine plays that comprise *The Orphans' Home* is the sense of identity and contentment Horace finds in his marriage to Elizabeth. As he tells her in *Valentine's Day*: "I am no orphan, but I think of myself as an orphan, belonging to no one but you. . . . I tell you I've begun to know happiness for the first time in my life. I adore you. I worship you . . . and I thank you for marrying me" (83). Such a passage is intended to be neither sentimental nor rhetorical. It expresses Foote's confirmed belief that love can be an active and powerful source of order amid the chaos of the human condition. As the writer explains: "I was trying to test her and her marriage against this chaos—the chaos of poverty, of lives that have no order. And you know, the chaotic people do sense there is some order in Horace and Elizabeth, whether it's from their love or wherever" (Sterritt 36). No such peace can be found, Foote's plays assert, under the rule of a divinity who replaces freedom with submission, compassion with contingent love.

This revision of a judgmental God in favor of a more nurturant one is indicative of Foote's personal and complex treatment of gender. While maintaining a Yeatsian respect for the order and continuity of the Victorian world, his plays recognize the need to move beyond the rigid, distant nature of patriarchy. Without Elizabeth's courageous rebellion against her parents in *Courtship*, Mr. Vaughn would repeat his tired male ways, crippling his daughters by his overly protective, controlling love. Though more cerebral than Mr. Vaughn, Mac Sledge has a similar need for control expressed in his round of unanswerable questions near the end of *Tender Mercies*. Even Foote's most interesting and complex men are handicapped by their limited, insulated emotional lives.

Foote's women are often stronger than these men because they tend to focus on the natural, more emotional rhythms of living and dying. As Foote says of Mac's wife, Rosa Lee: "She has a purer sense of what it's all about. . . . She has her own confusion, like the death of her husband. But she doesn't really doubt what she thinks is the final thrust of things" (Personal Interview with Wood). This belief in "the final thrust of things" gives his best, strongest women the rootedness sought by Foote's placeless people, especially his men. The purpose and meaning these women derive from such commitment makes them more courageous than the common Harrisonians. It is a form of female power that men would do well to emulate.

Best of all, Foote's heroines are willing to make peace with things beyond their control and understanding. Their "acceptance of everything that happened," as Foote says of the woman in *Old Man*, allows them to find "something in the journey itself to enjoy in spite of . . . the most horrifying conditions" ("On First Dramatizing Faulkner" 54). Living with a sense of accommodation and resilience, these "plains Madonnas," as Tess Harper describes them, sanctify whatever happiness comes to Foote's characters. Though sometimes interpreted as a debilitating passivity, these women express a radical acceptance of mystery as central to authentic human experience (Foote, "Horton Foote: An Interview" 10). Their example serves as both inspiration and moral norm for the other characters.

Belief carries such existential weight in Foote's dramas because, like many other southerners, he recognizes the loss of communal myth for the artist. According to this view, the twentieth century is marked by the absence, in Flannery O'Connor's words, of "a story of mythic dimensions, one which belongs to everybody, one in which everybody is able to recognize the hand of God and its descent" (202). This absence of sacred stories exacerbates the loneliness and disorder of the human condition. No longer connected by legendary records of meaning, writers and their readers/audiences are haunted by language's lack of mythopoeic power. According to Foote and other twentieth-century southern writers, the breakdown of shared values and beliefs makes loving connection and courageous action especially difficult (Wood, "Old Beginnings" 364–65).

But Foote's response to this alienation from religious mythology is not typical of southern writing. While recognizing, like William Faulkner, that Western civilization has retreated from its Judeo-Christian mythos, Foote does not imagine his characters as the victims of history. And, though some of his stories, like those of Katherine Anne Porter, record lives that fail to reach the Christian standards of love, other Foote characters find a peace unknown in Porter's work. More like Flannery O'Connor in his belief in a living sense of divinity, Foote nevertheless denies O'Connor's assertion that God's grace is indifferent to human will and freedom. Foote's stories, written in a tradition of southern mythic realism, are more interior than those of his fellow southerners (Wood, "Old Beginnings" 365).

For Horton Foote, God is neither absent nor controlling. Divinity is the order in the universe, often glimpsed in the movement of the natural world, a spiritual presence that lies just beyond the disorderly, fragmented experience of individual lives. Born into this sacred process—with its transcendent purity and innocence—the characters inevitably slide into the experience of fallen time. As Henry Vaughn, looking at his new grandchild, says near the end of *1918*: "Looking at them like this you can't imagine anything bad happening to them, can you? No bad habits, no sickness, no killings, no wars" (175). But Foote's best people are not paralyzed by such reality. They are asked to accept their personal limitations and face death. As Foote says in his interview with Irv Broughton, "I think . . . there's dignity in everyone. Certainly everybody is striving. . . . And if they're defeated, as many people are, that's moving, too" ("Horton Foote" 5). Whether the characters are strong or defeated, the endless pursuit of personhood is completed by the return to the spirit of God.

Within this process, which is physically limited but spiritually transcendent, Foote's people are given genuine freedom. Some are luckily born into loving families that offer protection and peace. But they are tempted, like Laura Lee in *Night Seasons*, to cling to such primitive connections, imagining the biological family as irreplaceable. More courageous characters, like Mary Catherine in *The Dancers*, risk the initial attachments in pursuit of more love and life. As Minnie explains in *Cousins*, "A family is a remarkable thing, isn't it? You belong. And then you don't. It passes you by. Unless you start a family of your own" (92). Others, like Horace Robedaux in *The Orphans' Home*, are orphaned by death and betrayal. They must control their bitterness and self-pity in order to find lost intimacy. For Horace and also for Mac Sledge in *Tender Mercies*, this search ends happily; for others, like Henry Thomas in *The Traveling Lady* and *Baby, the Rain Must Fall*, violent disconnection persists. Either way, Foote records their pursuit of freedom, selfhood, love, and courage.

Although the characters are generally unaware of the religious issues implied in such a call to personal responsibility, the writer suggests that religion can inspire graceful living. Without a focus on love, Foote's characters, like those at the rest stop in the film version of *The Trip to Bountiful*, drift from their traditions, confused about whether Corpus Christi means the body of Christ. At the other extreme, Sarah Eubanks and Jackson Fentry in *Tomorrow* realize the Christian ideal by loving each other in the face of brokenness, betrayal, and death. Their loving marriage not only rescues Sarah from loneliness, it inspires Fentry's later defense of their son. But while the language, images, and stories of Christianity surround Foote's characters with examples of loving community, the writer does not insist that they follow his beliefs. In the plays, religious experience is offered as a potential source of healing, but it "always must be willed, made real, by the love of human beings for each other and God" (Wood, "Old Beginnings" 370).

Key to the health and happiness of his characters, whether religious or not, is a powerful intimacy that inspires courage and offers peace in the face of death. In the teleplay *The Dancers*, for example, Horace is pressured by his older sister, Inez, to take Emily Crews, the prettiest and most popular girl in town, to a local dance. While seemingly a private matter, such action gains political significance when the audience learns that Emily's mother is using the date to undermine the girl's relationship with Leo, Emily's boyfriend. Such subterfuge is further politicized when Horace's sister joins the conspiracy to gain the approval and influence of Mrs. Crews, a powerful woman in Harrison. Fortunately, before all the intrigue develops, Horace meets Mary Catherine

Davis, another local girl, at the drugstore. The subsequent honest and open conversation between them gives Horace the courage, called confidence by the teenagers, to stand up to his sister and choose Mary Catherine (Wood, "Horton Foote's Politics" 50–51).

Both youngsters finally admit they are afraid of the dance, of appearing clumsy and unattractive in the public world. But sharing their mutual feelings of inadequacy strengthens their resolve. Able to accept themselves by sharing their doubts and fears, they practice dancing. Tempted to cling to each other and retreat from the world of risk and darkness, they nevertheless choose to venture out. The private moments of mutual vulnerability and mutuality—their intimacy—give them the courage to face the inevitable public trials and losses. They are ready to accept responsibility for their own lives and face death (Wood, "Horton Foote's Politics" 51–53).

A paradigm for Foote's political vision, *The Dancers* emphasizes healthy intimacy as prerequisite to all effective and lasting public action. While the writer continually records and criticizes sexual and racial injustice, he is careful to explore social inequality as an expression of failed loving connection. For example, Mamie Borden, the central character in Foote's early play *Only the Heart*, has, in the words of Mary Hunter (the play's director), "a deep fear of the give-and-take of love and the closeness of healthy personal relationships" that causes her to make herself "essential as a provider, as a controller of the destinies of those around her" (7). Such a person finds ingratitude rampant in the world; her private obsessions lead her to conclude that in the public world "people don't appreciate your trying to be nice to 'em. They'll turn against you every time when you try to help 'em. . . . Why, look at how those foreign countries we tried to help and loan money are acting" (Foote, *Only* 39).

Foote's religious and psychological interest in his characters' capacity or failure to love is integrated into his exploration of racism in plays like *Convicts* and of sexism in the one-acts *The Tears of My Sister* and *Blind Date* (Wood, "Boundaries" 163–65). Although the plays do not advocate or dramatize political action, they study the reasons why individuals want to control or violate others. The first cause is always failed intimacy; the "consequent loss of empathy and acceptance is the source of violence, either against oneself, the natural world, or others. Boundless competition and the obsessive need for wealth are not just political problems; they are also symptoms of a failure of emotion and imagination" (Wood, "Horton Foote's Politics" 57).

While still claiming intimacy as the benchmark for judging the characters' personal and public lives, Foote's later plays often add a remarkable note of benediction. Always more concerned with the subtleties of his people's emotional lives than with their actions, the writer throughout his career has repeatedly ignored or even betrayed traditional dramatic form. But in the past decade or so he often freezes the story line altogether, especially near the conclusion of his tales. While the resulting tableaus are, like his earlier work, not overtly religious, they imply a call for other contexts and realities than those discovered in earlier plays. Without becoming rhetorical, such scenes suggest an authorial presence, a more personal voice of disappointment and elegy.

In their darkest expression, these benedictory dramas portray an irremediable failure to achieve loving community. Near the end of *The Habitation of Dragons*, for example, Virgil, an aging and somewhat senile man, describes a dream in which he returns to childhood and cries as a preacher repeatedly calls "forgiveness": "And I woke up to tell my mama and papa about the dream, and of course, they weren't there. No one was there, and I was alone. Who was there to forgive? . . . Forgiveness. That's all he said. But what was there to forgive, except myself, or ask forgiveness of? Nobody. Nobody. Except myself" (61). Disconnected from any nurturant powers, parental or spiritual, Virgil feels alone. Unsupported by mutuality or common care, even forgiveness becomes an exercise in narcissism.

Such isolation and unresolved conflict are magnified by the burden of time at the conclusion of *Habitation*:

> VIRGIL: I broke my brother's heart, and he died. By his own hand,
>   he died. Did you break your brother's heart?
> LEONARD: Yes, sir.
> VIRGIL: And did he die?
> LEONARD: No, sir. He is alive, and his heart has mended very
>   well.
> VIRGIL: Are you alive?
> LEONARD: Yes, sir, and my heart is broken.
> VIRGIL: Who broke it?
> LEONARD: I did. . . .
> VIRGIL: Do you think it will mend?
> LEONARD: I hope. In time. (61)

Without understanding the implications of their words, Virgil and his nephew Leonard offer their personal litany of brokenness. Living without spiritual options, they stagnate in a deadly "time" of hollow forgiveness and fitful hope.

Like *Habitation*, *Dividing the Estate* is concerned with the devolution of community values. But the second play focuses less on individual shortcomings than on a family—the Gordons—whose members are unable to cooperate while anticipating an inheritance. Troubled by the thought that Korean and Vietnamese immigrants live more harmoniously than the indigenous

Texans (167), the Gordons remain confused throughout the play. Once again the dilemma is summarized in a bittersweet final scene, in which Mary Joe prays for oil as Irene cautions that John Moon found no lasting security in material things. According to Harrison legend, John purchased cars for each of his children, only to watch his possessions rust as the oil lay useless:

> MARY JO: I'm praying every night on bended knees.
> IRENE: Ma'am.
> MARY JO: Praying every night for my deliverance on bended
>   knees. Praying for an oil lease.
> IRENE: Yes, Ma'am.
> LUCILLE: John Moon. Yes, I remember him.
> IRENE: All I say is, if you strike oil watch out for crooks from the
>   Valley. They will sell your land under water every time. Ev-
>   ery time.
> LUCILLE: John Moon. My I hadn't thought about him for the
>   longest kind of time.
> MARY JO: I'm praying . . . I'm praying . . . *(Curtain)*. (173)

Simultaneously compassionate toward the Gordons and critical of their stasis, *Dividing the Estate* concludes, like *The Habitation of Dragons*, with images of a dynamic but chronically broken emotional landscape. Unable to resolve their differences, to reestablish loving order, the Gordons breathe paralytic air and mark, choruslike, their own passing.

The most personal and complex of the benedictory dramas is *Alone*, Foote's original teleplay for Showtime, first aired in December 1997. In this play, John Webb, a farmer "in his seventies, handsome, well preserved" (1), struggles with the death of Bessie, his wife of fifty-two years. Feeling "lost without her" (2), John receives little comfort from his nephews, Carl and Gus Jr., and their families; the children obsessively watch television while the adults covet money from the sale of land, mineral rights, and oil. When a lease for mineral rights is secured, John pays off debts and buys a tractor. But no oil is found. And near the end of the drama the brothers' children are seen wasting their percentage of the allotment.

John receives better support from his own children and friends, however. His two daughters, Grace Anne and Jackie, and their respective husbands, Gerald Murray and Paul, return home to aid their father, not just to await their inheritance. Jackie and Paul even remain on the farm, helping with chores until Paul's new job leads the couple back to Houston. During their brief stay, Paul becomes a steady companion for his father-in-law, recognizing the continuing power of the love between John and Bessie:

JOHN: I loved her a lot.
PAUL: I know you did. And she loved you.
JOHN: I know that. I take comfort in that. (83)

As in many previous Foote plays, such remembered love is embodied in African American characters deeply in touch with the emotional lives of Harrison. One such person is Grey, an "African American, in his mid eighties . . . well preserved" and "very erect" (12), whose acceptance that "Things change" (13) makes him a valuable confidant for John. The other is Sarah Davis, once the Webbs' cook for thirty years, who brings flowers to "Miss Bessie's grave" (91) and offers daily prayers in her memory.

The love of these two people of color inspires the ritual that concludes *Alone*. Sarah joins John and Grey on the porch of John's home, offering "Mr. John" (103) the devil's food cake, which he always enjoyed, they remember. Taking a piece, John offers Grey one, which he accepts. After a brief pause and Grey's declaration that Sarah "is a cook—always has been," Sarah breaks out into spontaneous song, "half to herself," according to the stage directions:

> "Shall we gather at the river, Where bright angel feet have trod." That's the song Miss Bessie liked me to sing best of all. I'd be in the kitchen singin' an' she'd call out to me, "Sarah, come out here and sing while I play." I'd come out then and she'd play the piano and I'd sing.
> (*A pause.*)
> GREY: It's so quiet, my God it's so quiet. Blessed. Blessed. Blessed quiet.
> (*They sit in silence for a beat.*)
> JOHN: (*Singing half to himself*) "Shall we gather at the river, The beautiful, the beautiful the river."
> (*He stops singing. Again there is silence.*) (104)

The action has become nearly static, forming a snapshot of lonely but satisfied people meeting on a landscape of mutability and death. Taking courage and comfort from their shared memory and service, they participate in a natural communion informed by a nearly miraculous "Blessed quiet." On the wings of their song, which unites the living and the dead, they imagine the transcendence represented in water, a spiritual presence equal to the emotional needs of the characters.

Alone is a special case among these benedictory dramas. It is the rare instance in which Foote records more than the general biography of his family, town, and region. In this teleplay he becomes personal and, with some indirection, quite autobiographical. Written soon after the death of Foote's wife, Lillian Vallish, *Alone* describes an alter ego seeking comfort in the face of a similar loss. As in previous work, the writer recognizes the family as a potentially stabilizing place of love and generation. But *Alone* also recognizes the healthy necessity that children leave their biological family to establish their own families. Subsequently, for John Webb—and Foote himself—the most sustaining ally becomes the spiritual order that finally transcends all families and persons. It is food for the physical world's final hunger for something greater than the self.

The authorial sense of benediction in many recent Foote plays thus serves the writer in various ways. While *The Habitation of Dragons* ends with a call for forgiveness between individuals, the enmity in *Dividing the Estate* is more political. It imagines immigrant cultures achieving a greater degree of community than indigenous ones in contemporary America. Even as they empathize with the characters, both plays ask for healthier, more loving families as the basis of sane and orderly societies. But *Alone* goes one step further. As Foote's most personal expression of Christian values and the religion of transcendence, this teleplay dramatizes the natural human need to gain identity through shared memory and the ritualizing of time. It portrays the grace offered to Foote's characters, who identify with a spirit of love beyond the limitations of self and history.

While belief takes many forms in Foote's imaginative world, healthy religion is based on a call to personhood. Whether or not they experienced genuine intimacy in their early lives, Foote's characters are asked to face the reality of their personal pasts. If they were loved, they must leave the nurturing parent to gain their own sense of self and freedom—as Elizabeth Vaughn does in *The Orphans' Home*. Even if their initial experiences were violent, like Henry Thomas's in *The Traveling Lady*, or smothering, like Laura Lee's in *Night Seasons*, Foote's characters are asked to become responsible for their life histories. Never feeling like victims, such individuals gain the courage to face all human loss, including their own deaths. The reality of such final sacrifice creates a hunger for the spirit of love that transcends hard-won identity and even time itself.

Critics of southern literature and culture need to be especially careful in matters of religion. Outsiders and secularists tend to ignore or discount religious experience. But literary evangels are equally tempted to find a Christian analogue or parable in every character or dramatic event. In the case of Horton Foote, the critic should proceed with double caution for the writer has correctly asserted that his plays are not written "from that point of view" ("Certain Kind" 231). They begin with found art and stay as faithful as possible to natural and human history. When religion appears within the works, it is specific to and varies with the characters. Foote reflects the historical truth of his characters' religious experiences, even when those experiences are substantially different from his own.

Such accurate reporting facilitates the identification of the southern religious ethos of Foote's work. A sensitive reader or audience will discover, for example, a Catholic influence (from the writer's wife, Lillian) in his celebration of mystery and the feminine nature of the divine. There is a trace of Episcopalianism in his natural sacramentalism, a personalist and pietistic Methodism that serves his subtext, and, of course, a Christian Science focus on healing. But these patterns are not definitive, sometimes not even integral to Foote's work. His sense of history and humanistic acceptance of the varieties of human experience leave no room for dogma. Despite the subtle influences of many religious points of view on his work, Foote's dramas assert two central values: the efficacy of all belief and the redemptive power of love.

Notes

1. The cycle includes *Roots in a Parched Ground, Convicts, Lily Dale, The Widow Claire, Courtship, Valentine's Day, 1918, Cousins,* and *The Death of Papa.*

2. See, for example, under Foote: "Foote-Work" 40; "Going Home" 30; *Horton Foote: Four New Plays* xii; "Horton Foote's Many Roads" 111; "Horton Foote: A Writer's" 27. Also see Wood, "Introduction" xix.

Works Cited

Foote, Horton. *Alone.* Unpublished teleplay courtesy of Horton Foote. Aired on Showtime, December 1997. Starring Hume Cronyn, James Earl Jones, and Piper Laurie.

———. *Baby, the Rain Must Fall.* [adaptation of Foote play *The Traveling Lady*]. Prod. Alan J. Pakula, dir. Robert Mulligan. Starring Steve McQueen and Lee Remick. Columbia Pictures, 1965.

———. *Blind Date.* In *Selected One-Act Plays of Horton Foote.* 363–89.

———. "'A Certain Kind of Writer': An Interview with Horton Foote." By Gerald C. Wood and Terry Barr. *Literature/Film Quarterly* 14.4 (1986): 226–37.

———. *Courtship, Valentine's Day, 1918: Three Plays from The Orphans' Home Cycle.* New York: Grove, 1987.

———. *Cousins.* In *Cousins and The Death of Papa: Two Plays from The Orphans' Home Cycle.* 1–99.

———. *Cousins and The Death of Papa: Two Plays from The Orphans' Home Cycle.* New York: Grove, 1989.

———. *The Dancers.* In *Selected One-Act Plays of Horton Foote.* 233–64.

———. *Dividing the Estate.* In *Horton Foote: Four New Plays.* 115–73.

————. "Foote-Work." Interview by Samir Hachem. *Horizon* 29 (Apr. 1986): 39–41.

————. "Going Home to the Hidden God." Interview by David Neff. *Christianity Today* 30 (4 Apr. 1986): 30–31.

————. *The Habitation of Dragons.* In *Horton Foote: Four New Plays.* 1–61.

————. "Horton Foote." Interview by Irv Broughton. *The Writer's Mind: Interviews with American Authors.* Ed. Irv Broughton. Vol. 2. Fayetteville: U of Arkansas P, 1990. 3–23.

————. *Horton Foote: Four New Plays.* Newbury, Vt.: Smith and Kraus, 1993. [Includes *The Habitation of Dragons, Night Seasons, Dividing the Estate,* and *Talking Pictures*]

————. "Horton Foote: An Interview." By Gerald C. Wood. *Post Script* 10.3 (1991): 3–12.

————. "Horton Foote: A Writer's Journey." Interview by Amanda Smith. *Varia* July-Aug. 1987: 18–20, 23, 26–27.

————. "Horton Foote's Many Roads Home: An American Playwright and His Characters." Interview by Marian Burkhart. *Commonweal* 115.4 (26 Feb. 1988): 110–13, 115.

————. *Lily Dale.* In *Roots in a Parched Ground, Convicts, Lily Dale, The Widow Claire: Four Plays from The Orphans' Home Cycle.* 135–204.

————. *Night Seasons.* In *Horton Foote: Four New Plays.* 63–113.

————. *1918.* In *Courtship, Valentine's Day, 1918: Three Plays from The Orphans' Home Cycle.* 109–77.

————. "On First Dramatizing Faulkner." *Faulkner, Modernism, and Film: Faulkner and Yoknapatawpha.* Jackson: UP of Mississippi, 1979. 49–65.

————. *Only the Heart.* New York: Dramatists Play Service, 1944.

————. Personal interview with Gerald C. Wood. 24 Oct. 1985. Unpublished.

————. "Preface." *Harrison, Texas: Eight Television Plays by Horton Foote.* New York: Harcourt Brace, 1956. vii-ix.

————. *Roots in a Parched Ground, Convicts, Lily Dale, The Widow Claire: Four Plays from The Orphans' Home Cycle.* New York: Grove, 1988.

————. *Selected One-Act Plays of Horton Foote.* Ed. Gerald C. Wood. Dallas: Southern Methodist UP, 1989.

————. *The Tears of My Sister.* In *Selected One-Act Plays of Horton Foote.* 149–65.

————. *Tender Mercies.* Prod. Philip S. Hobel, dir. Bruce Beresford. Starring Robert Duvall and Tess Harper. Universal Pictures, 1982.

————. *Tomorrow.* Prod. Paul Roebling and Gilbert Pearlman, dir. Joseph Anthony. Starring Robert Duvall and Olga Bellin. Filmgroup, 1972.

————. *The Traveling Lady.* New York: Dramatists Play Service, 1955.

————. *The Trip to Bountiful.* Prod. Sterling Van Wagenen, dir. Peter Masterson. Starring Geraldine Page, John Heard, and Carlin Glynn. Island Pictures, 1985.

————. *Valentine's Day.* In *Courtship, Valentine's Day, 1918: Three Plays from The Orphans' Home Cycle.* 51–107.

Freedman, Samuel. "From the Heart of Texas." *The New York Times Magazine* 9 Feb. 1986, sec. 6: 30–31, 50, 61–63, 73.

Harper, Tess. Telephone Interview with Gerald C. Wood. 24 Apr. 1991. Unpublished.

Hunter, Mary. "Foreword." *Only the Heart*. By Horton Foote. New York: Dramatists Play Service, 1944. 5–7.

O'Connor, Flannery. *Mystery and Manners*. Sel. and ed. Sally Fitzgerald and Robert Fitzgerald. New York: Farrar, Straus and Giroux, 1980.

Sterritt, David. "Horton Foote: Filmmaking Radical with a Tender Touch." *Christian Science Monitor* 15 May 1986: 1, 36.

Watson, Charles S. *The History of Southern Drama*. Lexington: UP of Kentucky, 1997.

Wood, Gerald C. "Boundaries, the Female Will, and Individuation in *Night Seasons*." *Horton Foote: A Casebook*. Ed. Gerald C. Wood. New York: Garland, 1998. 163–77.

———. "Horton Foote's Politics of Intimacy." *The Journal of American Drama and Theatre* 9.2 (1997): 44–57.

———. "Introduction." *Selected One-Act Plays of Horton Foote*. xiii-xxii.

———. "Old Beginnings and Roads to Home: Horton Foote and Mythic Realism." *Christianity and Literature* 45.3–4 (1996): 359–72.

Richard Ford

The Postmodern Exile and the Vanishing South

Joanna Price

> *There may come to be new places in our lives that are second spiritual homes—closer to us in some ways, perhaps, than our original homes. But the home tie is the blood tie. And had it meant nothing to us, any other place thereafter would have meant less, and we would carry no compass inside ourselves to find home ever, anywhere at all. We would not even guess what we had missed.*
>
> Eudora Welty, *The Eye of the Story: Selected Essays and Reviews*

> *It could . . . be said that exile is the archetypal condition of contemporary lives.*
>
> Eva Hoffman, *Lost in Translation: Life in a New Language*

Richard Ford has been described as "possibl[y] America's most peripatetic fiction writer" (Weber 50, qtd. in Hobson 42). Ford was raised in Jackson, Mississippi, but early in his childhood he became familiar with an itinerant life. After his father had a heart attack when Ford was eight years old, the young Ford "was shuttled between Jackson and Little Rock, Arkansas," where his grandfather lived (Lee 226). Ford left Mississippi when he was eighteen to attend Michigan State University. Since then, he has spent his time living and writing in various states (Lee 227), returning temporarily to live in the Mississippi Delta after the death of his mother (Ford, "An Interview" 71; "Richard Ford" 72–73).

When questioned about why he left the South, Ford has emphasized his personal motivations rather than dwelling on historical events of the period, just as in *The Sportswriter* (1986) and *Independence Day* (1995), he would focus on the interiorized journey of his protagonist, Frank Bascombe, assimilating cultural references to the psychological landscape of Bascombe. Ford has explained that he felt he needed to leave the South because "I simply didn't understand some very fundamental things in Mississippi in the early sixties and fifties: why it was we went to separate schools, why all this violence. . . . I couldn't piece it out, couldn't make racism make sense." Moving away from this allusion to the political conflict of the period, he continued: "And it wasn't just about race. It was about wanting to get out of the South because I wanted to see the rest of the country. Television had alerted me to New York, Chicago, Los Angeles. . . . I knew that there were terrible things coming in Mississippi. . . . I just thought. . . . I've got to get out of here to save myself. To reinvent myself" ("Richard Ford" 59). When pressed further by his interviewer about whether the "anguish" caused by his response to the racial conflict in Mississippi has affected his fiction, Ford responded that it is present in that he writes about "dramatic, important things that engage my sympathies" ("Richard Ford" 60).

Despite his desire to leave Mississippi, Ford has also stated that he thinks of it as "home." This became evident to him, he has explained, when after the death of his mother he began to ask himself such questions as "Where are you from? Where do you live? Where are you going to claim to be your home?" ("Richard Ford" 72). Ford's comments about his departure from Mississippi and subsequent itinerant life suggest an ambivalence toward the South and the notion of "home." They express the belief that to create the freedom for his own identity to flourish, he must distance himself from the turbulent history of his home state and, possibly, from any emotional claims that "home" might make.

Ford's desire to distance himself from "the South" extends to his dismissal of the notion of "southern" writing as parochial and nostalgic for a construct that is no longer tenable. Ford has commented that "southern regionalism as a factor in the impulse that makes us write novels . . . has had its day. . . . The south has become the regrettable 'Sunbelt'. . . . The south is not a place any more: it's a Belt, a business proposition, which is the nearest thing to anonymity the economy recognizes" ("Walker Percy" 561–62). In Ford's view, "the South" has become primarily a concept circulated by the media to attract economic investment, rather than a geographical entity with shared historical and cultural traditions defined by a predominantly agrarian economy. Ford's skepticism about what the concept of "the South" can now connote is accompanied by the desire to dissociate his fiction from "the limits of so-called Southern writing" (Lee 229). When his first novel, *A Piece of My Heart* (1974), which was set in Arkansas and Mississippi, was reviewed as "another Southern novel," he resolved not to set any more of his fiction in the South (Lee 229).

It is consistent with Ford's desire for his work not to be circumscribed by what he perceives to be the limitations of "southern writing" that his fiction could be read as having disengaged itself from the cluster of concerns that have characterized "southern writing" from the Southern Renascence onward. In his excellent book *The Southern Writer in the Postmodern World*, Fred Hobson has suggested that these concerns might include "a religious sense, a closeness to nature, a great attention to and affection for place, a close attention to family, a preference for the concrete and a rage against abstraction" (3). Hobson goes on to argue that contemporary southern fiction by authors such as Richard Ford, Bobbie Ann Mason, Lee Smith, Barry Hannah, and Josephine Humphreys is distinguished partly by the apparent absence of such concerns as they write about a postmodern world whose subjects' everyday existence is shaped by popular and consumer culture. In particular, these authors appear to be writing about characters who do not feel the "burden" of history and racial guilt, and their fiction seems to lack the "tragic sense" that has often marked the work of southern writers since the Civil War (2).[1] This has occurred, Hobson observes, even though writers such as Ford came of age in the period "before and during the civil rights movement" (41). Yet, Hobson goes on to argue, the fiction of these authors might be read as engaging with precisely those distinctively "southern" concerns that are ostensibly notable by their absence.

The Sportswriter, as Hobson has suggested, and *Independence Day*, present extended meditations on such subjects as "a religious sense," "attention to and affection for place," "family," and the relation between "the concrete" and "abstraction," despite Ford's narrator's protestations to the contrary. One might add to this other related concerns, such as the nature of community and "home," changing gender roles and relations between men and women, and, particularly, the relation of an individual and a culture to "history." Ford's two novels are largely concerned with exploring how an individual (as represented by his narrator Frank Bascombe) can accommodate himself to the way in which such concepts are changing as they have ceased to be defined by regionally specific traditions and are increasingly being reshaped by the cultural and economic formations of postmodernity. Thus the novels are concerned with the contemporary process of "Americanization" as the regionally distinct is translated into the generically "American."

In *The Sportswriter* and its "sequel" *Independence Day*, the narrative pretext for Ford's exploration of an individual's accommodation to the changed cultural spaces of contemporary America is the need of his protagonist, Frank Bascombe, to adapt to a life that has been riven by various losses. Through his evocation of Bascombe's adaptation to personal loss, Ford explores broader cultural adjustments to change. These are inscribed with the loss of certainty as to what now constitutes such concepts as home, family, identity, and community. In *The Sportswriter*, we learn that Frank Bascombe's nine-year-old son, Ralph, had died, four years before, of Reye's syndrome. Unable to find a common accommodation to their loss, Frank and his wife, "X," have subsequently divorced. The narrative tells of Frank's attempt to construct a new identity, most of the coordinates of his former self now having been removed. Frank's narrative is a reflection on what it means to be a man when familiar concepts of marriage, home, community, family, and the relation between past, present, and future have been wholly undermined. The present events of the narrative take place over one Easter weekend, the beginning of which is marked by Frank and X meeting in the graveyard in Haddam, New Jersey, where their son is buried to commemorate the anniversary of his death. Here, Frank realizes that "I don't know how to mourn and neither does X" (17). He observes that "we have tried to stay a modern, divided family. Our meeting here is only by way of a memorial for an old life lost" (18). The narrative that follows will trace Frank's attempts to bring the process of mourning to closure through the acceptance of "an old life lost" and the projection of a new life in a different cultural space.

Frank's accommodation to his losses is wrought partly by the formation of a lexicon of concepts through which he can map his path through the cultural and psychic space in which he has found himself. Ford's elaboration of this lexicon and his exploration of the psychological state to which it refers are the subject of the book's extended and expansive reflection. Representation of the external world that Frank Bascombe inhabits is eventually subsumed into this interior landscape. Nonetheless, the details of the locations across which Frank journeys inform the cultural topography that he attempts to chart though his conceptual lexicon. Frank Bascombe was born in the South, a fact from which he infers little, but has chosen to spend his adult life in the (fictional) town of Haddam. Most of *The Sportswriter* is set in Haddam, with an interlude in Detroit, Michigan, and Frank's concluding reflections being written in Florida. Ford's evocation of the detail of Haddam is meticulous, but these details ultimately serve an abstract schema. Ford has acknowledged the productive interaction between particular, localized details and the conceptual map of his novels in his comments about the significance of place in his fiction. He has stated that "a piece . . . sets itself for me without ever being conceptualized; you can't abstract a sense of place . . . for me, a place makes itself felt entirely through particulars" ("An Interview" 71). It is partly a writer's need to keep noticing "particulars" that has motivated his itinerant life; he explains: "I try to go to places where I am willing to be attentive, where I am willing to participate in the life there . . . a writer's obligation is to pay attention" ("An Interview" 72). This view is echoed in his comment that "place is where we can gain dominion over our subject and make it convincing" ("An Interview" 71). Elsewhere, however, he has stated: "Usually places are backgrounds for me, contexts made of interesting language and maybe even evoking striking mental pictures, in front of which characters perform the important actions of the story. But in each case, there is some kind of dramatic abstract—call it a figure, shape, line—that the up-front goings-on make in relation to the setting. I feel it as kind of necessary tensiveness, and it's no less so as stories move from place to place" ("Richard Ford" 67).

While this comment suggests that Ford envisages a dynamic relation between the details of place evoked, the trajectory of the plot, and the identities of the characters in his fiction, it also points to the fact that details of place become subordinated to a reflexive attention to the workings of language. In *The Sportswriter* and *Independence Day*, Frank Bascombe's attempt to "read" the details of the landscapes in which he immerses himself becomes assimilated into his attention to language, through which he desires to orient himself in relation to other people and consumer culture. Ford's depiction of this process, while creating detailed images of particular (albeit fictionalized) regions of America, ultimately transcends the representation of material detail to offer an interpretation of a changing cultural topography and its bearing on the identity of an individual. This cultural space, which becomes translated into a psychic space through his narrator's reflections, is a liminal one. It is informed by the passage of the traditions of regional cultures into a postmodern American culture through the intervention into traditional cultures of such phenomena as the ideology of consumerism, the influence of the mass media and popular culture, changing formations of the family, and altered gender roles and the relation between the sexes. This liminal space, which Ford's own characters occupy, has been aptly delineated by Ford in his characterization of Walker Percy's novels. Percy's novels, which, unlike Ford's, are set in the South, "point us," Ford observes, "convincingly toward the rest of the country, watching through the eyes of lonely, wandering narrators stranded in the contemporary and slightly ludicrous malaise between orthodoxy (the Catholic Church, the stock market, the family, the South) and complete culturization; men and women stuck between transcendence and immanence, between engagement and cynicism; folks out of phase with what one of Percy's characters calls the 'actuality of themselves'" ("Walker Percy" 558). It is such a space into which Frank Bascombe is "exiled" as he mourns the death of his son and the losses resulting from this bereavement.

Frank's narrative is premised on his frequently professed disbelief in the power of language and "history" to order and interpret the present. His narrative turns on what Ford has termed the "double reflex," in that it performs what it purports to deny ("An Interview" 87). Despite Frank's disavowals, this is a narrative that is preoccupied with the consolatory nature of telling,[2] the relation between language and "reality," and the effect of the past on the present. Frank informs us that in his early twenties, he had written a well-received book of short stories, *Blue Autumn*, and "half of a short novel" (9), but then had given up "serious" writing to become a sportswriter. Ford has explained that by making his narrator a sportswriter who "would have been a writer, an imaginative writer" gave him "the opportunity to move from a sort of quotidian language to the language of introspection and speculation" ("An Interview" 83). Frank's role as a sportswriter has confirmed the belief that a brief period as a college professor in literature has suggested to him: "Transcendent themes" are simply a literary artifice, and are not to be found in life. Hence, when meeting X at their son's grave, he will not seek in art the illusion of permanence but instead reads as a tribute Theodore Roethke's "Meditations of an Old Woman," which is "about letting the everyday make you happy—insects, shadows, the color of a woman's hair" (25). Much of the narrative that follows charts Frank's attempt to find in language a way of valuing the transient and immanent when the belief in religious or other cultural discourses of transcendence and permanence has been largely lost.

Writing about sports, which Ford has called "the language of modern America" ("An Interview" 83), offers Frank a popularly valued discourse that celebrates the ephemeral and the everyday. Central to his conception of sportswriting is Frank's notion of the athlete, which serves as the prototype for the form of identity for which he is striving. Anticipating his interview with the disabled former athlete Herb Wallagher, Frank observes that "linemen often tend to be more within themselves" than other athletes (40). Like "linemen," Frank aspires to attain a state of unreflective self-completeness in the present moment. He seeks this to ameliorate the dissociation from himself and others that he has experienced since the death of his son and his subsequent divorce. One of the key terms in Frank's lexicon is "dreaminess" that he uses to describe this sense of alienation and detachment. He defines dreaminess as "among other things, a state of suspended recognition, and a response to too much useless and complicated factuality" (48). A recurrent symptom of his dreaminess is his tendency to observe himself in a situation, rather than immersing himself in it: "I could always see myself as though from outside. . . . An inbred irony seemed to haunt me . . ." (33), or, as he puts it elsewhere, "I was always able to 'see around the sides' of whatever I was feeling" (70). The effect of this ironic sense is that Frank claims to have been unable to attain "the *oneness of the writer's vision*" required by "real writing" and that he maintains a sense of relativity and provisionality that other people tend to interpret as an unacceptable changeability. Later, in *Independence Day*, X reproaches Frank with the fact that "truth didn't really exist to you" (253) and "you were never entirely there" (254).

Frank desires to assuage his dissociation by demarcating his identity in time and space. Part of the cause of "dreaminess," Frank muses, is the loss of "a sense of anticipation" (*Sportswriter* 49), which loss implies an inability to project a future based on some knowledge drawn from the past. Yet Frank presents himself as "a proponent of forgetting" (150), arguing that "all we really want is to get to the point where the past can explain nothing about us and we can get on with life. . . . My own history I think of as a postcard with changing scenes on one side but no particular or memorable messages on the back" (30). He regards the desire to find an explanation for oneself in one's past as a particularly American trait, observing: "In my view Americans put too much emphasis on their pasts as a way of defining themselves, which can be death-dealing" (30). Frank's desire to sever himself from his past informs his embrace of a culture that promotes the idea that what one sees, experiences, or consumes in the present moment is the "truth" (albeit relative) of the way things are.

This is one of the reasons why he enjoys living in the commuter suburb of Haddam, New Jersey, which he regards as quintessentially American. Frank's desire for a "readable" American landscape is closely connected to his notion of an identity that is self-complete in the present moment: "When you are fully in your emotions, when they are simple and appealing enough to be in, and the distance is closed between what you feel and what you might *also* feel, then your instincts can be trusted" (138). Frank appropriates the term "literalist" to describe one who has attained this unified and present-centered state of being. With his usual precision, he distinguishes between "a literalist" and "a factualist," giving the following example: "A literalist is a man who will enjoy an afternoon watching people while stranded in an airport in Chicago, while a factualist can't stop wondering why his plane was late out of Salt Lake, and gauging whether they'll still serve dinner or just a snack" (139). For Frank, a "literalist" is one who can "read" or "relent to"[3] the significance of things, places, or situations as they appear, without searching for some other meaning that might be connoted. In contrast, a "factualist" seeks the irreducible events or actualities of life, thus divesting them of "mystery." As a "literalist" rather than a "factualist," for instance, he prefers the landscape of New Jersey to that of Detroit, which confronts him with the "facts" of "the complicated urban-industrial mix." He observes ruefully: "So much that is explicable in American life is made in Detroit" (121). Frank, a would-be "literalist," welcomes the suburban landscape of Haddam, whose residents subscribe to the fiction of what that landscape represents, for example, civic behavior, community, neighborliness, security, and the impression that people are "living steadfast and accountable lives" (5). Frank states: "We all need our simple, unambiguous, even factitious townscapes like mine" (109). He is drawn to such "factitiousness" in that the "literalist" can participate in the consensus to accept the illusion of what the suburb represents. The suburban landscape of Haddam epitomizes consumer, and synecdochically, American culture to Frank. As Roger Silverstone has explained in *Visions of Suburbia*, "Suburban culture is a consuming culture. Fuelled by the increasing commoditization of everyday life, suburbia has become the crucible of a shopping economy" (8). A typical suburb, Haddam is "a town of mailers and home shoppers" (*Sportswriter* 55). Frank recalls how "in the deepest depths of my worst dreaminess, I began to order as many catalogs into the house as I could" (201). Refusing the consolation of the "incumbent themes" (229) of literature, Frank has sought solace in the "factitiousness" of consumption. To Frank, the pleasure and comfort of mail-order shopping lies in consent to the fiction of what a commodity represents through reading it "literally." He observes that the depiction in the catalogs of people wearing clothes such as "wool nighties" or "saddle oxfords," or using objects such as "cane fishing rods" or "boxes of kindling sticks," creates a reassuring impression of unchanging traditions.

The repetition of such images confers upon everyday life the timelessness of myth. It evokes a stable concept of "home," where men and women are defined by a static relation to each other, to labor, the domestic sphere, and the familiar objects of their daily lives. Always an ironist, Frank recognizes the disparity between the nostalgic vision of the family invoked by these commodities and "lived life" (Ford, "An Interview" 81), but he prefers to assent to the illusion rather than to dwell on his own "home," with its "dreaminess and silence in a big old house where unprovoked death had taken its sad toll" (203). Frank thus allows himself to be temporarily consoled by the myth of "home" while recognizing its fictive nature and, implicitly, the way in which consumer culture invites its subjects to buy into the myth while also drawing attention to its own "factitiousness."[4]

Frank's espousal of the "factitiousness" of sportswriting, suburbia, and consumerism in general is motivated not only by his personal losses but also by his realization that a sense of loss (of former certainties) is inscribed into the proliferation of choices that consumer culture presents all its subjects, particularly regarding who one can be and how and where one can be it. So, he explains: "In the world now, it's harder to judge what is and isn't essential" (57). All that one can be certain of is the relativity of the individual's point of view.

Frank's assent to the culture's of suburbia and sportswriting belies, however, the longing that his narrative expresses to find "meaning" beyond that which is offered by a superficial reading of the signifiers of commodities and the "lingua franca" of sports. The occurrence of the anniversary of his son's death on Good Friday draws Frank's attention to the lack of possibility, for him, of any belief in transcendence, whether this be drawn from religion or literature, yet it leaves him with a yearning for something to put in the place of the sacred. A self-declared "literalist," Frank evades "facts," seeking the "mystery" promised by people or things one knows little about. So, for example, rather than seeking the solace that psychoanalysis might offer through an interpretative narrative that connects his present condition to selected events of his past, Frank prefers to visit a clairvoyant, who offers him only "mystery . . . the *only* thing I find to have value at this stage in my life" (107). Frank's desire for "mystery" is prompted by his fear of finding himself stranded in "a long, empty moment" (12), or indeed of discovering that, consolatory narratives having been lost, such a "moment" is *all* that life in contemporary American culture can amount to. Yet divested of consolatory or explanatory literary, cultural, or ethical narratives, Frank feels "a conviction that I have no ethics at all and little consistency. . . . I feel as literal as I've ever felt—stranded, uncomplicated as an immigrant" (126).

A lack of "consistency" or an "ethics" in which he can believe characterizes Frank's interaction with the eighteen lovers he has taken during the period of his "dreaminess." These relations are marked by Frank's desire to espouse the "commoditization of everyday life," as Silverstone has referred to it (8). During his brief contact with them, Frank has encouraged each woman to offer "full self-disclosure," while withholding any significant information about himself, in the attempt to "simulate complete immersion," to get "*into* her life" and "simulate . . . closure" (*Sportswriter* 135). Vicky Arcenault, with whom Frank has sustained a longer relationship, also represents to him the achievement of the "commoditization of everyday life." He describes Vicky as "a girl for every modern occasion and I find I can be interested in the smallest particulars of her life" (61). He takes pleasure in Vicky's condominium, which she had "furnished in a one-day whirlwind trip to the Miracle Furniture Mile in Paramus," observing that "the idea appeals to me of starting life over in such a new and genial space with an instant infusion of colorful, fresh and impersonal furnishings" (63). Frank's pleasure in his association of Vicky with the commodities of everyday life, combined with his "dreamy" detachment from her, leads him to objectify Vicky herself. With his usual propensity for "seeing around" things, Frank offers a humorous self-parody of his meeting with her: "I can't help thinking of my life as a scene in some steamy bus station novel. *Big Sledge moved toward the girl cat-quick, trapping her where he'd wanted her, between his cheap drifter's suitcase and the pile of greasy tire chains against the back of the lube bay. Now she would see what's what. They both would*" (174). Despite his ironic recognition of his detachment from Vicky and the other women he encounters, an anxiety about masculinity and what a man's role can be in a culture where gender and relations between the sexes are being redefined is one of the most acutely felt manifestations of Frank's alienation.

As his tale unfolds, Frank increasingly expresses doubt about whether the "factitious" narratives to which he has willfully subscribed can continue to offer solace. When he joins "the Divorced Men's Club," he acknowledges that myths of community notwithstanding, "the suburbs are not a place where friendships flourish" (85) and "all of us were and are lost" (86), a view that seems to be corroborated by the suicide of another member of the club. His interview with the former athlete, Herb Wallagher, fails to illustrate sportswriting's myth of how "within himself" an athlete can be, for Herb, who is "as alienated as Camus," reveals "everything is minor key, subjunctive and contingent" (214). This prompts Frank to reflect that life cannot be made to fit even into the simplified ordering narratives of sportswriting and to conclude that "in the end this is all I ask for: to participate briefly in the lives of others at a low level; to speak in a plain, truth-telling voice; to not take myself too seriously; and then to have done with it. Since after all, it is one thing to write sports, but another entirely to live a life" (214).

The novel concludes, although without reaching closure, with Frank attaining some acceptance of his propensity to "see around the sides" of things (70). Although he experiences "a sudden unwanted grief" (341) at the abyss between how things appear and what they become, he finds some reconciliation with the recognition that "some life is only life, and unconjugatable" (375). In particular, he approaches an acceptance of the bearing of his past upon his present, after a narrative dedicated to disavowing this.

Independence Day opens with Frank Bascombe living once again in Haddam, after having spent time in Florida and France. He is now living in "the house formerly owned by formerly my wife," "X," now named as Ann Dykstra (7). Frank's decision to refer to his former wife by her proper name indicates that the "grief" occasioned by their divorce has now been tempered, although, as he notes at the end of *The Sportswriter*, "mourning can be long" (380). The narrative takes place in the election year of 1988, five years after the events related in *The Sportswriter*. Frank has given up sportswriting to become a realtor, which gives rise to some of the text's central metaphors. As in *The Sportswriter*, Frank is still preoccupied with a sense of his own transience and disconnectedness, although he has largely replaced the conceptual lexicon of his first narrative with one "philosophical construct" (Lee 234): "the Existence Period." He uses this to denote the maintenance of a state of protective distance and disengagement from other people and events, prompted by the pain and loss caused by prior events. In trying to achieve "the high-wire act of normalcy" (94), he notes, "interest can mingle successfully with uninterest . . . intimacy with transience, caring with the obdurate uncaring. Until very recently (I'm not sure when it stopped) I believed this was the *only* way of the world: maturity's balance" (76).

In this novel, Ford continues to explore some of the themes of his earlier work, such as the nature of identity, family, community, home, and the relation between past and present in a generalized "American" consumer society. In *Independence Day*, however, he introduces two new discourses through which to extend his exploration of these concepts. As *The Sportswriter* was set over an Easter weekend, this novel takes place over the Independence Day holiday, which allows Ford's narrator to reflect on the relation among such concepts as independence, isolation, freedom, the individual, and community. Intersecting with the discourse of "independence" is that of realty: Frank Bascombe's work as a realtor becomes the vehicle for Ford to explore the relationship between individual identity and place, property ownership, community, neighborhood, and home. As in *The Sportswriter*, reference to external events, here most notably the impending election, is assimilated into the overarching reflection on the novel's central philosophical concepts.

Various interwoven strands comprise the narrative pretext for this reflection. As the story opens, Frank Bascombe is planning to take his surviving teenage son, Paul, on a trip to Connecticut, where they will "visit as many sports halls of fame as humanly possible in one forty-eight-hour period (this being only two), winding up in storied Cooperstown" (15). These locations, Frank believes, will provide the "*ur*-father-son meeting ground" (18), where he hopes to be able to help his son overcome the trauma, as he diagnoses it, caused by the death of Paul's brother and the divorce of his parents, which has led to his current "delinquent" behavior. Inspired by the theme of Independence Day, Frank has armed himself with copies of Carl Becker's *The Declaration of Independence* and Emerson's *Self-Reliance*, believing an exposition of "independence" will aid his son's "recovery." He observes: "I believe his instincts are sound and he will help himself if he can, and that independence is, in fact, what he lacks—independence from whatever holds him captive: memory, history, bad events he struggles with, can't control, but feels he should" (16). This observation suggests that Frank is beginning this narrative from the premise that he established at the end of *The Sportswriter*: that the past does matter and that one must reflect on it before one can free oneself from it.

A second strand of the narrative traces Frank's attempts to persuade the Markhams, a couple from Vermont, to buy a house in Haddam. As in *The Sportswriter*, Ford's exploration of the significance of place moves from the representation of concrete details to abstract speculation. Suburbia is now interpreted through the eyes of the realtor, Frank Bascombe. From the outset, Frank is circumspect about some of the myths associated with suburbia: despite the illusion of security, he has been mugged and a fellow realtor murdered. Nevertheless, he still seeks some of the things that suburbia is expected to represent, such as a sense of "belonging and permanence" (27) and of civic responsibility. To this end he has become the landlord of two houses in a black neighborhood of Haddam, persuading himself with his customary irony that this is "reinvesting in my community, providing affordable housing options, maintaining a neighborhood integrity I admired . . . establishing a greater sense of connectedness" (27). His role as a realtor allows him to reflect on the fundamental connection between individual identity and property ownership for many Americans as he observes how the Markhams, in pursuing the possibility of purchasing a house, experience the familiar "realty dreads" (57). Considering the house they will buy, and what the location in which they will buy it signifies, occasions the Markhams to brood upon their own identities, past, present, and projected into the future, as also upon their relation as individuals to any putative community. Against the Markhams' preoccupation with what place, and specifically suburbia, can offer them, Frank maintains his usual ironic detachment, remarking that it is a "theme" of the circumspect "Existence Period" "to cease sanctifying places" for they leave "no sign of you, no mention in the air's breath that you were there or that you were ever, importantly you, or that you even *were*. We may feel they *ought* to, *should* confer something—sanction, again—because of events that transpired there once; light a warming fire to animate us when we're well nigh animate and sunk. But they don't. Places never cooperate by revering you back when you need it. . . . Place means nothing" (151–52).

Continuing his conversation about house-purchasing with the Markhams over the telephone, Frank undertakes the journey to Connecticut with his son. Frank wishes to use his exegesis of the American struggle for and Declaration of Independence to persuade his son of the necessity of both confronting and freeing himself from his past in order to achieve autonomy. Frank's plans to rehabilitate his son are, however, violently interrupted when Paul suffers a serious accident in a baseball batting cage and is rushed to the hospital in an attempt to save his sight. As in *The Sportswriter*, the intrusion of unforeseen and violent events forces Frank to reassess the "tenets" he has been using to sustain himself through what he now calls the "Existence Period." Foremost among these, as he had planned to explain to his son, is his commitment to "a future based on the postulate that independence and isolation were not the same" (369). Once again, Frank explores the supposition that in finding a workable relationship between the individual and society, he will also discover a way of reconciling himself to transience and contingency. Again, cultural topography is translated into psychic space as Frank attempts to define a viable subjective position for himself. Frank has frequently expressed skepticism about the concept of community, remarking, for example, that Joe Markham seeks in the house he will buy "a perfect sanction, a sign some community recognizes him in the only way communities ever recognize anything: financially . . ." (51). But the effect of contingency on his own life leads Frank to posit a new notion of community that can accommodate change. He reflects: "We want to *feel* our community as a fixed, continuous entity . . . as being anchored to the rock of permanence; but we know it's not. . . . We and it are anchored only to contingency like a bottle on a wave, seeking a quiet eddy. The very effort of maintenance can pull you under." With the worldliness that his present role confers upon him, he continues wryly: "Being a realtor . . . makes you come to grips with contingency and sell it as a source of strength and father to true self-sufficiency" (439). This acceptance of cultural and historical contingency is paralleled by Frank's need to accept mutability within himself: "I dearly wish I could speak from some established *place* . . . rather than from this constellation of stars among which I smoothly orbit, traffic and glide. Indeed, if I could see myself as occupying a fixed point rather than being in a process (the quiddity of the Existence Period), things might grow better" (285).

The novel concludes with Frank envisioning a time when he might attain external coordinates that would locate him in relation to, and for, others: "The Permanent Period, this would be, that long, stretching-out time when my dreams would have mystery like any ordinary person's; when whatever I do or say, who I marry, how my kids turn out, becomes what the world—if it makes note at all—knows of me, how I'm seen, understood, even how I think of myself before whatever there is that's wild and unassuagable rises and cheerlessly hails me off to oblivion" (450). Embedded in this vision of "the purely ordinary" are concepts of home, community and relation to place that, through the course of *The Sportswriter* and *Independence Day*, have been newly elaborated to accommodate the transitions that the contemporary subject, "exiled" into a generalized American consumer culture, must undergo. Frank Bascombe, experiencing a sense of loss in his recognition that these concepts themselves are in transition, has embraced the mythologization of "home" and "community" that he has found in consumer culture. This culture has allowed him to delineate a position of irony, from which he can both accept the consolation of the illusion of timelessness that its representations of the family, home, and community offer and also reconcile himself to the provisionality and contingency that recent events in his life have underscored. Through their protagonist's ironic vision, Ford's novels offer both "a memorial for an old life lost" (*Sportswriter* 18) and an accommodation to contemporary life, as they depict Frank Bascombe's "ethical" commitment to forging a conceptual map that can allow him to adapt to the new cultural spaces of postmodern America.

Notes

1. For an interesting interpretation of the changing place of a historical consciousness in recent literature of the South, see Gilman 3–21.

2. Ford discusses "the efficacy of telling" in Faulkner's work in his interview with Bonetti, 79.

3. See Dupuy for a discussion of Frank Bascombe as a reader of his culture.

4. For an excellent analysis of the appropriation of the myth of home by popular culture, see Bronfen 17–20.

Works Cited

Bronfen, Elisabeth. "Between Nostalgia and Disenchantment: The Concept 'Home' in Jayne Anne Phillips' Novel *Machine Dreams*." *Arbeiten Aus Anglistik und Amerikanistik* 13.1 (1988): 17–28.

Dupuy, Edward. "The Confessions of an Ex-Suicide: Relenting and Recovering in Richard Ford's *The Sportswriter*." *Southern Literary Journal* 29.1 (1990): 93–103.

Ford, Richard. *Independence Day*. 1995. London: Harvill, 1995.

———. "An Interview with Richard Ford." By Kay Bonetti. *Missouri Review* 10.2 (1987): 71–96.

———. "Richard Ford: The Art of Fiction CXLVII." Interview by Bonnie Lyons. *Paris Review* 140 (1996): 42–77.

———. *The Sportswriter*. 1986. London: Flamingo, 1987.

———. "Walker Percy: Not Just Whistling Dixie." *National Review* 29 (13 May 1977): 558–64.

Gilman, Owen J., Jr. *Vietnam and the Southern Imagination*. Jackson: UP of Mississippi, 1992.

Hobson, Fred. *The Southern Writer in the Postmodern World*. Athens: U of Georgia P, 1991.

Lee, Don. "About Richard Ford." *Ploughshares* 22.2–3 (1996): 226–35.

Silverstone, Roger, ed. *Visions of Suburbia*. London: Routledge, 1997.

Weber, Bruce. "Richard Ford's Uncommon Characters." *New York Times Magazine* 10 Apr. 1988: 50.

Contributors

Moira P. Baker, Professor of English at Radford University, teaches courses in English Renaissance literature, women writers, and lesbian/gay/bisexual studies. Her published work appears in *South Atlantic Review, English Renaissance Prose, Dictionary of Literary Biography, Virginia English Bulletin,* and *The Harvard Gay and Lesbian Review.*

Barbara Bennett is a visiting Professor of English at Wake Forest University in Winston-Salem, North Carolina. She is the author of *Comic Visions, Female Voices,* and the forthcoming book *Understanding Jill McCorkle.*

Robert H. Brinkmeyer Jr. is Professor of English at the University of Mississippi. His publications include *The Art and Vision of Flannery O'Connor; Katherine Anne Porter's Artistic Development: Primitivism, Traditionalism, and Totalitarianism;* and *Three Catholic Writers of the Modern South.*

Keith Byerman is Associate Professor of English and African American studies at Indiana State University. His publications include *The Short Fiction of John Edgar Wideman; Seizing the Word: History, Art, & Self in the Work of W.E.B. Du Bois; Alice Walker: An Annotated Bibliography, 1968–1986* (with Erma Banks); *Fingering the Jagged Grain: Tradition and Form in Recent Black Fiction;* and numerous articles and chapters on African American literature in journals and books.

Linda J. Byrd is Assistant Professor of English at Sam Houston State University. She has published essays in *Southern Literary Journal, Conferences of College Teachers of English Studies, The Texas Review,* and in the collection *TR5: To Research, To Read, To Reason, To Write, To Report: An Introduction to Research Writing.* Her interview with Lee Smith appeared in *Shenandoah: The Washington and Lee University Review.*

Gary M. Ciuba, Associate Professor of English at Kent State University, is the author of *Walker Percy: Books of Revelations.* He has published in *American Literature, The Flannery O'Connor Bulletin, Mississippi Quarterly, South Atlantic Review, Southern Literary Journal,* and *Southern Quarterly.* He has contributed essays to *Walker Percy: Novelist and Philosopher* and *Sacred Violence: A Reader's Companion to Cormac McCarthy.*

Jeffrey J. Folks is Professor of English at Doshisha University in Japan. His publications include *Southern Writers and the Machine: Faulkner to Percy; Remembering James Agee,* 2nd ed. (edited with David Madden); *Southern Writers at Century's End* (edited with James A. Perkins); and articles in numerous journals.

Nancy Summers Folks is a freelance editor with more than thirty years of experience. In addition to literary books and articles, she has edited medical, scientific, and technical publications and other documents.

Susan Goodman is Professor of English at the University of Delaware and the author of several books on Edith Wharton. Her most recent book is *Ellen Glasgow: A Biography*.

James Grove, Professor and Chair of the English Department at Mt. Mercy College, has published in *New England Quarterly, American Literature, Critique, Prairie Schooner, The Crab Orchard Review, The Review of Contemporary Literature,* and *The High Plains Literary Review.* He contributed an article on Anne Tyler for *Southern Writers at Century's End.*

Suzanne W. Jones is Professor of English at the University of Richmond. She is the editor of *Growing Up in the South: An Anthology of Modern Southern Literature* and *Writing the Woman Artist: Essays on Poetics, Politics, and Portraiture.*

John Lowe, Professor of English at Louisiana State University, is author of *Jump at the Sun: Zora Neale Hurston's Cosmic Comedy,* editor of *Conversations with Ernest Gaines,* editor of *Redefining Southern Culture,* co-editor of *The Future of Southern Letters,* and is currently completing *The Americanization of Ethnic Humor.*

Joanna Price is a lecturer in American Studies at Liverpool John Moores University, England. She is the author of a forthcoming book on Bobbie Ann Mason and has published articles on contemporary American fiction, feminist theory, and cultural memory.

Julius Raper is Professor of English at the University of North Carolina, Chapel Hill, and author or editor of three books on Ellen Glasgow. He has also published *Narcissus from Rubble: Competing Models of Character in Contemporary British and American Fiction* and coedited *Lawrence Durrell: Comprehending the Whole.*

Frank W. Shelton is former academic dean and Professor of English at the University of South Carolina–Salkehatchie. He has published essays and chapters on Ernest Gaines and other contemporary southern novelists in *Southern Review, Southern Quarterly, Southern Literary Journal,* and other journals.

Linda Watts is Director of Interdisciplinary Arts and Sciences and Professor of American Studies at the University of Washington, Bothell. She has published several books and essays on Gertrude Stein, including *Rapture Untold: Gender, Mysticism, and the Moment of Recognition in the Writings of Gertrude Stein* and *The Short Fiction of Gertrude Stein* (forthcoming, Twayne).

Gerald C. Wood, Professor of English and Chair of the English Department at Carson-Newman College, has published articles in *Keats-Shelley Journal, Byron Journal, Literature/Film Quarterly,* and other journals. He interviewed Horton Foote for *Post Script,* and his critical articles on Foote have appeared in the *Journal of American Drama and Theatre* and *Christianity and Literature.* He also edited *Selected One-Act Plays of Horton Foote* and *Horton Foote: A Casebook.* His study of Foote's writing, *Horton Foote and the Theater of Intimacy,* was published in 1999.

Index